PHOTOGRAPHER'S GUIDE TO

The Grand Canyon and Northern Arizona

JOSEPH K. LANGE

STACKPOLE BOOKS

For my wife, Bonnie, my companion on all of our adventures in northern Arizona

Published by
STACKPOLE BOOKS
5067 Ritter Road
Mechanicsburg, PA 17055
www.stackpolebooks.com

Printed in China

Cover design by Wendy Reynolds
Cover photos by Joseph Lange

10 9 8 7 6 5 4 3 2 1

First edition

Library of Congress Cataloging-in-Publication Data

Lange, Joseph K.
Photographer's guide to the Grand Canyon and northern Arizona / Joseph K. Lange—1st ed.
p. cm.
Includes bibliographical references.
ISBN 0-8117-2900-1 (alk. paper)
1. Grand Canyon National Park (Ariz.)—Guidebooks. 2. Arizona—Guidebooks. 3. Photography—Arizona—Grand Canyon National Park—Guidebooks. 4. Photography—Arizona—Guidebooks. I. Title.

F788 .L36 2001
917.91'32—dc21

00-039491

Contents

Preface

Although I was not introduced to the beautiful canyon and plateau country of northern Arizona until I was an adult, it rapidly became one of my favorite photographic destinations. In my opinion, two of the most appealing elements of memorable photographs are form and color, and the Grand Canyon, Monument Valley, and northern Arizona have an abundance of both.

I grew up in the Midwest, and my parents took our family west for vacations a number of times. We visited many beautiful areas such as the Tetons, Yellowstone and Glacier National Parks, and the Canadian Rockies, and my interest in scenic photography was born. However, we never visited Utah or Arizona. I attended college and graduated with a degree in geological engineering from Colorado School of Mines on the eastern side of the Front Range near Denver. During those years, I took a lot of photographs in the mountains of Colorado, Wyoming, and Montana but didn't visit northern Arizona or Utah.

After graduation from college and a two-year stint in the army, I started my career in the oil business as an exploration geologist for Chevron Oil Company in Denver. My initial assignment was in the plateau district. This was my first exposure to the canyon country of northern Arizona and southern Utah, and I was astounded at the great beauty I found there. I only wished that I had discovered it earlier. My understanding of the geologic forces that created the rocks and scenery in northern Arizona enhanced my appreciation for this area.

It was at this time that I joined my first camera club and my interest in nature photography in general and scenic photography in particular became a major part of my life. I learned from the more experienced members of the local camera clubs and the Photographic Society of America the fine points of composition and lighting.

The plateau country was an entirely new and exciting area to explore and photograph. It provided much of my photographic subject material during the 1970s and 1980s. I found that it was necessary to return to productive areas and even specific locations again and again to obtain the best results. I learned that by going to these areas in different seasons of the year, I could achieve the desired lighting and atmospheric conditions for truly memorable images.

My career in the oil business ended in 1990 due to a significant decline in worldwide oil prices and a corresponding lack of demand for the geologists and geophysicists exploring for new reserves. I had always wanted to devote full time to photography, and now I had an opportunity to do so. Since 1990, my wife Bonnie and I have been conducting nature photographic workshops throughout much of the western United States, Canada, and Africa. The plateau country, including northern Arizona, is a major focus of our effort. The long years of exploring the plateau country have served me well in guiding our clients to the best photographic locations.

In this book, I tell you my favorite locations in each area and the best season and time of day to photograph them. I do not write extensively about the artistic and technical aspects of scenic photography. I assume that you already have most of the basic skills necessary to obtain good photographs. If you want a more detailed explanation of composition, lighting, exposure, equipment, and proper attitude, I recommend *How to Photograph Landscapes* (Stackpole Books, 1998). For an informative guide to the history, ecology, botany, geology, and zoology of the Grand Canyon, I recommend *The Grand Canyon: A Visitor's Companion,* by George Wuerthner (Stackpole Books, 1998). It will help you understand and better appreciate the subject material you will be photographing.

This is the second book I have authored in Stackpole's Photographer's Guide series. I would like to thank Stackpole Books for the opportunity to share my knowledge of photographic locations with the thousands of amateur photographers who flock to these wonderful scenic locations each year. In particular, I would like to thank my editor, Mark Allison, whose enthusiasm and sage advice have been instrumental in the preparation of this book as well as my other books for Stackpole.

Why to Photograph the Grand Canyon and Northern Arizona

The Grand Canyon is recognized as one of the great scenic wonders of the world. Other countries try to compare their canyons with the Grand Canyon: Copper Canyon is called the Grand Canyon of Mexico. The Fish River Canyon is called the Grand Canyon of South Africa. But none of the great canyons in other parts of the world have the combination of size, form, and color for which the Grand Canyon of Arizona is justifiably famous. Combine these attributes with constantly-changing atmospheric conditions such as thunderstorms, rainbows, snow, and haze, and you have all the elements needed for spectacular photographs.

The rims of the Grand Canyon are most popular with the millions of people who visit each year. The South Rim is open year-round, whereas the higher and wetter North Rim is open only from mid-May to mid-October. The inner gorge of the Grand Canyon also offers outstanding scenery. Many people hike into or through the canyon to get a different perspective on the Colorado River and the cliffs, buttes, and temples that surround it. Commercial raft trips through the canyon negotiate some of the most thrilling rapids in the country. The Havasupai area to the west of Grand Canyon National Park contains some extremely photogenic waterfalls.

The other major scenic attraction of northern Arizona is Monument Valley, one of my favorite photographic locations in the world. In Monument Valley, colorful freestanding monoliths tower a thousand feet above the valley floor. Coral-colored sand dunes and gnarled juniper trees provide foreground interest. Sunrises and sunsets are especially photogenic with the spires and monuments silhouetted against

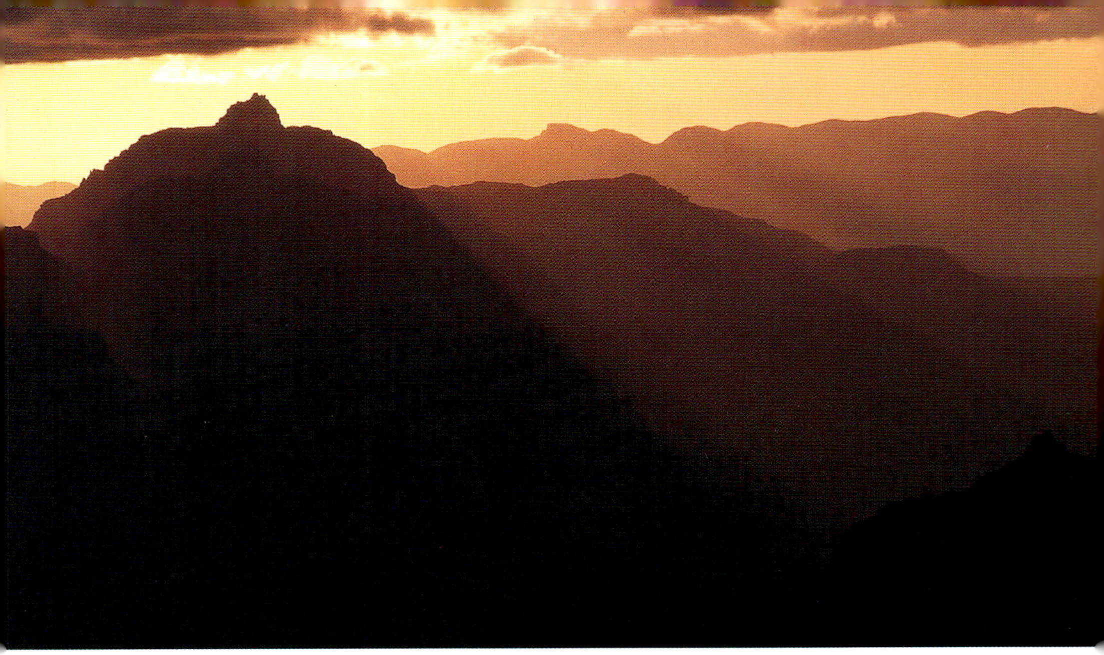

Grand Canyon at Sunrise, Grand Canyon National Park, Arizona. In this shot from Mather Point, the atmospheric haze in the canyon accentuates the rays and visual perspective in the picture. A gap in the clouds allows the rays to come through without flaring the lens. Backlit pictures at the Grand Canyon can be very effective. *Minolta 70–210mm lens, enhancing filter, Fuji Velvia film.*

Sunrise in Monument Valley, Monument Valley Tribal Park, Arizona. A sunrise at Monument Valley can be spectacular. The Mittens and other buttes in the valley make outstanding silhouettes. Just the right amount of thin clouds along the horizon added color to the sky and diffused the sun enough so that it didn't flare my lens. You must anticipate a sunrise or sunset and be set up at the proper spot before the color appears in the sky. *Minolta 70–210mm lens, enhancing filter, Fuji Velvia film.*

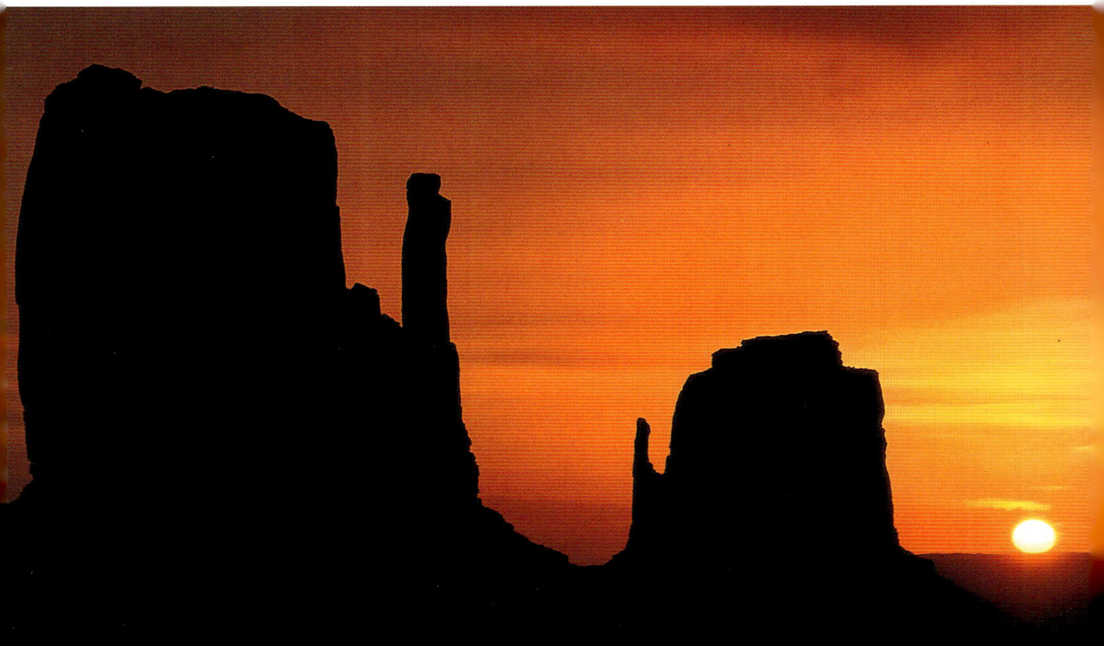

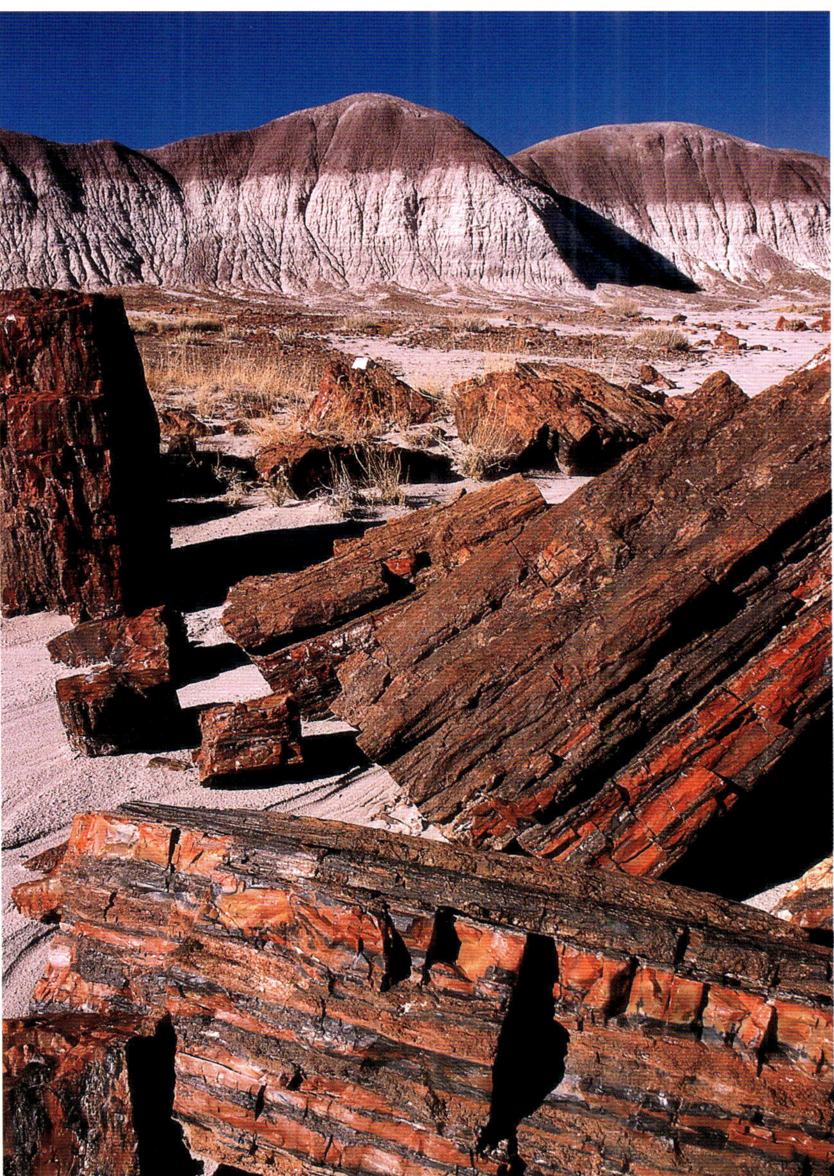

Petrified logs and Painted Desert, Petrified Forest National Park, Arizona. Interesting petrified logs and colorful badland buttes create outstanding photographic opportunities. By using wide-angle lenses with a small aperture and focusing at the hyperfocal distance, you can render both foregrounds and backgrounds sharp. *Canon 28–105mm lens, enhancing and polarizing filters, Fuji Velvia film.*

the colorful sky. The Navajo people who live in the valley add human interest to the spectacular scenery.

Many other destinations in northern Arizona provide excellent photographic opportunities. Petrified Forest National Park contains the colorful badlands of the Painted Desert and the largest concentration of petrified logs in the world. Canyon de Chelly National Monument is famous for its towering canyon walls, cliff dwellings, and spectacular spires such as Spider Rock. Wupatki and Montezuma Castle National Monuments preserve a variety of photogenic mesa-top ruins and cliff dwellings. Sunset Crater Volcano National Monument features some interesting cinder cones created by the geologically recent volcanic activity in the area.

The area around the town of Page contains many scenic attractions, including Glen Canyon Dam and Lake Powell, numerous slot canyons, and Horseshoe Bend. West of Page is the Paria Canyon–Vermillion Cliffs Wilderness, which features the Coyote Buttes Special Management Area, one of the most desolate and spectacular slickrock locations in the plateau country. South of Flagstaff, Sedona and Oak Creek Canyon exhibit outstanding red rock scenery.

The wealth of outstanding and varied subject matter found in the Grand Canyon and northern Arizona can form the basis for many productive photographic trips. Once you see the scenic potential of this area, you will want to return again and again. In this book, I give you the benefit of my experience to help you capture on film the beauty in color and form that you will find there.

ONE

Preparation, Clothing, Equipment, and Photographic Ethics

PREPARATION

Your photographic trip to the Grand Canyon and northern Arizona will be much easier and more productive if you follow a few simple guidelines. Many are just common sense. Acquainting yourself with the history, botany, geology, and zoology of the region is a good starting point. This knowledge will give you a greater appreciation and understanding of the scenery, plants, and wildlife that you will be photographing. The Resources and References section of the book lists suppliers of educational materials in the various parks.

Physical conditioning is also important in preparing for your photographic trip. Most of the destinations can be reached by anyone in reasonably good health. I find that walking several miles a day three days a week keeps me in condition to do the short hikes that photographing the Grand Canyon and northern Arizona requires. Check with your physician if you are in doubt about this level of physical activity. If you are planning to hike into and out of the Grand Canyon or Coyote Buttes, your level of conditioning must be much higher.

Even though you may not perspire as much at the Grand Canyon and northern Arizona because of the low humidity, your body is losing a lot of moisture. Drink large amounts of water to avoid heatstroke or heat exhaustion. When hiking away from your car, always take along a water bottle or canteen. At the Grand Canyon and throughout northern Arizona, the tap water is safe to drink, but some people prefer bottled water.

Rattlesnakes and scorpions are found in limited numbers in northern Arizona. Neither are common, but be aware that they may be present, especially in rocky areas. Usually a rattlesnake gives a warning before striking, but be alert and don't put your hands or feet anywhere that you can't see. If you are bitten, try to remain calm and send for medical help.

CLOTHING AND FOOTGEAR

When packing for your photographic excursion to the Grand Canyon and northern Arizona, remember that this area is mostly a high plateau where the weather can be severe and change quickly. During the time of year when most photographers visit northern Arizona, from April to early October, daytime temperatures can range from 40 to 90 degrees F. Rain is generally sparse except in late July and August, when afternoon thunderstorms known as "The Monsoon" are common. Some storms may be severe and accompanied by lightning and strong winds. In April and October, snow may fall at the rims of the Grand Canyon, although it usually melts quickly.

During the months of June, July, and August, the daytime temperatures are usually very warm except on the North Rim of the Grand Canyon. The sun may be intense due to the low humidity, and a hat with a brim and the use of sunscreen are necessary to avoid sunburn. Insects, especially cedar gnats, may be a problem during the summer months, but they usually die after the first cold night of autumn.

Layered clothing is the best way to cope with the large swings in temperature that may occur during the day. It is easy to stay comfortable by adding or subtracting layers such as sweaters, sweatshirts, or light jackets. A windbreaker is helpful to keep the wind from penetrating the layers below. A knit cap and light gloves may be needed early in the morning in early spring and late fall.

Comfortable, well-broken-in hiking boots are essential. Boots should be high enough to provide ankle support and have an aggressive lug sole for secure footing on rocks and trails. Consider wearing two pairs of socks—one thin inner pair and a heavier outer pair—for comfort.

If you plan to visit the Grand Canyon and northern Arizona in the wintertime, you can expect a large variety of weather conditions. Daytime temperatures usually range from 30 to 40 degrees F, and nighttime temperatures can drop to 0 degrees F or lower. Strong Pacific storms are possible, which could drop several inches of snow, especially at the South Rim of the Grand Canyon. The North Rim is closed from mid-October to mid-May. A heavy jacket, gloves, long underwear, a heavy sweater, and a wool hat should be added to your clothing list in the wintertime.

EQUIPMENT

Your photographic equipment will be governed by your specific interests, the time of year, and your budget. The following list assumes that you will want to photograph landscapes as well as some wildlife and close-ups.

Single-Lens Reflex Camera. Although a few folks will be using simple point-and-shoot cameras, most will want the versatility and quality of a good 35mm single-lens reflex. I own Canons and Minoltas, but Nikon, Pentax, and several other manufacturers make equally high-quality cameras. If your only interests are landscapes or flowers, a manual-focus camera and lenses are suitable. If you also plan to photograph wildlife, an autofocus camera and lenses are a distinct advantage.

I strongly recommend bringing an extra camera body along on any photographic trip. A camera body may be inadvertently dropped or broken, and sometimes camera bodies cease to operate properly for unknown reasons. You may want to shoot both negatives and slides of the same subject, and an extra body allows you to do this.

A larger camera that uses 120 or 220 film in 645, 2¼ square, or 6x7 format is also an option for landscape or close-up work. These formats give larger images, which are useful for making large prints, but they are typically more expensive, less versatile, heavier, and bulkier than 35mm equipment.

You should have a good working knowledge of how your camera functions, such as how to bracket exposures by half stops (or one-third stops if you are a Nikon user), how the metering system works, how filters affect exposure, and how to control depth of field. You should determine the correct ISO for your camera and film by shooting a test roll on "average" subjects at different ISOs before arriving at your photographic destination. It's a good idea to practice with your cameras, lenses, and filters at home so that you will be able to react quickly and precisely when photographing on location.

Landscape Lenses. On a 35mm camera, you need a range of lenses from 20mm on the wide-angle end to 200mm or even 300mm on the telephoto end. I firmly believe that zoom lenses are more versatile and cost-effective than an arsenal of fixed-focal-length lenses.

If you can afford the lenses made by the manufacturer of your camera, buy them; they will give more consistent color rendition than "off-brand" lenses. However, the quality of lenses manufactured by Tokina, Tamron, Sigma, and Vivitar is improving, and they offer good value. When purchasing off-brand lenses, choose apochromatic glass, which usually provides better sharpness and color rendition than normal glass. It's a little more expensive, but the greater quality is worth the extra money.

Close-up Lens or Macro Lens. Close-ups of many subjects, such as flowers, lichen patterns, and rock patterns, make powerful images. However, most lenses used for landscape or wildlife photography do not focus closely enough to allow the magnification that full-frame images of these small subjects demand.

A number of good solutions are available. The cheapest is to purchase a set of close-up lenses. These lenses look like filters and usually come in sets of three that can be used either separately or in combination to achieve the proper magnification. They are relatively inexpensive and can be used on one of your existing lenses.

Extension tubes or bellows can be inserted between the camera and the lens to allow closer focusing. Extension tubes also come in sets of three that can be used separately or together. Bellows can be thought of as variable extension tubes. Both extension tubes and bellows have the advantage of not adding any glass over the primary lens and thus may yield marginally sharper pictures than close-up lenses. However, both are more expensive and bulky than close-up lenses.

Macro lenses are simply lenses that focus much more closely than ordinary lenses. They yield high-quality images and are more convenient to use than the other options. However, macro lenses are also considerably more expensive than close-up lenses, extension tubes, or bellows.

Whichever option you choose, I recommend that the lens used for close-ups be at least 100mm in focal length. This allows you to set up farther from your subject and still get the same size image you would obtain using a shorter lens from a closer distance. By using a longer lens, you also minimize the background area and its potentially distracting elements.

Telephoto Lenses. Although northern Arizona is not famous for its wildlife, some interesting animals and birds are found at the rims of the Grand Canyon. For these subjects, I recommend a telephoto lens. Using a longer lens allows you to photograph your subject without frightening or disturbing it.

I do not recommend buying an expensive telephoto lens just to photograph wildlife at the Grand Canyon or northern Arizona. If you already have a medium-range telephoto zoom, such as a 75–300mm, it will be suitable for photographing the area's mule deer, wild turkeys, ground squirrels, and birds.

Film. A photographer's choice of film for a particular purpose is a personal one. A wide range of films exists, and new films are introduced every year. Each film has its unique blend of speed, grain, and color rendition. Which one you choose depends on the subject material and the way you see color.

For landscapes and close-ups, I recommend a relatively slow film (ISO 50 to 100) for either slides or negatives. These slow films have superior sharpness and very fine grain. Many films meet these requirements, but my personal choice for slides is Fuji Velvia (ISO 50). It has extremely good sharpness, fine grain, and enhanced color saturation. Its rich blacks give Velvia very good apparent contrast.

If greater film speed is required for wildlife photography or close-ups, I recommend Fuji Sensia 100 (ISO 100). It has the fine grain structure necessary, although the color saturation is less pronounced than with Velvia.

For negatives of landscapes, choose a film that gives good color saturation and contrast. Most negative films are made for photographs of people, in which exposure latitude (lack of contrast) is important. My personal choices are Agfa HDC 100 (ISO 100) and Agfa Ultra 50 (ISO 50), which provide the color saturation and contrast in prints that Velvia provides in slides. Other good negative films for scenics include Fuji Super G 100 and Kodak Royal Gold 100. For black-and-white shots of landscapes, an ISO 50 to 100 film is appropriate.

If you are shooting slides at the Grand Canyon and northern Arizona, plan on exposing five rolls of film per day. Negative shooters may need only three rolls per day. This is because slide makers need to bracket exposures to ensure the proper density; the exposure of negatives is not quite as critical. Although film is available at most visitor centers and photo shops in nearby towns, prices are high. It's better to buy plenty of film before you arrive and take a few rolls home if necessary.

Tripod. A sturdy tripod is a necessity for most scenic photographs. Putting your camera on a tripod forces you to be more careful and thoughtful about your composition. Many landscapes are taken during the low-light conditions that exist near sunrise and sunset. Polarizing and enhancing filters further reduce the amount of light that strikes the film. Because relatively slow films (ISO 50 to 100) are normally used for scenic photographs, the requirements for depth of field may necessitate small apertures with correspondingly slow shutter speeds. This combination of factors makes the use of a sturdy tripod mandatory.

A tripod is also useful for close-ups. At high magnifications, it is especially important to frame precisely in order to include the objects you wish to show and exclude any distractions. Great depth of field may be needed to render an entire flower or other subject sharp, which usually means using a relatively slow shutter speed.

Filters. For color landscape photography in northern Arizona, several filters are mandatory. A polarizing filter has the widest application. When oriented at a right angle to the sun, it effectively controls glare and reflections from nonmetallic surfaces. A polarizing filter makes skies darker and less distracting and make colors more saturated. When properly oriented, it also makes rainbows more vivid.

With Velvia film, I almost always use an enhancing filter along with a polarizing filter. It is a band-pass filter that works principally on the reds, oranges, browns, and purples in the spectrum. This makes an enhancing filter ideal for the red rock landscapes at the Grand Canyon and northern Arizona as well as autumn foliage, sunrises, and sunsets.

Split neutral-density filters even out the contrast so that both the bright and the dark parts of a scene can be exposed properly. This is often necessary when the sun is striking one part of a scene directly and another portion, where detail is desired, is in shadow. The split neutral-density filter is also useful with photographs that involve reflections, because the reflection is always a stop or two darker than the original scene.

For color photography, an 81A filter may be useful. It is slightly amber and is used to make autumn foliage a little more colorful or to warm up any scene.

For black-and-white photography at the Grand Canyon and northern Arizona, I recommend either an orange or a red filter. These filters darken the sky and lighten the red rock formations, making them stand out from the background.

Miscellaneous Equipment. I don't recommend taking a lot of doodads along on a serious photography expedition. Remember that you'll have to carry all this stuff around. However, some items are useful and are worth the extra weight. You should always carry extra batteries for your camera. Some cameras are harder on batteries than others, but I always have at least two spares. Also useful is a double-bubble level that attaches to the hot shoe of your camera (except Minolta Maxxum). By having two bubbles, you can level your camera for either horizontal or vertical pictures. I also carry a small set of flat-head and Phillips jeweler's screwdrivers. Another handy item is a film retriever in case you inadvertently wind the film leader back inside the cassette when changing film in midroll. Most photographers use a cable release to help keep camera shake to a minimum when exposing their pictures. Another useful item is a soft brush to remove dust from lenses and filters.

You may also want to carry a plastic card that contains hyperfocal distance information, which is important for landscape work. A hyperfocal chart tells you what distance to set on your lens, with a given focal length and aperture, to obtain maximum depth of field with infinity as the far distance.

Carrying Your Photo Gear. Although some photographs at the Grand Canyon and northern Arizona can be taken close to your car, many require a short walk. A camera bag, camera backpack, or photographer's vest can be used to carry cameras, lenses, filters, extra film, and other items. The choice is primarily a matter of personal taste.

Camera bags can hold and protect all your equipment, but they must be carried either in your hand or by a strap around your neck. This is okay for short distances, but carrying a camera bag on longer walks can be very tiring. A camera backpack does an equally good job of carrying your gear and is much more comfortable on longer jaunts. Depending on its size, a backpack may also hold water bottles, jackets, and food. The biggest advantage of a photographer's vest is quick and easy access to all your equipment. The disadvantages are limited capacity and the burden of carrying the weight on the front of your body, which may be hard on your back.

PHOTOGRAPHIC ETHICS

When visiting the Grand Canyon and northern Arizona, or any other natural area, you have a responsibility not to adversely affect the ecology. This means abiding by all park rules. Many things are obvious: Don't pick the flowers, don't remove artifacts or plants, and don't write on or remove rocks from the area.

You have to decide for yourself what is appropriate when photographing nature. Some people believe that removing distractions such as bright grass, twigs, or small rocks from the foreground of a landscape shot is wrong. I don't agree. I don't think these minor alterations affect the ecology of the region. However, my philosophy is that you should leave the area in the same condition that you found it. Remember that millions of people visit this area every year, and just a few thoughtless people can cause permanent damage. You came to the Grand Canyon and northern Arizona to photograph its beauty. Be sure that you do nothing to lessen that beauty.

TWO

The Grand Canyon

WHAT TO EXPECT IN THE PARK

The South Rim of Grand Canyon National Park, including all tourist facilities, is open year-round. The nearest major cities are Phoenix, Arizona, about 200 miles to the south, and Las Vegas, Nevada, about 275 miles to the west. The nearest town of any significant size is Flagstaff, Arizona, about 80 miles to the southeast. Flagstaff is served by commuter aircraft from Phoenix about half a dozen times a day. Rental cars from all the national chains are available in Las Vegas, Phoenix, or Flagstaff.

The South Rim can be reached from Flagstaff and from Williams, Arizona (59 miles to the south), via Interstate 40, US 180, and Arizona 64. The South Rim can also be reached from the east via US 89 and Arizona 64 from Cameron, Arizona (31 miles). The Grand Canyon Airport, located at Tusayan, just south of the park, provides access by small plane. The Grand Canyon Railway runs from Williams to the South Rim.

Access to the viewpoints along the most frequently visited portions of the South Rim is in a state of change. More than 5 million people visit the South Rim every year, and the existing transportation system and tourist facilities have been overwhelmed. In the future, during the peak season, the park plans to provide access to many of the viewpoints with a mass transit system combining light rail and buses. The overall transit system is expected to be fully operational by 2005. At present, the park transportation system is expected to operate only from the first of March through the end of October. During the summer months, overnight visitors will be able to drive to their hotels or campgrounds, but within the park, shuttles will be the primary form

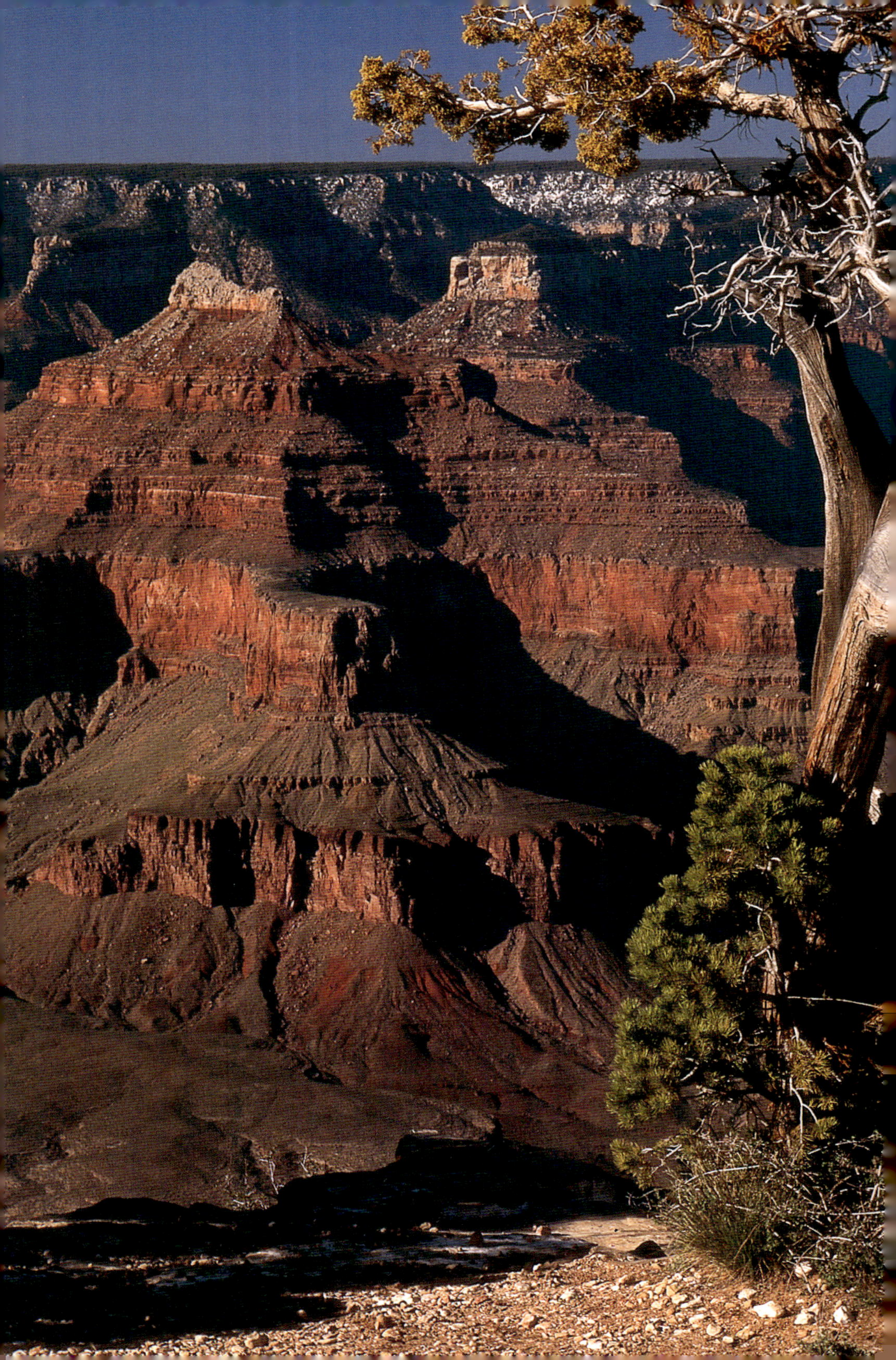

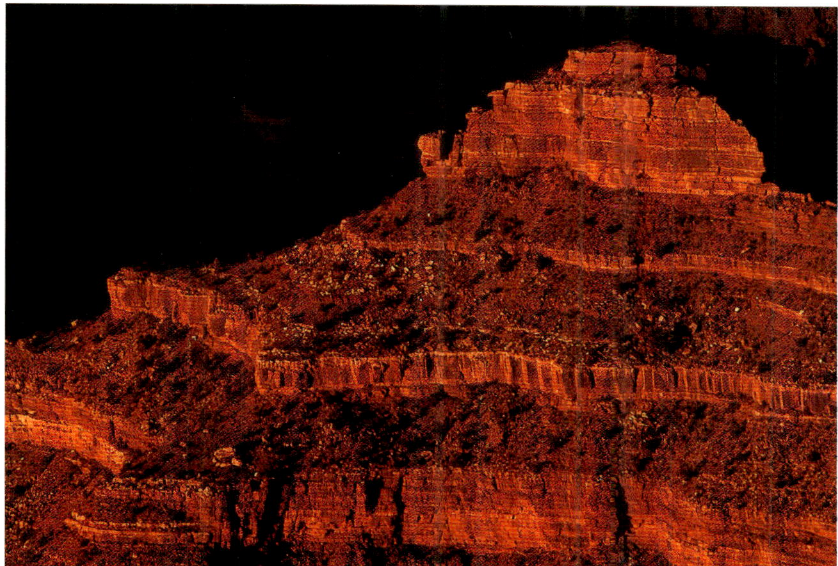

Butte at sunset, Mather Point, Grand Canyon National Park, Arizona. As the sun sets, individual buttes down in the canyon become isolated by the lengthening shadows. The sunset colors are made even more vivid by the use of polarizing and enhancing filters. Take a spot meter reading on the sunlit buttes so that the shadowed areas do not affect your exposure. *Minolta 70–210mm lens, enhancing and polarizing filters, Fuji Velvia film.*

of transportation. During the winter months, present plans call for all roads and viewpoints, even the West Rim Drive, to be open to private vehicles. When the park transportation system is fully operational, cars will still be able to drive along the eastern portion of the South Rim between Tusayan and Desert View. However, since many of the details of the new system were unresolved when this book was written, you should contact park headquarters before your visit or immediately upon your arrival.

Currently, during the peak season from March 1 to October 31, transit buses are scheduled to run from one hour before sunrise to one

Isis Temple from Hopi Point, Grand Canyon National Park, Arizona. Photographs of the Grand Canyon are more effective if you concentrate on one or two prominent buttes rather than on the whole canyon. Trees or plants close to the canyon's edge can be used for framing. *Minolta 70–210mm lens, enhancing and polarizing filters, Fuji Velvia film.*

hour after sunset. Since it takes a considerable amount of time to traverse the entire loop, you should plan to take a bus that will get you to your photographic destination with plenty of time to spare.

The North Rim is open only from mid-May through mid-October due to heavy winter snows. Las Vegas, the closest major city, is about 260 miles to the southwest. Access is via US 89A and Arizona 67 from Kanab, Utah, to the north (80 miles); US 89, US 89A, and Arizona 67 from Page, Arizona, to the northeast (125 miles); or US 89, US 89A, and Arizona 67 from Flagstaff (195 miles) to the south. Even though the South Rim and the North Rim are only 10 miles apart as the crow flies, they are 215 miles apart by road.

The Tuweep area of Grand Canyon National Park, which features Toroweap Point, is a primitive area on the North Rim at the western end of the park. It can be reached by several dirt roads from Arizona 389 and Utah 59, a paved road that connects Fredonia, Arizona and Hurricane, Utah. The distance to Tuweep on these dirt roads varies from 70 to 50 miles, depending on where you leave the pavement. These dirt roads are impassable when wet and should be traveled only when dry weather is anticipated.

Facilities Inside the Park. A wide range of accommodations inside the park on the South Rim are open year-round. Some of the units are rustic, and others are luxurious. Most of the facilities were built many years ago and offer historic value but may not be as comfortable as the newer motels just outside the park. Prices range from $44 at the Bright Angel Lodge to $279 at the El Tovar Hotel (1999 rates). Reservations are highly recommended throughout the year.

The Grand Canyon Lodge is the only accommodation available inside the park on the North Rim. Like its counterparts on the South Rim, it is an older hotel and somewhat pricey. Reservations are highly recommended.

A number of restaurants, snack bars, and cafeterias are located in Grand Canyon Village on the South Rim. General stores, which carry a wide selection of food and tourist supplies, are located in Grand Canyon Village and at Desert View. Other services available at Grand Canyon Village include a bank, a post office, a garage with mechanics on duty, kennels, a beauty and barber shop, a self-service laundry, and showers.

On the North Rim, the only eating facilities are located in the Grand Canyon Lodge. A general store carries groceries and other staples. Gas stations are located inside the park on both rims. The station at Grand Canyon Village is open year-round. The gas station on the North Rim and the one at Desert View on the South Rim are open only during the summer months. The stations on the South Rim may close when the shuttle system is fully implemented.

Two national park campgrounds and a trailer village are available on the South Rim. The Mather campground and the trailer village, near Grand Canyon Village, are open year-round. The National Park Service campground on the North Rim is open from mid-May to mid-October. Reservations for the Grand Canyon Village and North Rim campgrounds can be made through Biospherics by calling (800) 365-2267. A campground at Desert View is on a first-come, first-served basis and is open only during the warmer months.

Facilities Outside the Park. Flagstaff is the major gateway city for the South Rim. It contains a wide variety of motels, restaurants, and shopping facilities. The University of Northern Arizona is located at Flagstaff. Flagstaff is the only nearby location with a significant selection of photographic equipment.

Williams, west of Flagstaff, has a number of motels and restaurants but is much smaller than Flagstaff and does not offer the same variety of goods and services. A motel and restaurant are also located at Bedrock City (Valle) about 30 miles south of the park entrance.

The small town of Tusayan, located just south of the park boundary, is the best staging location for photographing the South Rim. It is only 10 miles from Mather Point and provides easy access to the new shuttle system. Tusayan is expanding rapidly and already offers a wide variety of services. Prices are high because of the location and because all the water used in Tusayan has to be trucked in. At the present time, eight motels offer accommodations year-round. Reservations are highly recommended. Several campgrounds and trailer parks are located in or near Tusayan. Dining facilities include McDonald's, Wendy's, Subway, Denny's, Pizza Hut, and Taco Bell, as well as several more expensive sit-down restaurants. An Imax Theater shows films of the Grand Canyon. A general store and service stations are also available. Flights over the Grand Canyon can be booked at the Grand Canyon Airport at Tusayan.

Cameron and Grey Mountain, Arizona, east of the South Rim, also offer accommodations, dining facilities, gasoline, and other tourist services. The Cameron Trading Post has one of the best collections of Native American rugs, pottery, and jewelry in the region. Costs for

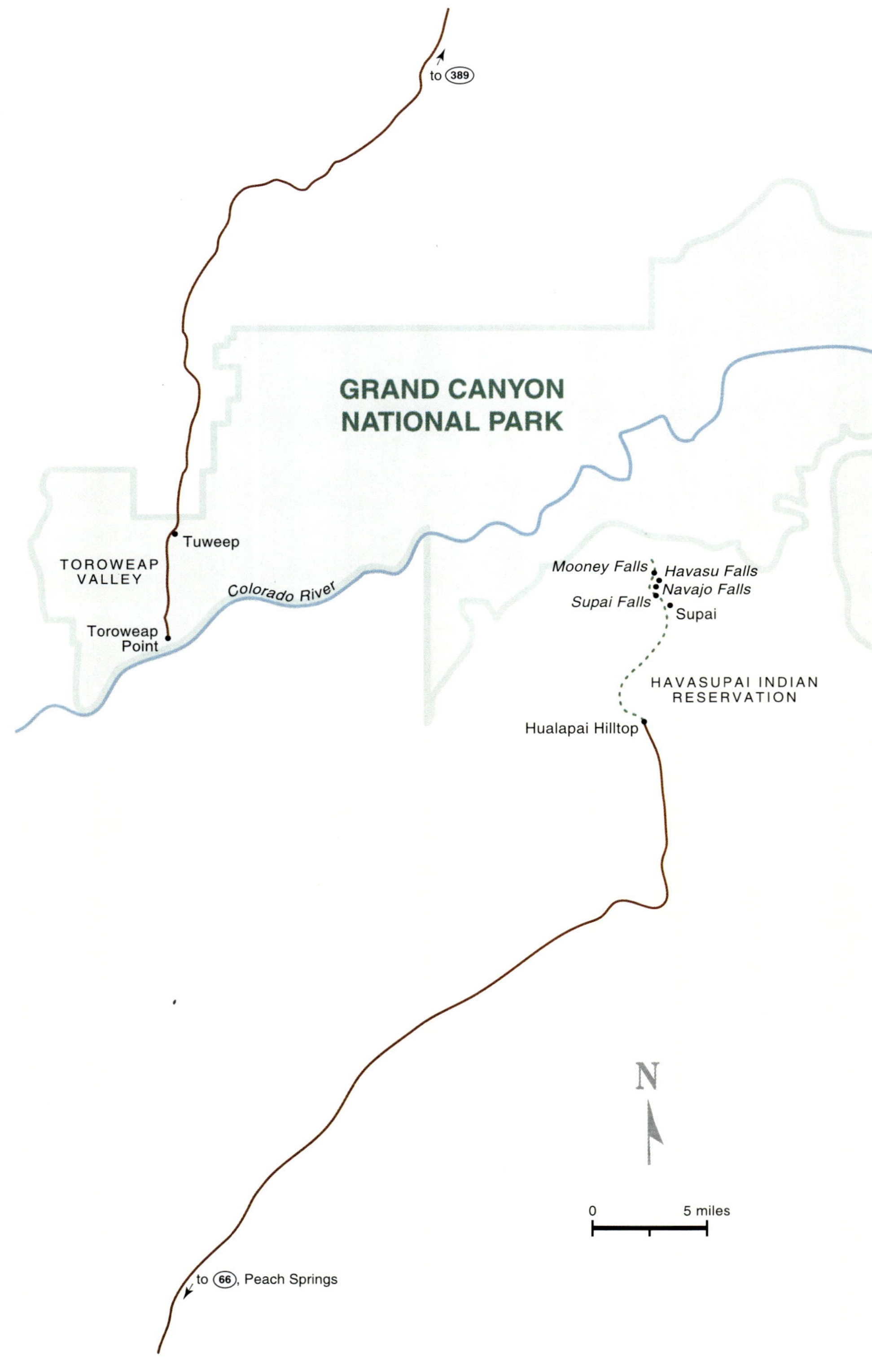

to 389
GRAND CANYON NATIONAL PARK
Tuweep
TOROWEAP VALLEY
Colorado River
Toroweap Point
Mooney Falls
Havasu Falls
Navajo Falls
Supai Falls
Supai
HAVASUPAI INDIAN RESERVATION
Hualapai Hilltop
N
0
5 miles
to 66, Peach Springs

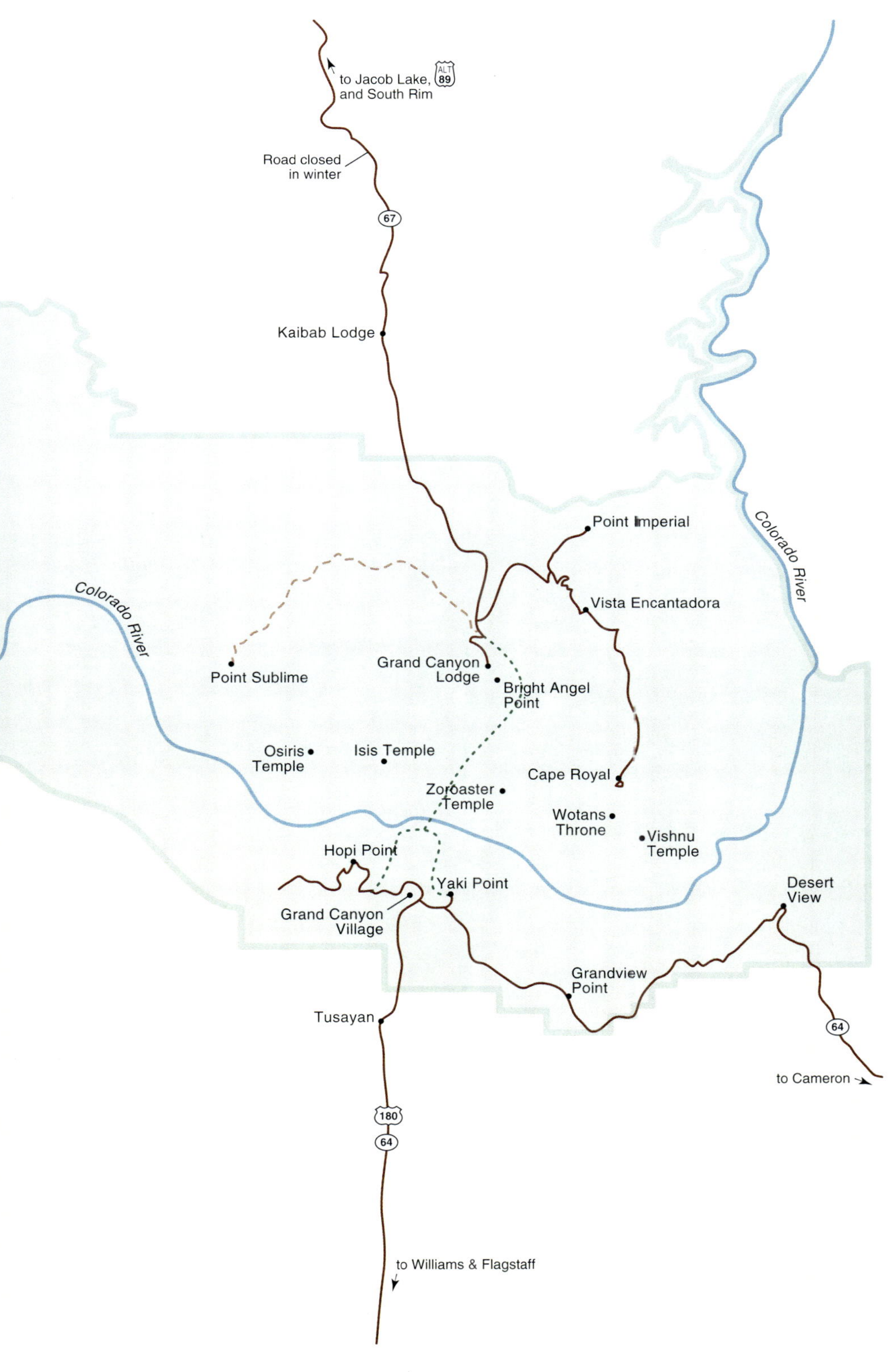

to Jacob Lake, ALT 89
and South Rim
Road closed
in winter
67
Kaibab Lodge
Colorado River
Point Imperial
Vista Encantadora
Colorado River
Point Sublime
Grand Canyon
Lodge
Bright Angel
Point
Osiris
Temple
Isis Temple
Cape Royal
Zoroaster
Temple
Wotans
Throne
Vishnu
Temple
Hopi Point
Yaki Point
Desert
View
Grand Canyon
Village
Grandview
Point
Tusayan
64
to Cameron
180
64
to Williams & Flagstaff

services are generally lower in Cameron than in Tusayan. However, Cameron is located more than 50 miles from the best photographic viewpoints on the South Rim, which makes photographing sunrises and sunsets more difficult.

At the North Rim, the nearest facilities outside the park are at the Kaibab Lodge about 5 miles north of the park boundary. The accommodations are rustic but clean and comfortable. The Kaibab Lodge

Autumn color at Vista Encantada, Grand Canyon National Park, Arizona. On the higher and wetter North Rim, autumn color can add to the impact and interest of pictures of the canyon. In early October, the color of the aspen and underbrush is at its best. These aspen were intentionally isolated against a dark portion of the canyon to make them stand out better. *Minolta 35–70mm lens, enhancing and polarizing filters, Fuji Velvia film.*

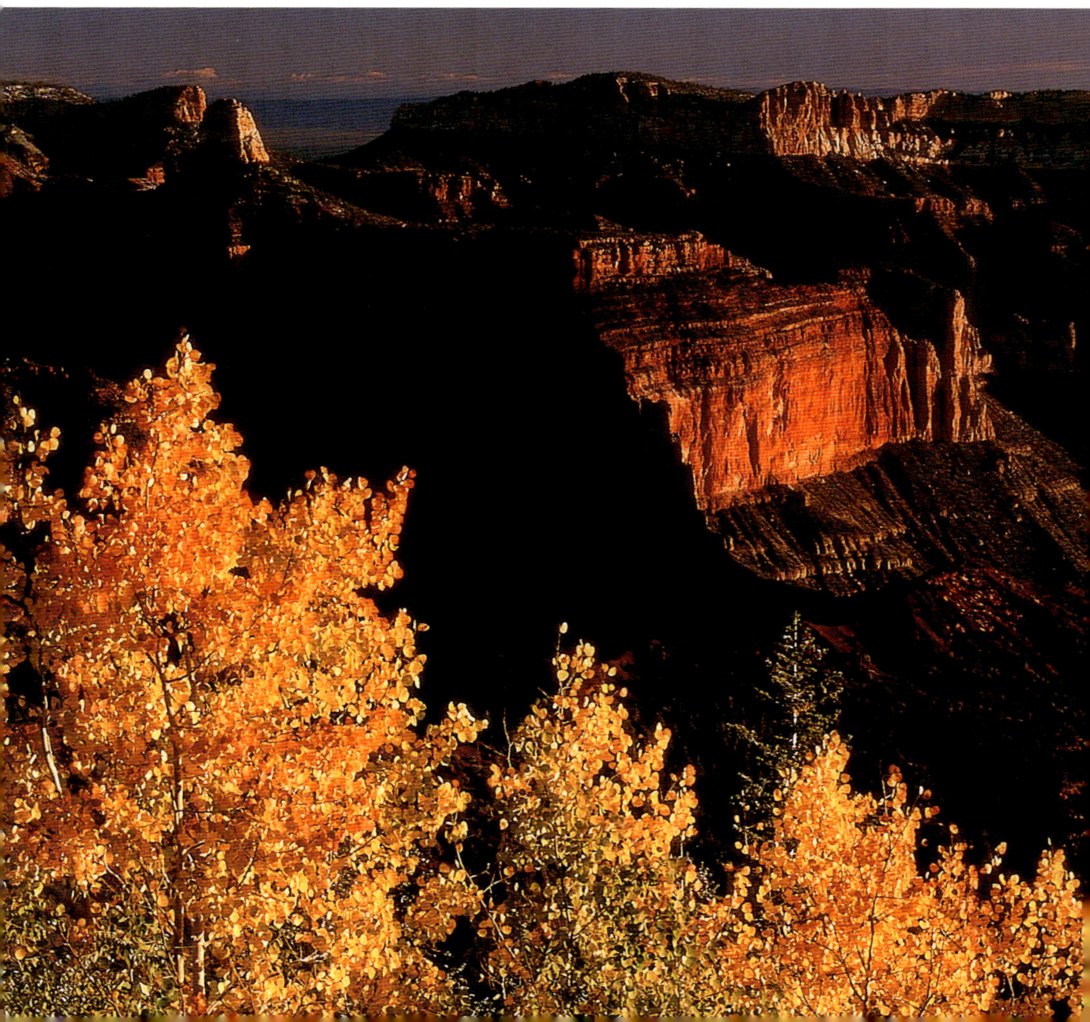

also features a good restaurant and a gas station. A motel, restaurant, gas station, and general store are also available at Jacob Lake, about 30 miles north of Grand Canyon National Park. Several National Forest Service campgrounds are located between Jacob Lake and the North Rim. Complete tourist facilities with a wide assortment of motels, restaurants, stores, and services can be found in the towns of Fredonia, Arizona, and Kanab, Utah, about 60 and 67 miles, respectively, north of the park boundary.

Arriving at the Grand Canyon. Entrance stations on the South Rim are open 24 hours a day year-round but may not be staffed at night. The fees are $20 for a private vehicle and its occupants for a week; $50 for a Golden Eagle Pass, which admits the holder and the other occupants of a private vehicle to all federal lands for one year; and $10 for a Golden Age Pass, which admits a person aged 62 or older to all federal lands for life (1999 rates). Park personnel compare signatures on driver's licenses with signatures on Golden Eagle and Golden Age Passes to verify identity.

At your first opportunity you should stop at the visitor center on the South Rim, where you can obtain books, maps, and information that will make your visit to the park more enjoyable. Information can also be obtained at the Desert View information center, the Tusayan Museum, the Yavapai observation station, and the Kolb Studio. On the North Rim, information can be obtained at the entrance station.

PHOTOGRAPHING THE GRAND CANYON

The Grand Canyon offers limitless photographic possibilities, but capturing the beauty and immensity of the canyon on film is a challenge. Most people are overwhelmed by the size of the canyon and try to include too much in one picture. It is best to concentrate on smaller parts of the canyon and make them the focal point of the picture. A number of prominent buttes such as Shiva Temple, Osiris Temple, Isis Temple, Zoroaster Temple, Wotan's Throne, and Vishnu Temple make excellent centers of interest, depending on the viewpoint. When possible, try to include trees, rocks, or shrubs in the foreground to frame the buttes and give depth to the picture. Either eliminate the sky entirely or include only a sliver of sky above the horizon; a little sky can be useful to provide perspective, but too much sky is usually distracting.

Lighting conditions are just as important as good composition in obtaining memorable pictures of the canyon. Sunrise and sunset

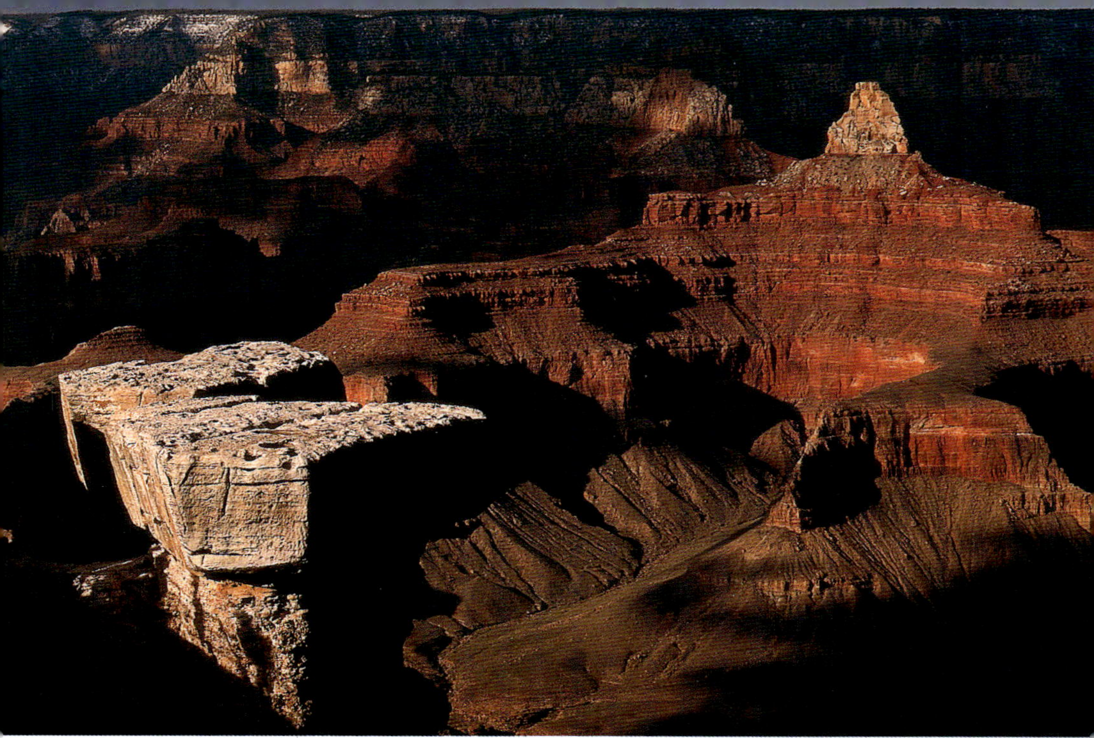

Zoroaster Temple from Mather Point, Grand Canyon National Park, Arizona. This afternoon shot of the canyon includes Mather Point in the lower left which balances the sunlit butte in the upper right part of the photograph. The shadows from scattered clouds darken the less interesting parts of the background and spotlight the butte. Time and patience are both required to obtain the best lighting on any subject. *Minolta 70–210mm lens, polarizing and enhancing filters, Fuji Velvia film.*

produce glowing colors and long shadows. Be sure to stop down (use negative compensation; give less light) when exposing photographs with large shadow areas. Flat lighting and overhead lighting are uninteresting and should be avoided. The middle of the day, when the sun is too high for good lighting, is an excellent time to explore and look for other interesting compositions and framing of the canyon.

Sidelighting, which provides texture to canyon features, or backlighting, which adds drama, should be used whenever possible. Polarizing and enhancing filters should always be considered in red rock country when the lighting is from the side. The enhancing filter is especially important when using Fuji Velvia film. For backlit shots, remove the polarizer, since it has little or no effect. Special weather conditions such as thunderstorms, snow, or haze produce interesting moods. Overall cloudiness usually produces lighting that is dull and uninteresting.

Besides photographing my favorite spots, I encourage you to look for other compositions. In addition to the grand scenics, patterns that include rocks, gnarled trees, and flowers make good subjects. As you walk along the rim, continually look for interesting compositions. That's how you develop your photographic eye.

From the South Rim. Photographing on the South Rim will be much more challenging when the shuttle system becomes the only means of transportation to the viewpoints in 2002. It will impair your ability to react quickly to changing atmospheric conditions and slow you down when lighting conditions are optimal. You will need to identify your photographic locations much further in advance and allow extra time to reach them. The exclusive use of the mass transportation system will necessitate more days of photography to achieve the same results and will also make carrying your camera equipment more difficult. Knowing in advance where the best pictures can be obtained will be more important than ever.

Mather Point. When you arrive at the South Rim from Tusayan, your first stop should be Mather Point. Currently, you can park your own vehicle at Mather Point, but when the shuttle system becomes operational, you will need to take a short trail to the viewpoint. Mather Point is one of the finest locations for photographing the canyon at either sunrise or sunset.

At sunrise, Wotan's Throne and Vishnu Temple provide interesting silhouettes, but colorful clouds just above the horizon are needed for a successful shot. A telephoto lens allows you to concentrate on the most dramatic portions of the sunrise. An enhancing filter makes the colors in the sky more vivid. If you want to include detail in the canyon below and still have good color saturation in the clouds, you need to use about four stops of split neutral density on the portion of the picture above the horizon. Also, look for shafts of light that combine with the atmospheric haze to separate the different planes in the canyon.

Shortly after sunrise, walk northwest from the overlook along the rim for about 100 yards to a spot that features a view of Isis Temple in the background and a particularly interesting rock formation on the rim in the foreground. Be sure to reach this viewpoint while shadows still separate the foreground and the background. I also recommend taking a telephoto shot concentrating on this interesting cliff with the shadowed canyon in the background. The light is somewhat flat in winter, but in spring and autumn there is good sidelighting.

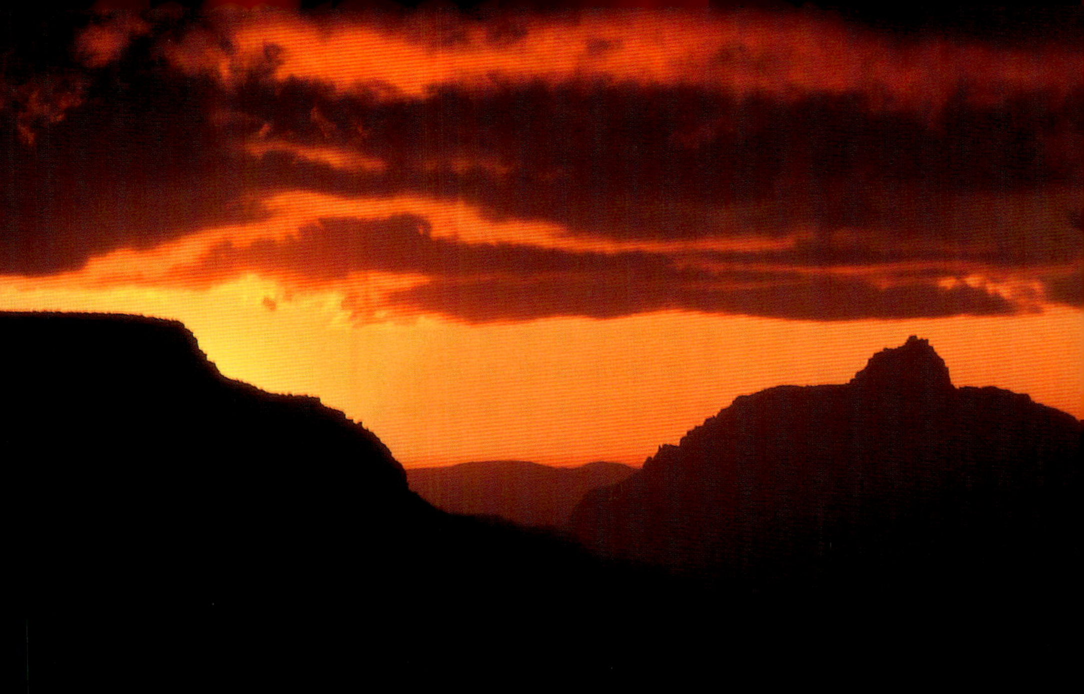

Sunrise at Mather Point, Grand Canyon National Park, Arizona. Sunrise at the Grand Canyon can be spectacular if you are fortunate enough to have some clouds in the east and clear sky immediately above the horizon. Everything below the horizon will be black, so devote most of your frame to the sky and take a spot meter reading on the colorful clouds. Try to choose an interesting butte for the center of interest. *Minolta 70–210mm lens, polarizing and enhancing filters, Fuji Velvia film.*

In the afternoon, I prefer shots along the rim east of the point that include Mather Point as framing for either Zoroaster Temple or Isis Temple. Be sure not to get the railing or shadows of people on the point in your picture.

As sunset approaches, position yourself either on Mather Point or along the rim several hundred yards east of the point. From these vantage points you can shoot unobstructed views of the canyon or portions of it as the shadows lengthen. Additionally, I like to use a telephoto lens to concentrate on several interesting buttes in the canyon as the area around them becomes shadowed.

Viewpoints West of Mather Point. A number of viewpoints west of Mather Point offer good photographic possibilities, including Yavapai Point, Maricopa Point, Powell Point, Hopi Point, Mohave Point, Pima Point, and Hermit's Rest. The Rim Trail runs from Yavapai Point to Hermit's Rest and provides many additional views. At present, Yavapai

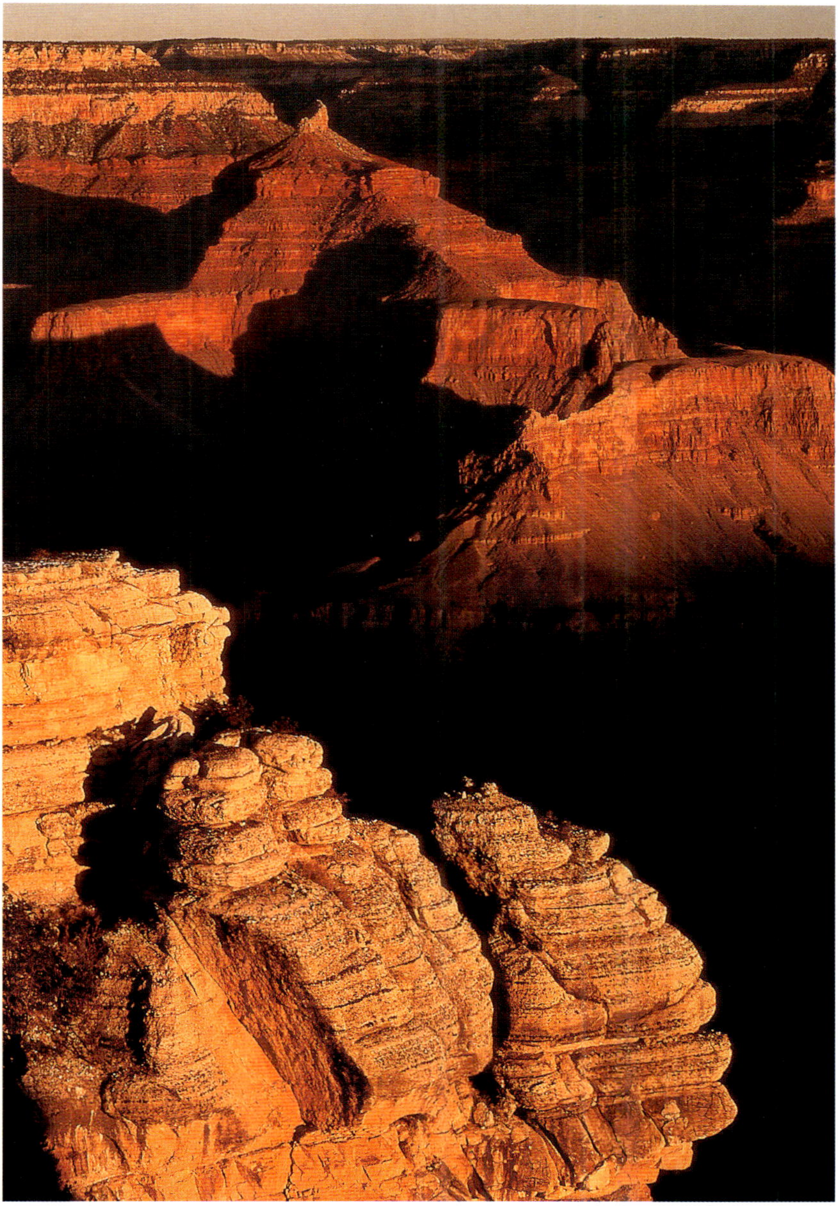

Sunrise at Mather Point. One of the best viewpoints on the South Rim for sunrise photography is Mather Point. This shot, from a trail along the rim just west of the main overlook, was taken while a shadow still separated Isis Temple from the interesting cliff in the foreground. *Minolta 35–70mm lens, polarizing and enhancing filters, Fuji Velvia film.*

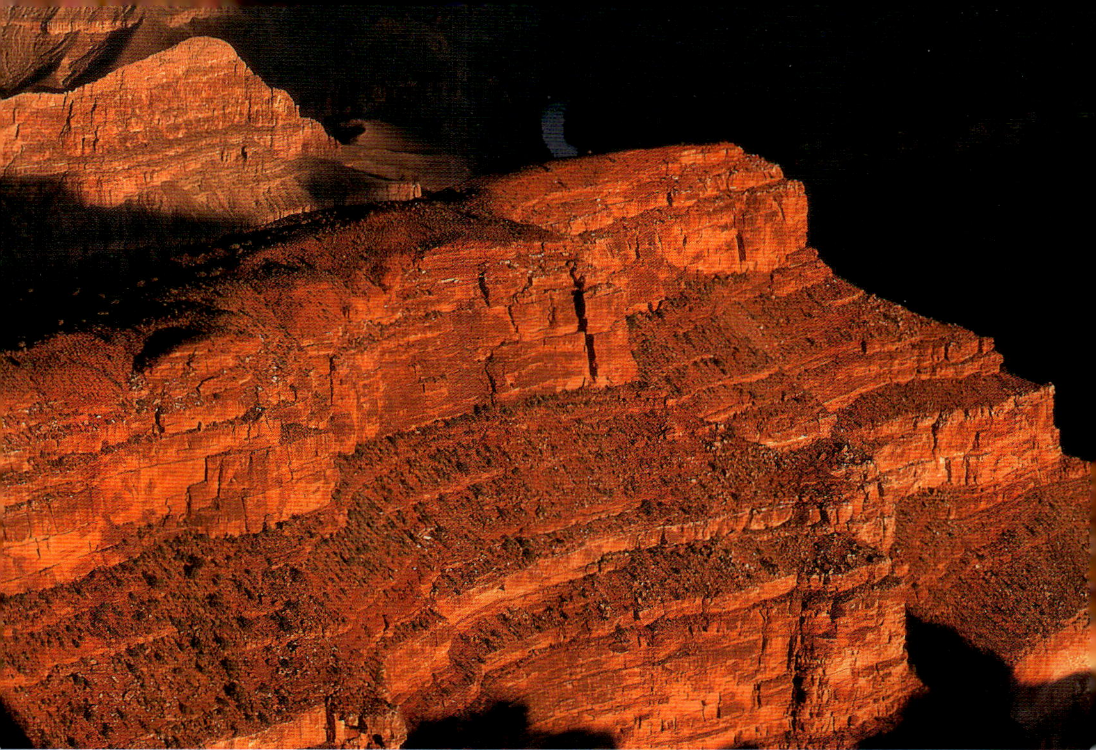

Sunrise at Hopi Point, Grand Canyon National Park, Arizona. Although Hopi Point is justifiably famous for its sunsets, sunrises can also be productive. For this shot, I pointed down into the canyon to the west of the overlook to capture the warm early light on a prominent cliff above the Colorado River. *Minolta 70–210mm lens, polarizing and enhancing filters, Fuji Velvia film.*

Point is accessible by car year-round; the other viewpoints are accessible by car from November through February but must be reached by shuttle the rest of the year. When the park transportation system becomes fully operational, you will be required to park your car at the Canyon View Information Plaza near Mather Point and take the free shuttle to all the West Rim viewpoints.

Although good photographs can be obtained at any of the West Rim points with the right lighting and atmospheric conditions, my favorite location is Hopi Point. Hopi Point protrudes farther north into the canyon than any of the other viewpoints on the South Rim, which makes it a particularly good location for unobstructed views up and down the canyon at sunrise or sunset. Hopi Point is extremely popular, so plan to arrive early, especially for sunset photos.

From Hopi Point at sunrise, either Shiva Temple or Osiris Temple is a good center of interest, depending on the time of year. I have also had good results catching the warm sunrise light on some of the cliffs just above the river.

In the late afternoon, walk east from the parking lot about 100 yards to several picturesque trees close to the rim. A short telephoto lens can be used to photograph Isis Temple framed by either of these trees. To achieve the required depth of field, focus at the hyperfocal distance. Polarizing and enhancing filters make the colors more vivid.

As sunset approaches, position yourself on the northeasternmost part of Hopi Point about 200 yards from the parking lot. This allows you the most expansive unobstructed view of the canyon when the color and patterns are best.

My second choice for photographs along the West Rim is Powell Point just east of Hopi Point. It has almost the same view of the canyon as Hopi Point but is not as well known or as crowded. At Powell Point, however, I haven't found any outstanding trees along the rim for framing.

Sunset from Hopi Point, Grand Canyon National Park, Arizona. Since Hopi Point protrudes farther north into the canyon than any of the other South Rim vantage points, it is a great place to photograph a sunset. Arrive early, because there may be competition for a good camera position. Wide compositions of the canyon or close-ups of specific features are both rewarding. *Minolta 35–70mm lens, polarizing and enhancing filters, Fuji Velvia film.*

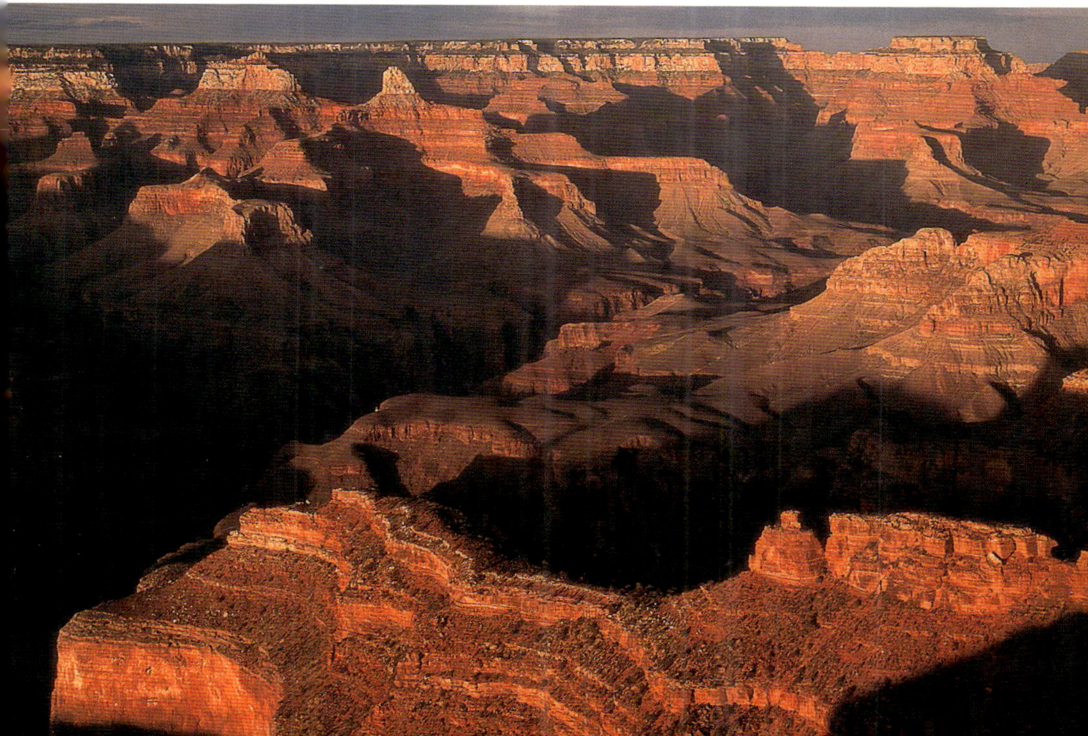

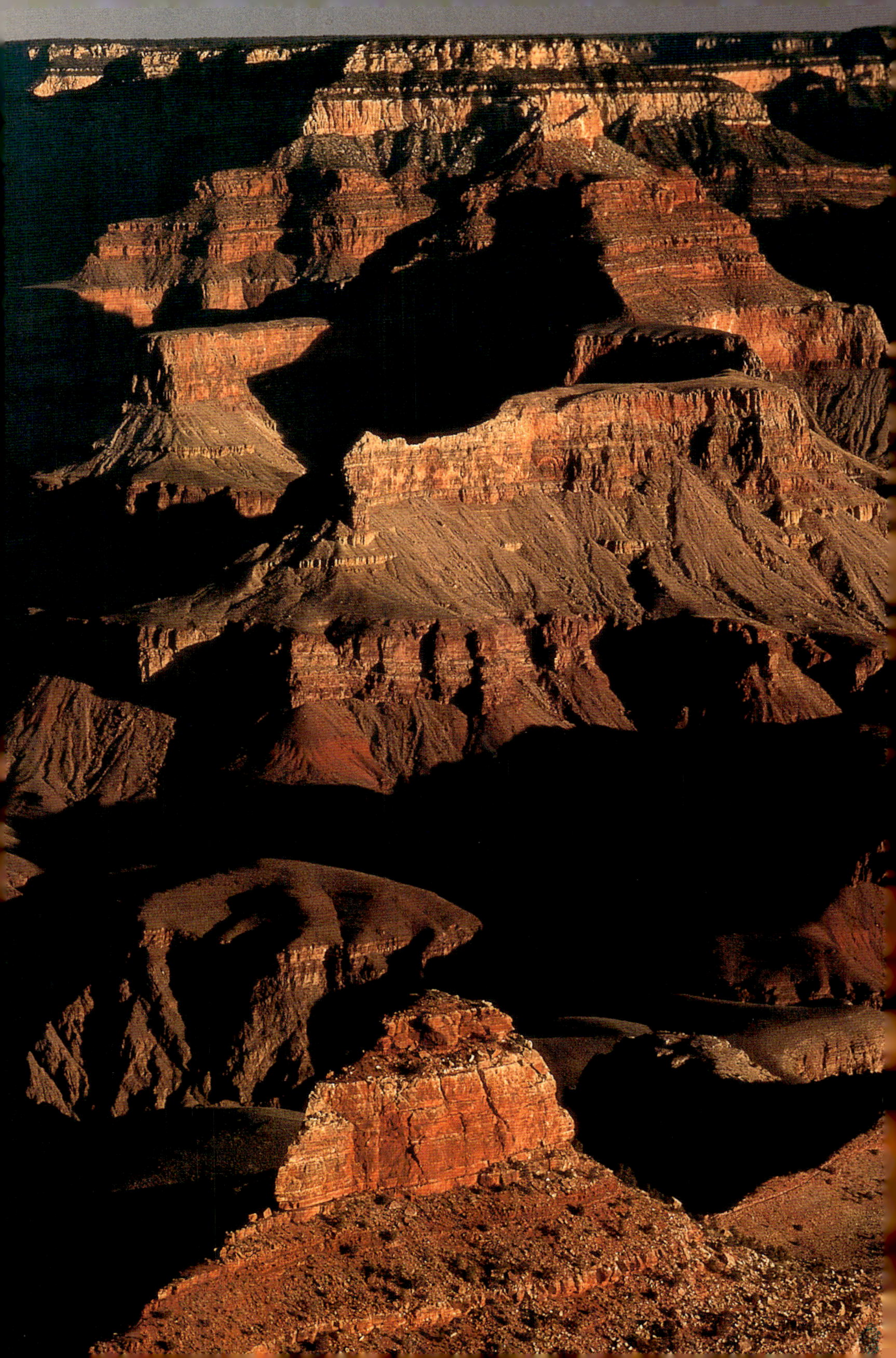

Viewpoints East of Mather Point. Turnouts and viewpoints along the South Rim east of Mather Point provide additional photographic opportunities. My favorite viewpoints east of Mather Point are Yaki Point, Grandview Point, and Desert View. Other viewpoints include Moran Point and Lipan Point. At the present time, all these locations can be reached by private vehicles with the exception of Yaki Point, which can be reached only by shuttle or on foot. When the new transportation system goes into effect, shuttle buses may provide the only access to these viewpoints.

Yaki Point, which protrudes about a mile into the canyon, provides excellent views both up and down the river and is a good spot in both early morning and late afternoon. From the parking lot at Yaki Point, walk east along the rim about 100 yards to a photogenic tree on the canyon rim. This tree can be used either as the center of interest, with the canyon as a backdrop, or as framing for Isis Temple. The challenge is to compose the shot so that the bright rock on the rim does not dominate the picture.

Farther east along the rim at Yaki Point, a good early-morning shot looks to the west and includes Isis Temple, along with a prominent butte in the canyon below. If you look east from this spot in the morning hours, several interesting foreground rocks provide good framing for backlit shots of the canyon. Yaki Point also provides an alternative to Hopi Point and Mather Point for late-afternoon and sunset pictures with Wotan's Throne and Vishnu Temple as the centers of interest.

From Grandview Point, an early-morning shot featuring Wotan's Throne makes an interesting image. Strong sidelighting provides good shadow detail in the canyon and helps to separate the buttes. Desert View provides one of the best views of the inner gorge and the Colorado River on the South Rim. Just west of the observation tower, look for an unusually picturesque tree along the canyon rim that frames the canyon and the river. Midmorning is a good time to photograph this composition. The potential for late-afternoon and sunset pictures from Grandview Point and Desert View is not as good as from Hopi, Mather, or Yaki Points.

View from Yaki Point, Grand Canyon National Park, Arizona. Yaki Point, just east of Mather Point, is an excellent destination for either morning or afternoon pictures. In this shot, the butte in the lower left balances Isis Temple in the upper right. *Minolta 70–210mm lens, polarizing and enhancing filters, Fuji Velvia film.*

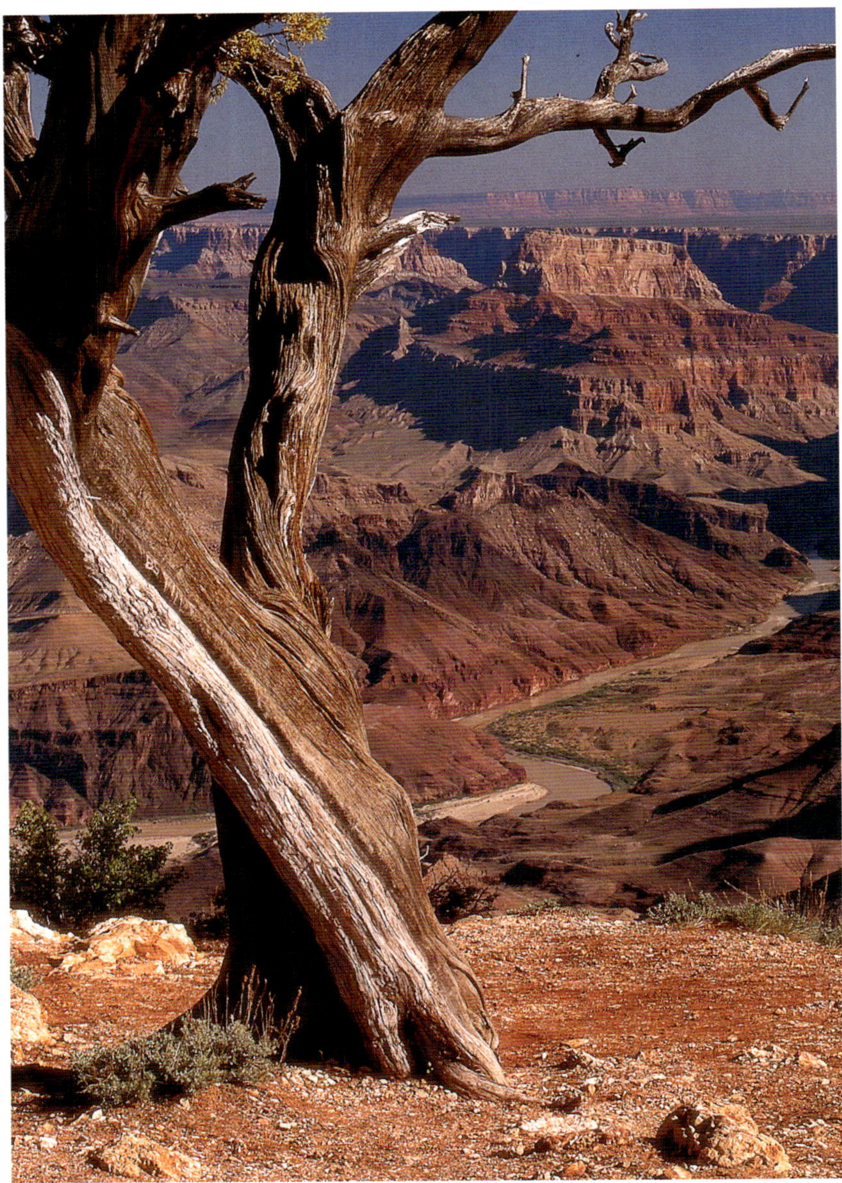

Colorado River from Desert View, Grand Canyon National Park, Arizona. Desert View, near the eastern entrance to the South Rim, provides excellent vistas of both the canyon and the Colorado River. Look for interesting juniper trees along the rim to frame the canyon. At Desert View, sunlight does not reach the river until midmorning. *Minolta 35–70mm lens, polarizing and enhancing filters, Fuji Velvia film.*

From the North Rim. The North Rim of the Grand Canyon has an entirely different personality than the South Rim. At an elevation of about 8,000 feet, it has colder temperatures and receives more precipitation than the South Rim. This additional moisture supports a forest of blue spruce and aspen, in contrast to the ponderosa pine and juniper on the South Rim. In early October, the aspen on the North Rim turn gold and provide excellent subject material either by themselves or with the canyon as a backdrop. The North Rim is open from mid-May to mid-October. Comparatively few people visit the North Rim, and a shuttle system to provide public transportation is neither needed nor planned.

The views of the Grand Canyon from the North Rim are at least as good as those from the South Rim. The buttes seen from the South Rim such as Isis Temple, Zoroaster Temple, Vishnu Temple, and Wotan's Throne, are all on the north side of the Colorado River. As a result, they

Sunset at Bright Angel Point, Grand Canyon National Park, Arizona. This image features Zoroaster Temple. I waited until the shadows crept up to the bottom of the frame so that the colors would be as warm and saturated as possible. I eliminated the sky because the Park Service was doing a "controlled burn" on the South Rim. *Minolta 70–210mm lens, polarizing and enhancing filters, Fuji Velvia film.*

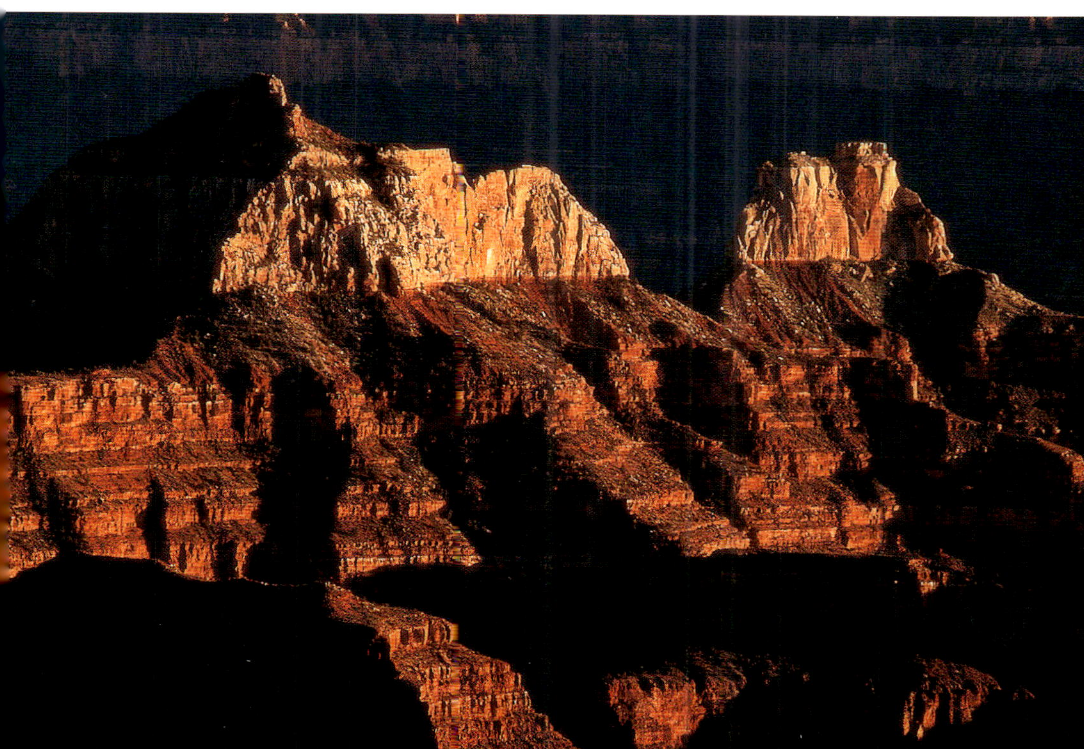

are more prominent and make even better centers of interest when seen from the north.

North Rim Viewpoints. The main road from Kanab and Jacob Lake to the north rim ends at Bright Angel Point. A number of good vantage points are available along the rim below the Grand Canyon Lodge. At sunrise and during the early morning, I recommend views of the canyon that feature Isis Temple. In late afternoon and at sunset, Zoroaster Temple and Wotan's Throne provide excellent centers of interest.

The road to Cape Royale and Point Imperial, which branches off the main highway several miles north of Bright Angel Point, winds through a beautiful forest of aspen and blue spruce. This stretch of road has good photographic potential, especially when the aspen are turning. Mule deer, blue grouse, and wild turkeys are often seen, although they are usually difficult to photograph.

Autumn on the North Rim, Grand Canyon National Park, Arizona. An attractive grove of aspen is situated at the edge of the canyon just west of Point Imperial. In October, the golden leaves produce a striking contrast with the purples of the canyon. Backlighting makes the color of the aspen more brilliant and emphasizes the different planes in the background. *Canon 75–300mm lens, enhancing filter, Fuji Velvia film.*

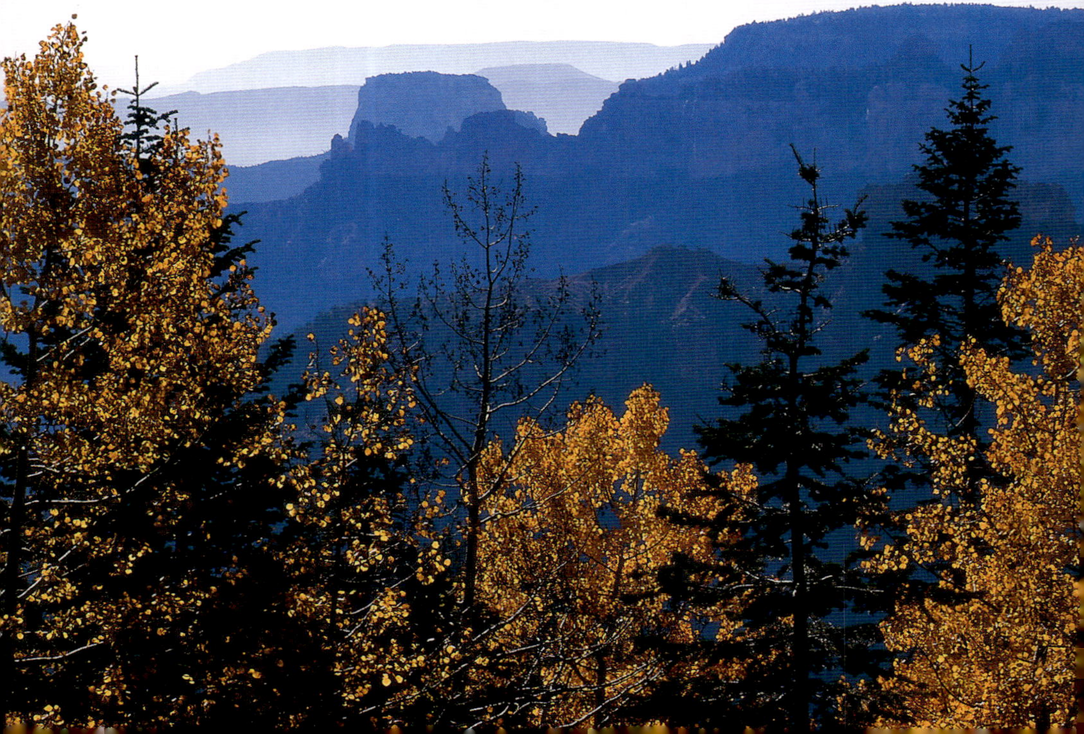

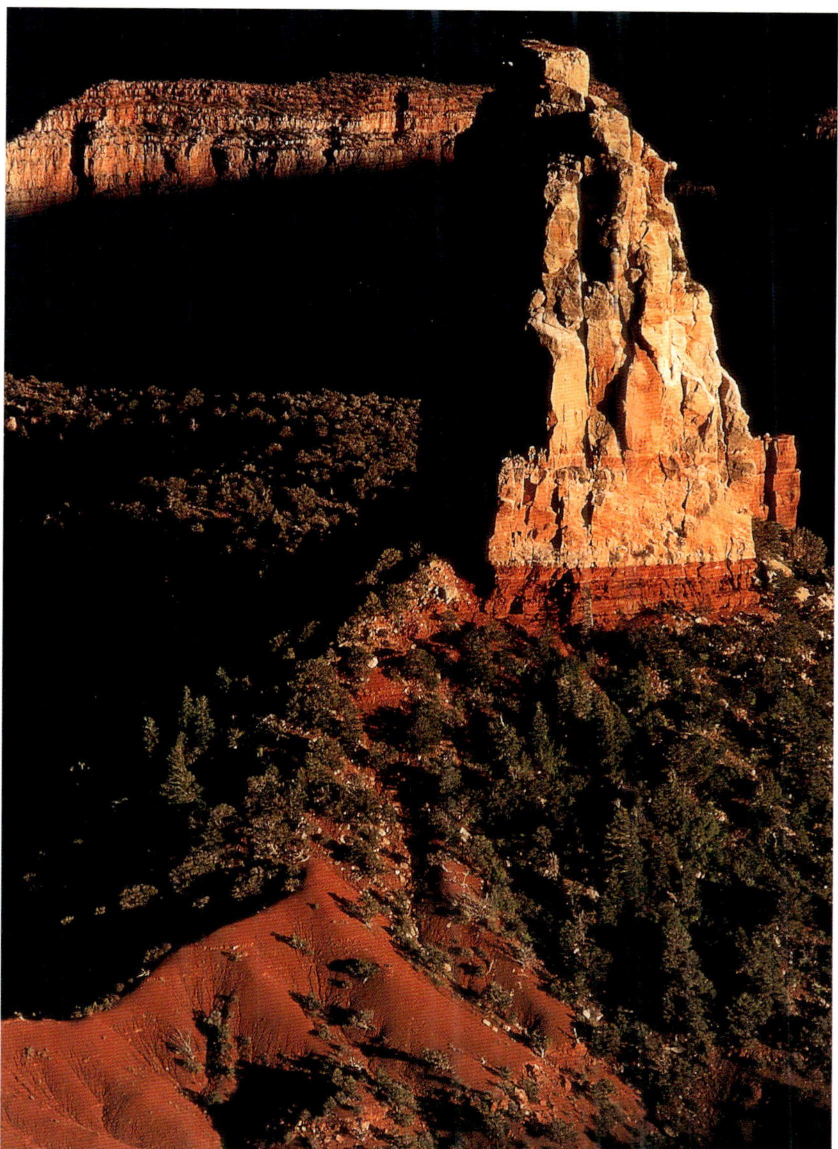

Mount Hayden from Point Imperial, Grand Canyon National Park, Arizona. Mount Hayden is the most prominent butte seen from Point Imperial and makes a good center of interest. As the sun sets, this promontory becomes increasingly separated from the darkening canyon in the background. The red ridge leads up from the lower left to Mount Hayden in the upper right portion of the picture. *Minolta 70 – 210mm lens, polarizing and enhancing filters, Fuji Velvia film.*

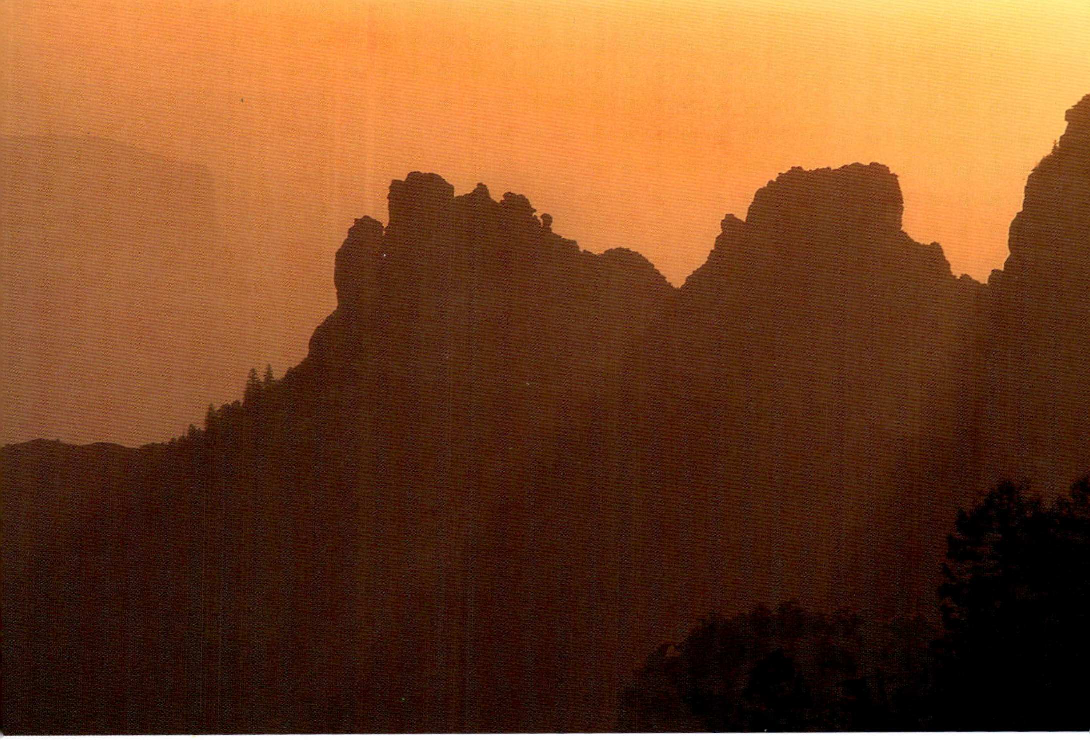

Sunrise from Vista Encantada, Grand Canyon National Park, Arizona. The combination of backlighting and haze in the canyon at sunrise created this special image. I used the trunk of a tree to shade my lens so that I wouldn't have to worry about lens flare. A long lens accentuated the haze and allowed me to concentrate on the most interesting buttes in the canyon. *Minolta 70–210mm lens, enhancing filter, Fuji Velvia film.*

At the road intersection about 5 miles from the main highway, take a left to go to Point Imperial. About half a mile before reaching this viewpoint, look for a view to the south that features a number of aspen trees; in early October, the golden leaves contrast beautifully with the canyon buttes beyond. In mid to late morning, backlighting provides the most vivid color.

From Point Imperial, the view to the southeast includes Mount Hayden, a picturesque butte that makes a wonderful center of interest. Sunrise and early-morning pictures are well lit in midsummer, and late-afternoon and sunset pictures are best in autumn. You can use a wide range of lenses at Point Imperial, from normal to moderate telephoto, depending on how prominent you want to make Mount Hayden in the composition.

To reach Cape Royale, return to the previous intersection and stay to the left. The first viewpoint you encounter, several miles from the intersection, is Vista Encantada, which looks back toward Point Imperial.

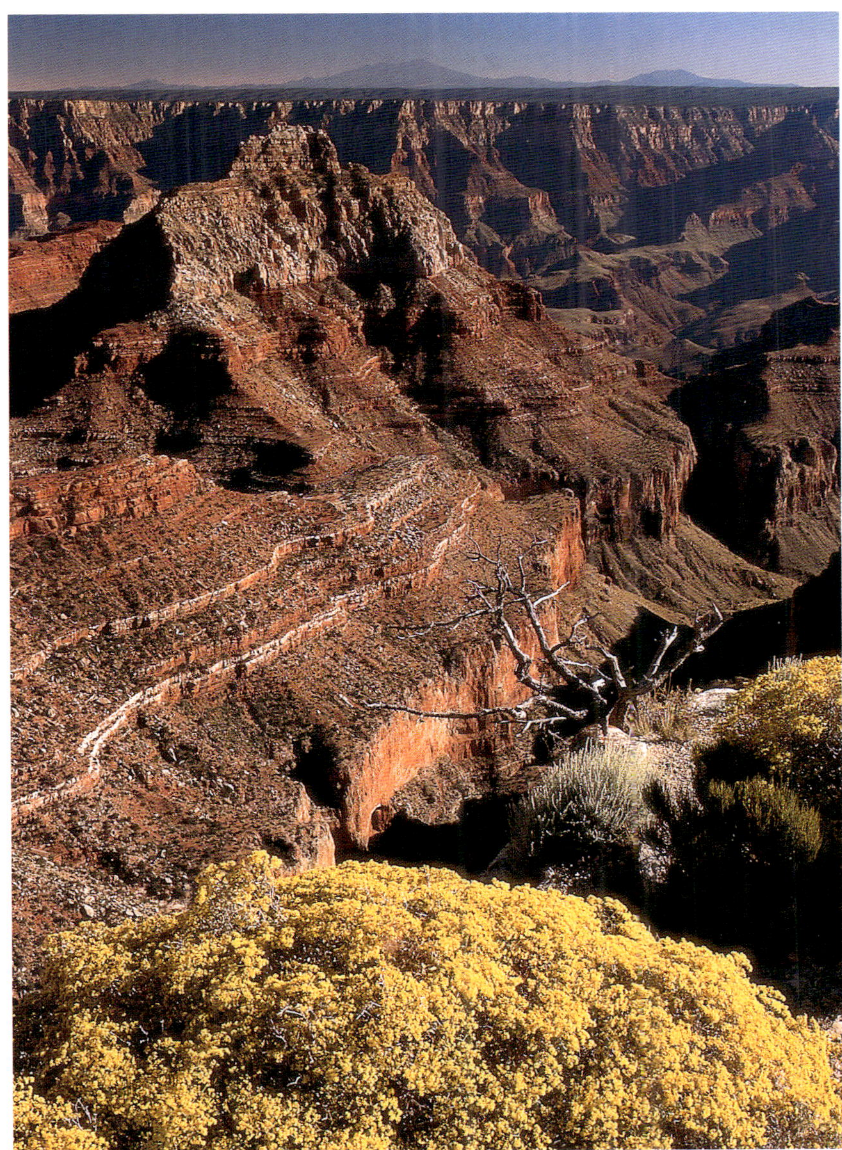

View from Cape Royale, Grand Canyon National Park, Arizona. Cape Royale provides some of the best views on the North Rim. This late-afternoon shot of Vishnu Temple was made more interesting by the inclusion of the colorful shrub in the foreground. By using a wide-angle lens and a small aperture and focusing at the hyperfocal distance, I obtained sharpness throughout. *Minolta 35–70mm lens, polarizing and enhancing filters, Fuji Velvia film.*

At sunrise, photographs of the backlit buttes to the east of the viewpoint can be very effective. Be sure to shade your lens to prevent lens flare. Just below the north side of the parking lot is a grove of aspen trees that can be photographed with the canyon in the background. This provides one of the best opportunities to combine the beauty of the canyon with autumn colors. Sunrise and early morning are the best times to photograph this scene.

From Vista Encantada, the road continues south along the Walhalla Plateau to Cape Royale. The other turnouts and viewpoints along this stretch of road, including the Walhalla Overlook, have only average photographic potential. A short trail leads from the parking lot at Cape Royale out to the viewpoint. Along the trail is a view of Angel's Window, which frames a portion of the canyon. Early morning in the summer is a good time to photograph Angel's Window, since it is mostly shadowed in the afternoon. Although Angel's Window is an interesting subject, the railing along its top can't be avoided, which is a definite negative.

Sunset at Point Sublime, Grand Canyon National Park, Arizona. Point Sublime is difficult to reach, but the panorama at sunset is interesting. *Canon 75–300mm lens, polarizing and enhancing filters, Fuji Velvia film.*

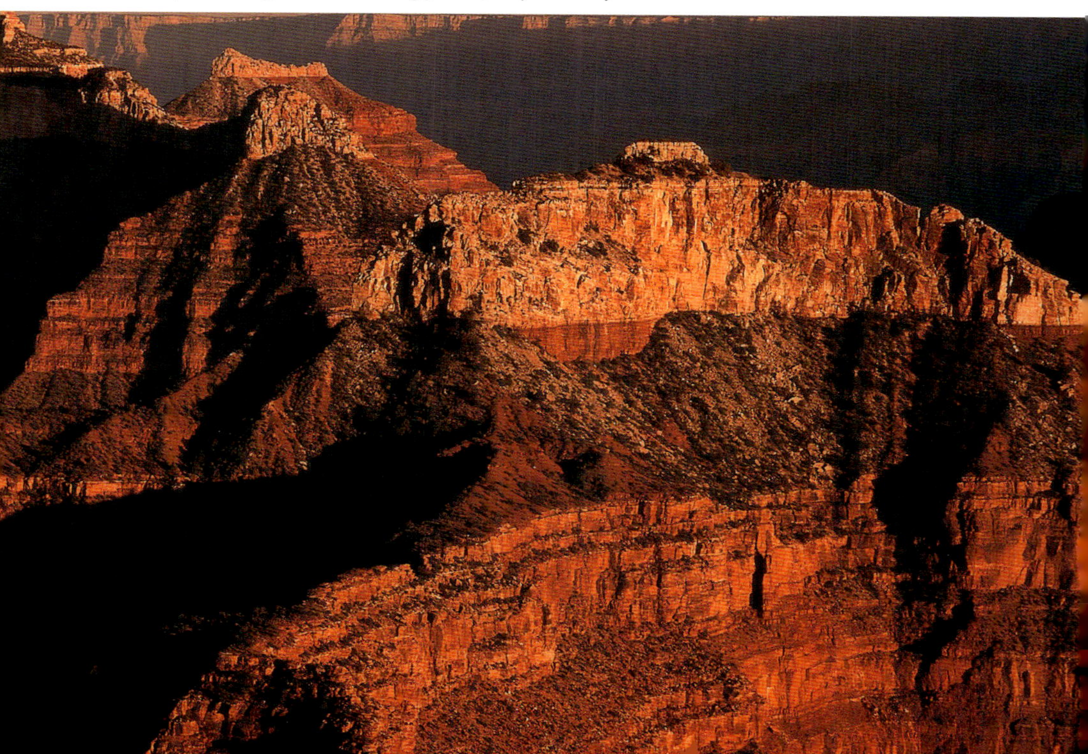

The view from Cape Royale includes Vishnu Temple and Wotan's Throne. At sunrise, a prominent cliff below the point makes a good subject with the dark canyon in the background. In late afternoon, Vishnu Temple provides a good center of interest. In the autumn, look for colorful shrubs along the rim for framing material.

A dirt road branches off Arizona 67 near the Cape Royale–Point Imperial Junction and leads 17 miles west to Point Sublime. This road is very rough and should be attempted only in high-clearance or four-wheel-drive vehicles. Anticipate at least an hour and a half one way to reach Point Sublime. The photographic possibilities are good, especially at sunset, but because of the long, rough drive, Point Sublime is not high on my list of priorities.

From the Tuweep Area. The Tuweep area of the North Rim is remote and primitive and has good but limited photographic possibilities. It can be reached from Fredonia by a 70-mile dirt road and from Colorado City by a 50-mile dirt road. These roads are impassable when wet. The best view is from Toroweap Point, at the end of the road. From the parking lot, walk east to a viewpoint that overlooks a sheer cliff towering above the Colorado River. Early to midmorning, before the sun reaches the river, yields the best light for this shot. A wide-angle lens captures the cliff and the river far below. Staying overnight at the primitive campground located at Tuweep makes early-morning photography more convenient.

From Below the Rim. ***The Inner Canyon.*** By far the most effective pictures of the Grand Canyon are taken on the rims. My wife, Bonnie, has hiked all the way through the Grand Canyon from the North Rim to the South Rim. Although she enjoyed the experience, she would be the first to tell you that the photographic potential isn't very high. Some good pattern and wildlife shots are possible, but the grandeur and majesty of the canyon can't be captured when you're looking up from below.

Hiking in the Grand Canyon is not for everyone. Day hikes may involve an elevation loss and gain of 1,000 feet or more. An overnight hike to the bottom of the canyon and back out requires a 4,000- to 5,000-foot elevation loss and gain, depending on whether you leave from the North Rim or the South Rim. The temperatures inside the canyon are usually 20 to 30 degrees F higher than at the rims.

For day hikes, no permits are required. For camping below the rim, a permit must be obtained. Since the number of permits granted in

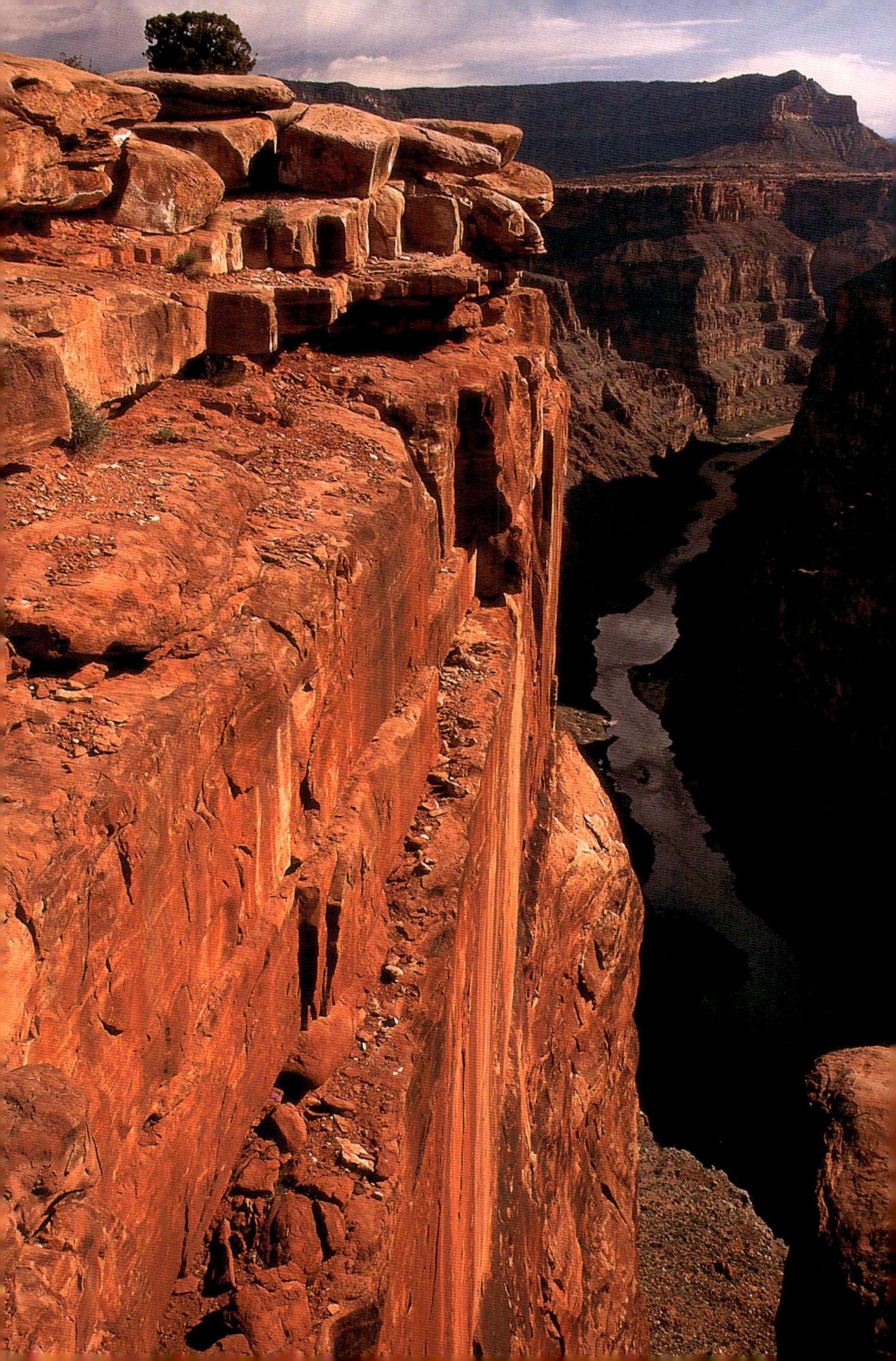

relation to the number requested is small, it is wise to apply for permits at least four months in advance. Even that is no guarantee that you will be fortunate enough to get one. The backcountry office that grants permits is open from 1 to 5 P.M. daily and can be reached at (520) 638-7875. Fees are $20 plus $4 per person per night (1999 rates).

One- or two-day mule trips into the canyon are also possible, but it's hard to take photo gear on a mule. Mule trips are for grab shots and not for serious photography. On mule trips, riders have a 200-pound maximum weight restriction, including photo equipment. For information, call the Bright Angel Transportation Desk at (520) 638-2631.

Phantom Ranch Lodge, near the Colorado River at the bottom of the canyon, provides accommodations and food. Facilities are very limited, so reservations should be made a year in advance. An overnight camping permit is not required if you have advance reservations at Phantom Ranch. Reservations can be obtained from AmFac Parks & Resorts at (303) 297-2757.

If you do hike into the canyon, take plenty of water and snacks. Allow twice as much time to hike up as to hike down. Take rain gear along to keep yourself and your equipment dry during thunderstorms.

The Havasupai Area. The Havasupai Indian Reservation features four beautiful waterfalls in a tributary canyon on the southern side of the Colorado River. It is in a remote area west of the South Rim of Grand Canyon National Park. The Havasupai area is not on national park land and is administered by the Supai people.

The Supai village and the four waterfalls can be reached only by foot or on horseback. To reach the Havasupai area, drive 66 miles on a paved road from Peach Springs to the Hualapai Hilltop and park your car. The trail distance to the Supai village, where lodging and food are available, is 8 miles. Reservations should be obtained well in advance.

The hike to Supai involves a considerable loss of elevation that must be regained when returning to your car. Horses can be rented for the trip to Supai for fairly reasonable rates ($115 round-trip in 1999). A campground is also available 2 miles below the village. The campground is located between Havasu Falls and Mooney Falls.

Canyon from Toroweap Point, Grand Canyon National Park, Arizona. The spectacular view of the Colorado River from Toroweap Point makes the long drive on a dirt road worthwhile. Sunrise and early to midmorning light are best for this shot. *Minolta 35–70mm lens, polarizing and enhancing filters, Fuji Velvia film.*

Entry fees are $20 per person. Fees for the campground, which are in addition to entry fees, are $10 per person per night. All facilities at Supai operate on a *cash only* basis. Traveler's checks, credit cards, and personal checks are not accepted.

Since all the falls face north, direct sunlight doesn't hit them from October to March. This means that the best light can be obtained only during the hotter months of the year. These waterfalls are beautiful, but getting to them involves a lot of planning, expense, and physical exertion. In addition, flash floods have damaged some of the beautiful travertine formations around the base of the falls, making them less attractive.

Rafting Through the Grand Canyon. Another way to access the inner gorge of the Grand Canyon is to take a float trip through all or part of the canyon. The rapids in the Grand Canyon are some of the most exciting in the country. Many options are available, including putting in at Lee's Ferry and floating the entire canyon, hiking down to Phantom Ranch and rafting the lower canyon, and putting in at Lee's Ferry and hiking out from Phantom Ranch. The best rapids, including Lava Falls, are downstream from Phantom Ranch. Companies that offer raft trips through the Grand Canyon are listed in the Products and Services section of the book.

The river and inner canyon have some good photographic possibilities if you have the time to take advantage of them. One of my favorite photographic books is *Time and the River Flowing* by Eliot Porter, which contains many outstanding images taken along the river. However, on most commercial float trips, you have neither the time nor the freedom to do much serious photography. Most of the rafts are quite large and rarely capsize, but keeping your photographic equipment dry and safe is a legitimate concern. I haven't floated the Grand Canyon, but I have run the rapids in Cataract Canyon on the Colorado River above Lake Powell, and although rafting is a lot of fun, it doesn't have much photographic potential, unless you happen to specialize in outdoor activity.

THREE

Monument Valley

WHAT TO EXPECT IN MONUMENT VALLEY

Monument Valley is one of the most dramatic landscapes to be found anywhere in North America. Its fantastically shaped buttes, towering spires, colorful mesas, and coral-colored sand dunes have been immortalized in countless movies and commercials. The Navajo Indians who live in the valley add a human element to the spectacular scenery. Contiguous areas such as Mystery Valley also provide outstanding photographic material.

Monument Valley isn't close to any cities—either large or small. It's in the middle of nowhere. To me, that's one of its biggest attractions. It's part of the Navajo Nation, which encompasses a large section of northeastern Arizona, southern Utah, and northwestern New Mexico.

The closest major towns are Flagstaff, Arizona, 150 miles to the southwest; Grand Junction, Colorado, 250 miles to the northeast; and Cortez, Colorado, 125 miles to the east. Access is provided by US 160 from the east and west and by US 163 from the north. Tourist facilities and gasoline are available at Mexican Hat, Utah, 22 miles to the north; Kayenta, Arizona, 25 miles to the south; and Goulding's Trading Post just west of the Tribal Park. A modest landing strip for small private planes is located near Goulding's.

The Monument Valley Tribal Park is administered by the Navajo Nation and is *not* a part of the U.S. national park system. Golden Eagle Passes, good in all national parks and monuments are *not* accepted in Monument Valley. However, entry fees are quite reasonable at $3.00 per person. Children under the age of 7 are admitted free. Monument Valley is open every day of the year except Christmas Day and the afternoon of Thanksgiving Day.

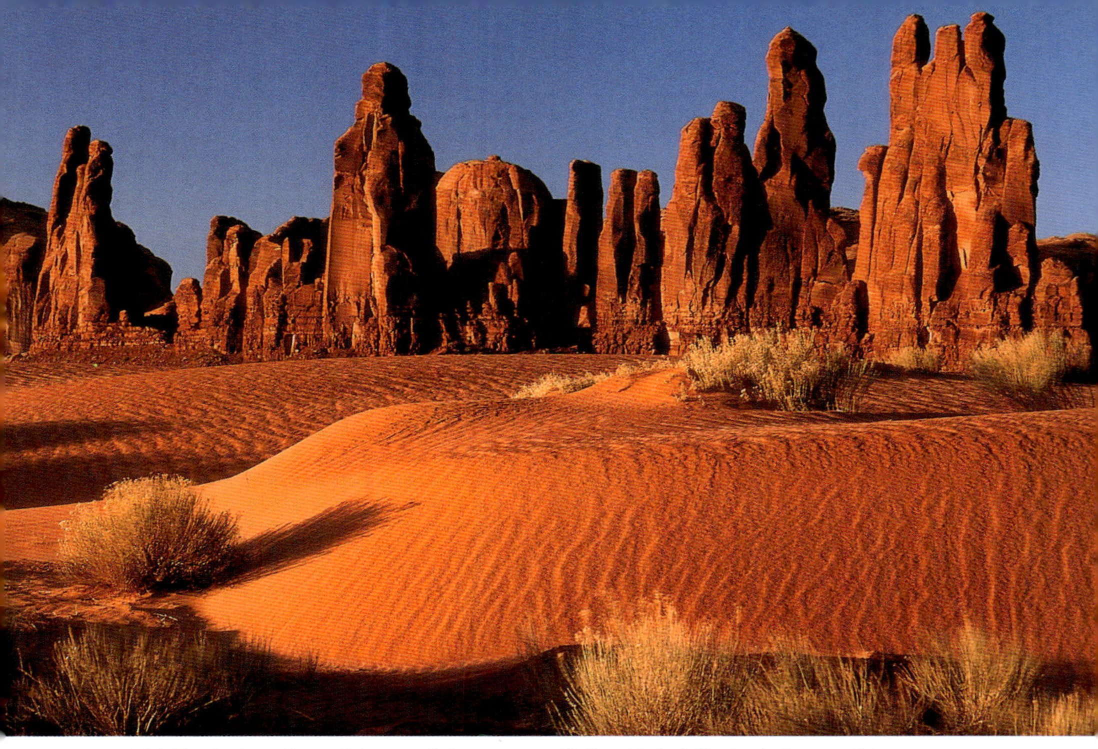

Yei bi Chei and sand dunes, Monument Valley Tribal Park, Arizona. Monument Valley has some of the most beautiful scenery in the United States. Its monoliths, spires, and arches provide outstanding subject material. Coral-colored sand dunes contrast beautifully with maroon-colored rocks. Sunrise and sunset light adds even more magic to the landscape. *Minolta 70–210mm lens, polarizing and enhancing filters, Fuji Velvia film.*

Located at the rim of Monument Valley are a visitor center, a restaurant, and a campground. The campground has 99 sites and a comfort station with showers. Rates are $10 for up to six persons per site, $20 for six to thirteen persons, and $2 for each additional person. In the winter, the sites are half price, but the comfort station is closed. Also at the rim are about a dozen kiosks whose owners offer guided tours into the valley.

PHOTOGRAPHING MONUMENT VALLEY

It's difficult to take a bad photograph in Monument Valley. The landforms and foregrounds are superb, and the colors are magnificent. In reviewing my photographs of Monument Valley, the best were taken within an hour of sunrise or sunset. The ability to visit Monument Valley at different seasons of the year is crucial in obtaining good early or late light on all the different scenes.

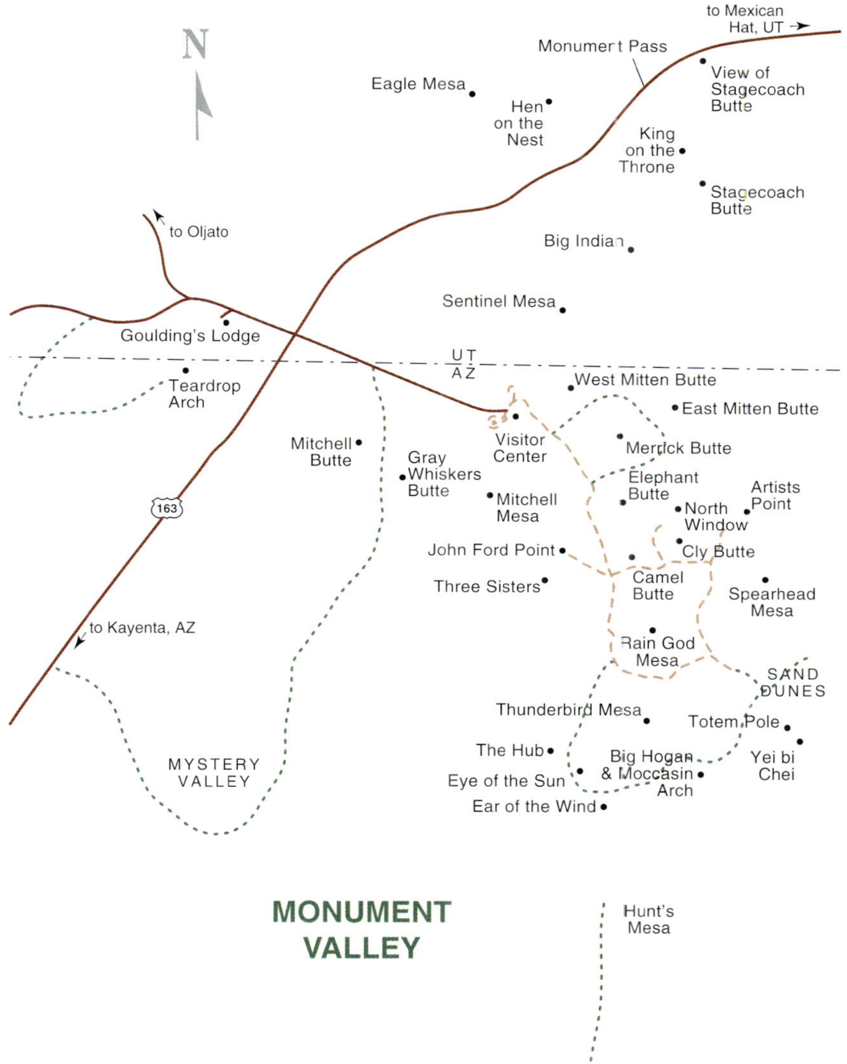

I find that concentrating on only one or two landforms usually makes a more effective composition than trying to get the whole valley in one picture. In the foreground, use gnarled junipers, sand dunes, and rocks to give depth and framing to the buttes and spires. Most of the colors in Monument Valley are of average reflectance, so you can generally trust your meter readings. The use of a polarizing filter is highly recommended, and an enhancing filter (especially if you are using Fuji Velvia Film) adds saturation and warmth to your images.

From US 163. US 163 is the main highway providing access to Monument Valley from Moab, Monticello, Blanding, Bluff, and Mexican Hat, Utah, to the north and from Kayenta, Arizona, to the south. A number of interesting photographs of some of the buttes of Monument Valley can be obtained from this scenic highway.

Approaching Monument Valley from the north, you can identify some of the spectacular buttes from about 50 miles away, but the first spot to shoot from is at the top of a hill between mileage markers 13 and 14 south of Mexican Hat. This view of a long stretch of highway with several Monument Valley buttes in the distance was made famous by the movie *Forrest Gump.*

One of my favorite shots north of the valley on US 163 is between mileage markers 7 and 8 and features Stagecoach Butte to the south of the road. A rough dirt road turns off the pavement at this location.

Stagecoach Butte, Monument Valley Tribal Park, Utah. The sandstone butte in the lower left balances Stagecoach Butte in the upper right. Sunrise or sunset provides attractive lighting on Stagecoach Butte from this location. *Minolta 70–210mm lens, polarizing and enhancing filters, Fuji Velvia film.*

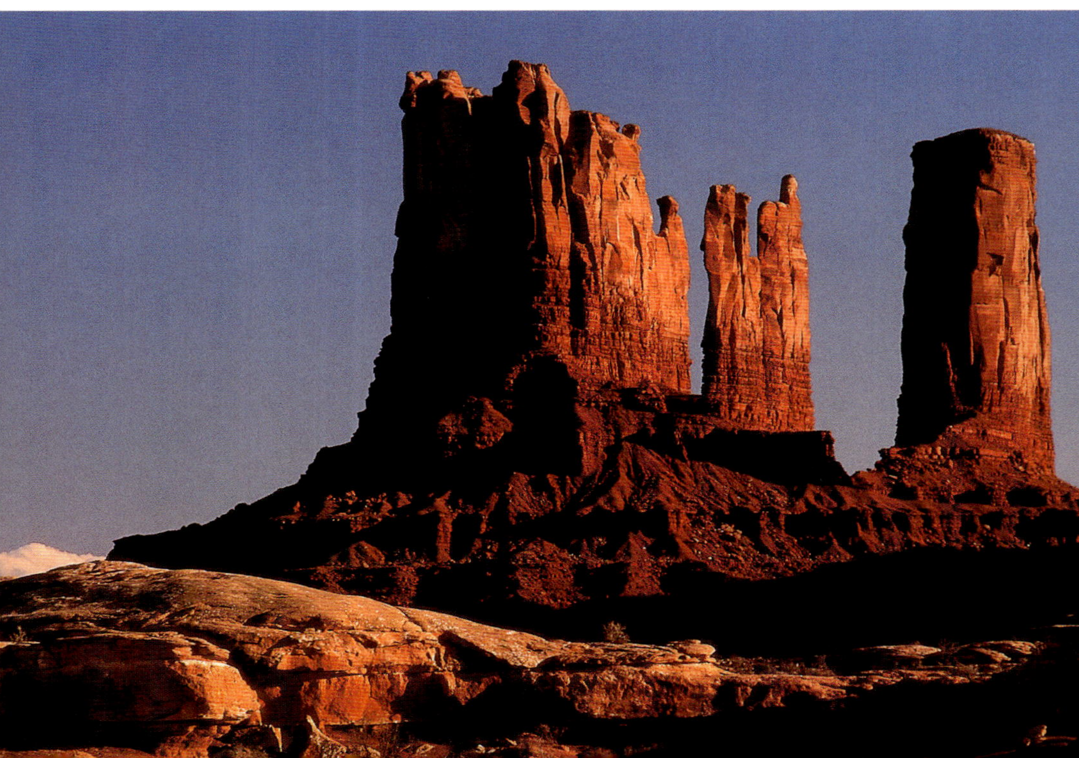

Using a telephoto lens and including an attractive foreground butte provide compositional balance for Stagecoach. Sunset or sunrise in the spring or autumn provides the best lighting for this shot.

Just beyond this location, US 163 crosses Monument Pass and descends toward Monument Valley. To the west of the road is the Hen on the Nest. A silhouette of this rock with a beautiful sunset is very effective. Choose a parking spot along the road so that the sun goes down directly behind the Hen. My favorite spot to photograph sunlit pictures of this interesting butte is between mile markers 5 and 6, a location that includes some interesting rock formations in the foreground. Since the Hen on the Nest faces southeast, it can be photographed from morning until about 2:00 P.M. throughout the year, but the morning light is rather flat.

To the east of the road, before you reach the Monument Valley Junction, there are many good views of Stagecoach, Big Indian, King on His Throne, and the Bear and the Rabbit. Many of the buttes in Monument Valley have several names, depending on the point from which they are viewed. These interesting buttes can be photographed as silhouettes at sunrise or in the late afternoon and at sunset when they are bathed with beautiful, warm light. A summer thunderstorm may even produce a rainbow. You may need a long lens to come in tight on the buttes and eliminate some of the houses that are being built in this area by the Navajo people.

Just north of the Utah-Arizona state line is Monument Valley Junction. A number of kiosks selling jewelry, tourist goods, and food are located just east of the junction. From here, the crossroad leads southeast about 4 miles to the rim of Monument Valley and northwest to Goulding's Trading Post.

After crossing the state line, proceed south on US 163 toward Kayenta. From milepost 404 to milepost 401, a large, dark volcanic plug named Agathla Peak is prominent to the east of the road. Although not as colorful as the other buttes in Monument Valley, Agathla Peak is a worthwhile photographic subject. As with most subjects, sunrise or sunset provides the most interesting lighting. Your choice of camera position will be dictated by the time of day and the season.

Another interesting formation is Owl Rock, best photographed between mileage markers 403 and 402. It is perched on top of the red cliff to the west of the highway. Owl Rock can be shot either very tightly with a long telephoto lens or with a shorter lens in a composition that includes the colorful strata at the base of the cliff. Midmorning provides good lighting for Owl Rock.

From the Rim of the Valley. The rim of the valley offers some excellent photographic opportunities. It is reached from US 163 by turning southeast at Monument Valley Junction onto an approximately 4-mile-long paved road that leads to the visitor center. The public is allowed to photograph from this road or from the rim of the valley near the visitor center at any time of day.

Just north of the visitor center are two large, striated rocks on the rim overlooking the valley. These rocks make an excellent foreground for sunset photographs of the Mittens and Merrick Butte. Your photograph can include one mitten, two mittens, or all three buttes with one or both foreground rocks. The choice depends on the lighting and your imagination. The light on this scene is rather flat at sunset during the winter months but becomes progressively more sidelit during the late

The West Mitten and rocks, Monument Valley Tribal Park, Arizona. On the rim of the valley just north of the visitor center, several attractive rocks can be used to frame the West Mitten, the East Mitten, and Merrick Butte. Compositions can include one butte, two buttes, or all the buttes. Sunset in the late spring and summer provides the best sidelighting at this location. *Minolta 70–210mm lens, polarizing and enhancing filters, Fuji Velvia film.*

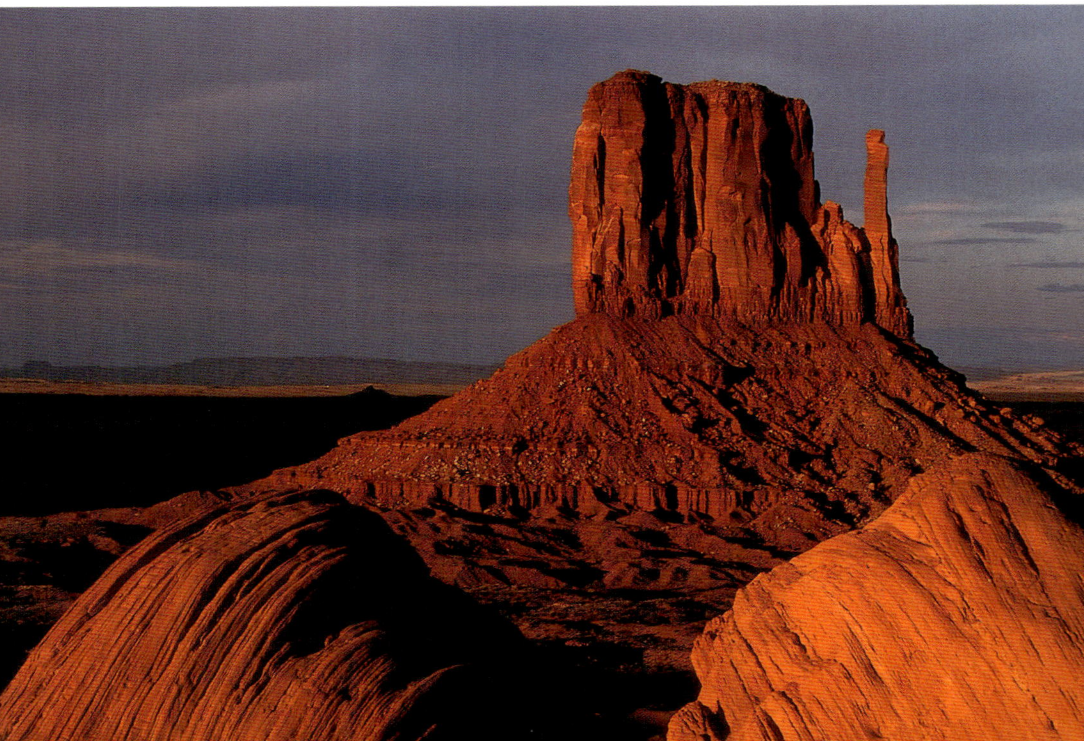

spring and summer. This is an excellent spot to observe and photograph interesting atmospheric conditions such as thunderstorms and rainbows with the Mittens as a backdrop. Dark skies add drama to the scene. Be sure to set up far enough from the foreground rocks so that your shadow does not fall on the rocks. Also try to avoid several areas on the rocks where thoughtless individuals have carved their names. As the sun sets, the whole valley is engulfed in shadow, except for the Mittens and Merrick Butte providing a truly magnificent view.

Several interesting juniper trees on the rim of the valley provide excellent framing for the Mittens and Merrick Butte. My favorite tree is north of the parking lot, north of the gate to the valley road, and just a few yards north of the road junction where the valley road turns east. With a wide-angle lens, any of the buttes can be completely framed by the tree. Your lens should be set at a small aperture and at the hyperfocal distance to obtain sharpness on both the tree and the butte. Late in the day in the wintertime, the lighting on Merrick Butte is excellent.

Anywhere along the rim is a good place to photograph silhouettes of the Mittens or Merrick Butte at sunrise. I usually try to arrive at the rim at least a half hour before the sun breaks the horizon. The park brochure gives the times of sunrise and sunset for each month. Cloud conditions are the key to good sunrise shots at Monument Valley or, for that matter, anywhere else. If no clouds are present in the eastern sky, you won't have a good shot because the sun will flare your lens as soon as it breaks the horizon. Too many clouds will obscure the sun, but be patient and be prepared. Sometimes, even though it looks like the sunrise will be poor, a shaft of light breaks through the clouds and creates a dramatic image.

My favorite place to photograph a sunrise from the rim is from the old campground about a quarter mile north of the visitor center. From this vantage point, the Mittens are closer together and make a better composition than from near the overlook. On days close to the spring and autumn equinoxes, (March 21 and September 21), the sun comes up either between the Mittens or very close to them. You won't be able to drive your car to the old campground because the valley road gate will still be locked, so allow yourself an extra 5 minutes to walk there.

Your choice of lens depends largely on the extent of colorful clouds in the sky. Remember that the area below the horizon will be black, so don't include much of it in your picture. Take a meter reading off the colorful clouds, and use an enhancing filter to make the sunrise even more colorful.

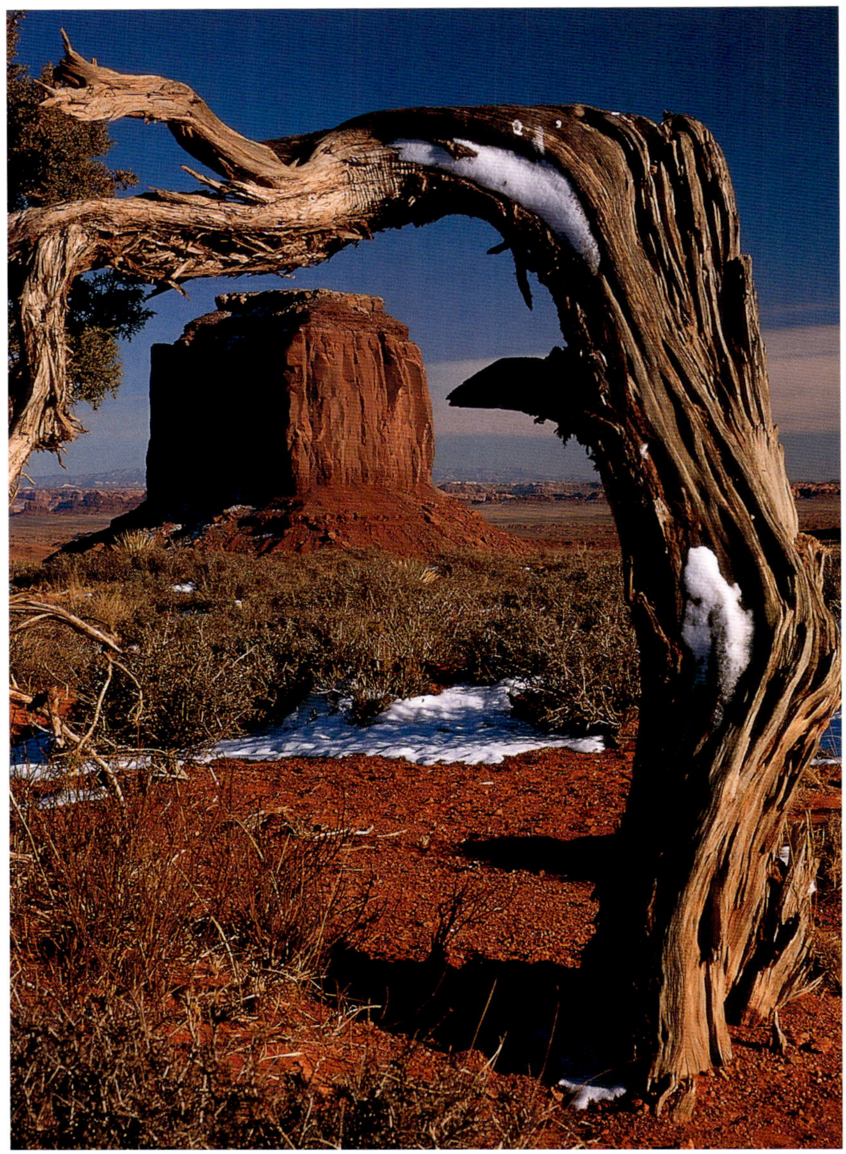

Merrick Butte, Monument Valley Tribal Park, Arizona. Just north of the junction where Valley Drive turns east and drops off the rim is a little juniper tree that can be used to frame either of the Mittens or Merrick Butte. In this shot of Merrick Butte, I focused at the hyperfocal distance at f/22 to obtain sharpness in both the foreground and the background. The snow on the tree and the ground adds to the contrast and helps tell the nature story. *Canon 28–105mm lens, polarizing and enhancing filters, Fuji Velvia Film.*

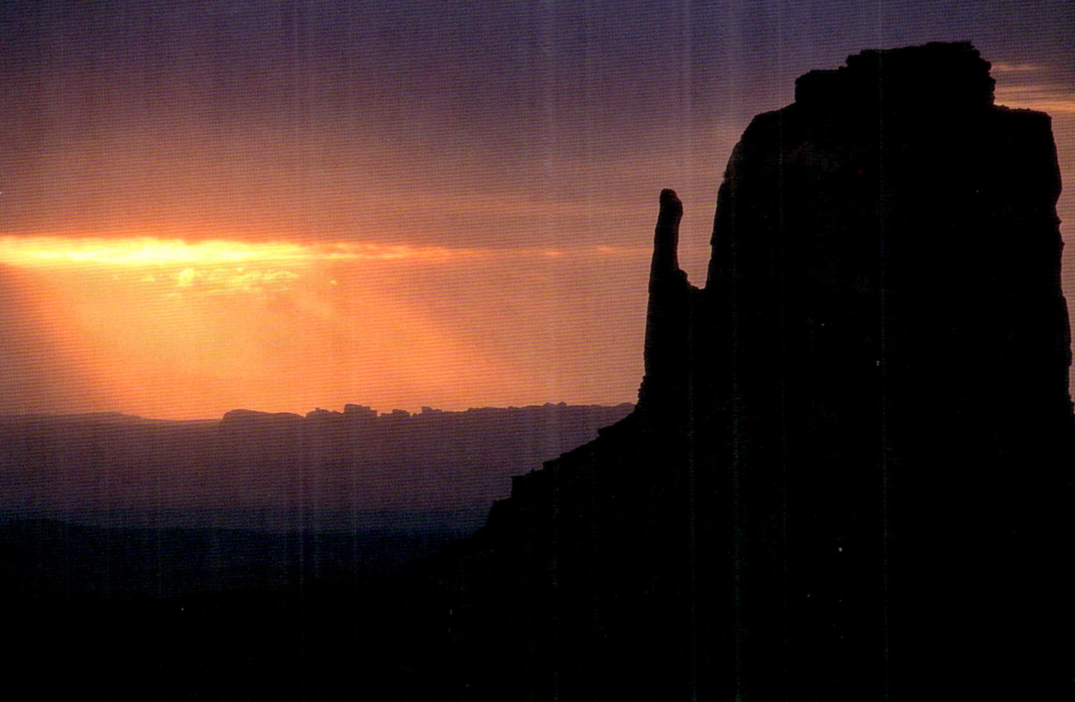

Sunrise in Monument Valley, Monument Valley Tribal Park, Arizona. Never give up on a sunrise at Monument Valley. On the morning that this image was taken, the sky looked totally overcast, and sunrise appeared to be a bust. However, hoping for the best, I set up my cameras, and when a shaft of light broke through the clouds, I was ready. The enhancing filter made the colors even more spectacular than they appeared at the time. *Canon 75–300mm lens, enhancing filter, Fuji Velvia Film.*

From the Monument Valley Road. A gravel and dirt road descends from the rim into Monument Valley. This loop road is approximately 11 miles long (excluding spur roads) and leads to good views of many of the main features in the valley, including the Mittens, the Three Sisters, and the Totem Poles. Portions of this road are one way. The valley road is open from about an hour after sunrise to about an hour before sunset. It has been greatly improved over the last decade and is passable to most vehicles. However, it is still rough in places and should be driven slowly. After a snowstorm or thunderstorm, the valley road may be impassable and temporarily closed.

The public is not allowed to drive on any side roads in or around Monument Valley or hike from the main highways or loop road. The maximum distance that one can go away from the road without a guide is about 100 yards. Please respect the privacy and customs of the Navajos who live in the valley, and do not enter their property without permission. Permission is also needed to photograph the Navajo people or their property. A gratuity is expected. Commercial photography requires a permit from the Department of Broadcast Services, P.O. Box 308, Window Rock, AZ 86515.

Monument Valley Road Log

0.0 mile Set the trip meter on your odometer to 0.0. From the rim, the road descends via a series of switchbacks into the valley. Please exercise caution on this rough road.

0.55 mile On the hill just east of the road, you will see a picturesque juniper tree. This tree makes an excellent frame for the West Mitten. Sunset light is best for this composition. The light is flat at sunset during the winter months but is very good in May, June, and July.

0.75 mile When the road tops the next hill, park in the parking lot north of the road. There may be several tables here with Navajos selling jewelry. To the east and down the hill, you will see some sand dunes and juniper trees. These elements provide a good foreground for the West Mitten. Since the sand moves continually, the location and quality of the dunes change constantly. Late afternoon in the spring or autumn provides the strong sidelighting needed for good texture on the sand dunes and on the West Mitten.

1.3 miles Two outstanding juniper trees on the east side of the road frame the West Mitten. Late afternoon in the spring and autumn provides the best light.

1.5 miles Two juniper trees on the west side of the road provide the same function. Late afternoon in the spring or autumn is best.

2.5 miles This is the best spot for pictures of the Three Sisters, which are prominent southwest of the road. Some interesting low buttes in the middle distance can be used for framing and compositional elements. Sunrise or early morning in the wintertime provides the best lighting from this location.

3.2 miles Look to the east for interesting views of Camel Butte. You can use the patterns in the hills and drainages below the butte for framing. Early afternoon in the wintertime is the best time to photograph Camel Butte.

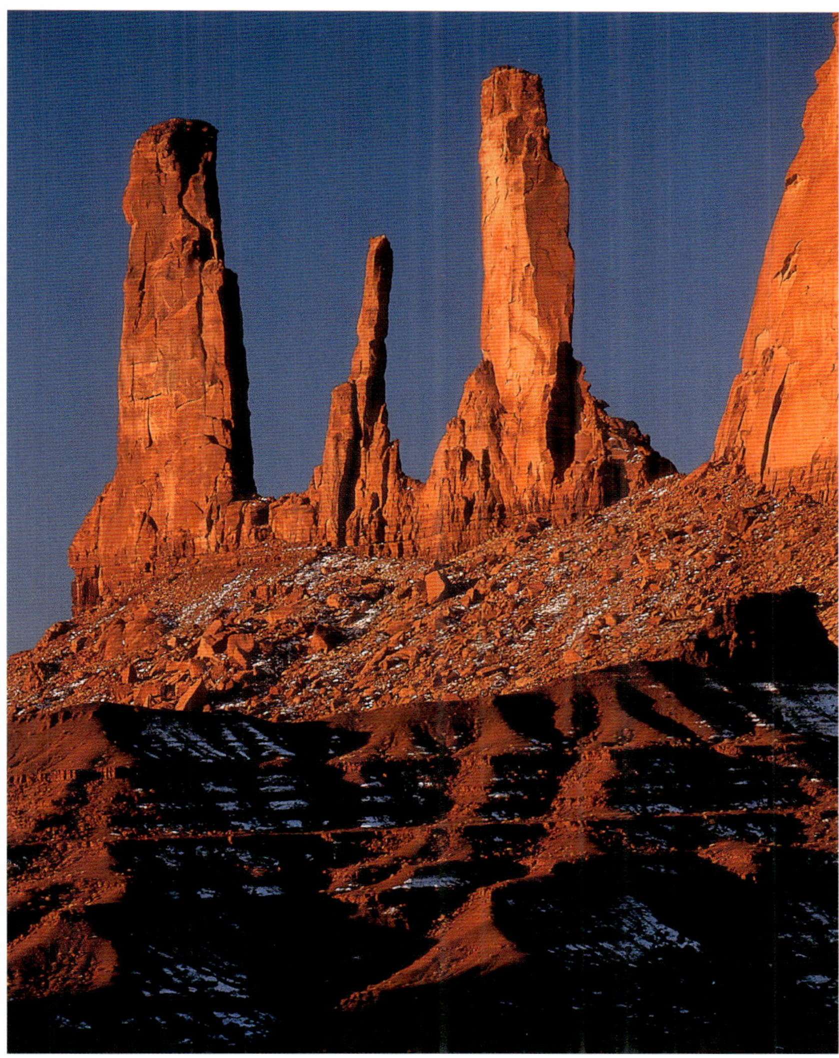

The Three Sisters at sunrise, Monument Valley Tribal Park, Arizona. Sunrise in the wintertime provides ideal lighting for the Three Sisters, one of the most interesting landforms in Monument Valley. The buttes in the foreground were positioned to add interest and framing. To enter the valley at sunrise, you need a Navajo guide. *Minolta 70–210mm lens, polarizing and enhancing filters, Fuji Velvia Film.*

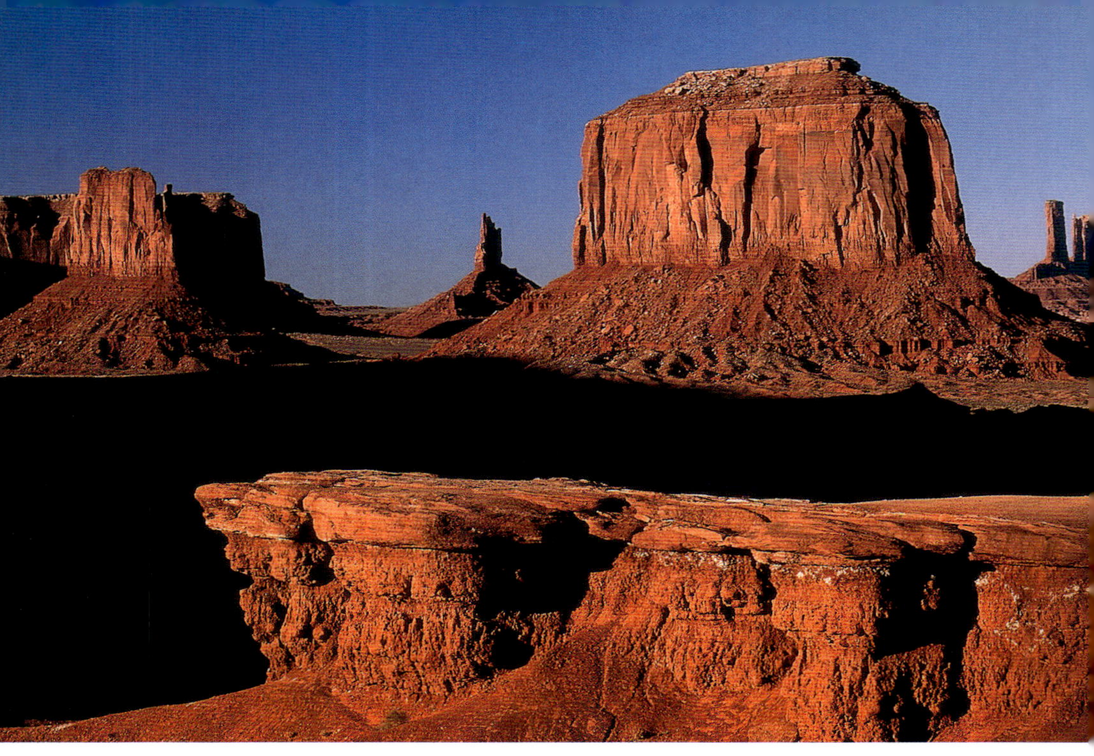

View from John Ford Point, Monument Valley Tribal Park, Arizona. Late in the afternoon in autumn or spring, long shadows separate John Ford Point (in the foreground) from the West Mitten, Merrick Butte, and Stagecoach Butte. *Canon 28–105mm lens, polarizing and enhancing filters, Fuji Velvia film.*

3.3 miles Take the turnoff to John Ford Point, named for the famous Hollywood director who brought Monument Valley to the attention of the outside world in the late 1930s. This location offers excellent views of both Mittens, Merrick Butte, and Stagecoach Butte and is justly recognized as one of the best photographic locations in the valley. John Ford Point lies in the foreground of this panorama and can be used as a compositional element with one, several, or all of these buttes. Usually a Navajo on a horse is available to pose out on the point for a modest fee. A light-colored horse is preferable to a dark-colored one, and colorful Navajo garb is mandatory for the rider. Since the views from John Ford Point are to the north, good photographs can be obtained at most times of the day and year. I particularly like to photograph from this location near sunset in the spring and autumn, when the cliff to the west throws long shadows across the scene, isolating John Ford Point from the buttes in the distance.

0.0 mile Return to the Monument Valley Road, reset your trip meter to 0.0, and turn right. This is where the one-way portion of Monument Valley Road begins.

1.15 miles Immediately ahead is a fine view of Hand Rock, the Totem Pole, and Yei bi Chei. Proper camera positioning on the north side of the road hides the road and a Navajo hogan from view. Early afternoon in the wintertime provides the best lighting for this shot.

1.6 miles On the north side of the road is a large, attractive rock that can be used to frame the Totem Pole and Yei bi Chei. Early afternoon in the wintertime is good for this shot. I recommend a moderate telephoto lens and hyperfocal distance to ensure that both the distant formations and the rock in the foreground are sharp.

Totem Pole and rock, Monument Valley Tribal Park, Arizona. On the south side of Rain God Mesa is an interesting rock that can be used to frame the Totem Pole and Yei bi Chei. Midafternoon in the wintertime provides ideal lighting for this scene. Focusing at the hyperfocal distance and stopping down to f/22 were necessary to obtain sharpness throughout. *Minolta 70–210mm lens, polarizing and enhancing filters, Fuji Velvia film.*

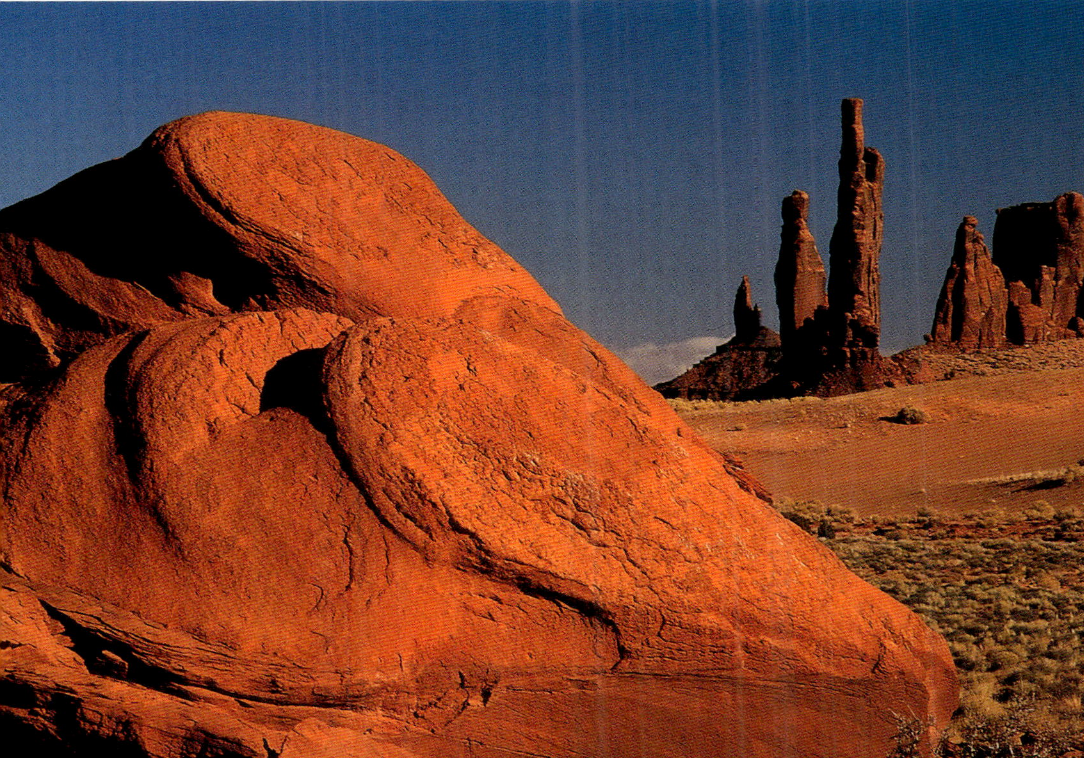

1.7 miles Straight ahead is a very attractive view of the Totem Pole and a small formation on the left known as Mother and Child. A long telephoto vertical shot of these two formations makes an attractive composition. Backlighting in the morning produces a strong silhouette; for strong sidelighting, early afternoon in the winter is best.

2.05 miles On the south side of the road is a wash that frames the Totem Pole, Yei bi Chei, and the sand dunes. An overhanging rock in the wash and shrubs in the foreground provide good framing and compositional elements. Mid to late afternoon in the spring, autumn, or winter is the best time to photograph this scene. Just beyond this wash, a short spur leads to another viewpoint of the Totem Pole, Yei bi Chei, and the sand dunes. I prefer the views from the wash.

0.0 mile Reset you trip meter to 0.0 and proceed north along the one-way Monument Valley Road.

1.1 miles An old hogan is situated just east of the road. The fence around it makes the hogan unsuitable for photography, but it is interesting to visit.

1.2 miles A spur road to the right leads to Artist's Point. To the north are fine views of the Mittens, Merrick Butte, and Stagecoach Butte. Midmorning and midafternoon are the best times to photograph from Artist's Point. I have never been able to identify any good framing elements at the point itself, but bushes and trees between the road intersection and the point can be used to good effect, especially in the autumn, when the bushes may be gold.

0.0 mile Return to Monument Valley Road, reset your trip meter to 0.0, and turn right.

0.75 mile A spur road leads to North Window, which features good views of the major buttes in the valley. At the start of the spur road is a picturesque dead tree that can be used to frame one or more of the buttes that can be seen through North Window. Another shot that includes these buttes as well as the cliffs on both sides of North Window can be taken from the clear area east of the spur road. I usually try to include one of the juniper trees in the foreground of this shot. At the parking area at the end of the spur road are several interesting rocks that can be used either as

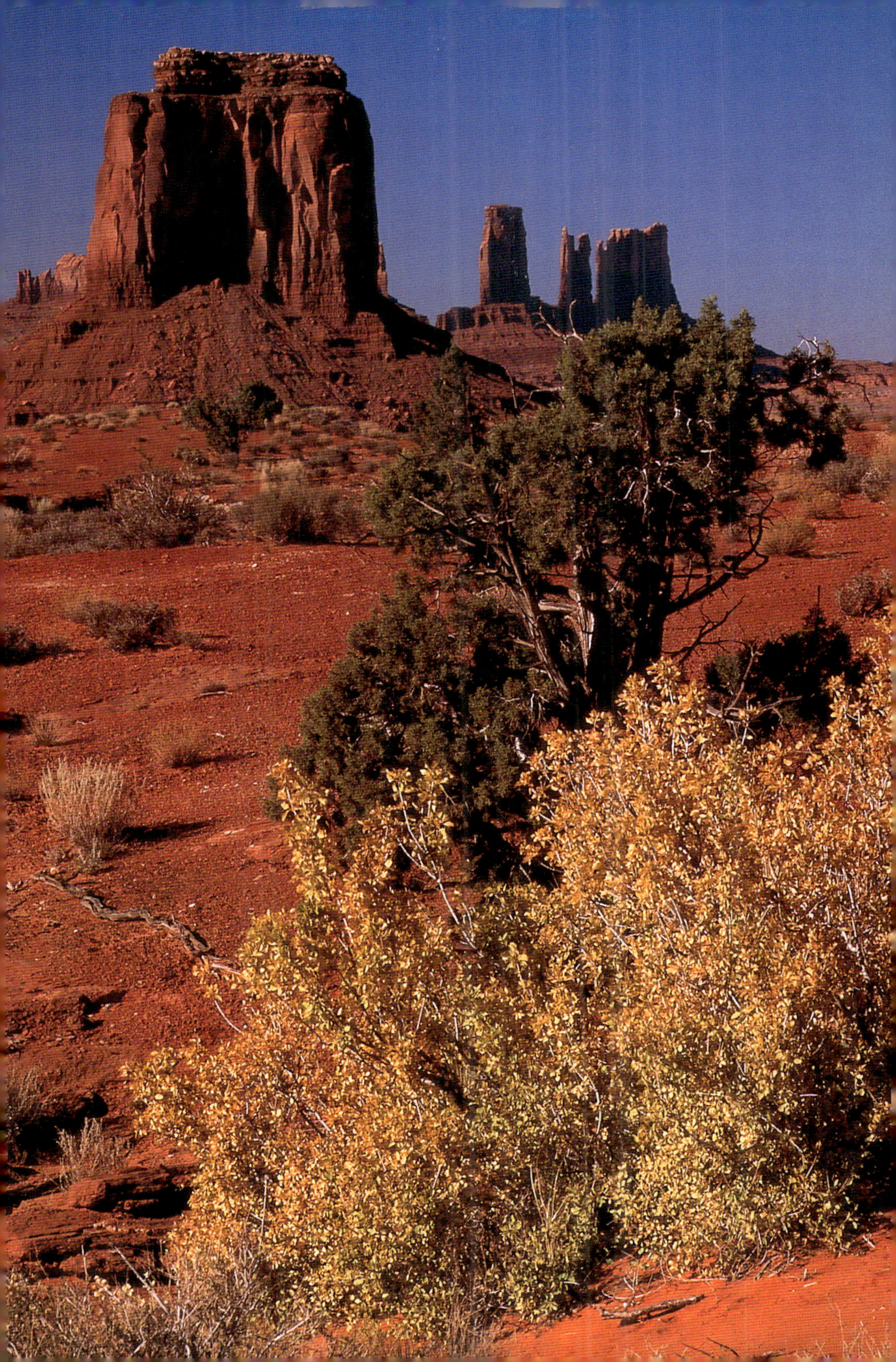

framing for the buttes to the north or as the main subject of the picture. Although morning and afternoon provide good lighting for all the shots from North Window, sunset light is especially attractive for the views at the north end of the spur road.

0.0 mile Return to Monument Valley Road, reset your trip meter to 0.0, and turn right.

0.10 mile To the north of the road is Thumb Rock. I recommend an early-morning or late-afternoon wide-angle shot that includes some of the boulders in the foreground.

0.55 mile Arrive at the John Ford Point intersection. Turn right, rejoin the two-way traffic portion of Monument Valley Road, and drive back to the visitor center at the rim of the Valley. You may want to revisit some of the spots you noted on your way in. If so, reset your trip meter at this intersection and reverse the mileages previously given.

Off-Road Locations with Guides. To drive on any of the side roads, hike away from the main road, or enter Monument Valley at sunrise or sunset, you need a Navajo guide. One can be engaged at the rim of the valley at the aforementioned kiosks. A complete list of authorized guides is available at the visitor center. Rates for guides are relatively modest, especially considering that they furnish the vehicle. I usually pay about $40 per person for an entire morning or afternoon and about $20 per person for the two hours around sunrise and sunset. All-day tours or tours to more remote destinations such as Hunt's Mesa cost more, but the spectacular photography makes it worthwhile. With the large number of guides available, competition will probably keep prices low.

Several of the guides that I have worked with over the years have been especially attuned to photography. Even though I have photographed in the valley about 100 times, they still show me new angles

Previous page: View from Artist's Point, Monument Valley Tribal Park, Arizona. Artist's Point is a good place to view many of the buttes in the northern part of Monument Valley. Although autumn color is not abundant, colorful bushes can add interest to your pictures. Midmorning or midafternoon lighting works best for pictures from Artist's Point. *Canon 75–300mm lens, polarizing and enhancing filters, Fuji Velvia film.*

and locations. I especially recommend Fred Cly of Fred's Adventure Tours and Tom Phillips of Keyah Hozhoni Tours. Many of my best photographs of Monument Valley were taken under their guidance.

Probably the most rewarding excursion away from the main road with a Navajo guide is a morning at the sand dunes and in the area south of Thunderbird Mesa. Make arrangements for this tour in advance, and have your guide meet you at the rim of the valley about an hour before sunrise. I recommend the following itinerary.

Drive immediately to the sand dunes and choose a vantage point, depending on the time of year, where the sun will come up at a right angle to the Totem Pole and Yei bi Chei. You will probably have to drive down Sand Creek a short distance to reach the right position. Since the dunes change from year to year and even from day to day, you need to find your own exact locations. At sunrise, the colors are vivid, and the ripples on the sand dunes make beautiful patterns.

After shooting the sand dunes, position yourself west of the Totem Pole in a spot where the sun is hidden behind this delicate spire. This shot produces a powerful silhouette of the Totem Pole, along with the nearby rocks. Try to get just a pinpoint of sun emerging from behind the Totem Pole. If you use the smallest aperture (f/22 or f/32), your image will have a starburst caused by the interaction of this pinpoint of light with the leaves of the diaphragm of the lens.

The next destination (about 9:00 A.M.) is Ear of the Wind, a beautiful arch with a sand dune in the foreground. I recommend three compositions of Ear of the Wind. The first is from a location a short distance southeast of the parking area, where a beautiful dead tree can be used as a silhouette in front of the left abutment of the arch. Be sure to reach this point before the sun illuminates the tree. The second view is up the draw to the southwest of the parking area and includes several picturesque juniper trees as well as the sand dune below the arch. The third is along the dirt road north of the parking area, where several groups of yucca provide framing and balance for the arch.

From Ear of the Wind, proceed to the Big Hogan, a large pothole arch on the south side of Thunderbird Mesa. I recommend that you photograph this scene from beneath the overhanging cliff using a wide-angle lens, and include the hole in the roof (which is lit) along with the beautiful rock varnish pattern emanating from it. Bounce light from the opposite wall illuminates this shot beautifully.

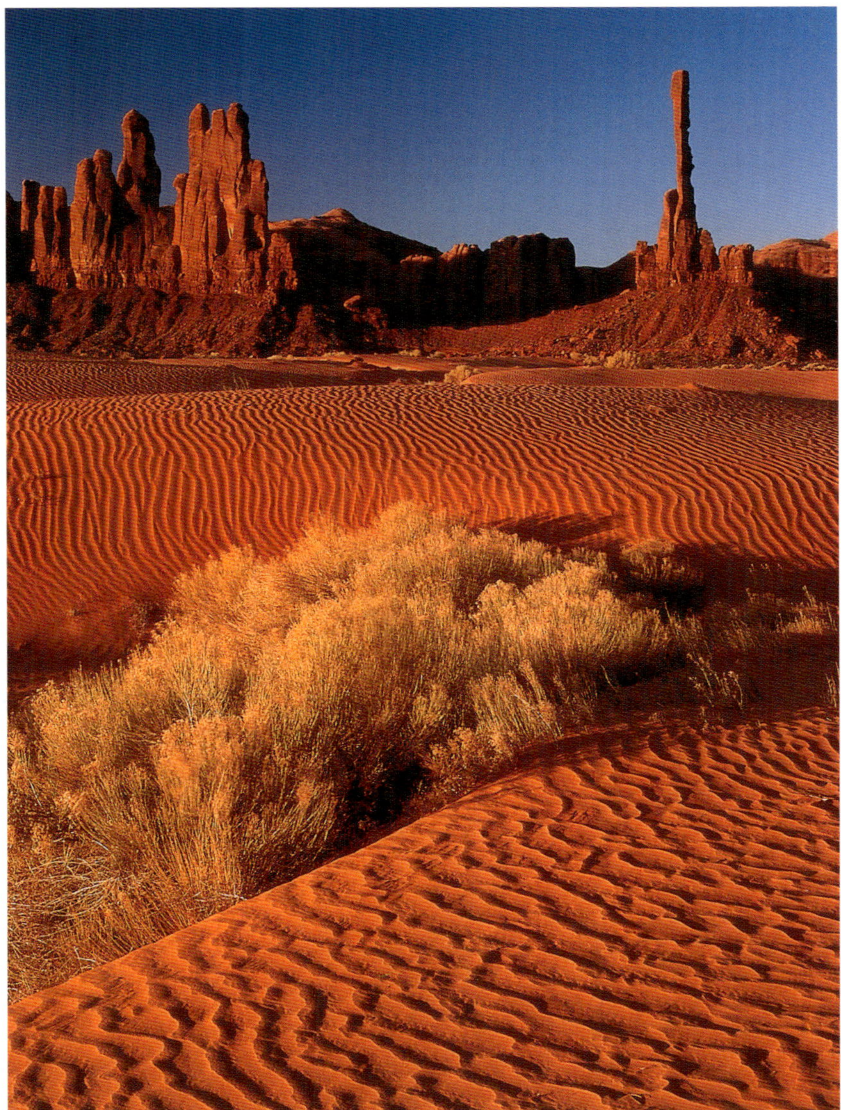

Totem Pole and sand dunes at sunrise, Monument Valley Tribal Park, Arizona. Sunrise on the sand dunes can produce many beautiful images with the Totem Pole and Yei bi Chei as centers of interest. The shrubs on the dunes add color and interest to the scene. The vivid color and strong shadow detail on the sand last for only about half an hour after sunrise. To photograph on the sand dunes or anywhere away from Valley Drive, you must be accompanied by a Navajo guide. *Minolta 35–70mm lens, polarizing and enhancing filters, Fuji Velvia film.*

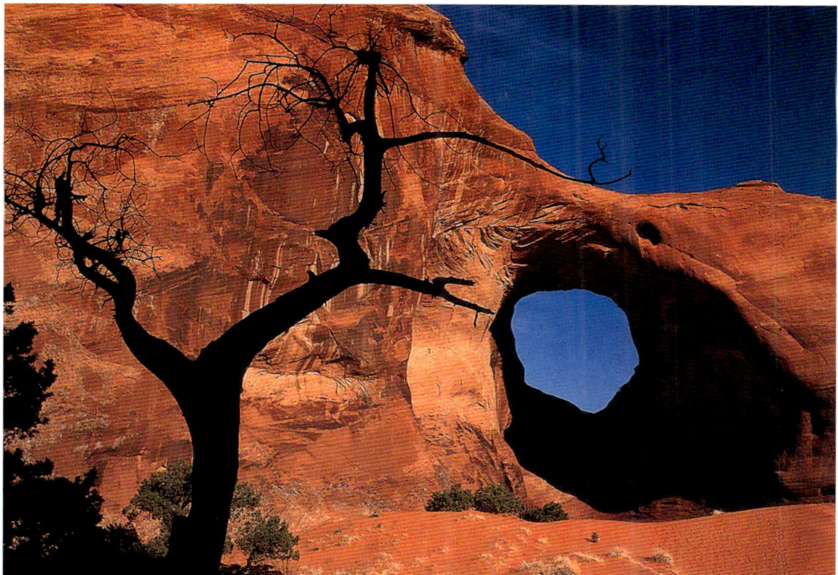

Ear of the Wind, Monument Valley Tribal Park, Arizona. One of the most interesting features you can visit on a guided tour is Ear of the Wind. Early to midmorning is a good time to photograph this beautiful arch. The silhouette of the juniper tree adds depth, contrast, and interest to this photograph. Be sure to look for other good compositions that include yucca plants, junipers, and sand dunes as foreground elements. *Minolta 35–70mm lens, polarizing and enhancing filters, Fuji Velvia film.*

Within 100 yards of the Big Hogan is Moccasin Arch, an attractive feature best photographed at about 10:00 A.M. Many good compositions are possible here. My favorite includes the arch along with the top of the sand dune below it. Another composition includes some picturesque rocks to the left of the arch in the foreground with the arch in the background. Tight shots of just the opening of Moccasin Arch are also interesting.

The last major location for the morning is Eye of the Sun, an attractive opening high above the valley floor. Depending on the time of the year, Eye of the Sun is also a good early-afternoon destination. Tight shots, as well as wider shots including more of the cliff below the arch, provide good compositions. Some interesting rocks east of Eye of the Sun offer potential framing but are hard to arrange in an attractive composition with the arch. On the rock wall below Eye of the Sun is a

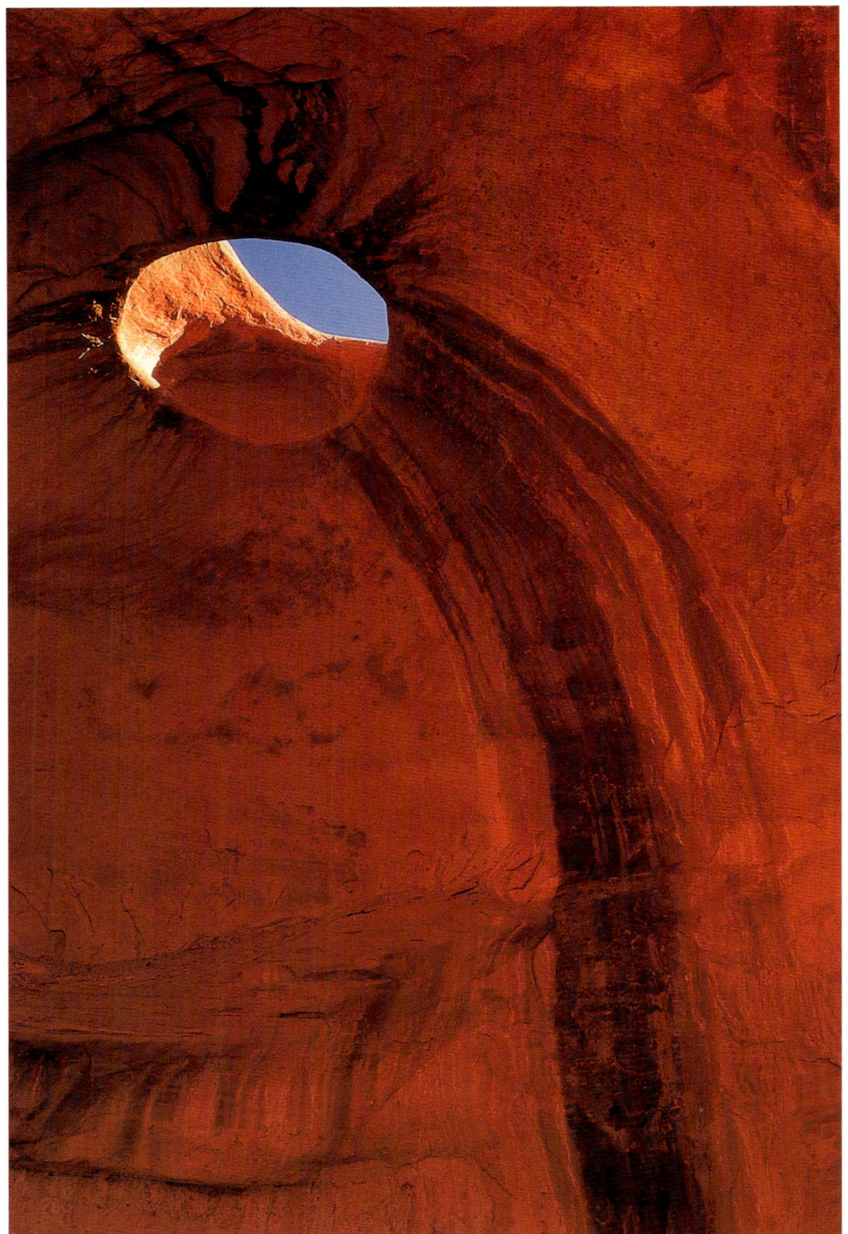

The Big Hogan, Monument Valley Tribal Park, Arizona. Not far from Ear of the Wind is the Big Hogan, a large overhanging cliff with a pothole arch in the roof. In midmorning, bounce lighting illuminates the interior of this feature beautifully. My Navajo guides have told me that the desert varnish around and below the opening in the roof resembles a Native American dancer. *Minolta 24–35mm lens, polarizing and enhancing filters, Fuji Velvia film.*

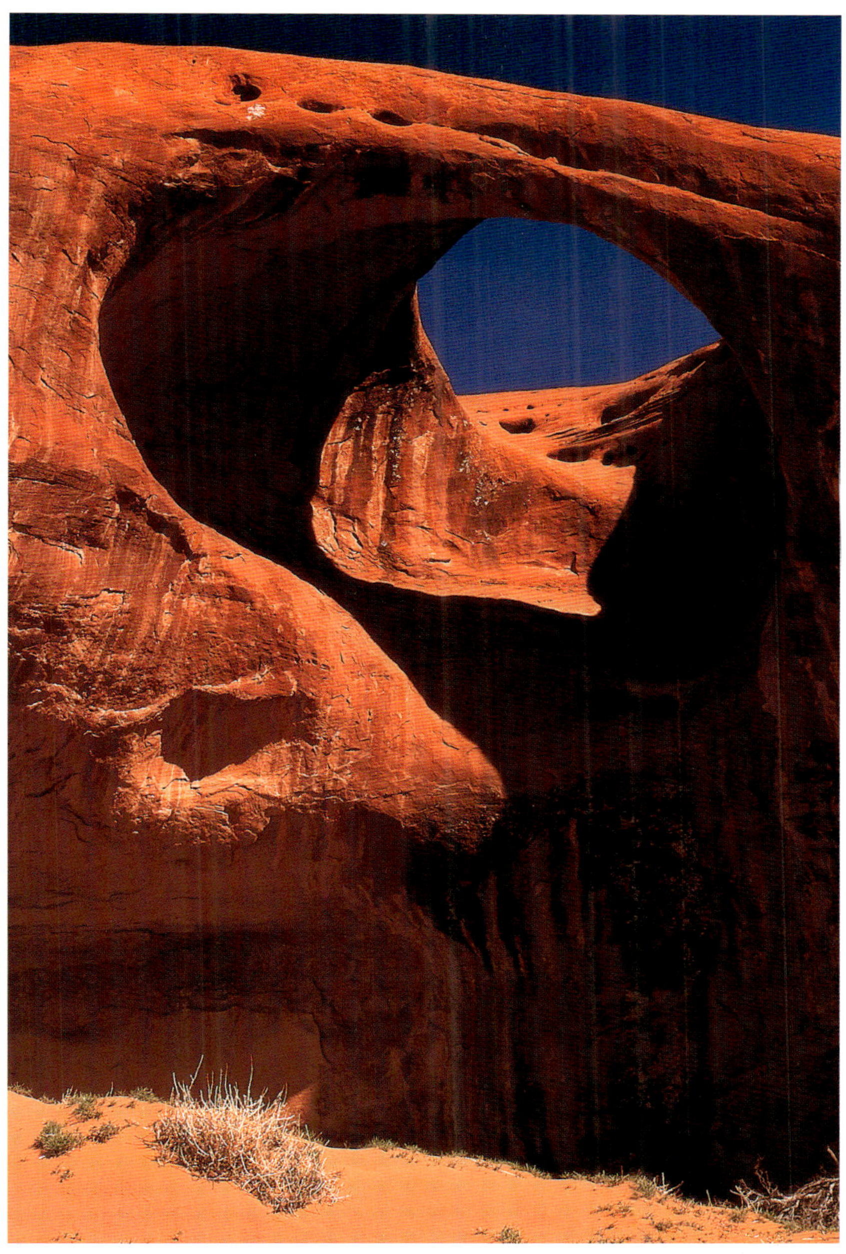

Moccasin Arch, Monument Valley Tribal Park, Arizona. Moccasin Arch is located only a few yards west of the Big Hogan. Mid- to late-morning light provides just the right proportions of light and shadow. I usually try to find some vegetation growing on top of the small sand dune below the arch to help balance the composition. *Minolta 35–70mm lens, polarizing and enhancing filters, Fuji Velvia film.*

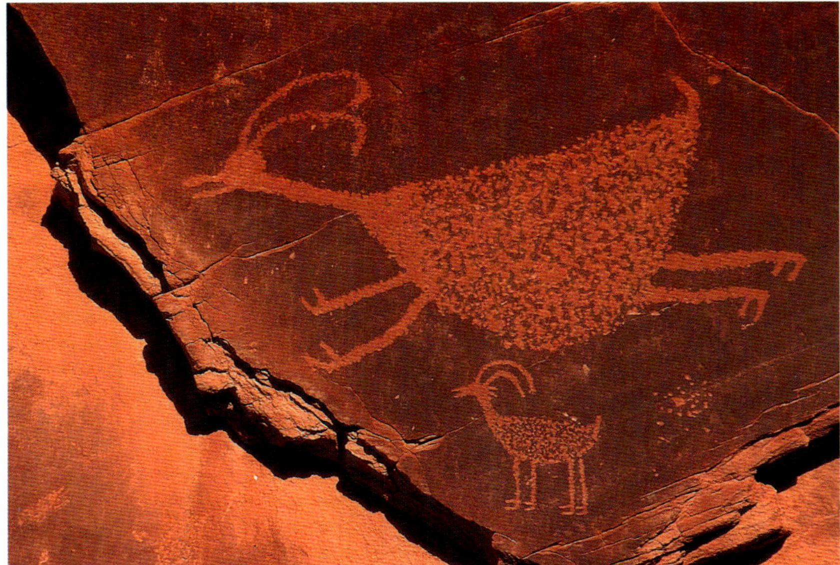

Petroglyph, Monument Valley Tribal Park, Arizona. This petroglyph, located on the cliff just below the Eye of the Sun, is my favorite rock art in Monument Valley. Although the sun illuminates the drawings from late morning to mid-afternoon, they can also be photographed effectively in the shade. Since the desert varnish on which the petroglyphs were drawn is dark, be sure to underexpose your pictures by about half a stop. *Minolta 70–210mm lens, polarizing and enhancing filters, Fuji Velvia film.*

petroglyph of several bighorn sheep that should not be missed. A moderate telephoto lens captures a tight composition of this rock art.

Another sunrise destination features a side view of the West Mitten framed by a photogenic tree. To reach this location, have your guide turn east off Monument Valley Road about 1 mile from the visitor center. The tree is located about half a mile east of the main road. From this vantage point, the West Mitten looks like a slender spire instead of a hand. Pleasing compositions can be achieved with the tree on either the right or the left of the spire. At sunrise, the light is flat during the winter months, but the West Mitten becomes increasingly sidelit in the late spring and summer.

If you choose to take a guided tour in the afternoon, several good destinations are available. One location that should not be missed is

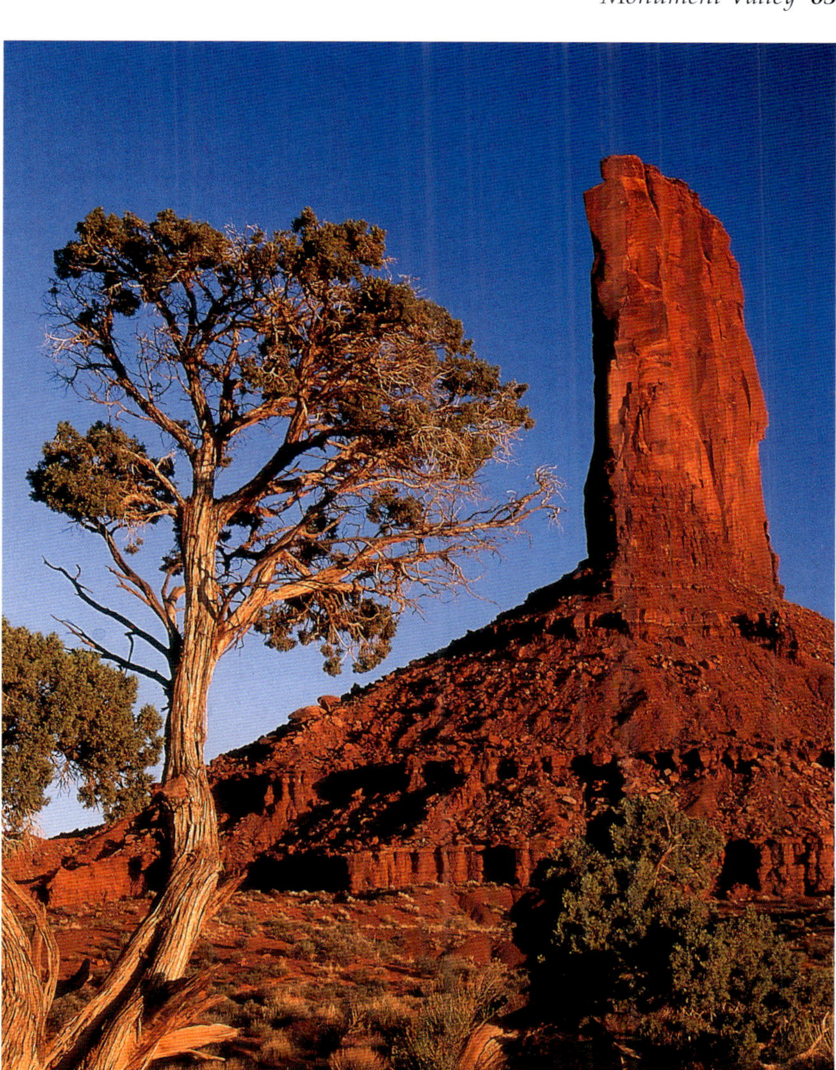

Side view of the West Mitten, Monument Valley Tribal Park, Arizona. The West Mitten is one of the most recognizable and photographed buttes in Monument Valley, but from this viewpoint, which can be reached only with Navajo guides, it looks like a slender spire. The picturesque juniper tree, which can be used to frame the Mitten on either side, adds to the appeal of this image. Sunrise in the late spring or summer provides the best lighting. *Minolta 35–70mm lens, polarizing and enhancing filters, Fuji Velvia film.*

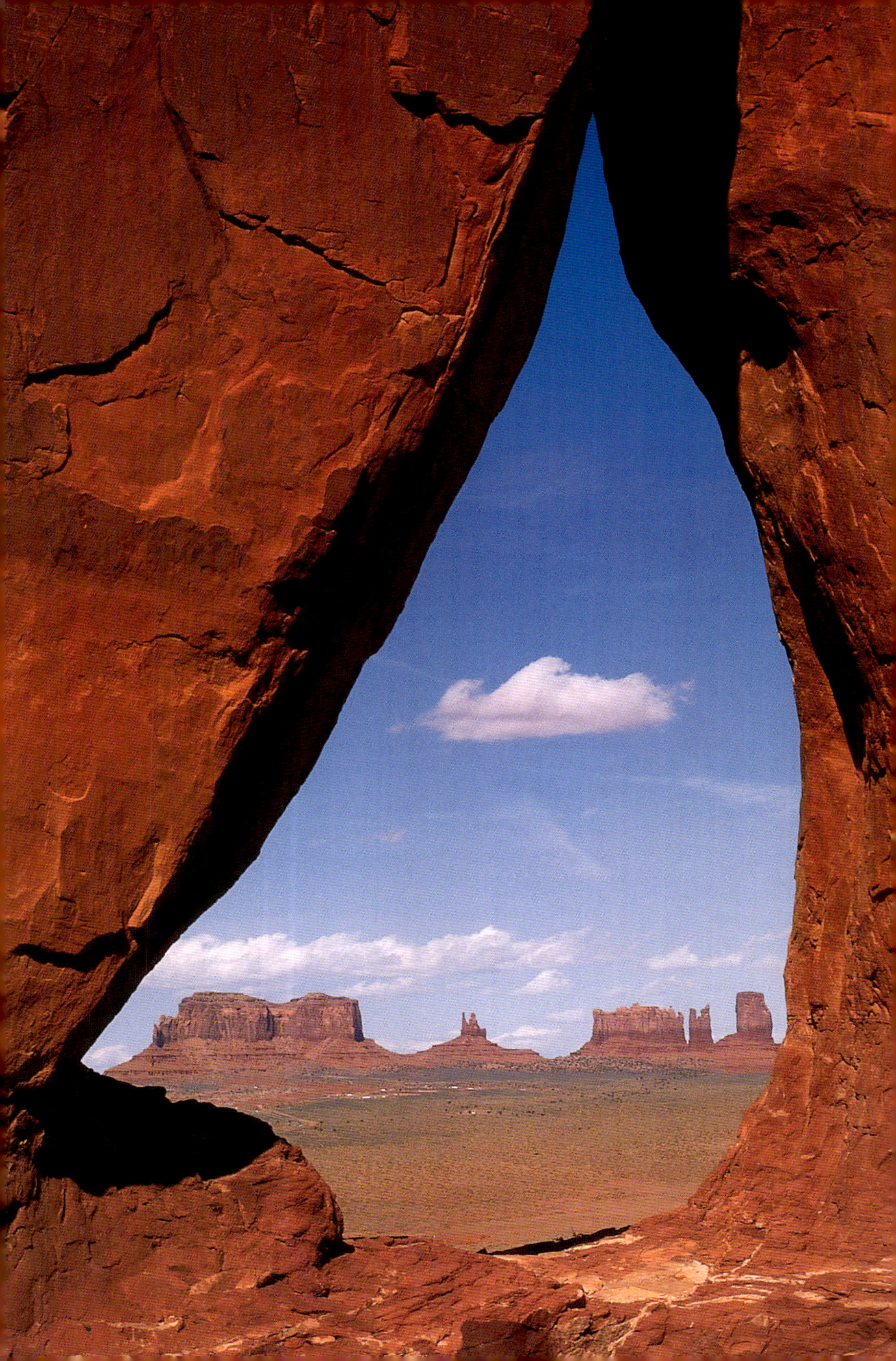

Teardrop Arch, one of the most beautifully shaped arches anywhere. From exactly the right camera position, many of the buttes in the northern portion of Monument Valley can be framed inside the opening. Teardrop Arch, which is not in Monument Valley Tribal Park, is situated high on a ridge above Goulding's Trading Post. Late afternoon in the spring, summer, and early autumn provides the best lighting. If you arrive too late in the afternoon, the arch starts to go into shadow. During the winter months, the shadow of a nearby cliff covers the arch, rendering it in silhouette. However, Teardrop Arch in silhouette is still an attractive image, with the sunlit buttes framed in the dark opening.

Another good late-afternoon and sunset destination for a Navajo guided tour is the sand dunes with the Totem Pole and Yei bi Chei as your center of interest. Since the prevailing wind in Monument Valley is from the west, the steepest face of the dunes is to the east. Therefore, the rippled patterns in the sand are even stronger in the late afternoon than in the morning. Your exact location on the dunes, ideally at a right angle to the sun, depends on the time of year.

I also strongly recommend spending an afternoon with your guide in Mystery Valley, about 7 miles south of Monument Valley. Mystery Valley contains a number of attractive arches, Anasazi ruins, and picturesque rocks. Half Moon Arch is appealing in the early to mid-afternoon. Honeymoon Arch is well lit in mid to late afternoon. I recommend that you scramble up inside the arch to photograph a small ruin named Honeymoon House. The mid- to late-afternoon sun bounces off the opposite wall of the arch and back onto the ruin. The strong rock patterns, interesting ruin, and beautiful lighting combine to create great images. Try a number of different compositions from tight to wide angle, but avoid putting any of the light-colored sky in your picture.

Teardrop Arch, west of Monument Valley Tribal Park, Arizona. Teardrop Arch is one of the most beautifully shaped arches in the canyon country. It frames several buttes in the northern end of Monument Valley, including Stagecoach and King on the Throne. It can be reached only on guided tours and is best photographed in mid to late afternoon in the spring, summer, and early autumn. Although the winter sun does not illuminate Teardrop Arch, the arch can still be used effectively as a silhouette to frame the distant buttes. Having a few clouds in just the right places adds to the beauty of this image. *Minolta 70–210mm lens, polarizing and enhancing filters, Fuji Velvia film.*

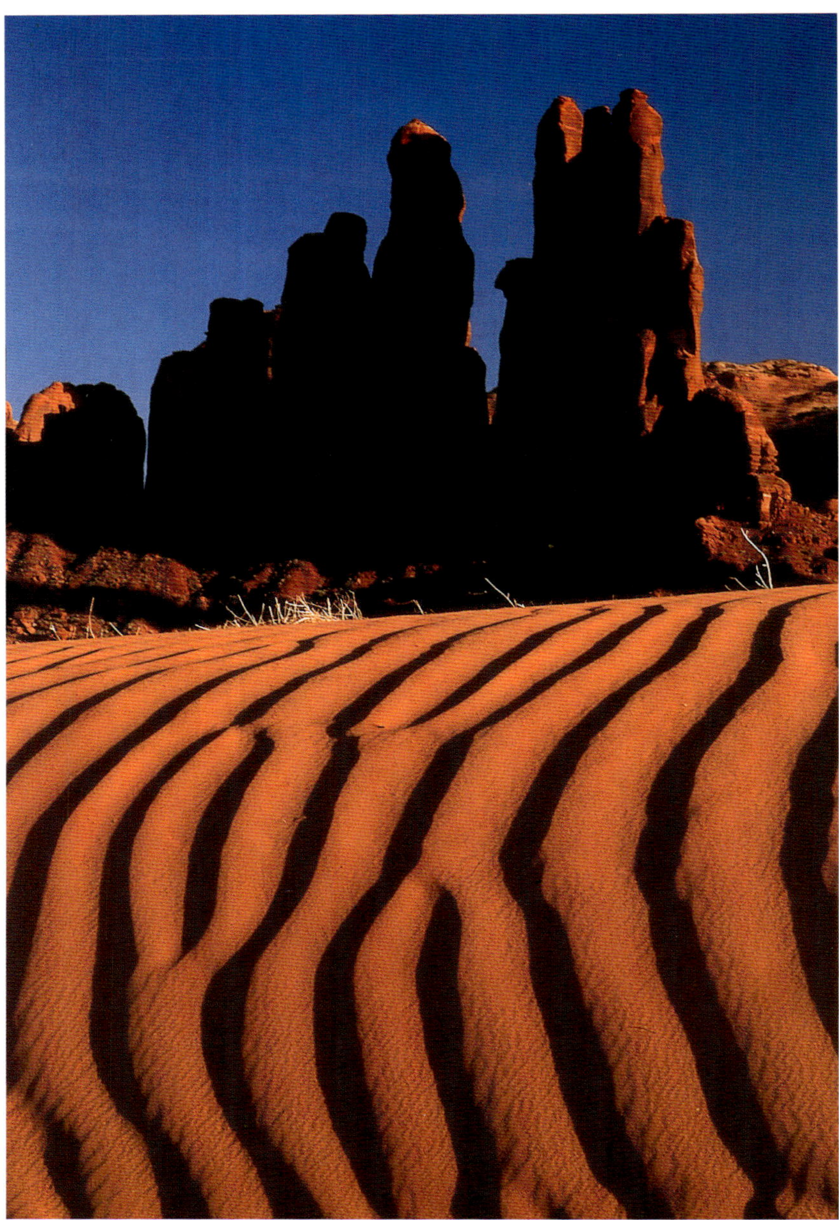

Yei bi Chei and sand dunes, Monument Valley Tribal Park, Arizona. Late afternoon and sunset provide good opportunities to photograph the patterns on the sand dunes, along with the Totem Pole and Yei bi Chei. Strong side-lighting is mandatory, so the portion of the dunes you photograph depends on the time of year. Since the prevailing winds in Monument Valley are from the west, the steep side of the dunes is to the east. This means that shadows on the dunes are even stronger at sunset than at sunrise. *Minolta 70–210mm lens, polarizing and enhancing filters, Fuji Velvia film.*

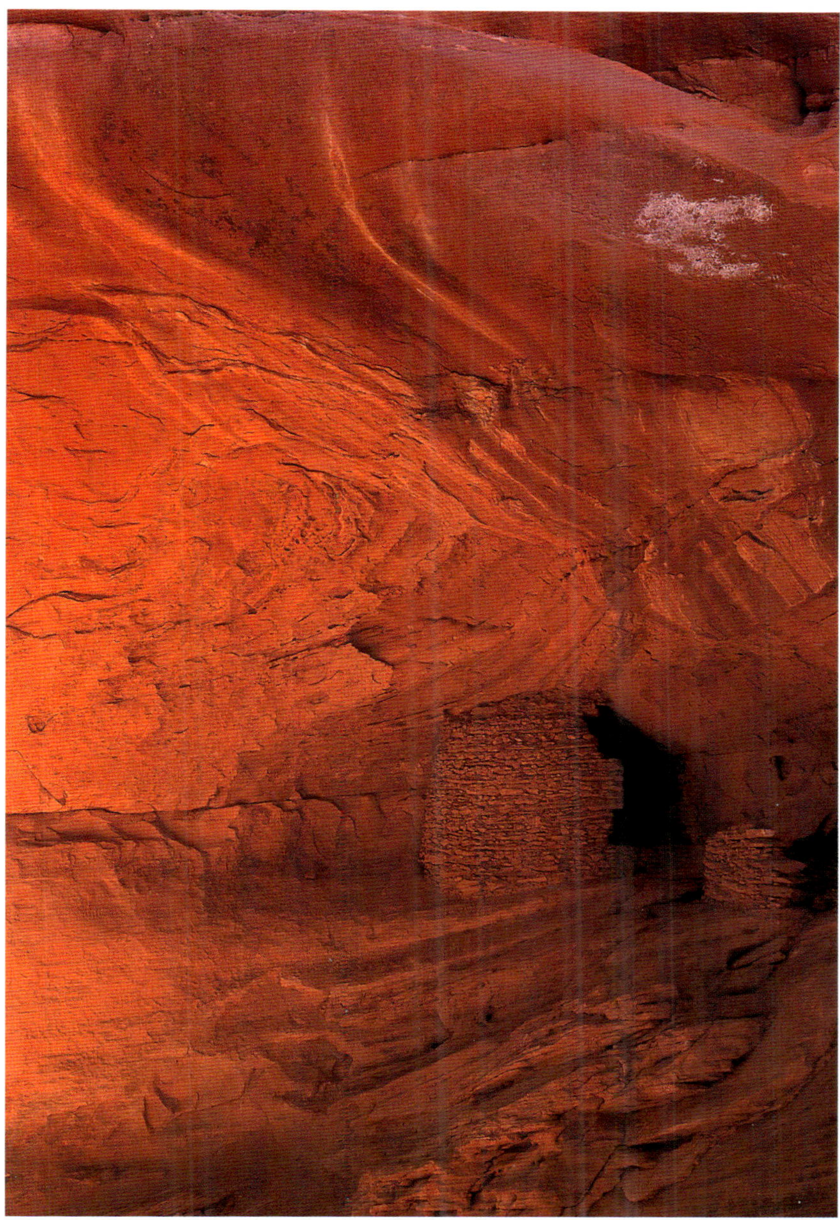

Honeymoon House, Mystery Valley, Monument Valley Tribal Park, Arizona. Mystery Valley, south of Monument Valley, features interesting arches, ancient ruins, and spectacular rock formations. Inside Honeymoon Arch is a small structure known as Honeymoon House. In the afternoon, especially in the autumn and winter months, the sun hits the rock on the opposite side of the opening and bounces across to create beautiful lighting on the ruin and the rock patterns around it. *Minolta 24–35mm lens, enhancing filter, Fuji Velvia film.*

Another good late-afternoon destination in Mystery Valley is Many Hands Ruin, which features a number of fine pictographs, including numerous hand prints, near the ruin. As sunset approaches, ask your guide to take you to the Saucers area, where an interesting foreground of disc-shaped rocks combines with the distant buttes of Monument Valley to make a spectacular scene. The light on the Saucers is a little flat during the winter months but is ideal in spring and autumn.

For an outstanding half-day guided tour, ask about a trip to Hunt's Mesa, which lies south of and overlooks Monument Valley. You will need to start early in the afternoon, as it takes a considerable amount of time to reach your destination. One way to reach Hunt's Mesa is by climbing up the cliff from Monument Valley on a crude trail, but this route is very strenuous and slightly dangerous. The preferred route approaches Hunt's Mesa from the south and can be negotiated by four-wheel-drive vehicles. Be sure that your guide is familiar with this route and is aware of current conditions. The excursion to Hunt's Mesa costs

The Saucers in Mystery Valley, Monument Valley Tribal Park, Arizona. Another interesting view in Mystery Valley includes the disc-shaped rocks known as the Saucers and the distant buttes of Monument Valley. Late afternoon in the spring, autumn, and winter provides the best lighting for this scene. *Minolta 70–210mm lens, polarizing and enhancing filters, Fuji Velvia film.*

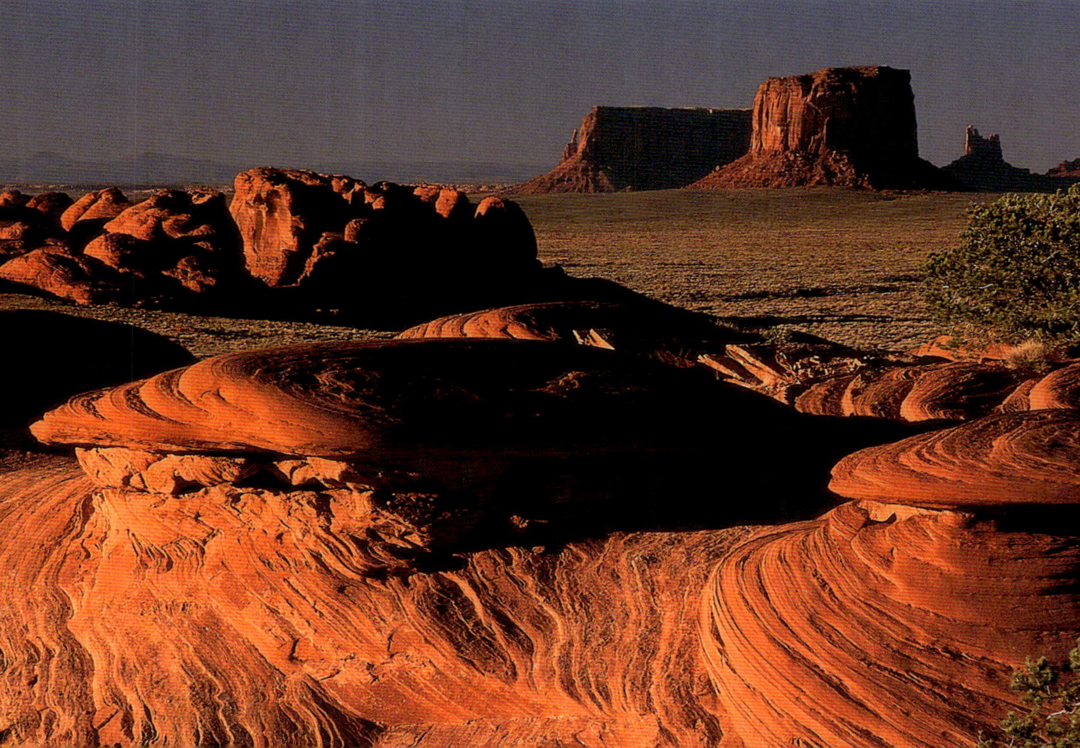

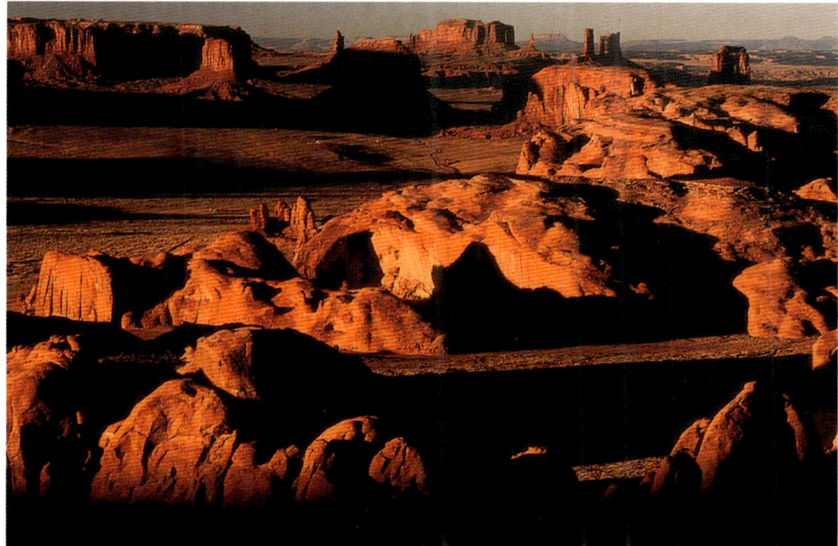

Monument Valley from Hunt's Mesa, Monument Valley Tribal Park, Arizona. The long four-wheel-drive trip to Hunt's Mesa is well worth the effort and expense. From this vantage point, all the features of Monument Valley are spread out below you. At sunset, the lengthening shadows swallow up the buttes and mesas in a sea of darkness. *Minolta 70–210mm lens, polarizing and enhancing filters, Fuji Velvia film.*

more than some of the tours to more easily reached destinations, but the photographs you will obtain make it worthwhile.

From the rim of Hunt's Mesa, the entire expanse of Monument Valley with all its buttes, sand dunes, and mesas lies before you. Late-afternoon lighting is best at this location in autumn, winter, or spring. At sunset, the buttes glow like molten embers, and the shadows lengthen until they finally engulf Monument Valley in a sea of darkness.

FOUR

Other Photographic Locations in Northern Arizona

PETRIFIED FOREST NATIONAL PARK

About 225 million years ago, large pinelike trees grew on a vast tropical floodplain in what is now northeastern Arizona. When they fell, the trees were covered by silt and volcanic ash. Silica-laden waters seeped through the logs and encased the original wood tissues. The silica crystallized into quartz, and the logs were preserved as petrified wood. Erosion of the surrounding mudstones by water and wind exposed this ancient forest and created the spectacular topographic forms known as the Painted Desert. Petroglyphs and ruins left by the Anasazi are plentiful in this area. These archaeological treasures, along with the petrified logs and spectacular badlands, are preserved in Petrified Forest National Park.

Petrified Forest National Park is located in northeastern Arizona about 25 miles from the small town of Holbrook. The northern (Painted Desert) portion of the park can be reached from Holbrook on Interstate 40. The southern (Petrified Log) portion of the park is most easily accessed from Holbrook on US 180. A 28-mile scenic drive connects the northern and southern portions of the park. All the traditional tourist facilities, including numerous motels, restaurants, and gas stations, are available in Holbrook.

Petrified Forest National Park is open year-round but is closed at night to discourage the theft of petrified wood. The park has a zero-loss-tolerance policy for petrified wood. If you remove even the smallest piece, you could be subject to a fine, arrest, or both. The park is usually open from about half an hour after sunrise to half an hour before sunset. The hours of operation change every month and are usually posted at business establishments in Holbrook, along the major access roads, and at the park entrances. Arizona does not go on daylight

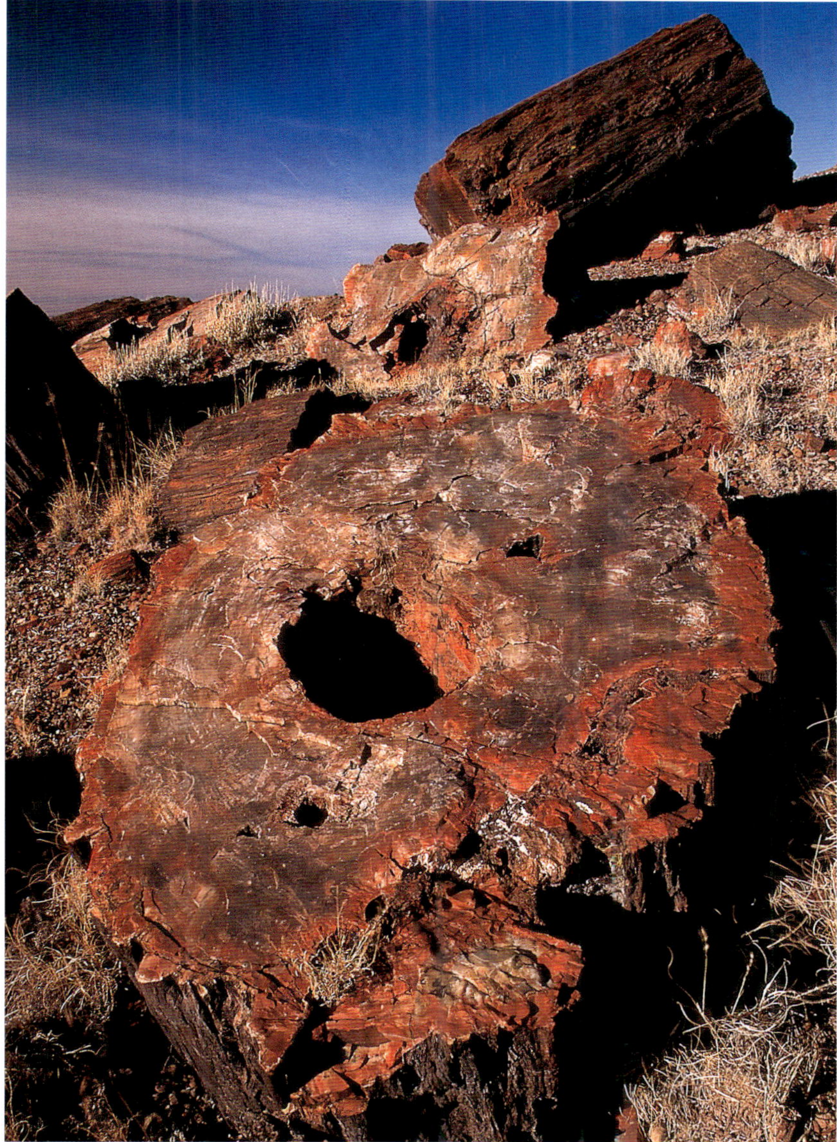

Petrified logs, Giant Logs Trail, Petrified Forest National Park, Arizona. The photographic opportunities at Petrified Forest are endless. The logs are colorful and plentiful and, depending on the direction of the light, can be combined in many attractive ways. In most areas, including Giant Logs Trail, Long Logs Trail, Crystal Forest Trail, Jasper Forest, and the paved trail at Blue Mesa, you can wander around among the logs looking for good compositions. *Canon 28–105mm lens, polarizing and enhancing filters, Fuji Velvia film.*

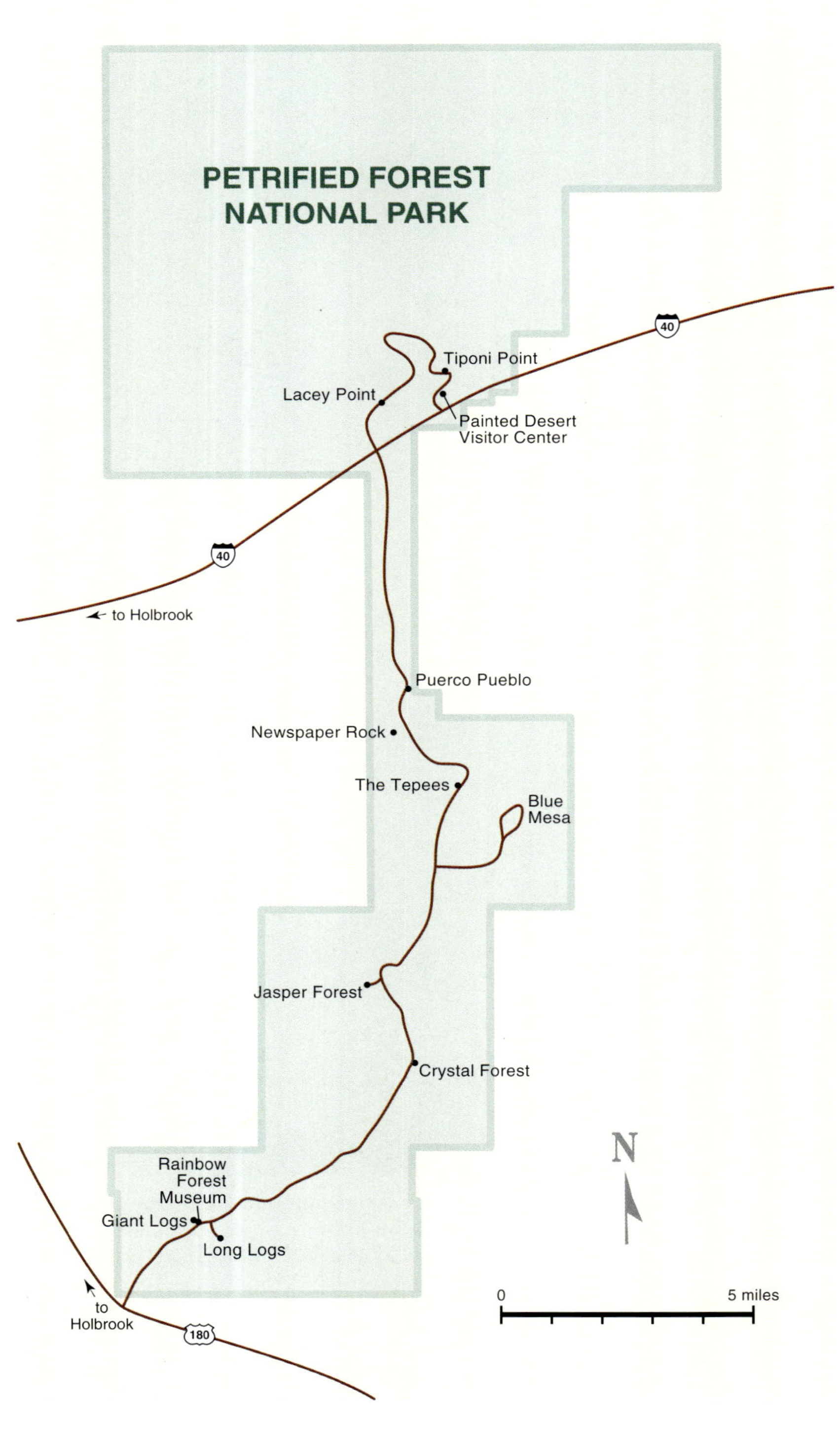
PETRIFIED FOREST
NATIONAL PARK
40
Tiponi Point
Lacey Point
Painted Desert
Visitor Center
40
to Holbrook
Puerco Pueblo
Newspaper Rock
The Tepees
Blue
Mesa
Jasper Forest
Crystal Forest
N
Rainbow
Forest
Museum
Giant Logs
Long Logs
0
5 miles
to
Holbrook
180

saving time during the summer months, so park opening and closing times are mountain standard time.

Although fees may change from time to time, entry to Petrified Forest National Park is currently $10 per car. Golden Eagle and Golden Age Passes are accepted. Petrified Forest is relatively uncrowded, especially in the early morning and the late afternoon. This means that you will be able to do a lot of serious photography without other people getting in your way.

Petrified Forest National Park has outstanding photographic potential. The petrified logs have interesting shapes and are both colorful and plentiful. In most of the park, photographers have the freedom to walk among the logs and find the best composition and lighting. Close-ups of the logs and the lichens growing on them are rewarding. The patterns and colors of the Painted Desert provide an interesting background for the logs or can even serve as the main focus.

I use a wide-angle lens and shoot with a vertical format much of the time when photographing petrified logs. Usually, I try to put an arrangement of interesting logs in the foreground and a colorful butte in the background. This requires the use of hyperfocal distance to get everything sharp from front to back. For Painted Desert vistas, I usually favor horizontal formats and use a wide assortment of focal lengths from wide angle to moderate telephoto.

For both petrified logs and badlands, I try to shoot within two hours of sunrise or sunset for the most pleasing light. I insist on subject material that is oriented at a right angle to the sun for good texture. I almost always use polarizing and enhancing filters to make the colors more vibrant and to darken the sky.

The principal locations where petrified logs can be photographed are, from south to north, the Giant Logs Trail by the Rainbow Forest Museum, the Long Logs Trail, the Crystal Forest Trail, Jasper Forest, and Blue Mesa. Most of these trails are about half a mile round-trip and, with the exception of the trail at Blue Mesa, mostly flat. All these areas offer good photographic possibilities and should be examined carefully in both early morning and late afternoon.

Perhaps my favorite area for photographing petrified wood is the Long Logs Trail near the southern entrance to the park. If your time in the Petrified Forest is short, make this your primary photographic location. As the name Long Logs implies, many nearly complete petrified trees can be found here. In addition, some colorful badlands are located

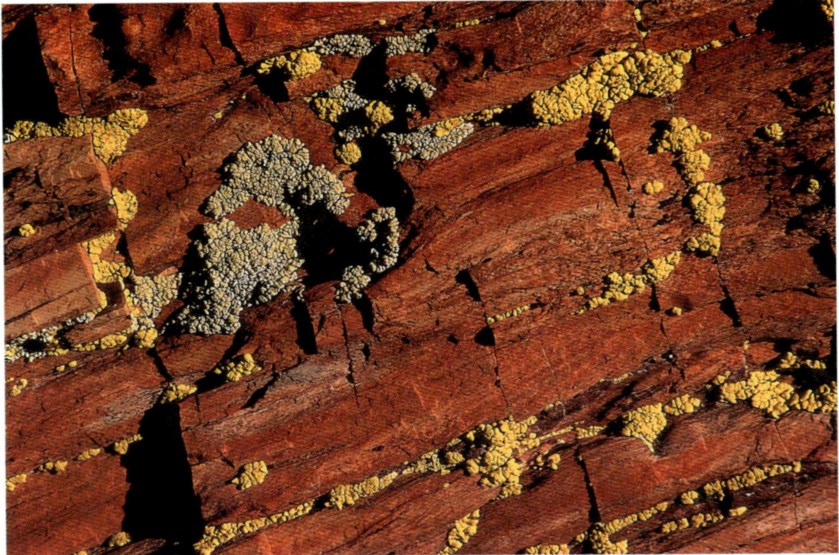

Lichens on petrified log, Petrified Forest National Park, Arizona. When walking among the petrified logs, don't overlook the smaller features. Cross sections of logs often have dramatic colors and designs. The lichens that grow on the logs contrast beautifully with the petrified wood. A successful pattern shot usually has a center of interest, such as the yellow-green lichen in the upper left portion of this picture. *Canon 75–300mm IS lens, polarizing and enhancing filters, Fuji Velvia film.*

just east of the trail and can be used as background elements in your photographs.

A few areas just off the Long Logs Trail close to the parking lot are being restored and have been fenced off, but as of late 1999, you could still wander around most of the area looking for good compositions. A spur off the main Long Logs Trail leads to Agate House, a partially restored pueblo built many years ago from petrified wood. In my opinion, Agate House is just a curiosity and not a photographic destination.

My other favorite area in Petrified Forest is Blue Mesa, reached by a 3-mile loop road about halfway along the main scenic drive. In the early 1990s, it was possible to descend into the valley on the southeast side of the mesa to an area that featured a number of pedestal logs. You can still see the pedestal logs from a parking area on the Blue Mesa road, but the public is no longer allowed to descend into this valley.

On the north side of Blue Mesa is a paved trail leading down into another area below the rim. Although portions of this trail are somewhat steep, the 1-mile round-trip hike is well worth the effort. No pedestal logs can be seen along this trail, but the colorful badlands and petrified logs combine to present some excellent photographic opportunities.

Just beyond the trailhead is a parking area and an overlook of the badlands surrounding Blue Mesa. The patterns and colors from this vantage point are outstanding. I also recommend walking from the parking area for several hundred yards in each direction along the rim looking for other compositions. My favorite time to photograph from this vantage point is late afternoon, but the light in midmorning is also acceptable.

Painted Desert–Blue Mesa, Petrified Forest National Park, Arizona. The colorful badlands of the Painted Desert portion of Petrified Forest make an interesting photographic subject. Early or late light is highly desirable, and strong sidelighting is mandatory if you want to capture the texture and shape of the buttes. One of the best places to photograph the Painted Desert is from or near the overlooks on the Blue Mesa Loop. *Canon 28–105mm lens, polarizing and enhancing filters, Fuji Velvia film.*

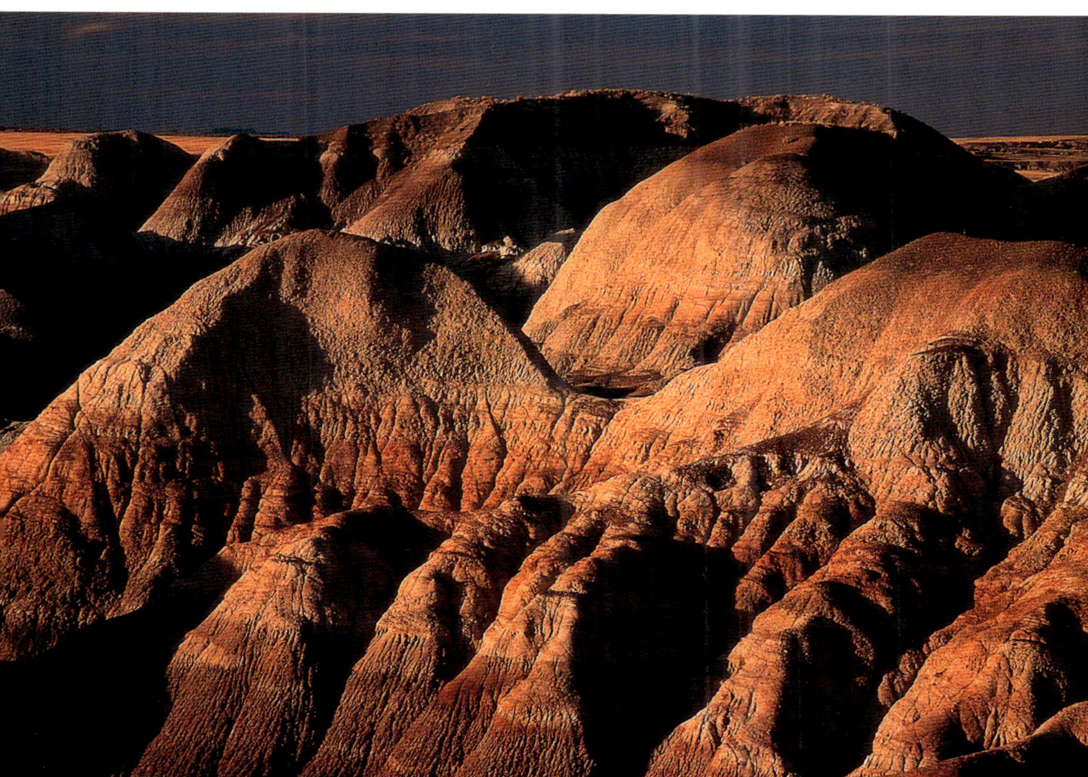

After returning to the scenic drive, turn north and proceed to the Teepees, an area with a number of colorful buttes exhibiting interesting erosional patterns. The most interesting buttes are northeast of the main parking area. I usually try to include some of the stream patterns in the foreground leading up to the Teepees in the background. Early to midmorning is the best time to photograph the Teepees, but late afternoon in the autumn and winter is also good.

Farther north is a spur road to Newspaper Rock, a huge sandstone boulder covered with petroglyphs. The public can no longer go down to the rock, but a viewpoint allows observation from a moderate distance. A long telephoto lens is required to obtain good images of these ancient drawings from the overlook. Midmorning is when the best light falls on Newspaper Rock. Puerco Pueblo, just north of Newspaper Rock, was built by the ancient inhabitants of the Petrified Forest. Puerco Pueblo doesn't have much photographic potential, but some petroglyphs can be found on the rocks below an overlook south of the ruins. You can get to them by following an old dirt road from the north side of the parking lot and around the east side of the bluff.

The scenic road proceeds north, crosses over Interstate 40, and enters the Painted Desert portion of Petrified Forest National Park. The badlands in this area contain mostly reddish hues and are quite attractive early or late in the day. My favorite overlook in late afternoon is Lacey Point, and my favorite near sunrise is Tiponi Point.

You may be fortunate enough to see and photograph some pronghorn antelope during your visit to Petrified Forest National Park. I have seen them quite often, usually in the southern end of the park. In the autumn, the coats of the pronghorn are in prime condition, and they are very involved in mating activity and not concerned about photographers. To obtain good pictures of these beautiful but wary animals, I recommend at least a 300mm lens, but a 500 or 600mm lens would be better.

CANYON DE CHELLY NATIONAL MONUMENT

Canyon de Chelly National Monument contains spectacular canyons, soaring monoliths, and some of the most interesting Anasazi ruins and rock art in the plateau country. Canyon de Chelly is located in northeastern Arizona and is completely surrounded by the Navajo Reservation. Many Navajo families still live and farm in the canyon. The monument can be reached from either the north or the south on US 191.

In the small town of Chinle, located just west of the monument, lodging, food, gasoline, and other services are available. Thunderbird Lodge, located within the park, offers lodging, food, and guided tours. A public campground, maintained by the National Park Service, is located within the park boundaries, but no hookups are available. Since Canyon de Chelly and Chinle are on the Navajo Reservation, daylight saving time is observed during the summer months. The rest of Arizona stays on mountain standard time year-round.

Canyon de Chelly is one of the few entities in the National Park System that does not collect entry fees or camping fees. A visitor center at the entrance to the monument has staff on duty to answer your questions. The visitor center also features informative exhibits, a good assortment of books, and other interpretive materials. *Visitors are warned not to leave valuables in their cars if they visit an overlook, hike on a trail, or take a guided tour. Any suspicious activity should be reported to the visitor center.*

Visitors can explore Canyon de Chelly in a number of different ways. Probably the most productive, from a photographic point of view, involves guided tours of Canyon de Chelly and Canyon del Muerto in four-wheel-drive vehicles. The vehicles drive right up the riverbeds of the two canyons, and the water level determines the extent and duration of the tours. During the spring runoff, the guided tours may be limited to half a day or canceled altogether. Visitors are not allowed to enter the canyon by themselves, even if they have their own four-wheel-drives.

Guided half-day or all-day tours in six-wheel-drive trucks are available at Thunderbird Lodge. Prices, which are subject to change, range from about $40 for a half-day tour to $60 for an all-day tour. The half-day tour goes into Canyon del Muerto as far upstream as Antelope House Ruin or Standing Cow Ruin and into Canyon de Chelly as far as White House Ruin. The full-day tour continues up Canyon del Muerto to Mummy Cave Ruin and up Canyon de Chelly to Spider Rock.

Reservations are not needed for the Thunderbird tours. If more people show up, they just add more trucks. The trucks can carry up to 20 passengers, and the itinerary is controlled by the driver. Although there is some flexibility, the needs of the entire group prevail over the wishes of an individual photographer. On the Thunderbird tours, you will learn about the history and geology of the canyon, but you may not arrive at the best photographic locations at the proper time for good pictures or stay as long in one location as you might desire.

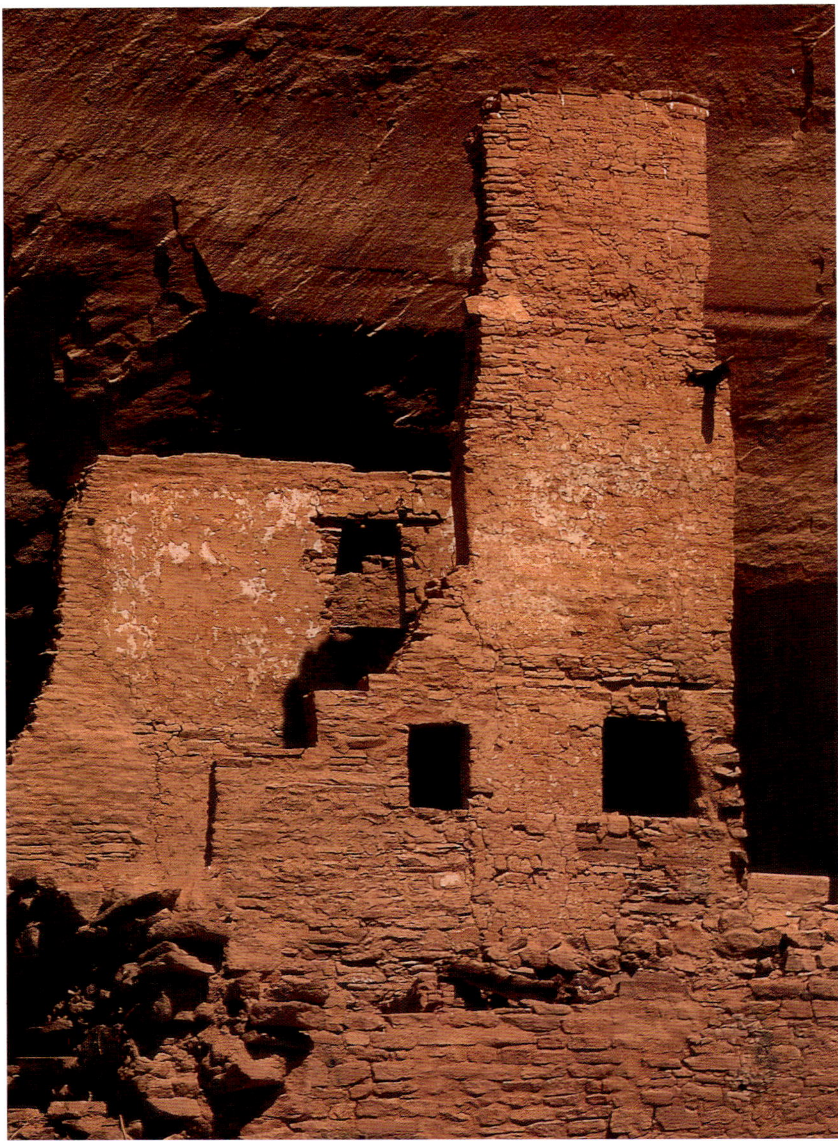

Antelope House, Canyon de Chelly National Monument, Arizona. Antelope House should be your first major destination on a guided tour of Canyon del Muerto and Canyon de Chelly. Sunlight hits this attractive feature from midmorning to early afternoon. My favorite composition at Antelope House concentrates on the most prominent tower in the ruin. *Minolta 70–210mm lens, polarizing and enhancing filters, Fuji Velvia film.*

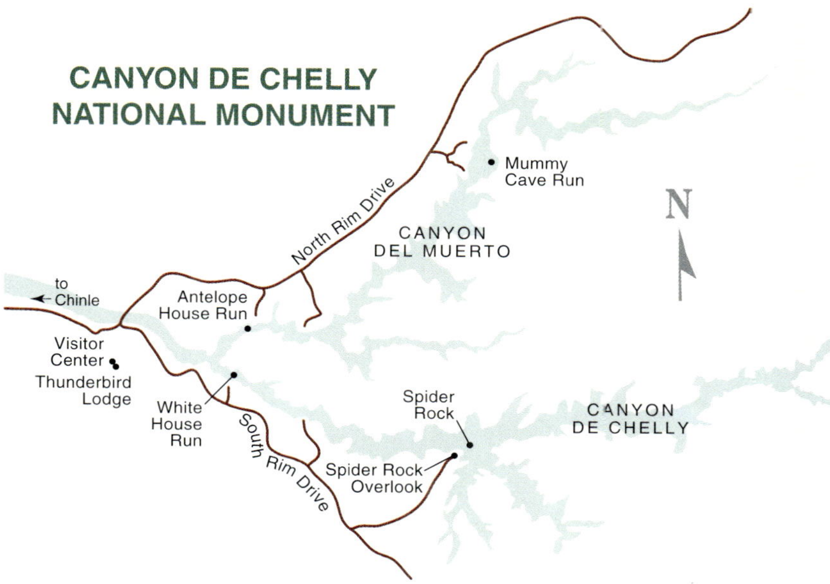

The second way of exploring the canyons is with a smaller vehicle and a smaller group. De Chelly Tours provides drivers and four-wheel-drive vehicles that carry four to six people. I recently took an all-day tour with two clients. We paid $70 per person, for a total of $210. The larger the group, the lower the cost per person; if you charter a vehicle by yourself, the cost would be more than $70. You can engage De Chelly Tours at the Holiday Inn just west of the visitor center or call for reservations at (520) 674-3772.

There are many advantages to exploring Canyon del Muerto and Canyon de Chelly with a smaller group and in a smaller vehicle. You have greater control over the itinerary and can spend as much time as necessary at each location. The small vehicles are much faster than the big trucks, and you waste less time going from one photographic location to another. Since the driver does all the driving, you are free to enjoy the beauty of the canyons and look for photographic opportunities. This is the option I recommend for serious photographers.

The third option is to use your own four-wheel-drive vehicle. You must still have a Navajo guide with you in the canyon and pay for a minimum of three hours. To engage a member of the Tsegi Guide Association, either inquire at the visitor center or call (520) 674-5500.

The advantage of providing your own vehicle is the slightly lower cost. The disadvantages are that you have to do a lot of tough driving yourself and may incur a lot of wear and tear on your own vehicle. Also, you must keep your eyes on the road at least part of the time and may miss some photographic opportunities.

Whichever means you choose to explore Canyon del Muerto and Canyon de Chelly, you will be amazed at the photographic possibilities. I mention only the major photo stops, but an unlimited number of pattern shots are also available. These include the beautiful cottonwood trees against the tan sandstone cliffs, desert varnish patterns on the walls of the canyon, quaint Navajo farms nestled below the cliffs, and reflections of the trees or cliffs in shallow or still portions of the stream. In the springtime, the light green cottonwoods are particularly attractive. My favorite time of year in the canyons is late October, when many of the cottonwoods are gold.

Start your tour at about 9:00 A.M. Shortly after entering the canyon near the visitor center, you pass several groups of interesting petroglyphs. These are worth a stop and can be successfully photographed either in the morning, when they are in the shade, or on your return trip, when they may be in the sun. First Ruin is the initial cliff dwelling you encounter and is only a prelude of things to come; if time is short, you can wait to photograph it on your return trip.

Several miles up the canyon, where the streams divide, is a cliff dwelling appropriately named Junction Ruin. It is more impressive than First Ruin and can be photographed either from the streambed or from the far bank of the stream. Midmorning light is good for Junction Ruin. From the stream junction, follow Canyon del Muerto upstream to Antelope House Ruin. On the way, notice a number of small ruins and granaries on the canyon walls. Anytime you spot a small cave or overhang, the odds are good that an Anasazi ruin is located there.

Antelope House Ruin was named for some prominent pictographs of antelope on the canyon wall near the ruin. The antelope and other interesting rock art at this location are of Navajo rather than Anasazi origin. These pictographs are sunlit during the morning hours and can be photographed successfully with a 300mm lens.

Antelope House is one of the major ruins in the monument and receives midmorning to early-afternoon sunlight. I usually try to reach this spot at about 10:00 A.M. A wire fence in front of Antelope House has been erected to keep people from entering it. With a little maneuvering, you can adjust your tripod to either shoot through the openings in the wire or, if you are tall enough, shoot over the fence. My favorite composition is a tight shot of the tallest tower taken with a telephoto lens, but wider-angle shots that include more of the ruin should also be tried.

Proceeding a mile upstream in Canyon del Muerto, you reach Standing Cow Ruin. The pictographs, including the cow, are of Navajo origin. The ruin has been rebuilt with a door and a roof and is not a good photographic subject. The ruin and the pictographs are several hundred yards from the road, on private property, and cannot be approached closely on a guided tour.

About 5 miles farther upstream is Mummy Cave Ruin. I recommend crossing the stream and photographing this interesting ruin from just outside the log fence that surrounds it. During the late spring and summer, the sun is too high in the sky to illuminate the most interesting portion of the ruin completely. However, in autumn and winter, the sun reaches Mummy Cave Ruin about 11:30 and illuminates it until midafternoon. My favorite composition is taken at about 70mm and includes the slope and juniper trees to the right of and below the ruin. This gives some perspective to the size of the ruin and its height above the valley floor. I also like a tight vertical composition of just the prominent tower on the right side of the ruin, but this shot works best with a 400 to 500mm lens.

After leaving Mummy Cave Ruin, retrace your route back down Canyon del Muerto past Antelope House Ruin to the junction with Canyon de Chelly. This drive takes about an hour. Proceed upstream in Canyon de Chelly, pass White House Ruin, and drive to the base of Spider Rock.

On the way to Spider Rock, you pass an attractive arch high on the cliff above the stream. This arch can be photographed from the west side or approached on the east side after an arduous scramble up the rocky slope. You can photograph this arch on your return trip down Canyon de Chelly.

Spider Rock is a narrow spire that towers 600 feet above the canyon floor. In the spring and summer, it is sunlit from midmorning to sunset, but in the autumn and winter, the sun goes behind the canyon wall early in the afternoon. In late October, you may not be able to reach Spider Rock in time to have sun on the foreground, even if you leave Mummy Cave Ruin by noon. I recommend a camera location near the base of Spider Rock looking up a side canyon, isolating it against the sky, and separating it from the canyon walls. In the autumn, several

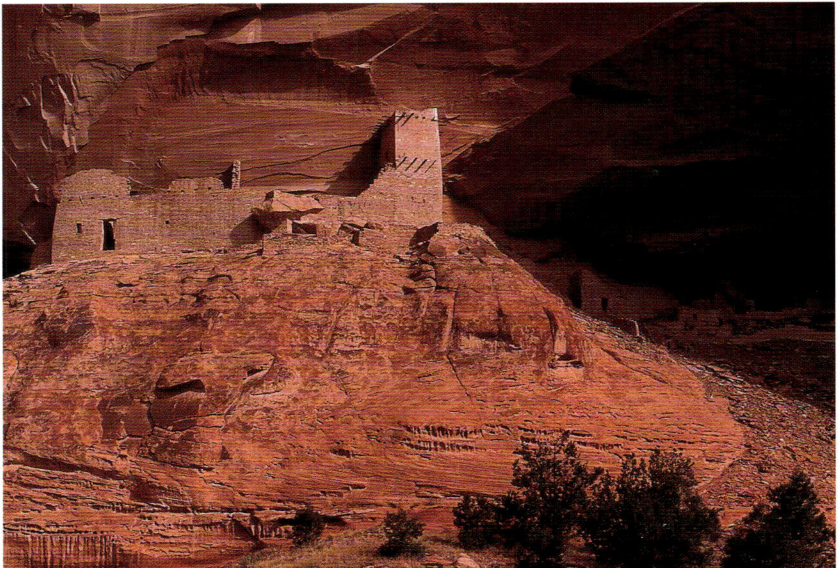

Mummy Cave Ruin, Canyon de Chelly National Monument, Arizona. If you are taking an all-day tour, be sure to visit Mummy Cave Ruin at the far end of Canyon del Muerto. Late morning to midafternoon provides the best lighting for this feature, but only in the late fall and winter is the sun low enough in the sky to reach below the overhanging cliff and illuminate the entire ruin. To give a perspective on how far this feature rises above the valley floor, I recommend including the slope and the group of juniper trees below Mummy Cave Ruin in your composition. Teleshots of the prominent tower are also effective. *Canon 75–300mm IS lens, polarizing and enhancing filters, Fuji Velvia film.*

colorful trees near the base can be used for framing. A very wide angle lens is needed for this shot.

After photographing Spider Rock, drive back down the canyon to White House Ruin, the crown jewel of Canyon de Chelly National Monument. Midmorning to midafternoon, from October through March, provides the best lighting for this ruin. During the spring and summer months, the sun is too high in the sky, and the white portion of the cliff dwelling is always in shadow.

I recommend a variety of compositions of White House Ruin. Actually, this site includes a ruin at the base of the cliff as well as the more famous ruin higher on the cliff. One powerful view, taken from about 200 yards downstream, includes the entire expanse of the desert varnish–streaked cliff above the ruin. Telephoto views of the cliff portion of White House Ruin framed by cottonwood trees also have good

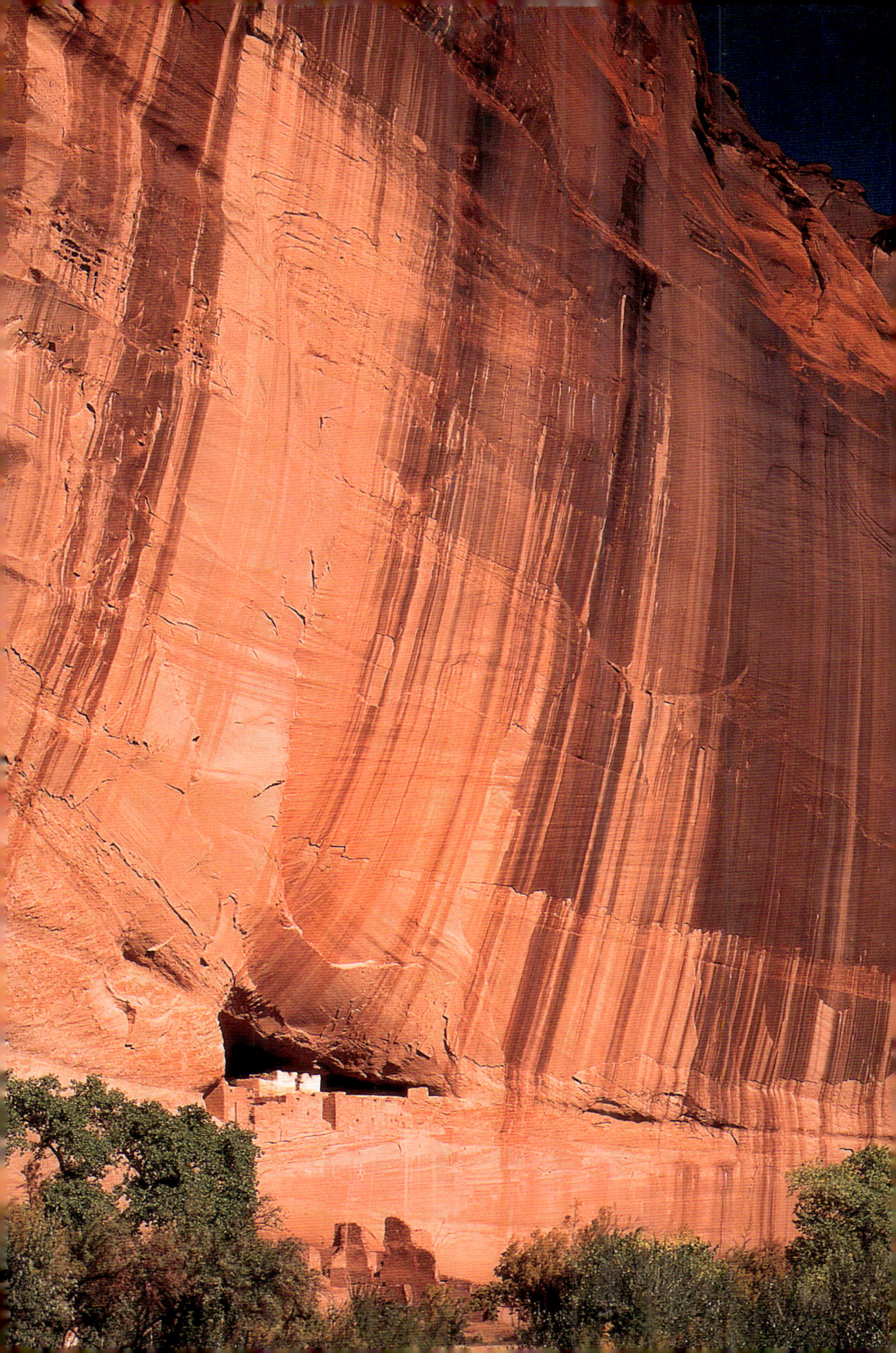

potential. Wide-angle shots that include both the upper and the lower ruins can be taken through the wire fence at the base of the cliff.

Not far downstream from White House Ruin are some large, cross-bedded rocks that exhibit strong patterns. Late-afternoon light is ideal for photographs at this location. This may be your final stop in the canyon unless you want to visit some of the lesser petroglyphs and ruins on the way out.

If you don't have the time, money, or inclination to take a guided tour into Canyon del Muerto or Canyon de Chelly, you can still see many of the major features from the two roads that follow the rims of the canyons. North Rim Drive follows Canyon del Muerto for about 15 miles. Along the way are parking areas with short trails that lead to overlooks providing distant views of Ledge Ruin, Antelope House Ruin, Mummy Cave Ruin, and Massacre Cave Ruin. The perspective from the rims is not nearly as good as that from the floor of the valley, and you need at least a 300mm lens to document these ruins. For features seen from North Rim Drive, lighting is generally better in the mid to late morning.

South Rim Drive follows the rim of Canyon de Chelly to Spider Rock Overlook, about 16 miles from the visitor center. Many of the overlooks provide interesting views of the small farms and sheer canyon walls. I recommend photographing from several spots on South Rim Drive even if you have seen Canyon de Chelly from below.

At White House Overlook, you can photograph White House Ruin from the rim. The best light is from midmorning to midafternoon, but the view from the rim is not nearly as good as the view from the base. From the north side of this overlook, you can also look down on and photograph the cross-bedded sandstone buttes that are just west of White House Ruin. The view from above actually gives a better perspective than the one from the floor of the canyon. Late afternoon is best for photographs of these interesting rocks.

Previous page: White House Ruin, Canyon de Chelly National Monument, Arizona. White House Ruin is the most photogenic feature in Canyon de Chelly. My favorite composition is a wide-angle shot that includes the desert varnish-stained cliff above the ruin. Telephoto shots of the upper ruin or wide-angle shots that include the ruins at the base of the cliff are also effective. Although sunlight reaches White House Ruin from midmorning to midafternoon, only from October to March is the sun low enough in the sky to completely illuminate the upper portion of the cliff dwelling. *Minolta 35–70mm lens, polarizing and enhancing filters, Fuji Velvia film.*

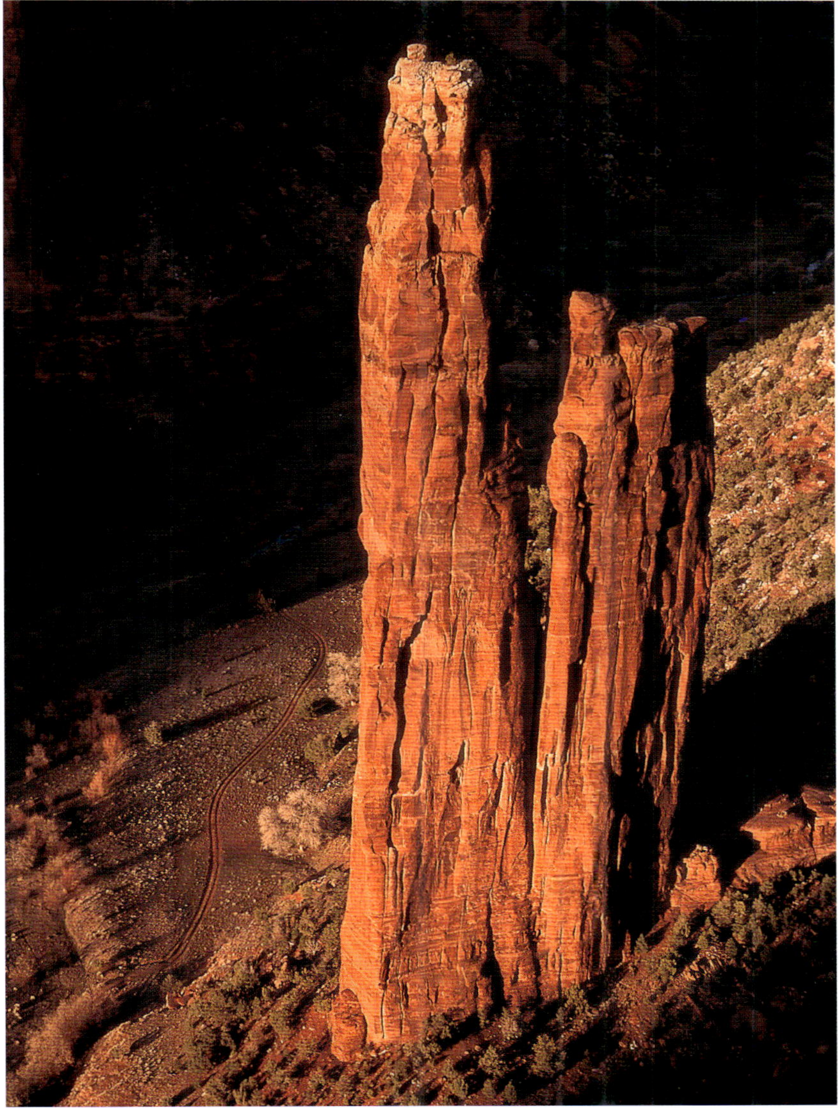

Spider Rock at sunset, Canyon de Chelly National Monument, Arizona. Spider Rock is a spectacular 600-foot-high spire that can be photographed effectively either from its base in Canyon de Chelly or from an overlook on South Rim Drive. My favorite time to photograph Spider Rock is at sunset during April or September. During those months, the setting sun is aligned with Canyon de Chelly; at other times of the year, the sun dips below the canyon walls and leaves Spider Rock much earlier in the afternoon. *Minolta 70–210mm lens, polarizing and enhancing filters, Fuji Velvic film.*

The White House Trail leads from White House Overlook down into Canyon de Chelly and allows visitors the opportunity to photograph this outstanding ruin from the floor of the canyon. The trail is moderately strenuous and is about 2.5 miles round-trip, with a vertical gain and loss of over 600 feet. If you plan to hike this trail, take plenty of water.

The other South Rim Drive viewpoint that should not be missed is the Spider Rock Overlook at the end of the paved road. A short trail leads from the parking area to the overlook high above Canyon de Chelly. In late spring and summer, sunlight reaches Spider Rock and its surroundings from midmorning to late afternoon. In autumn and winter, the sun is on Spider Rock only from midmorning to early afternoon.

The best photographs of Spider Rock from the overlook are taken at sunset during April and September, when the direction of the setting sun coincides with the orientation of Canyon de Chelly. In all the other months, including summer, the sunlight disappears from Spider Rock long before the actual sunset. Excellent photographs of Spider Rock from the overlook can also be taken from 9:30 to 11:00 A.M. in the wintertime. Since Canyon de Chelly National Monument is at an elevation of 6,000 to 7,000 feet, snow is often found on the rims and in the canyons during the winter months.

WUPATKI AND SUNSET CRATER VOLCANO NATIONAL MONUMENTS

In A.D. 1064, Sunset Crater was born as cinders and volcanic ash spewed high into the sky out of a crack in the ground. Over the next 200 years, the bombs and cinders formed a 1,000-foot-high cone. The lighter materials dusted 800 square miles of northern Arizona with volcanic ash. The eruptions were accompanied by two lava flows that destroyed everything in their paths. The eruptions ceased about A.D. 1250. This colorful cinder cone and the lava flows at its base have been preserved as Sunset Crater Volcano National Monument.

The dwellings and farmlands of the Anasazi and Sinaguan people living in the immediate vicinity of the new volcano were destroyed. They were forced to relocate about 20 miles to the north in the area that is now Wupatki National Monument. The volcanic ash from Sunset Crater made their farmlands more fertile, and they built a number of attractive mesa-top pueblos. Due to a combination of factors, including

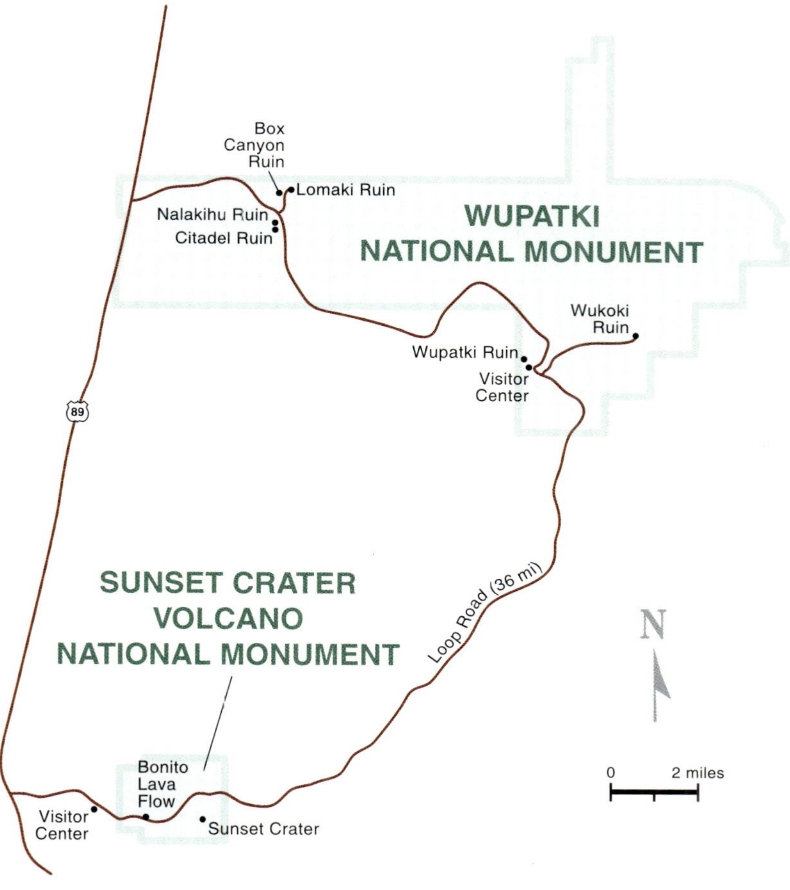

disease, depletion of natural resources, and drought, the Sinaguan and Anasazi peoples abandoned the Wupatki area about A.D. 1225. The remnants of this ancient civilization are preserved in Wupatki National Monument.

Wupatki National Monument and Sunset Crater Volcano National Monument are located just north of Flagstaff along US 89. A 36-mile paved loop road, which connects on both ends to US 89, winds through both monuments. The entrances to this road are 12 miles and 27 miles north of Flagstaff. Both national monuments have visitor centers. A National Park Service campground is located near the Sunset Crater Volcano visitor center. The only entrance station is located at the south end of the loop near Sunset Crater Volcano. Golden Eagle and Golden Age Passes are accepted for entry to both monuments.

Sunset Crater is an interesting geological feature but is difficult to photograph. The dark color and low contrast of the cinder cone and the lava beds surrounding it don't yield many exciting images. My best results have been from the west side of Sunset Crater and include portions of the Bonito Lava Flow in the foreground. At one spot in particular, the white trunks of some small aspen trees growing on the flow add contrast in an otherwise dark-colored landscape.

Snow can also add contrast and interest to the scene. Since Sunset Crater is at an elevation of 8,000 feet, frequent snowfalls occur during the late autumn, winter, and early spring. Early afternoon is the best time of day to photograph Sunset Crater from the Bonito Lava Flow. Be sure to intentionally underexpose the scene by at least half a stop since your picture contains a predominance of dark rock.

Sunset Crater, Sunset Crater Volcano National Monument, Arizona. Sunset Crater is difficult to photograph effectively because of its predominantly dark colors. My best images were taken with snow on the ground to add contrast to the scene. The Bonito Lava Flow, northwest of the cinder cone, provides some foreground interest. *Minolta 35–70mm lens, polarizing and enhancing filters, Fuji Velvia film.*

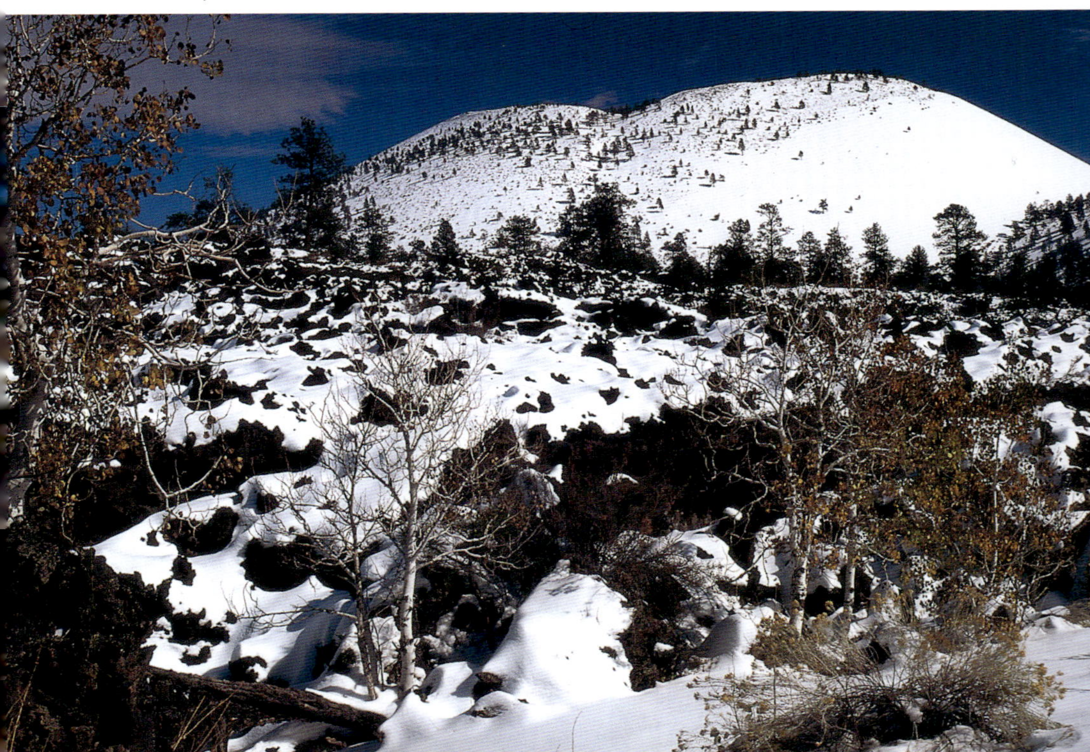

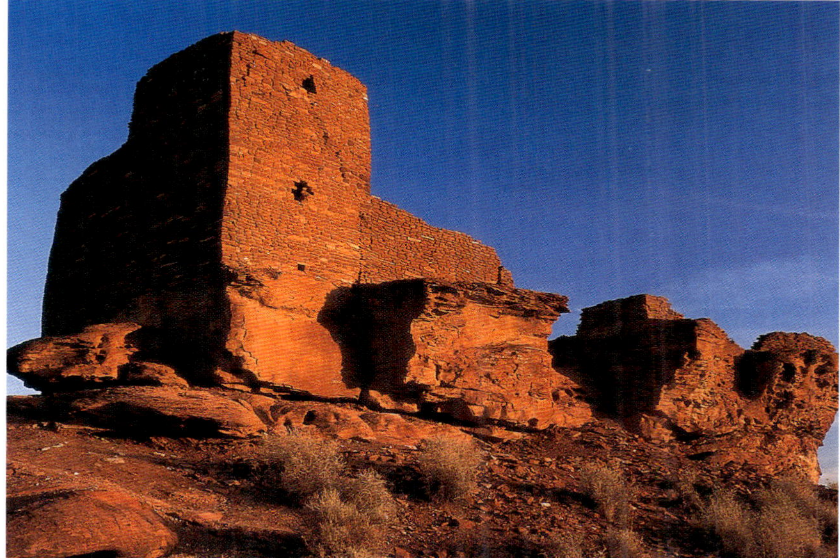

Wukoki Ruin at sunset, Wupatki National Monument, Arizona. Wukoki Ruin, east of the visitor center at Wupatki, is an appealing photographic subject. Because the north and west sides of the ruin are more attractive than the south and east sides, late afternoon and sunset provide the best lighting. This shot was taken from the drainage just below the ruin, but some interesting rock formations nearby can also provide good foreground material. *Minolta 35–70mm lens, polarizing and enhancing filters, Fuji Velvia film.*

The mesa-top pueblos in Wupatki National Monument are very attractive and are built from a reddish brown rock that adds a lot of color to photographs. Early-morning or late-afternoon light increases this color saturation. The rock work at Wupatki is very good, and many of the ruins are well preserved.

The largest pueblo in the monument is Wupatki Ruin near the visitor center. Since it faces south, good photographs can be obtained at any time of day. My favorite time for photographing Wupatki Ruin is at sunrise, when the colors are rich and the shadow detail is excellent. I usually walk down the paved path and photograph the ruin from the southwest side with some low rock walls in the foreground. Be sure to complete the half-mile round-trip trail around Wupatki Ruin and look for pattern shots with the walls and windows.

A 2-mile spur road leads from the vicinity of the visitor center to Wukoki Ruin. This pueblo sits on top of a hill and is surrounded by interesting rock formations that make attractive foregrounds. I like the

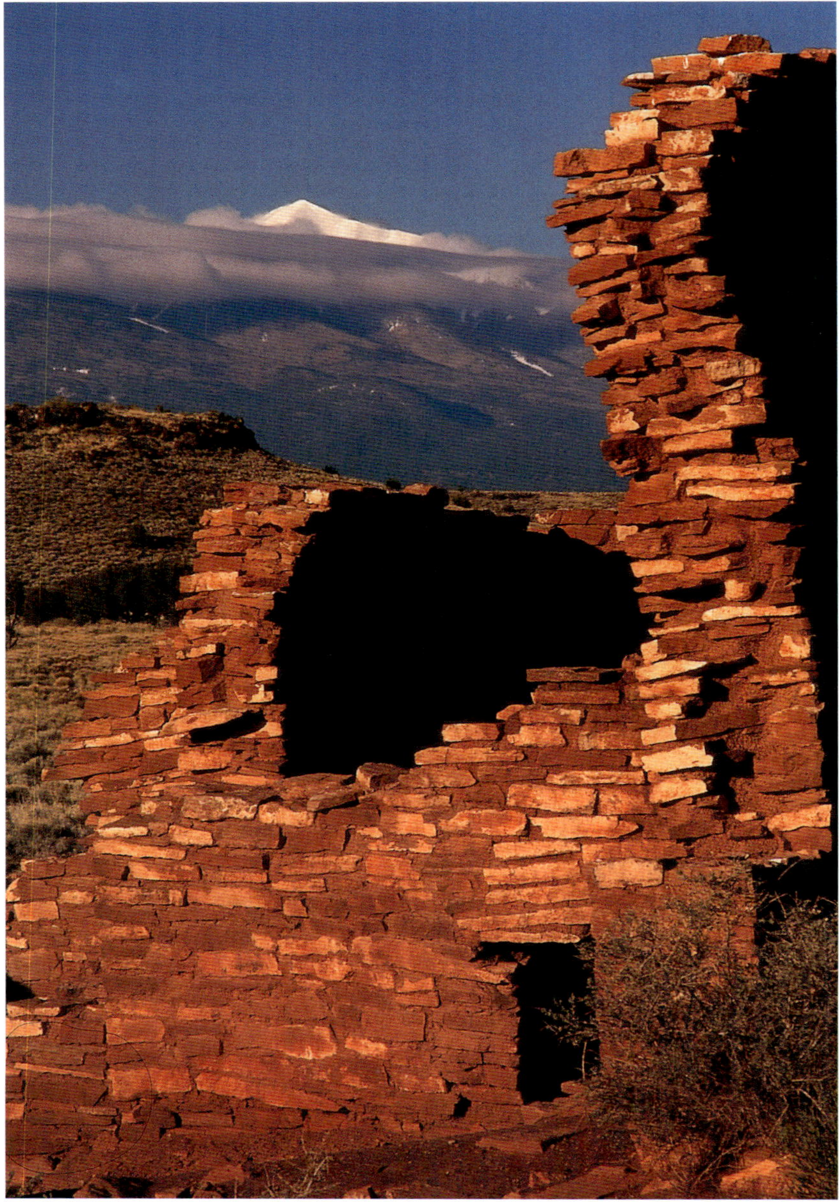

Lomaki Ruin, Wupatki National Monument, Arizona. The Lomaki and Box Canyon Ruins, at the north end of Wupatki, should not be missed. Sunrise and early morning provide the best lighting for these features. Including the distant, snow-covered San Francisco Peaks adds to the overall interest. *Minolta 70–210mm lens, polarizing and enhancing filters, Fuji Velvia film.*

views from the north side of Wukoki Ruin. Late afternoon or sunset provides the best lighting for photographs of this feature.

Northwest of the visitor center along the main loop road are Citadel Ruin and Nalakihu Ruin. If time is short, you can skip these features, as they do not yield outstanding pictures. Three miles east of US 89, near the north end of the loop road, a short spur road leads to Box Canyon Ruin and Lomaki Ruin. Reached by a short trail, these attractive features should not be missed and are best photographed in early-morning light. The snow-covered San Francisco Peaks to the southwest can be included in compositions of both these ruins and provide added interest.

PAGE AND LAKE POWELL

North-central Arizona boasts a wide variety of spectacular scenery, including Glen Canyon, Lake Powell, and many deep, narrow "slot" canyons. The town of Page, on a bluff overlooking the Colorado River and Lake Powell, makes a good headquarters for exploring and photographing this area. Page contains a wide range of tourist facilities, including numerous motels and restaurants, a hospital, an airport, a golf course, and 12 churches.

Lake Powell. Glen Canyon Dam, constructed in the late 1950s and early 1960s, impounded the waters of the Colorado River to form Lake Powell. It created a lake 186 miles long with a shoreline of 1,960 miles. Towering buttes, natural bridges, arches, Anasazi ruins, and petroglyphs can be photographed from the shores of Lake Powell and its 96 major side canyons.

Lake Powell and its surroundings can be explored by a combination of boat and trail. If you don't own a boat, you can rent one at the four major marinas on Lake Powell: Wahweap Marina near Page, and Bullfrog, Hall's Crossing, and Hite Marinas near the upper end of the lake. Rates are much lower from November 1 through the end of April at Wahweap and from November 1 to May 15 at the other three marinas. Many types of boats are available, including houseboats and motorboats. Making an advance reservation for your boat rental is highly recommended. The toll-free number for information and reservations is (800) 528-6154.

Since Lake Powell is so vast, the best way to explore it is from a houseboat, which enables you to spend several days on the lake in relative comfort. Some people like to tow motorboats and use them to enter canyons too narrow for houseboats. A number of locations along

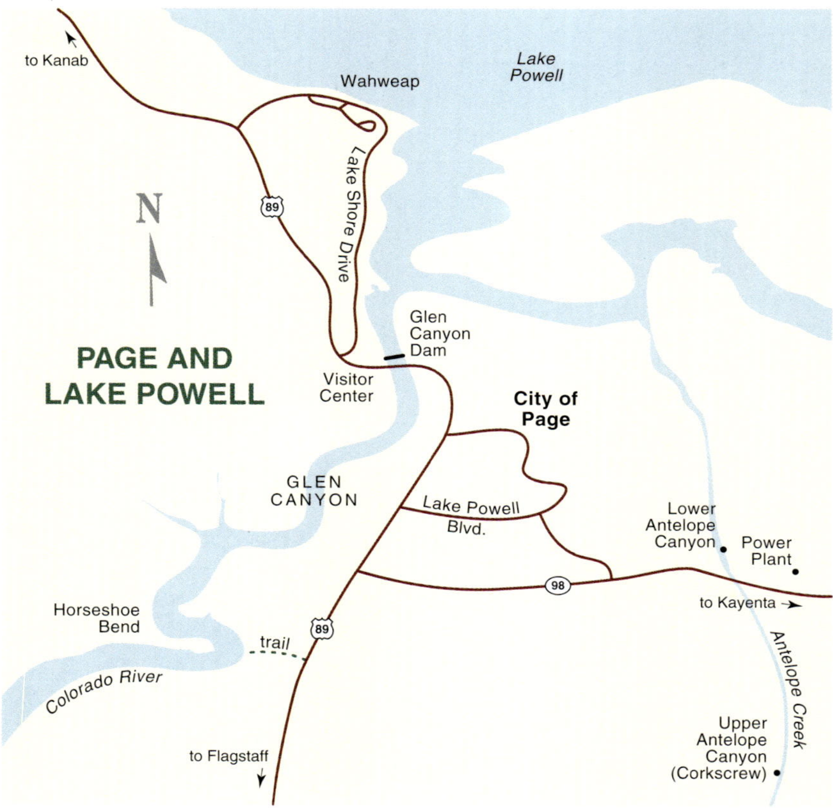

the shore have been designated for camping or for anchoring houseboats overnight. Gasoline, groceries, and other supplies are available at Wahweap, Hall's Crossing, Bullfrog, and Hite Marinas, as well as at the Hanging Rope Marina near Rainbow Bridge.

The best photographic destination on Lake Powell is Rainbow Bridge, just north of the Arizona-Utah boarder. It lies about 50 miles northeast of Wahweap Marina, 45 miles southwest of Hall's Crossing and Bullfrog Marinas, and 89 miles southwest of Hite Marina. This beautiful 290-foot-high span was formed millions of years ago when the waters of Bridge Creek cut through the narrow wall of an entrenched meander in the stream. Subsequent erosion by floodwaters, combined with erosion by wind, moisture, and freezing and thawing, enlarged the opening to its present size. The photographic appeal of Rainbow Bridge is based on its color, size, shape, and setting.

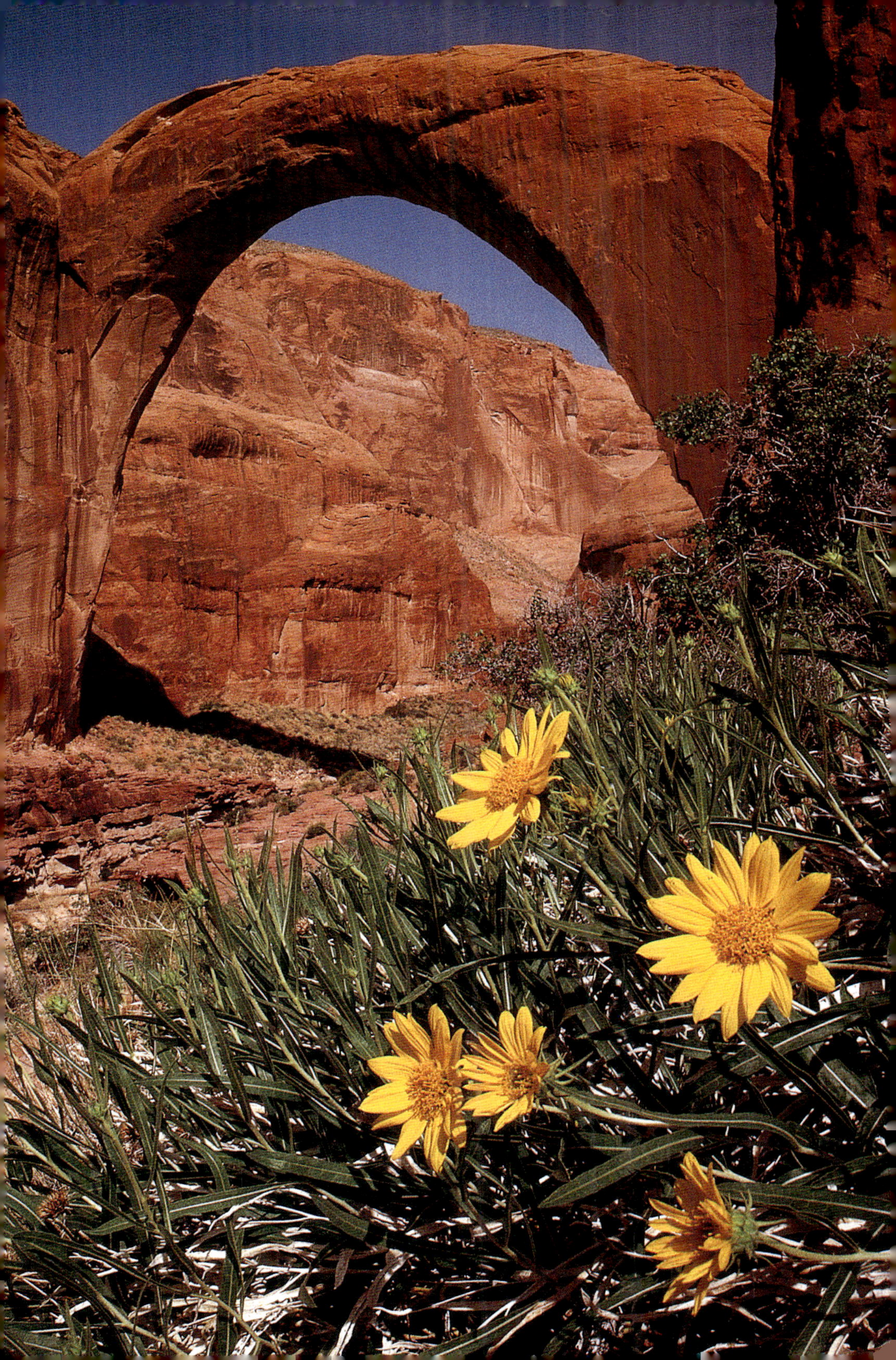

An easy trail of about half a mile one way leads from the boat dock in Bridge Canyon to Rainbow Bridge. The best times to photograph Rainbow Bridge are midmorning and midafternoon. In the early morning, the light is quite flat, and by late afternoon, the sun sinks behind the towering canyon walls. I especially enjoy photographing Rainbow Bridge in early May when the yellow blossoms of the mule ears add to the beauty of the foreground. Many good compositions from both sides of the bridge can be obtained with foregrounds that include rocks, juniper trees, and flowers. To separate Rainbow Bridge from the background, I recommend shooting from a vantage point that puts some sky underneath the bridge.

Another interesting excursion is up the Escalante River arm of Lake Powell, 69 miles from Wahweap or 25 miles from Bullfrog and Hall's Crossing. LaGorce Arch and Stevens Arches are both very impressive. The San Juan River arm of the lake, 57 miles from Wahweap or 38 miles from Hall's Crossing and Bullfrog, also has much to offer.

Lake Powell boasts many other worthwhile photographic subjects. Exploring all the side canyons could take a lifetime. Sunrise and sunset light on the rocks can be spectacular. Reflections in Lake Powell itself or in the quiet waters of the side canyons present wonderful colors and patterns. Many of the lesser-known arches provide good subject material with the right lighting. Desert varnish on the canyon walls makes interesting abstract patterns.The photographic opportunities are limited only by your imagination.

If you can't spend several days on Lake Powell, you can join a full-day cruise on a tour boat that departs from Wahweap or Bullfrog Marina year-round. It takes you to and from Rainbow Bridge, but you will be at this beautiful feature during the middle of the day, which is not ideal for photography. You can also get some decent photographs of Lake Powell and Wahweap Bay from the roads that follow the lakeshore near Wahweap Marina. I especially recommend the road

Previous page: Rainbow Bridge in springtime, Rainbow Bridge National Monument, Utah. Rainbow Bridge is probably the most outstanding photographic subject with easy access from Lake Powell. Early May is a good time to visit, because temperatures are moderate and colorful spring flowers may be blooming. For this shot, I used a wide-angle lens and a small aperture and focused at the hyperfocal distance to obtain sharpness throughout. *Minolta 35–70mm lens, polarizing and enhancing filters, Kodachrome 200 film.*

from the Carl Hayden Visitor Center to the marina. Sunrise and sunset lighting produces the best results.

One minor problem you might encounter when photographing on Lake Powell is the "bathtub ring" on the canyon walls that corresponds with the high-water level of the lake. It is light colored and not very attractive. Most of the rocks surrounding the lake are naturally red, the result of a small amount of iron oxide deposited with the sediments. The waters of the lake leach out all or part of the iron and make the rock either white or pink. In the springtime, when the reservoir is full, you might not even see the ring. To minimize or eliminate the ring, crop reflections and cliffs as tightly as possible.

For more information about destinations on the lake, I recommend Stan Jones's *Boating and Exploring Map of Lake Powell and Its 96 Canyons.*

The Slot Canyons. The slot canyons are narrow, deep, convoluted gorges carved into the sandstone formations of the Colorado Plateau by itermittent streams. Direct sunlight seldom penetrates into the depths of these canyons but bounces around on the canyon walls, creating patterns that are renowned for their color and form. These patterns change constantly with the movement of the sun. Capturing outstanding images in the slot canyons requires considerable technical and artistic expertise.

Although slot canyons are numerous and can be found throughout southern Utah and northern Arizona, the most spectacular and best known are in the Page area. I discuss only Upper and Lower Antelope Canyons, because they are the best for photography and are the easiest to get to. Many of the other slot canyons require a lot of dangerous rock scrambling or ropes to enter and exit. Most of the slot canyons near Page are on the Navajo Reservation, and you need permission to enter them.

By far the most spectacular and popular slot canyon near Page is Upper Antelope Canyon, sometimes known as the Corkscrew. It has the best photographic potential of the slots and is the easiest to enter. The floor of the canyon is flat and sandy throughout its quarter-mile length. Its only drawback is its well-deserved popularity. You may encounter a number of other photographers and sightseers in the Corkscrew, but since most pictures are taken pointing upward, other people shouldn't be much of a problem.

Access is from a gate on the south side of Arizona Highway 98 about 5 miles east of Page and just west of the Navajo power plant. A

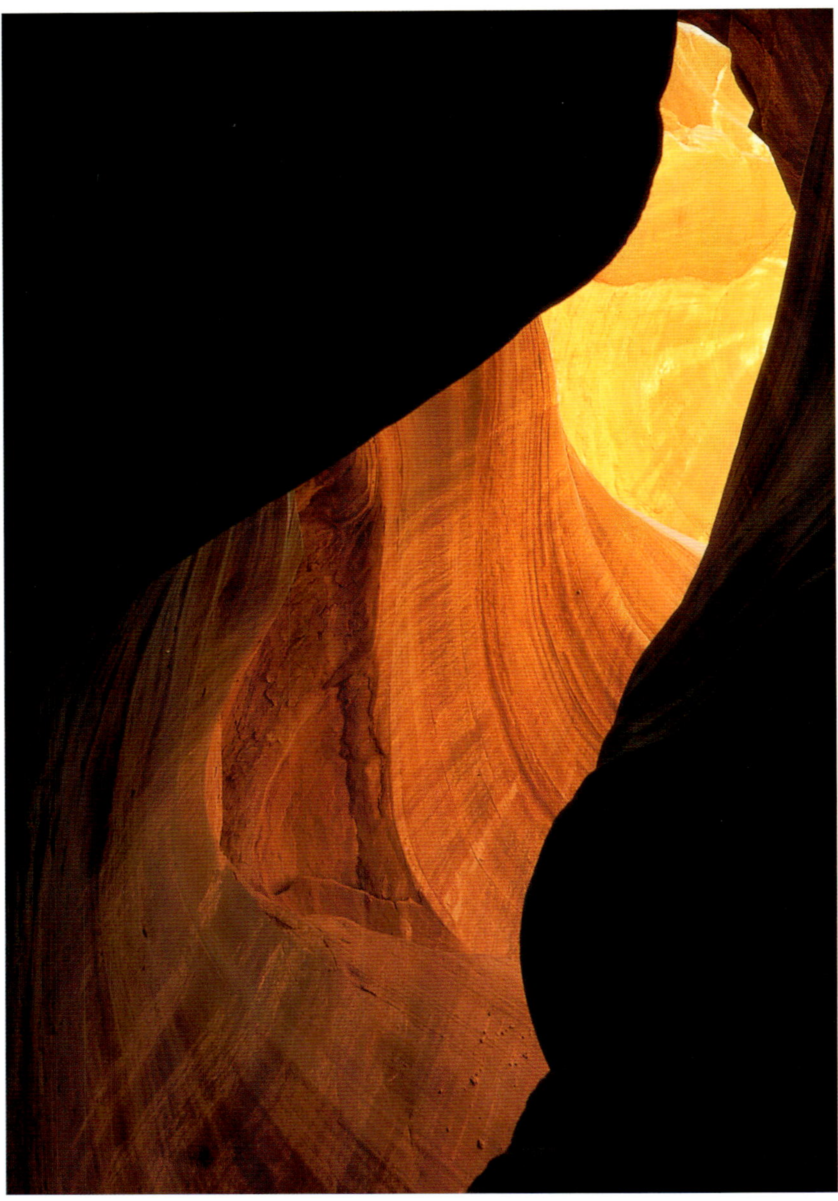

Upper Antelope Canyon pattern, near Page, Arizona. When looking for a pattern to photograph in any of the slot canyons, try to choose one with a wide range of light intensities. An area that looks drab to the eye will look drab in a photograph. Also try to enclose the lighter areas with dark rock to prevent the eye from being drawn out of the frame. In this shot, the diagonal orientation adds interest to the composition. I took a spot meter reading on an area of average brightness (the orange rock) and bracketed exposures around it. *Canon 28–105mm lens, 81A filter, Fuji Velvia film.*

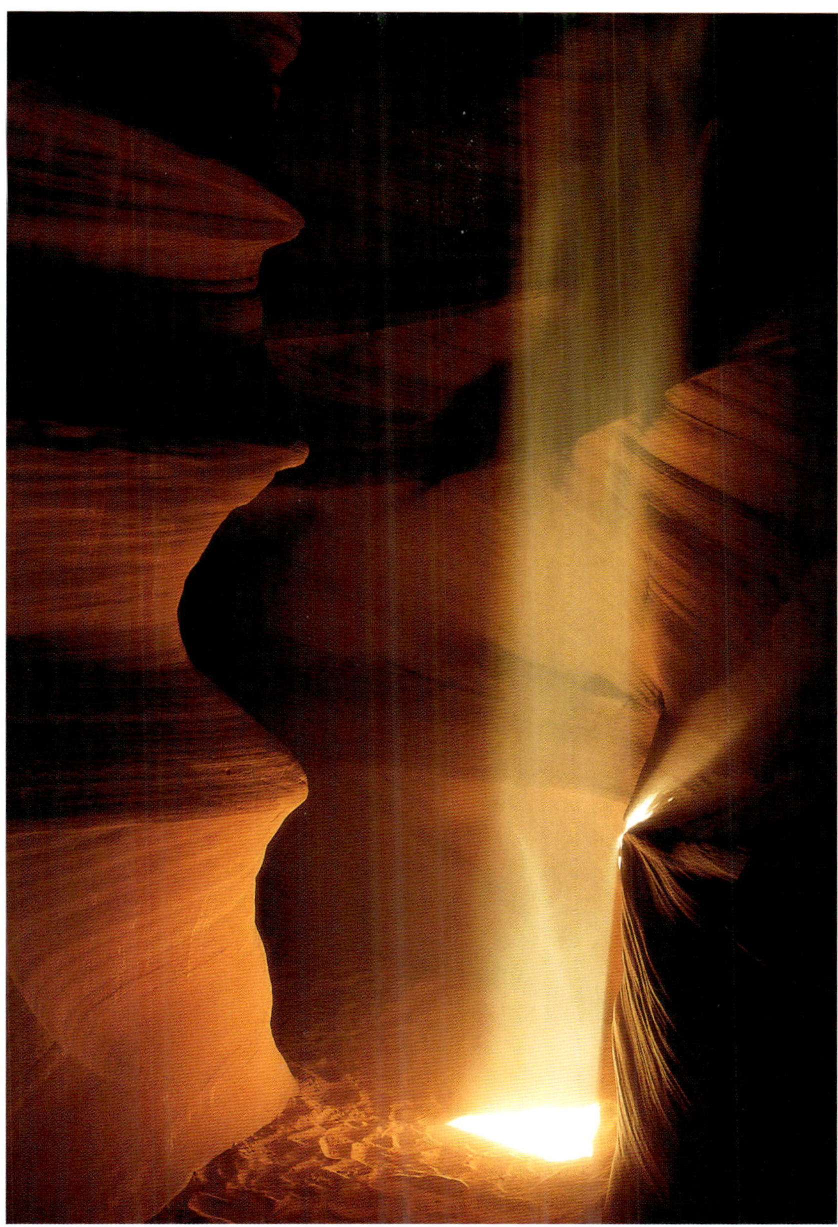

Upper Antelope Canyon sunspot near Page, Arizona. From April to September, the sun is high overhead, and beams of direct sunlight may briefly reach the floor of Upper Antelope Canyon. You must anticipate these fleeting and spectacular moments and be ready to shoot. Unless there is dust in the air, the beam of light won't show up. You can toss dirt from the floor of the canyon into the beam to help nature out a bit. *Canon 28–105mm lens, 81A filter, Fuji Velvia film.*

sign identifies the proper spot to turn off the highway. From this gate, a 3-mile road leads up the sandy riverbed to the Corkscrew. Even if you have your own four-wheel-drive vehicle, you are not allowed to drive this road yourself. To visit the Corkscrew, you can go to the gate (if anyone is there to unlock it that day) and have the Navajos transport you to and from the entrance of the canyon. Current prices are about $17.50, which includes a fee paid to the Navajo Nation. Alternatively, you can have Lake Powell Jeep Tours in Page (see the Products and Services section) transport you to the Corkscrew. They will drop you off and then pick you up about four hours later for around $25, including the Navajo fee. The biggest advantage of going with Lake Powell Jeep Tours is that they have a key to the gate, guaranteeing access.

Probably the best months to photograph in the Corkscrew are March, April, September, and October. I usually plan to arrive at the canyon at about 10:00 A.M. and depart at 2:00 P.M. During the middle of the day in these months, more sunlight penetrates the gorge and produces colorful bounce-lighting patterns on the walls. At times, shafts of direct sunlight may briefly reach the floor of the canyon and light up the canyon walls. During the winter months, the sun is lower in the sky and never reaches very far into the narrow gorge. This causes the colors to be more muted. Cloudy days also produce less contrast and softer colors. During the summer months, the danger of flash floods is always present.

The other slot canyon that I recommend is Lower Antelope Canyon. You do not need a four-wheel-drive to reach it, and you can park close to the entrance, which is on the north side of Arizona Highway 98 just east of the gate into the Corkscrew and before you get to the Navajo power plant. The last time I visited Lower Antelope, the turnoff was well marked. Lower Antelope Canyon is open from 9:00 A.M. to 4:00 P.M. From spring to autumn, a Navajo is usually on duty to take your entry fee ($17.50 per person in 1999).

To enter Lower Antelope, you descend a series of metal staircases into the canyon. Until recently, ladders were used, and the permanent stairs are a big improvement. In Lower Antelope, the canyon walls are not as high or as steep as in the Corkscrew, but the patterns are great. Midmorning and late afternoon are good times for photography. During the middle of the day, too much direct sunlight may be present. The canyon floor in Lower Antelope is somewhat rocky and irregular but can be negotiated if proper care is exercised.

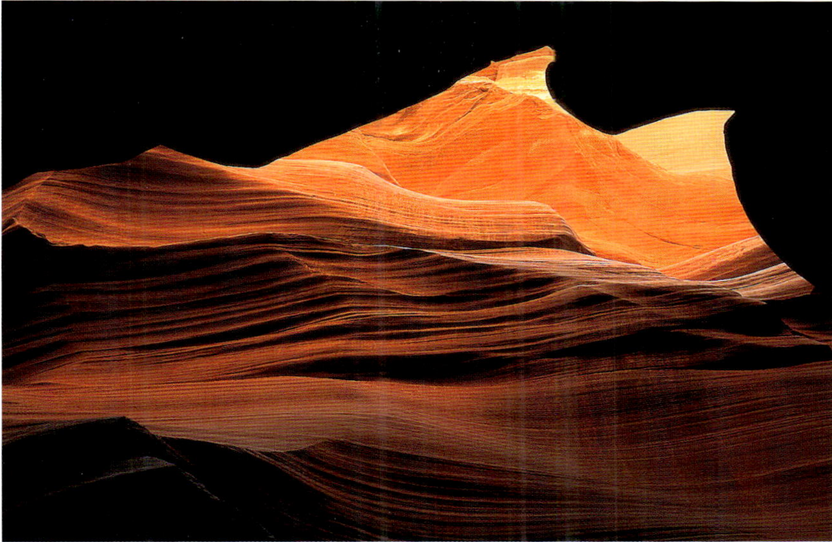

Lower Antelope Canyon pattern, near Page, Arizona. Lower Antelope Canyon is not as narrow or as deep as Upper Antelope Canyon, but it contains a lot of exciting patterns. A wide range of tones is found in this picture, including yellow, orange, red, and violet. On a cloudy day, the colors would be more muted. The light patterns in all the slot canyons change from hour to hour, and new compositions can be found no matter how often one visits. *Canon 28–105mm lens, 81A filter, Fuji Velvia film.*

Lower Antelope Canyon continues from the stairs until it reaches Lake Powell about a mile to the north. How far you can go safely depends on the water level in the lake. I have found good subject material in the first quarter mile from the entrance. Some people like Lower Antelope even better than the Corkscrew. Both are worth visiting if you have the time.

Here are a few important hints for photographing in slot canyons:

1. Never enter slot canyons if thunderstorms are in the area. Flash floods might kill you.
2. Use a sturdy tripod. Most of your exposures will be longer than 1 second.
3. Use a cable release for sharper pictures.
4. Use f/16 to ensure adequate depth of field.
5. Carry lenses with focal lengths of 28 to 200mm (for 35mm photography).

6. Take spot meter readings on an area of "average" brightness. Bracket exposures widely.
7. Use Fuji Velvia film with an 81A filter. It has good properties with long exposures.
8. Electronic flash is unnecessary.
9. Take a small flashlight to see in dark passages and to read your camera's controls.
10. Take a sweater or sweatshirt even if it's hot outside. Temperatures inside are cool.
11. Concentrate on brightly lit areas. Dull areas will look dull in your pictures.

Horseshoe Bend. The view of the Colorado River from the rim of Glen Canyon 1,000 feet above Horseshoe Bend is one of the most awe-inspiring scenes in northern Arizona. To reach this spot, go south of

Horseshoe Bend, Colorado River, near Page, Arizona. The overlook above Horseshoe Bend on the Colorado River provides an awe-inspiring view that is not for the faint of heart. To include the entire bend in the river and the cliffs on either side, you need at least a 20mm lens. The best lighting is in the late morning during spring and summer, when the sun is high enough to illuminate all the riverbanks. *Vivitar 17–28mm lens, polarizing and enhancing filters, Fuji Velvia film.*

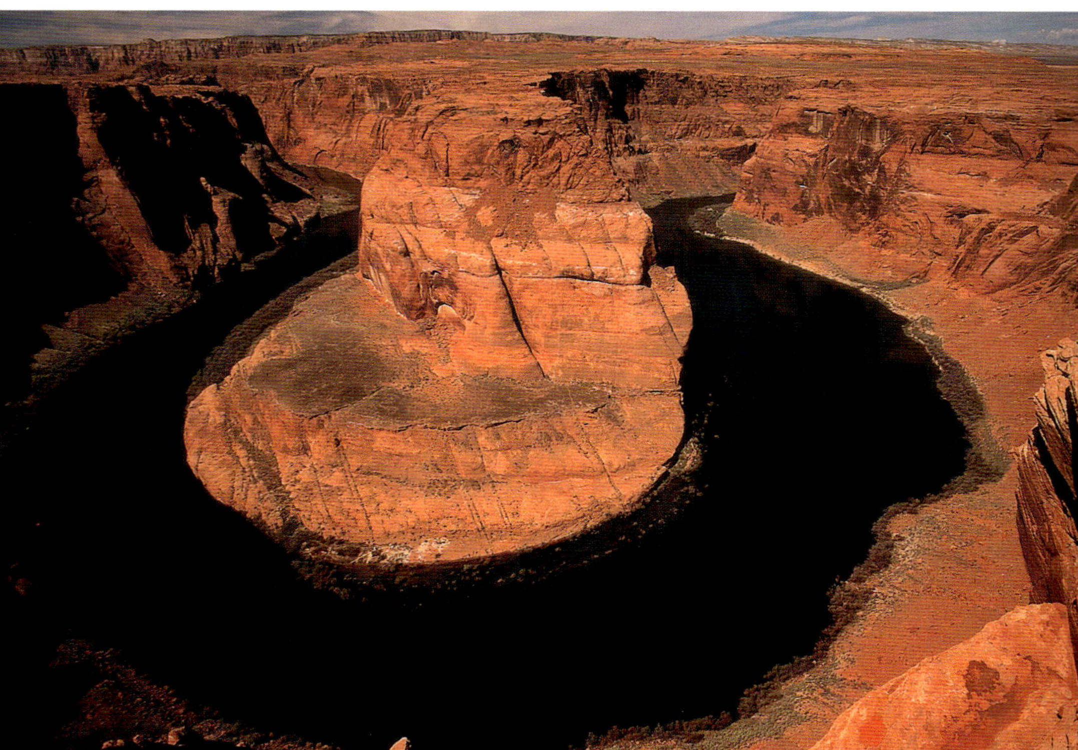

Page to the junction of US 89 and Arizona Highway 98. From this intersection, go south another 1.5 miles on US 89 to a small parking area just west of the road between mileage markers 544 and 545. From here, hike west along an old jeep road for about a mile to the rim of the canyon. Parts of this hike are moderately strenuous, but the spectacular views are worth the exertion.

Late morning is the best time to photograph Horseshoe Bend. Because of the almost vertical canyon walls, sunlight does not illuminate the riverbank to the south of the bend until almost noon. From September to March, the sun is too low in the sky to ever provide ideal lighting. Without sunlight on *all* the banks of the river, the dark river merges with the shadows, and the photograph is not effective.

Look for a vantage point on the rim where you can see the near shore of the river at the bottom of the canyon. This is no place for someone who is fearful of heights. You need an extremely wide angle lens (at least 20mm) to include the river at the base of the cliff and the river on both sides of the bend. Polarizing and enhancing filters add color and saturation to the scene. If you are using more than one filter, be especially wary of vignetting.

If you have extra time to spend around Page, you might want to ask Gail or Norm at Lake Powell Jeep Tours to take you out to some lesser-known areas. They know a lot of great photographic subjects off the beaten path.

COYOTE BUTTES

The Coyote Buttes area is one of the most spectacular scenic locations in the western United States. The form and color of the rocks are outstanding, but what makes Coyote Buttes unique are the delicate ridges in the rock formations, which create powerful leading lines and patterns. This banding is caused by differential hardness in the sandstone and is much more pronounced at Coyote Buttes than at any other location in canyon country.

Visiting the Coyote Buttes area requires about 8 miles (round-trip) of moderately strenuous hiking over terrain that is almost never flat. A crude trail exists for only the first mile of the 4-mile one-way hike into the best part of the area. The route is typically uphill, downhill, and sidehill on slickrock and sand, and it takes a toll on your legs and knees. No drinking water is available in Coyote Buttes, and all-day hikers should carry one full gallon of water. Very little shade is available. For these reasons, only persons in reasonably good physical shape should even *think* about hiking into Coyote Buttes.

Coyote Buttes lies in the Paria Canyon–Vermillion Cliffs Wilderness on the border between Utah and Arizona and is almost equally distant from Kanab, Utah, and Page, Arizona. The Paria Canyon–Vermillion Cliffs Wilderness is administered by the Bureau of Land Management (BLM), with offices in Kanab. Coyote Buttes is divided into a North Area and a South Area, and only ten people per day in groups of six people maximum are allowed to enter each area. I recommend visiting the North Area because of its easier access. In the South Area, a long stretch of four-wheel-drive road, much of it through deep sand, must be negotiated before the hiking even begins.

Visit Coyote Buttes in either early spring or autumn (March and April or September and October). During the summer, the temperatures are unbearably hot, and during the winter (November through February), the sun is too low in the sky to get above the high ridge that rises steeply to the south of The Wave.

Permits must be obtained from the BLM before entering the Coyote Buttes area. Request your permit at least six months in advance to ensure that you get the days you want. It's a good idea to request two back-to-back days so that if the weather is bad on the first day, you'll have another chance the following day. Permits cost $5 per person per day. Dates can be reserved on-line through the Paria Canyon Project at *http://paria.az.blm.gov/* or by calling the Arizona Strip Interpretive Association at (435) 688-3230.

To access Wire Pass, the trailhead for the Coyote Buttes North Area, drive east from Kanab 38 miles on US 89 or west from Page 35 miles on US 89 to the House Rock Road, a dirt road that connects US 89 on the north to US 89A on the south. Wire Pass Trailhead is 8.3 miles south of US 89 and should be accessed from this direction rather than from US 89A. The House Rock Road may be impassable after a heavy rain, and flash flooding during the summer months can wash out stream crossings. Call the BLM office in Kanab at (435) 644-2672 for the latest road information prior to your visit.

I usually arrive at Wire Pass about an hour before sunrise and start up the trail as soon as I can see. Take a flashlight along; you may need it before sunrise, as well as on the return trip at the end of the day. For the first half mile, the trail follows the streambed of Wire Pass Wash to a sign that points east to Buckskin Gulch. Just before you reach the

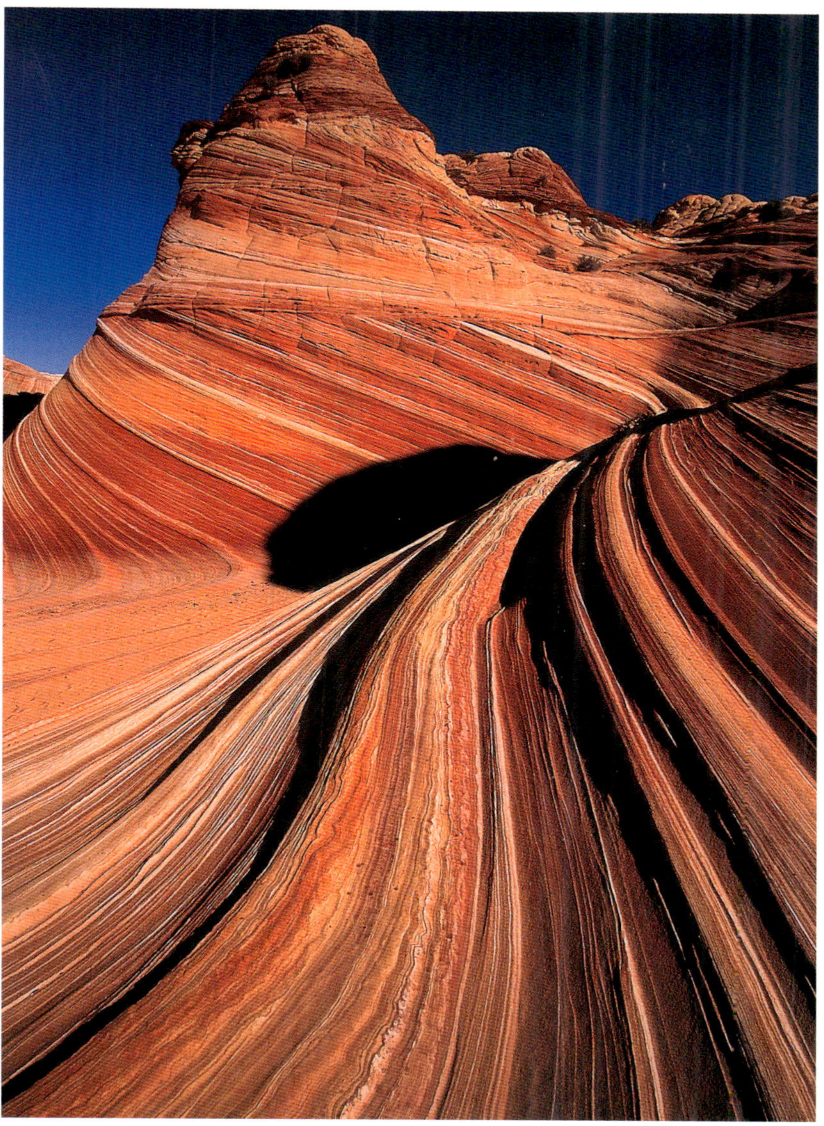

Pattern at The Wave, Paria River–Vermillion Cliffs Wilderness, Arizona. The Coyote Buttes area is unique in a region that features many red sandstones. The spectacular rock banding, which creates powerful leading lines, is caused by differential hardness in the Navajo sandstone—the rock in which the Coyote Buttes are carved. The Wave is the culmination of the scenery created by this rare sedimentary feature. In this picture, a very wide angle lens was used to accentuate the banding in the foreground leading up to the butte in the background. *Vivitar 19–35mm series 1 lens, polarizing and enhancing filters, Fuji Velvia film.*

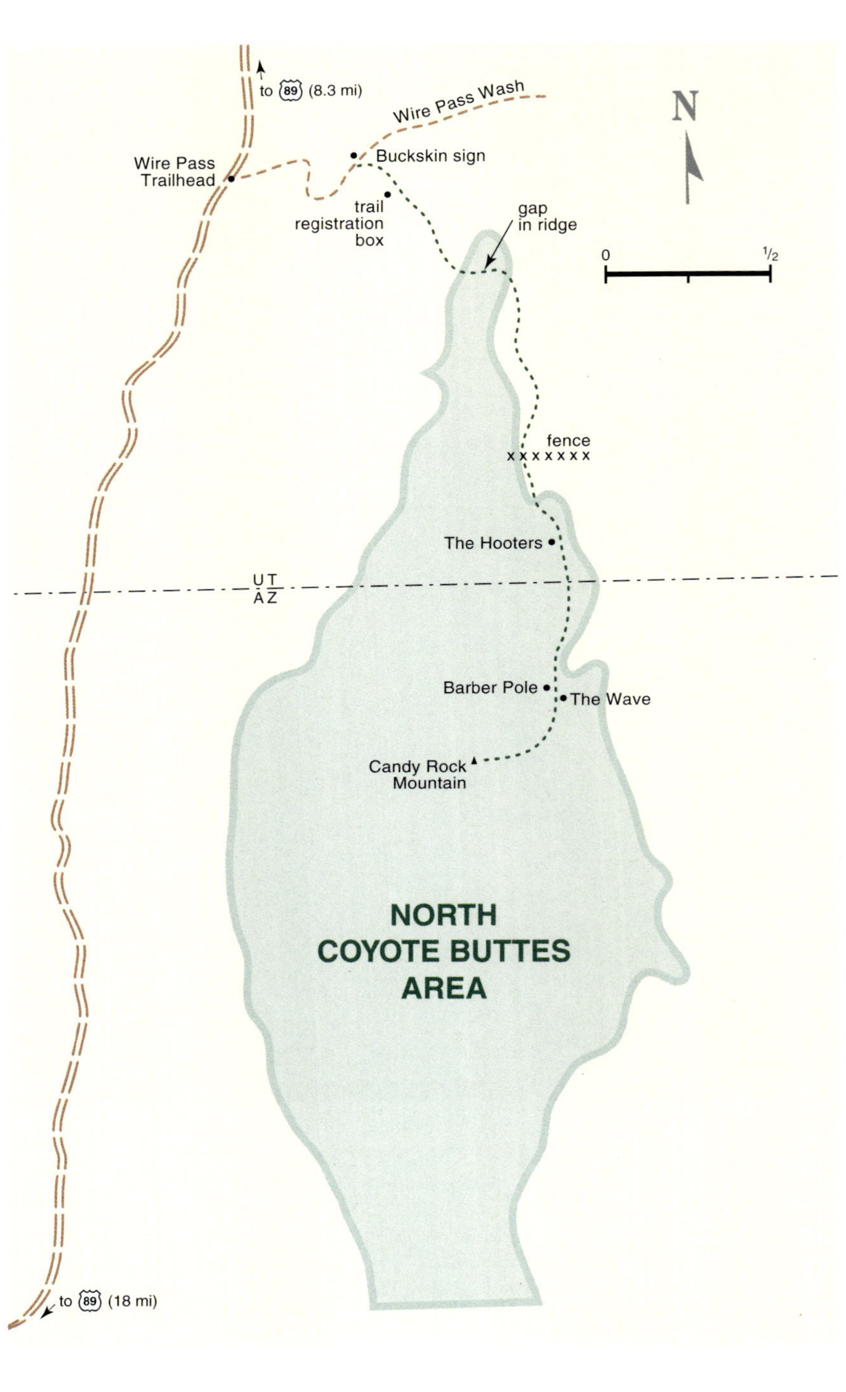
to 89 (8.3 mi)
Wire Pass Wash
N
Buckskin sign
Wire Pass
Trailhead
trail
registration
box
gap
in ridge
0
1/2
fence
The Hooters
UT
AZ
Barber Pole
The Wave
Candy Rock
Mountain
NORTH
COYOTE BUTTES
AREA
to 89 (18 mi)

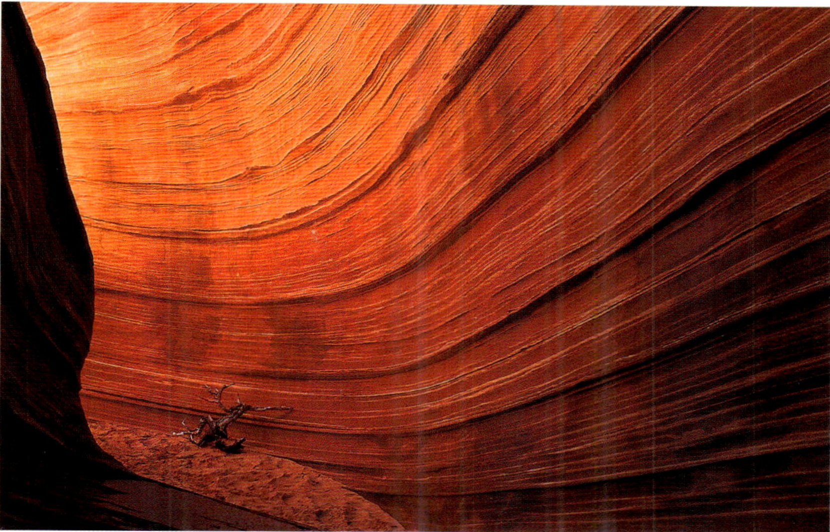

Coyote Buttes pattern, Paria River–Vermillion Cliffs Wilderness, Arizona. In the mini-slot canyon adjacent to The Bowl, a variety of sedimentary structures are exposed on the walls. In the morning hours, sunlight bounces off the opposite wall of this little canyon, creating patterns that are outstanding in color and form. *Canon 28–105mm lens, enhancing filter, Fuji Velvia film.*

"Buckskin" sign, leave the streambed on an old jeep road that climbs southeast over a low ridge and descends into another wash. This portion of the trail is about a mile in length and passes a trail registration box along the way. From the far wash, climb up through the low point in the ridge to the east. This is the end of the semimarked trail.

After coming through the gap in the ridge, spend some time becoming familiar with and marking this location (with rock cairns), as you will need to find it again on your return trip. Turn south and parallel the main ridge, trying to maintain elevation as much as possible. *Do not go down into the river valley to the east.* I usually arrive at the gap in the ridge as the sun is breaking the horizon. The buttes to the southwest make good subject material at sunrise, especially if they are reflected in pools of water left by recent rains. You need a split neutral-density filter to even out the exposure between the scene and its reflection.

From the top of the first rise south of the gap (about a quarter mile), you can see several prominent buttes directly ahead and a large vertical gash on the cliff about 2 miles ahead. The Wave (the best photographic location) is directly below this gash. Keep it in view as you go south. While passing the previously mentioned buttes on the left, you cross a barbed-wire fence.

Beyond the buttes, continue south and note a minor drainage that leads up into a beautiful swirled sandstone area below the main ridge to the southwest. You might want to take a short detour into this area, as it contains some outstanding material. Returning to the main route beyond this drainage, you pass several rounded buttes, affectionately known as The Hooters. From the high area south of The Hooters, you are about 1 mile from The Wave, and the gash in the cliff is very prominent.

Descend south into the next drainage (avoid the soft sand and stay on the rock as much as possible), climb up toward the gash on a sand dune, and follow the minor drainage to The Wave. I usually try to arrive at The Wave by about 9:00 to 10:00 A.M., when the sun tops the cliff and illuminates the area.

This is the most productive area in North Coyote Buttes. The Wave provides a multitude of wonderful rock patterns. If there have been recent rains, a pool of water just below The Wave may reward you with stunning reflections. A narrow canyon just west of The Wave provides exciting rock patterns, beautiful bounce lighting, and much-needed shade during the middle of the day. A spire west of this slot canyon, nicknamed the Barber Pole, provides an interesting center of interest for the sandstone patterns surrounding it. Explore the areas around The Wave and you will discover many other exciting compositions.

In the late afternoon, hike up above The Wave to the southwest about a quarter mile to find a colorful butte surrounded by delicate sandstone filigree. The leading lines here are magnificent. This formation, informally named Candy Rock Mountain, can be photographed from the high ground just south of the butte as well as from next to the butte. Take these photographs as late in the afternoon as possible to get good shadow detail on the delicate ridges. This should be your last photographic location of the day, as it takes the better part of two hours to return to your car. Don't stay too late and get lost in the dark on the way back.

You need a variety of lenses at Coyote Buttes, with an emphasis on wide-angle lenses to capture the lead-in lines. I typically carry two lenses into Coyote Buttes: a 19 to 35mm lens and a 28 to 105mm lens. A polarizing filter and a tripod are necessary, and an enhancing filter is mandatory, especially with Fuji Velvia film.

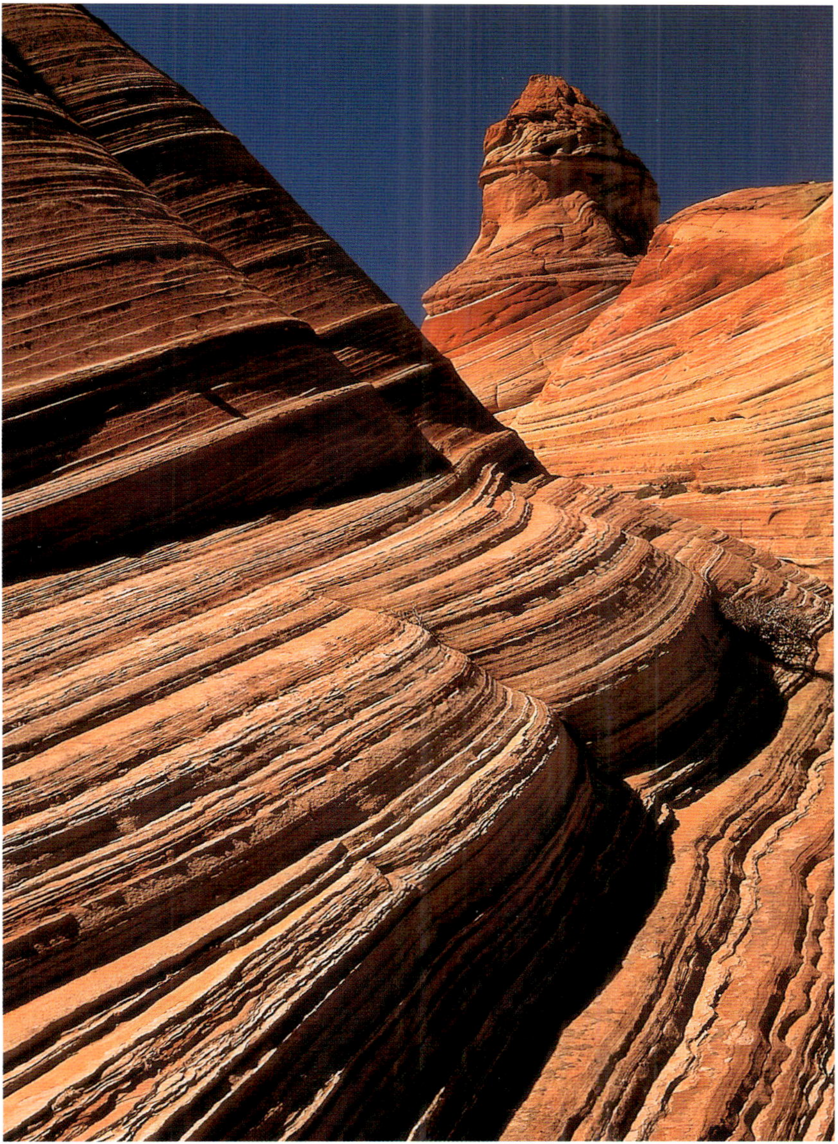

The Barber Pole, Paria River–Vermillion Cliffs Wilderness, Arizona. Just west of The Wave is a slender tower nicknamed the Barber Pole. The banding leading up to it is outstanding, and with good sidelighting in late morning, all the individual beds are beautifully highlighted. The strong diagonals add immeasurably to the effectiveness of this picture. *Minolta 35–70mm lens, polarizing and enhancing filters, Fuji Velvia film.*

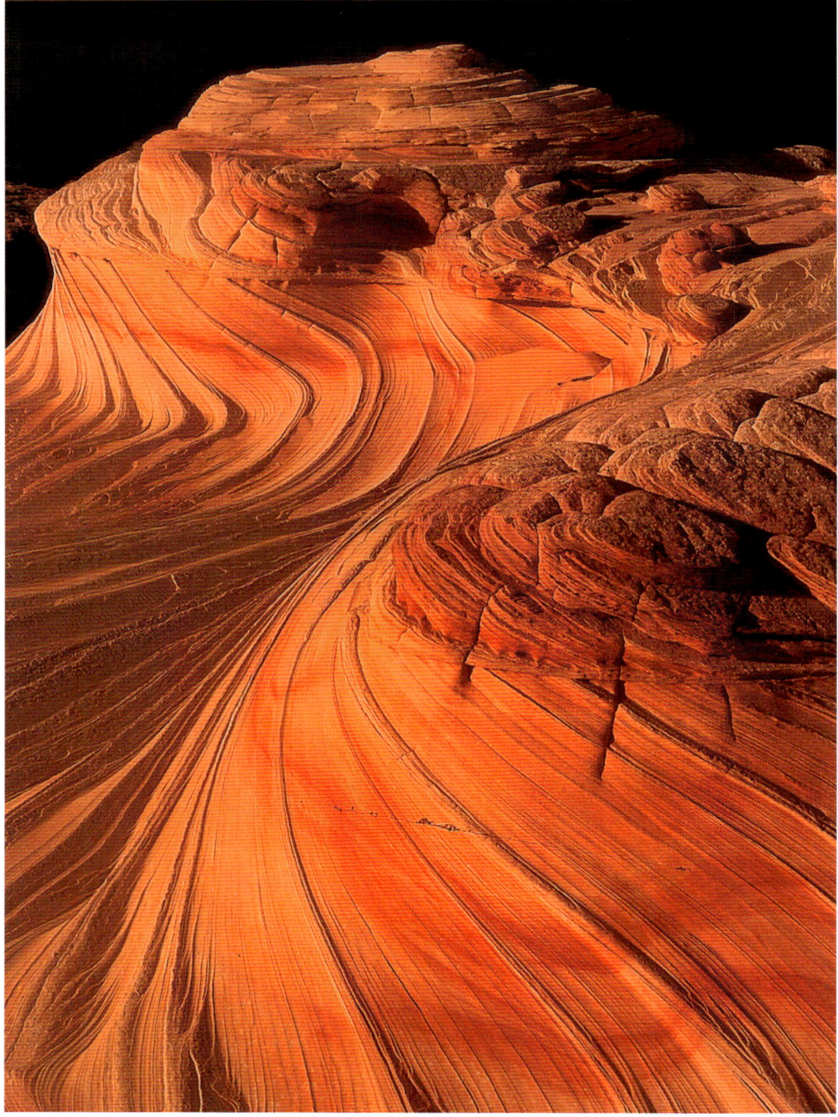

Candy Rock Mountain at sunset, Paria River–Vermillion Cliffs Wilderness, Arizona. The best late-afternoon subject at Coyote Buttes is the rock I call Candy Rock Mountain. It is lighter colored than many of the other rocks in Coyote Buttes and glows a golden color at sunset. The rock banding here is breathtaking. Please keep in mind that these rare sedimentary features are fragile. Exercise extreme care so that the beauty of this area will be preserved for future generations to enjoy. *Canon 28–105mm lens, polarizing and enhancing filters, Fuji Velvia film.*

MISCELLANEOUS

Several other locations that you may want to visit in northern Arizona include the Sedona area and Montezuma Castle National Monument. Both are located south of Flagstaff. You can reach Sedona on Interstate 17, but I recommend taking US 89A south from Flagstaff through scenic Oak Creek Canyon. Although you may not take many photographs in Oak Creek Canyon, this route is considerably shorter and certainly more enjoyable than the interstate.

Sedona is the southernmost red rock area of the Colorado Plateau. Although many locations in and around Sedona are scenic, for photography, I recommend one spot in particular: Red Rock State Park. At this location, about 7 miles southwest of Sedona, the red buttes known as the Courthouse Rocks tower above Oak Creek.

To reach Red Rock State Park, start at the intersection of US 89 and State Highway 179 in the middle of Sedona. Drive 4.1 miles southwest on US 89 and turn off on a side road that leads southeast down the hill to Red Rock State Park. You will pass several confusing intersections on the way to the park, so look for and follow the park signs. There is a small fee to enter Red Rock State Park.

The Courthouse Rocks make excellent subjects by themselves but are most effective when combined with Oak Creek. Walking southwest from the parking lot, you reach an area where the stream is very quiet and can be used to reflect the Courthouse Rocks. Many other good compositional elements are present, including cottonwood trees and interesting foreground rocks. A primitive bridge crosses the stream at this spot and provides access to other picturesque foreground rocks on the south bank.

My favorite spot at Red Rock State Park can be reached by walking upstream from the parking lot about a quarter mile. At this location, Oak Creek cascades over a ledge of red rock and makes an excellent foreground for the Courthouse Rocks. In early November, the trees along Oak Creek turn yellow and add extra color to all the scenes. Late-afternoon or sunset light is best for all pictures taken at Red Rock State Park. During autumn and winter, good sidelighting can be obtained late in the day, but during the spring and summer, the light is rather flat as sunset approaches.

The major problem with photographing at Red Rock State Park is its popularity. It's a small area, and a lot of local people, as well as folks from Flagstaff and Phoenix, visit the park. People picnicking on the rocks and wading in the stream may interfere with your shots. I would

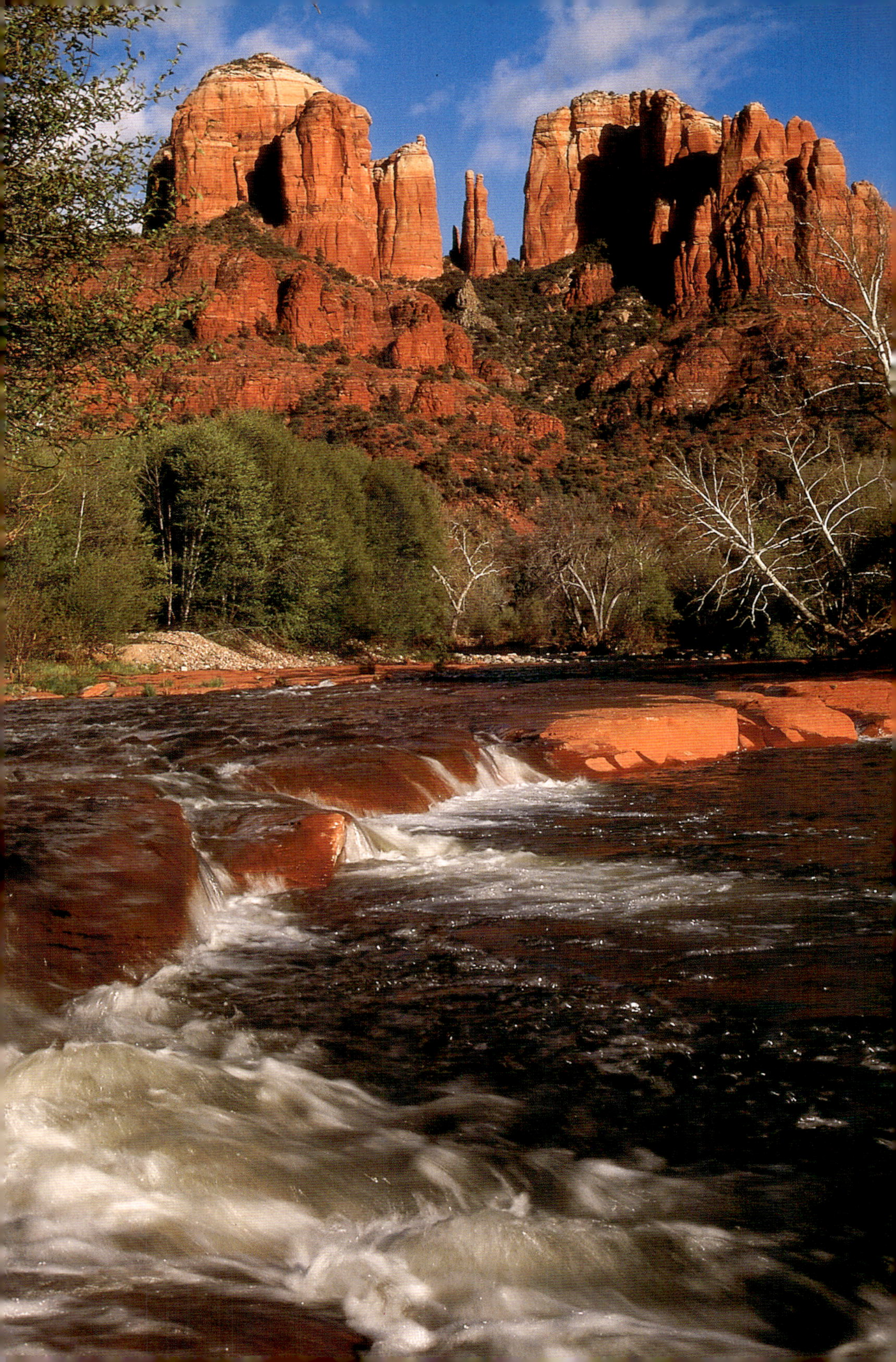

not even consider going to Red Rock State Park on a weekend. Fortunately, as sunset approaches, many of the sightseers and picnickers leave, and in the late autumn and winter months, visitation is much lower. If you can't wait for the people to leave, a more telephoto shot of the Courthouse Rocks framed by trees makes a good image.

The other good photographic destination south of Flagstaff is Montezuma Castle National Monument. It features a five-story, 20-room cliff dwelling 100 feet above the valley floor. It was built by the Sinagua people in the early twelfth century. Montezuma Castle is well preserved, and its size, form, and setting are all impressive.

To reach Montezuma Castle National Monument, drive south of Flagstaff on Interstate 17 about 50 miles to the town of Cape Verde. The monument is only a couple of miles east of the interstate.

Since Montezuma Castle was constructed in a recess in the cliff, in spring and summer, when the sun is high in the sky, all or part of the ruin is always in shadow. The best photographs of Montezuma Castle are taken in the autumn and winter, when the sun illuminates the ruin completely. Even when the sun is low in the sky, full illumunation is not achieved until midmorning, and shadows begin to engulf the ruin by midafternoon. The cliff that houses Montezuma Castle is light colored, so to prevent underexposure, use positive exposure compensation.

Courthouse Rocks, Red Rock Crossing, Red Rock State Park, Arizona. My favorite spot to photograph the Courthouse Rocks near Sedona is from the little cascade on Oak Creek upstream from the parking lot. A wide-angle lens, a small aperture, and hyperfocal distance are needed to obtain the necessary depth of field. Mid to late afternoon in the fall and winter provides good side-lighting for this scene. At this time of year there are also fewer people around to interfere with your picture. *Minolta 35–70mm lens, polarizing and enhancing filters, Fuji Velvia film.*

Resources and References

Grand Canyon National Park
Park Headquarters
P.O. Box 129
Grand Canyon, AZ 86023
(520) 638-7888
(general information)
(520) 638-7875
(backcountry office)
Web site: *www.thecanyon.com/nps*
Park information, visitor center.

Grand Canyon Association
P.O. Box 399
Grand Canyon, AZ 86023
(800) 858-2808
(520) 638-2494 (fax)
Web site: *www.grandcanyon.org*
Park information, books (list available on request).

AmFac Parks & Resorts
14001 E. Iliff, Suite 600
Aurora, CO 80014
(303) 297-2757
(303) 297-3175 (fax)
Grand Canyon Park lodging and Trailer Village.

Biospherics
(800) 365-2267
Grand Canyon Village and North Rim camping.

Havasupai Tourist Enterprises
Supai, AZ 86435
(520) 448-2121
Tourist office and campground in Havasupai Reservation.

(520) 448-2111
Lodging in Havasupai Reservation.

Navajoland Tourism Department
P.O. Box 663
Window Rock, AZ 86515
(520) 871-6436 or 7371
(520) 871-7381 (fax)
Web site: *www.atiin.com/navajoland*
Information on Navajo Nation parks.

Monument Valley Tribal Park
P.O. Box 360289
Monument Valley, UT 84536
(435) 727-3353 or 3287
Park information, visitor center.

Petrified Forest National Park
P.O. Box 2217
Petrified Forest, AZ 86028
(520) 524-6228
Web site: *www.nps.gov/pefo*
Park information, visitor center.

Petrified Forest Museum Association
P.O. Box 2277—Park Road One
Petrified Forest, AZ 86028
(520) 524-6228 ext. 239
Park information, books (list available on request).

Canyon de Chelly National Monument
P.O. Box 588
Chinle, AZ 86503
(520) 674-5500 or 5513
Web site: *www.nps.gov/cach*
Park information, visitor center.

Southwest Parks & Monuments Association
P.O. Box 588
Chinle, AZ 86503
(520) 674-5502
Web site: *www.spma.org*
E-mail: *info@spma.org*
Park information, books (list available on request).

Wupatki and Sunset Crater Volcano National Monuments
2717 N. Steves Blvd., Suite 3
Flagstaff, AZ 86004
(520) 679-2365
Park information, visitor center.

Red Rock State Park
Red Rock Loop Rd.
Sedona, AZ 86336
(520) 282-6907
Park information.

Glen Canyon National Recreation Area
1000 US Highway 89
Page, AZ 86040
(520) 645-3978
Lake Powell park information, visitor center.

Montezuma Castle National Monument
P.O. Box 219
Camp Verde, AZ 86322
(520) 567-3322
Web site: *www.nps.gov/moca*

Bureau of Land Management
Kanab Resource Area
318 N. First East
Kanab, UT 84741
(435) 644-2672
Web site: *http://paria.az.blm.gov/*
Information on and permits for Coyote Buttes.

Arizona Strip Interpretive Association
(435) 688-3230
Information on and assistance in getting Coyote Buttes permits.

Products and Services

Transportation
Grand Canyon Airlines
Tours of Grand Canyon
(800) 528-2413

Grand Canyon Railway
From Williams, AZ, to Canyon Village
(800) 843-8724
Web site: *www.thetrain.com*

Kenai Helicopters
Tours of Grand Canyon
(800) 541-4537

Nava-Hopi Tours
Buses from Phoenix to Flagstaff
Scenic tours of northern Arizona
(800) 892-8687 or (520) 774-5003

Trans Canyon Shuttle
Grand Canyon rim to rim
(520) 638-2820

River Concessioners (Grand Canyon)
Aramark–Wilderness River Adventures
(800) 992-8022 or (520) 645-3296

Arizona Raft Adventures, Inc.
(800) 786-RAFT or (520) 526-8200

Arizona River Runners, Inc.
(800) 477-7238 or (602) 867-4866

Canyon Explorations/Canyon Expeditions
(800) 654-0723 or (520) 774-4559

Canyoneers, Inc.
(800) 525-0924 or (520) 526-0924

Colorado River & Trail Expeditions, Inc.
(800) 253-7328 or (801) 261-1789

Diamond River Adventures, Inc.
(800) 343-3121 or (520) 645-8866

Grand Canyon Dories
(800) 877-3679 or (209) 736-0805

Grand Canyon Expeditions Co.
(800) 544-2691 or (435) 644-2691

Hatch River Expeditions, Inc.
(800) 433-8966 or (435) 789-3813

High Desert Adventures, Inc.
(800) 673- 1733 or (435) 673-1733

Moki Mac River Expeditions, Inc.
(800) 284-7280 or (801) 268-6667

O.A.R.S.
(800) 346-6277 or (209) 736-2924

Outdoors Unlimited
(800) 637-7238 or (520) 526-4546

Tour West, Inc.
(800) 453-9107 or (801) 225-0755

Western River Expeditions, Inc.
(800) 453-7450 or (801) 942-6669

Mule Trips (Grand Canyon)
Grand Canyon Trail Rides
(435) 679-8665

Monument Valley Tour Guides
Bennett Tours
Tom Bennett
(800) 862-8270

Black's Van & Hiking Tours
Roy Black
(800) 739-4226

Crawley's Tours
(520) 697-3463

Fred's Adventure Tours
Fred Cly
(435) 739-4294

Goulding's Tours
(800) 874-0902

Keyah Hozhoni Tours
Tom Phillips
(520) 674-1960

Roland's Navajoland Tours
(435) 727-3313

Sacred Monument Tours
(520) 691-6199

Totem Pole Tours
Vergil Bedoni
(800) 345-8687

Canyon de Chelly Tour Guides
De Chelly Tours
(520) 674-3772 or 3724

Thunderbird Lodge Canyon Tours
(800) 679-2473

Tsegi Guide Association
(520) 674-5500

Page Area Tour Guides
Lake Powell Jeep Tours
Gail and Norm
(520) 645-3142

Lake Powell Services
Lake Powell Resorts and Marinas
(800) 528-6154 or (888) 272-5131
Web site: *www.visitlakepowell.com*
Boat rentals, guided tours, and accommodations.

MOTELS

Flagstaff, AZ
Flagstaff has more than 50 motels with varying degrees of luxury and cost. All the national chains are represented, including Best Western, Comfort Inn, Days Inn, Hampton Inn, Holiday Inn, Howard Johnson, Motel 6, Super 8, Travelodge, Econo Lodge, and Ramada Inn.

Williams, AZ
Williams has more than 25 motels with varying degrees of luxury and cost. Most of the national chains are represented, including Best Western, Days Inn, Holiday Inn, Howard Johnson, Motel 6, Super 8, Travelodge, Econo Lodge, and Ramada Inn.

Tusayan, AZ
Grand Canyon Squire Inn
AZ 64 and US 180
(520) 638-2681

Grand Canyon Suites
AZ 64 and US 180
(520) 638-3100

Grand Hotel
AZ 64 and US 180
(520) 635-9203

Holiday Inn Express
AZ 64 and US 180
(520) 638-3000

Moqui Lodge
AZ 64 and US 180
(520) 638-2424

Quality Inn
AZ 64 and US 180
(520) 638-2673

Red Feather Lodge
AZ 64 and US 180
(520) 638-2414

Seven Mile Lodge
AZ 64 and US 180
(520) 638-2291

Valle (Bedrock), AZ
Grand Canyon Days Inn Motel
AZ 64 and US 180
(520) 635-9203

Jacob Lake, AZ
Jacob Lake Inn
AZ 67 and US 89A
(520) 643-7232

Kaibab Lodge
AZ 67 (5 miles north of park)
(520) 638-2389

Cameron, AZ
Cameron Trading Post and Motel
US 89
(800) 338-7385 or (520) 679-2231

Gray Mountain, AZ
Anasazi Inn
US 89
(520) 679-2214

Fredonia, AZ
Blue Sage Motel and RV
330 S. Main St.
(520) 643-7125

Grand Canyon Motel
175 S. Main St.
(520) 643-7646

Kanab, UT
Best Western Red Hills Motel
124 W. Center St.
(435) 644-2675

Brandon Motel
223 W. Center St.
(435) 644-2631

Holiday Inn Express
815 E. US 89
(435) 644-8888

Kanab Mission Inn
386 E. 300 South
(435) 644-5373

Shilo Inn
296 W. 100 North
(435) 644-2562 or (800) 222-2244

Super 8 Motel
70 S. 200 West
(435) 644-5500 or (800) 800-8000

Kayenta, AZ
Hampton Inn
West US 160
(520) 697-3170

Holiday Inn
US 163 and US 160
(520) 679-3221

Wetherill Inn
North US 163
(520) 679-3231

Mexican Hat, UT
San Juan Inn
US 163 and San Juan River
(520) 683-2220 or (800) 447-2022

Valley of the Gods Inn
US 163
(520) 683-2221

Monument Valley, UT
Goulding's Lodge
West of US 163
(801) 727-3231

Holbrook, AZ

Holbrook has more than 25 motels with varying degrees of luxury and cost. Most of the national chains are represented, including Best Western, Comfort Inn, Days Inn, Holiday Inn, Super 8, Econo Lodge, and Ramada Inn. Most of the prices are quite reasonable, especially during the fall and winter.

Chinle, AZ

Canyon de Chelly Best Western
100 Main St.
(520) 674-5875

Holiday Inn
East of US 191
(520) 674-5000

Thunderbird Lodge
Next to the Monument Campground
(800) 679-2473 or (520) 674-5841

Page, AZ

Arizona Inn Best Western
716 Rim View Dr.
(520) 645-2466

Best Western at Lake Powell
208 N. Lake Powell Blvd.
(520) 645-5988

Comfort Inn
649 S. Lake Powell Blvd.
(800) 228-5150

Courtyard by Marriott
600 Clubhouse Dr.
(520) 645-5000

Days Inn
961 US 89
(520) 645-2800

Empire House
100 S. Lake Powell Blvd.
(520) 645-2406

Holiday Inn Express
751 S. Navajo Dr.
(800) 465-4329

Motel 6
637 S. Lake Powell Blvd.
(800) 466-8356

Page Boy Motel
150 N. Lake Powell Blvd.
(520) 645-2416

Ramada Inn
287 N. Lake Powell Blvd.
(520) 645-8851

Super 8
75 7th Ave.
(800) 800-8000

Sedona, AZ
Sedona has more than 25 motels with varying degrees of luxury and cost. Many of the national chains are represented, including Best Western, Comfort Inn, Days Inn, Holiday Inn, Super 8, and Hampton Inn. Since Sedona is a very trendy place, costs for the same lodging are much higher in Sedona than in Flagstaff.

CAMPGROUNDS

Tusayan, AZ
Grand Canyon Camper Village
US 180 and AZ 64
(520) 638-2887

Jacob Lake, AZ
Jacob Lake Campground
US 89A and AZ 67
(520) 643-7232

Holbrook, AZ
KOA Campground
102 Hermosa Dr.
(520) 524-6689

Page, AZ
Page/Lake Powell Campground
849 S. Coppermine Rd.
(520) 645-3374

Wahweap Campground and
Trailer Village
100 Lake Shore Dr.
(520) 645-1004

RESTAURANTS

Flagstaff, AZ
Flagstaff has more than 100 restaurants that serve just about every kind of food, with a wide range of prices. Consult the Yellow Pages on arrival.

Williams, AZ
Buckles Family Restaurant
995 N. Grand Canyon Blvd.
(520) 635-2224

The Cowboy's Kitchen
117 E. Bill Williams Ave.
(520) 635-2708

Doc Holliday's
950 N. Grand Canyon Blvd.
(520) 635-2111

Miss Kitty's Steak House
and Saloon
642 E. Bill Williams Ave.
(520) 635-9161

Pine Country Restaurant
107 N. Grand Canyon Blvd.
(520) 635-9718

Rod's Steak House
301 E. Bill Williams Ave.
(520) 635-2671

Tusayan, AZ
Denny's
AZ 64 and US 180

Quality Inn
AZ 64 and US 180
(520) 638-2673

Steakhouse at the Grand Canyon
AZ 64 and US 180
(520) 638-2780

We Cook Pizza and Pasta
AZ 64 and US 180
(520) 638-2278

Valle, AZ
Grand Canyon Inn
Jct. US 180 and AZ 64
(520) 635-9203

Jacob Lake, AZ
Jacob Lake Inn
AZ 67 and US 89A
(520) 643-7232

Kaibab Lodge
AZ 67 (5 miles north of park)
(520) 638-2389

Cameron, AZ
Cameron Trading Post
US 89
(800) 338-7385 or (520) 679-2231

Gray Mountain, AZ
Anasazi Inn Coyote's
US 89 (520) 679-2214

Fredonia, AZ
Nedra's Too
US 89A
(520) 643-7591

Kanab, UT
Chef's Palace
176 W. Center St.
(435) 644-5052

Escobar's Mexican
373 E. 300 South
(435) 644-3739

Fernando's Hideway
332 W. 300 North
(435) 644-3222

Frontier Bar-B-Q and Steak
1143 S. 175 East
(435) 644-5346

Houston's Trail End
32 E. Center St
(435) 644-2488

Nedra's Cafe
Jct. US 89 and US 89A
(435) 644-2030

Parry Lodge
89 E. Center St.
(435) 644-2601

Kayenta, AZ
Blue Coffee Pot Restaurant
West US 160
(520) 697-3396

Holiday Inn
Jct. US 160 and US 163
(520) 697-3221

Mexican Hat, UT
San Juan Inn
US. 163 at San Juan River
(435) 683-2220 or (800) 447-2022

Burch's Cafe
US 163
(520) 683-2221

Monument Valley, UT and AZ
Goulding's Lodge/Restaurant
West of US 163
(435) 727-3231

Haskeneini Restaurant
Monument Valley Visitor Center
(435) 727-3312 or (520) 871-4108

Holbrook, AZ
Butterfield Stage Company
Steak House
609 W. Hopi Dr.
(520) 524-3447

Denny's
2510 N. Navajo Blvd.
(520) 524-2893

Jerry's
2602 N. Navajo Blvd.
(520) 524-2364

Mandarin Beauty
2218 N. Navajo Blvd.
(520) 524-3663

Mesa Italiana
2318 N. Navajo Blvd.
(520) 524-6696

The Plainsman
1001 W. Hopi Dr.
(520) 524-3345

Roadrunner Cafe
1501 N. Navajo Blvd.
(520) 524-2787

Romo's Cafe
121 W. Hopi
(520) 524-2153

Chinle, AZ
Holiday Inn
East of US 191 just outside
monument
(520) 674-5000

Junction Restaurant
100 Main St.
(520) 674-8443

Thunderbird Lodge Cafeteria
Next to monument campground
(520) 674-5841

Page, AZ
Bella Napoli's
810 N. Navajo Dr.
(520) 645-2706

Butterfield Stage Co.
704 Rim View Dr.
(520) 645-2467

Dam Bar and Grille
644 N. Navajo Dr.
(520) 645-2161

Dos Amigos
608 D Elm St.
(520) 645-2161

Ken's Old West
718 Vista Ave.
(520) 645-5160

Mandarin Gourmet
683 S. Lake Powell Blvd.
(520) 645-5516

Peppers
600 Clubhouse Dr.
(520) 645-5000

Stromboli's
711 N. Navajo Dr.
(520) 645-2605

Sedona, AZ
Sedona has a large number and a wide variety of restaurants from pricey to modest. Check in the Yellow Pages for one that sounds good to you.

PHOTOGRAPHIC STORES

Flagstaff, AZ
Photo Outfitter
25 North San Francisco
(520) 779-5181
Equipment, supplies, and processing.

Four Seasons Color, Inc.
2604 North Steves
(520) 773-7408
Film processing and printing.

Kanab, UT
Caine-Alderman and Son Photography
19 W. Center St.
(435) 644-5981
Photo equipment, supplies, and repair.

Cottonwood, AZ
Art's Shutterbug Camera Shop
1632 E. Cottonwood
(520) 634-8855

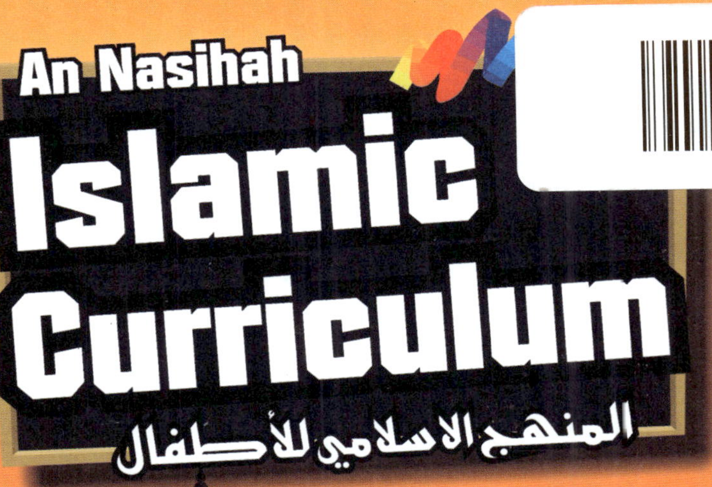

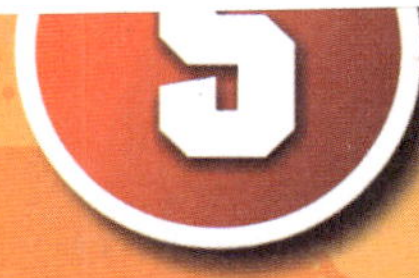

When Allāh wishes good for someone, He bestows upon him the understanding of dīn. From Ṣaḥīḥ al-Bukhārī.

"And say: My Lord increase me in knowledge."
Qur'an - Surah 20, Verse 114

علم

إيمان

- Fiqh
- Aḥādīth
- Sīrah
- Tārīkh
- `Aqā'id
- Akhlāq
- Ādāb

An Nasihah Publications

7th edition November 2021

British Library Cataloguing in Publication Data. A catalogue record for this book is available from the British Library.

Every effort has been made to ensure the correctness of the content. The publishers will gladly receive information enabling them to rectify any error or omission in subsequent editions.

An Nasihah Publications Ltd.
58 Buckland Road
Leicester LE5 0NT
United Kingdom

+44 (0)116 2966 442
+44 (0)7414 044 561
www.an-nasihah.com
admin@an-nasihah.com

Distributor in the UK
Azhar Academy, London
020 8911 9797
www.azharacademy.com
sales@azharacademy.com

Distributor in Canada
Hayaat Collection
647-781-7313
hayaat.ca
info@hayaat.ca

Distributors in Australia
Melbourne, Victoria
Mufti Zeeyad Ravat
0499 559 199
zravat@hotmail.com

Perth, Western Australia
Shaykh Burhaan Mehtar
0452 217 866
iqraacademyperth@gmail.com

Printed by Imak Offset in Turkey

Name: ______________________________

Class: ______________________________

Foreword

Over the years, the makātib (religious evening classes) have unanimously played a vital role in preserving the dīn of Allāh سبحانه وتعالى by disseminating it to our future generations throughout the world. In England too, in the 1960s when the first immigrants from the Indian subcontinent settled down for a better future and livelihood, a prime objective was to cater for the religious and educational needs of themselves and their offspring. As a result, the first masājid together with makātib were founded.

Initially, the syllabus adopted in these makātib was more or less based on material and syllabus of the Indian subcontinent, as the children were familiar with the Urdu language. Alḥamdulillāh, this went a long way in fulfilling the objectives of the makātib at that time. However, as time passed, the needs of the subsequent generations, together with the ever-changing world, demanded that changes be brought into the syllabus, teaching methods be reviewed and the setup of classes revised, in order to provide the best teaching and learning for our children. The early 1990s witnessed the makātib gradually evolve to a more structured educational entity. A period system for each subject, i.e. fiqh, sīrah, tārīkh, akhlāq and ādāb, was being introduced and the teaching was now being conducted in the English language, which had gradually become the main spoken language of our children.

This transition can be attributed to two main factors. Firstly, many individuals born and bred in England took the path of Islamic education and after graduation began serving their communities as imāms and teachers. Secondly, the availability of Islamic books and literature in the English language became more common and easily accessible. The latter served as a stepping-stone for this transition period.

Foreword

Alḥamdulillāh, the exemplary efforts of the 'ulamā' of South Africa, especially the textbooks prepared by Madrasah Islamia Benoni, Waterval Islamic Institute, and eventually the Tasheel Series and its syllabus prepared by the Jamī'atul 'Ulamā have played a significant role in this regard. Many makātib throughout the UK have benefited from these efforts.

As this new system of teaching became more widespread and well established, many new books and different methods of teaching came to the fore. This was primarily based on teaching experiences and meeting the needs of pupils.

Alḥamdulillāh, the 'Islamic Curriculum' by An Nasihah Publications is also part of this great effort that has come into the public domain. Madrasah An Nasihah has prepared this commendable syllabus with much effort and hard work. It is very pleasing to learn that the young 'ulamā' have worked together cohesively and with perseverance to make this syllabus a reality. They have tried to cover in much detail the core and most important aspects of a child's learning from the age of 4 to 14 years. This has been done adopting a method, which makes learning more interesting and enjoyable for children.

I pray that Allāh (سبحانه وتعالى) accept this work, make it a success and a means of salvation in both worlds. May He enable them to continue authoring beneficial books and literature long into the future. Amīn.

(Shaykh) Muḥammad Saleem Dhorat, Leicester, UK
Islāmic Da'wah Academy

Rajab 1436/May 2015

Foreword

الحمد للہ و الصّلوۃ والسلام علی رسول اللہ صلی اللہ تعالی علیہ وسلم ، اما بعد

مجھے بڑی خوشی ہوئی کہ ہمارے ادارے کے عزیز فارغین نے ملکر برطانیہ کے مکاتب میں پڑھنے والے ہمارے مسلمان بچوں کے لئے موجودہ ماحول اور تقاضوں کو سامنے رکھتے ہوئے اور ان نونہالوں کی عمر اور اذہان کا خیال کرتے ہوئے بہترین نصاب مرتب کیا ہے اور احقر کو بھی اس پر نظر ثانی کی درخواست کی گئی ، چونکہ احقر کو پچھلے بیس سال سے یہاں کے مکاتب اور بچوں اور انکی تعلیمی نظام اور نصاب سے واسطہ رہاہے، اور دل میں کئی بار یہ خیال بھی آتا رہا کہ ان مکاتب میں پڑھنے والے ہمارے نونہال بچے بچیاں ان مکاتب میں رہتے ہوئے بہت کچھ اسلامی دینی اھم اھم ضروری تعلیمات اور مسائل کو سیکھ کر جائیں اور عملی نمونہ بنیں اور اسکے لئے ماحول کے تقاضی کے مطابق بہترین نصاب تیار ہو جائے،

الحمد للہ ہمارے ان عزیز دوستوں نے اسلامی درسی نظام کے نام سے یہ آٹھ سالہ نصاب تیار کیا ہے جسے دیکھکر بڑی خوشی ہوئی اور دل سے دعائیں دی کہ اللہ تعالی اسے قبول کرے اور پورے ملک میں پھیلادے اور ہمارے ایک ایک مسلمان بچہ بچی میں ایمانی اسلامی روح پھونک دے، وما ذالک علی اللہ بعزیز

میں نے ان کتابوں کو دیکھا اور اسے برطانوی اذہان کے بچوں کے لئے مفید پایا اور کچھ ضروری مشورے بھی دئے، اس نصاب میں ایک خیال یہ رکھاگیاہیکہ اھم اھم مضامین ایک ہی جلد میں آجائے اور عمر کے اعتبار سے ان مضامین میں زیادتی کی جائے، اور ہر کتاب کے ساتھ ایک تمرین کی بوک بھی رکھی گئی ہے تاکہ اسباق کا مشق بھی ہوتارہے، میری مکاتب کے ذمہ داروں سے درخواست ہے کہ اسے اپنی درسیات میں داخل کریں اور فائدہ اٹھائیں ، اور اسکا ھدیہ بھی دوسری کتابوں کے مقابلہ میں کم رکھا گیا ہے تاکہ ماں باپ پر بوجھ نہ ہو؛ ہماری دعا ہے

تقبل اللہ تعالی سعیهم وجعل سعیهم مشکورا، وینفع بها الناس جمیعا، آمین

(شیخ الحدیث مولانا) محمد ادریس الفلاحی
ذوالحجہ - اکتوبر

Foreword

All praise belongs to Allāh (سبحانه وتعالى). May His choicest blessings and salutations be upon the beloved Messenger of Allāh (صلى الله عليه وسلم).

It brought me great happiness when I learned that graduates of our institute had embarked on the task of preparing a comprehensive syllabus for the makātib here in the UK, tailoring it for the needs of today's growing generation.
This humble servant has been working within the makātib system for the past twenty years and throughout this many a time a wish came to heart that a complete syllabus be prepared for these young innocent children who can learn the beautiful teachings of Islām in a fun and interactive way.

Alḥamdulillāh when the team at An Nasihah Publications requested that this humble servant take a look at the books that were prepared under the name of The Islamic Curriculum -which spans across eight years- I was delighted when I went through them and prayers escaped my heart that Allāh (سبحانه وتعالى) grant it acceptance and spread it across the lands.

Going through the books, I found them to be of benefit to our children. After giving some points of advice I noted that all the important topics have been combined in one book per year which have corresponding workbooks. The topics are then developed progressively according to the age of the child. It is my humble advice to the responsible people of the makātib to enter these books into their curriculum and take advantage of these books. The price has been kept low so as not to burden parents with large sums of money being spent on books.

Finally I pray to Allāh (سبحانه وتعالى) to accept and reward their efforts granting benefit to all of Mankind. Āmīn

(Shaykhul Ḥadīth Mawlānā) Muḥammad Idrīs Falāḥī, Leicester
Senior Lecturer of Ḥadīth at Darul Uloom Leicester

Dhul Ḥijjah 1436/October 2015

Foreword

For many years Raḥma has been operating madāris across the Balkans. After the fall of communism, dīn was still very new to the people hence we initially only had a basic syllabus in place. Over a decade had passed when in 2012 we decided it was time to introduce a more advanced, more informative and interactive syllabus for the students. We contacted An Nasihah Publications expressing our concerns and they gladly took up this noble project.

After a year of consultation and careful planning the 'Islamic Curriculum' series of coursebooks and workbooks were first published. A set of books for the 5 years of maktab were compiled by the team at An Nasihah and then translated into the Albanian language. It covered all the major topics that a Muslim child ought to learn in his/her years at madrasah in a fun and innovative way.

In 2013 the An Nasihah Publications Team launched these books in Albania and Kosovo. Alḥamdulillāh these books have proven to be inspirational. Students and teachers alike have benefited greatly and the Raḥma team of 'Ulamā' have seen a great improvement in the level of education. In 2015 An Nasihah launched a revised edition with additional books for adults too. Just as these books have been successful in Albania and Kosovo, I pray to The Almighty Allāh (سبحانه وتعالى) that the English version of these books prove to be a greater success in the English speaking world. Āmīn.

(Shaykh) Khalīl Patel, Leicester
Amīr at Raḥma (Mercy)

Rabī' ath-Thānī 1437/January 2016

Foreword

All praise belongs to Allāh (سبحانه وتعالى) and Salutations be upon his honourable Messenger (صلى الله عليه وسلم).

I was greatly pleased upon seeing the Islamic Curriculum by An Nasihah Publications.

Mā shā Allāh this syllabus has been prepared in a child-friendly manner with great effort over the course of eight years.

In addition to this many scholars have looked through it thoroughly.

I pray Allāh (سبحانه وتعالى) accepts this and grants the writers and those associated with it a great recompense. Āmīn

(Shaykh) Abdul Raheem Limbada, Bury

Rabī' ath-Thānī 1437/January 2016

In the name of Allāh (سبحانه وتعالى), All praise belongs to Him and salutations be upon his honourable Messenger (صلى الله عليه وسلم).

The people of knowledge know very well the importance a curriculum has in the Islamic upbringing of the child. Keeping this point in mind Mā shā Allāh a few scholars from Darul Uloom Leicester have put together this simple syllabus which is relevant to the needs and age of our children.

This humble one had a brief look over the books and was greatly pleased.

May Allāh (سبحانه وتعالى) grant this syllabus acceptance and benefit the ummah through it.

Muftī Mūsā Badat, Dewsbury

Rabī' ath-Thānī 1437/January 2016

Foreword

الحمد للہ برطانیہ میں مکاتب کا نظام ایک معیاری اور مثالی صورت اختیار کر گیا ہے، اور اکثر شہروں اور قصبات میں بہترین مکاتب وجود میں آگئے ہیں، اس لئے ضرورت تھی کہ یہاں کے مکاتب کے لئے کوئی معیاری نصاب ترتیب دیا جائے۔ مبارکبادی اور شکریہ کی مستحق ہیں لیسٹر کے علماء کی وہ جماعت جنھوں نے برسوں کی محنت اور توجہ سے آٹھ سالہ ایک نصاب ترتیب دے کر امت مسلمہ اور خصوصا اہل برطانیہ پر عظیم احسان کیا۔ چونکہ یہ نصاب انگریزی زبان میں ہے، اس لئے میں اس سے استفادہ نہ کرسکا، لیکن اکابر علماء نے اس پر نظر فرمائی اور اس کو بہتر سے بہتر بنانے کے لئے اپنی اپنی رائے مرحمت فرمائی۔ امید ہے کہ یہ نصاب ملک کے مکاتب کے لئے ایک بہترین نصاب ہوگا، اورانشاء اللہ مرتبین کے لئے صدقۂ جاریہ اور ذخیرۂ نجات ہوگا۔

بعض اہل علم نے اس کے مطالعہ کے بعد فرمایا کہ: بہت جامع نصاب ہے ،ایک ہی کتاب میں مختلف سات قسم کے مضامین جمع کئے گئے ہیں، اس میں طلباء اور اساتذہ کے لئے آسانی اور بڑی سہولت ہے۔

اللہ تعالی سے دلی دعا ہے کہ ان نوجوان علماء کی محنت کو شرف قبولیت عطا فرمائے، اور مکاتب کے ذمہ داروں اور صدر مدرسین کو ان کی حوصلہ افزائی کی توفیق مرحمت فرمائے۔
اللہ کرے پورے ملک کا ایک نصاب ہو ،اور یہاں کے ارباب انتظام کو یہ مناسب لگے تو اور اسی کو داخل نصاب کرلیں۔ اور اس معاملہ میں کسی تعصب کے بغیر غور کریں کہ اس نصاب کو اپنے مکاتب میں داخل کیا جائے یا نہیں؟ اس لئے کہ عصبیت بڑے سے بڑے ہنر اورمفید سے مفید کام کو بھی قبول کرنے سے مانع بنتی ہے ۔

اس نصاب کی تیاری میں جن جن علماء نے محنت فرمائی اللہ تعالی ان کو دارین میں بہترین بدلہ عطافرمائے، آمین ۔

(مولانا) مرغوب احمد لاجپوری ۔ ڈیوزبری
جمادی الثانیۃ - مارچ

Foreword

In the name of Allāh (سبحانه وتعالى) the Most Beneficent, the Most Merciful.

Iqra' was the first word of revelation from the Lord of the Worlds to our Beloved Messenger Muḥammad (صلى الله عليه وسلم) through the Angel Jibra'īl. This was the first lesson to light the lantern of knowledge to mankind which was drowned in ignorance and darkness and it is through this very word that we see many libraries in existence today brimming with books.

Blessed are those scholars and thinkers who, in every era, worked tirelessly for the growing needs of the future generation to protect their knowledge and actions.

From these very scholars our young graduates of Britain from An Nasihah Publications came together to prepare this year by year syllabus according to the needs of our children.

I strongly feel that the children's minds and hearts will find them appealing and this syllabus, along with filling a gap, will be a means of fulfilling the need.

May Allāh (سبحانه وتعالى) increase the team in knowledge and practice and make these books beneficial and full of blessings. Āmīn

Shaykhul Ḥadīth Mawlānā Muḥammad Ayyūb Sūrtī
Senior lecturer of ḥadīth at Darul Uloom Falāḥ e Darayn, India
Director of Majlis e Dawatul Haq, UK

Jumadā ath-Thāniyah 1437/March 2016

Foreword

Alḥamdulillāh, I was very pleased to meet the group of scholars from An Nasihah Publications. The Islamic Curriculum books have been compiled in a very beautiful and easy-to-understand method.

May Allāh (سبحانه وتعالى) accept the hard work of the young 'ulamā' and make it beneficial for our youngsters and students of maktabs and madrasahs.

I would really recommend these books to all our children who want to know about our beautiful religion.

Shaykh Muftī Saiful Islām
Founder, Principal and Director of Jāmiah Khātamun Nabiyeen (JKN), Bradford, UK
Editor of the family magazine 'Al Mu'min'

Jumadā ath-Thāniyah 1437/March 2016

The presentation of these books is dyslexia-friendly and they will appeal to all the children who use them. The layout is clear and uncluttered, with key texts often contained within information boxes. The use of pastel colours and clear text is helpful to children who find reading difficult.

Fiona Hossack
Teaching Coordinator
Leicester Dyslexia Association

Foreword

Alḥamdulillāh this curriculum by An Nasihah Publications is a unique gift for the growing need of today's generation.

The team from Darul Uloom Leicester have worked tirelessly to make these books fun and engaging according to the age and need of the child.

I humbly request the management of the institutes to implement this curriculum into their madāris & Islamic schools through which our children will benefit greatly in shā Allāh.

Together the syllabus can go from strength to strength through your constructive feedback making it a Ṣadaqah Jāriyah for us all.

May Allah accept this humble effort. Āmīn

Mawlana Ismail Ahmad Patel
Principal and founder of Darul Uloom Leicester

Sha'bān 1437/May 2016

Testimonials

Testimonials obtained from parents whose children are studying the Islamic Curriculum.

"Having taken time out to look over the books, I find them to be inspiring, student-friendly and highly educational. It is clearly well-researched and covers all the needed topics. May Allāh (سبحانه وتعالى) reward all those included in the publication of these books."

"Mā shā Allāh the books cover a wide range of topics and contain essential material on every subject. This should give a solid foundation in obtaining necessary knowledge of dīn."

"Very pleased with the coursebooks. They're very child and parent-friendly for the whole family to learn and brush up on basic knowledge, Mā shā Allāh. Encourages one to learn."

"I'd like to thank you and your team for all the time and effort you have put into making these Islamic books for our children. The books are very educational, beautiful to look at and easy to understand. I myself will gain knowledge from the books as well as the children."

"This comprehensive syllabus program for the madāris on preparing children for life and beyond is published beautifully with colour & illustration. The way the syllabus has been printed in the first few pages gives parents an insight into what ages will learn what subjects. I see my children excited to learn the different subjects, due to it being filled with fun and activities. It is also beneficial to us, parents, who haven't been lucky enough to learn in this manner, especially with regard to the aḥādīth. May the Almighty reward everyone who made this publication possible, āmīn."

Preface

All praise is due to Allāh (سبحانه وتعالى), Lord of the heavens and earth. May peace and blessings be upon our Noble Messenger, Muḥammad (صلى الله عليه وسلم).

It is a great blessing of Allāh (سبحانه وتعالى) that He has made this dream into a reality. For many years our team at An Nasīhah have been working on a comprehensive syllabus program for the madāris to prepare the pupils for life and beyond. We wanted to give our children a series of books with colourful yet fruitful content to allow them to grasp the key elements of their dīn with love and devotion.

Alḥamdulillāh when Moulāna Khalīl (May Allāh (سبحانه وتعالى) protect him) approached us in 2012 on behalf of Raḥma (Mercy) with a proposal of setting out something similar for the pupils of Albania, we were able to see the benefits of such a system. Alḥamdulillāh 50 thousand books were printed and rolled out across all the madāris operating under Raḥma (Mercy) in Albania and Kosovo. The feedback we received from the teachers and pupils was highly positive. This motivated us to push for the initial English version and - with all praise to Allāh (سبحانه وتعالى) - after many hard years of effort from our team, you now have the books before you.

Each of the eight books in the series corresponds with a workbook to assist in understanding the topics thoroughly. Seven subjects are covered progressively across the years.

Preface

At the end of the eight-year course, In shā Allāh pupils will have mastered the five pillars of Islām along with a large amount of fiqh necessary for them to lead their lives as Muslims. They will have memorised 85 aḥādīth in Arabic and English, understood the basic creed ('aqā'id) of a Muslim, covered approximately 100 akhlāq & ādāb, learnt about many Prophets, covered the whole life of our Beloved Messenger Muḥammad (صلى الله عليه وسلم) along with the 4 Khulafā and many more anecdotes and achievements from the annals of our history.

I pray Allāh (سبحانه وتعالى) accepts this humble work in His court, rewards all those who were part of this publication in anyway, their families and their associates with His pleasure and success in both worlds. Āmīn

If you find any fault, then correct it I pray,
For no one is faultless except Allāh
(Imām Jalāl-ud-dīn Suyūṭī)

Shaykh Muḥammad Yaḥyā
Director - An Nasihah Publications

Rabi' al-Awwal 1436/January 2015

Transliteration Key

Vowels

A	Short vowel as in 'Ago'	I	Short vowel as in 'Sit'
Ā	Long Vowel as in 'Heart'	Ī	Long vowel as in 'See'
AY	Diphthong as in 'Page'	AW	Diphthong as in 'Home'
'	Abrupt start or pause	U	Short vowel as in 'Put'
Ū	Long vowel as in 'Food'		

Consonants

ب	B	'B', no 'H' attached	ص	Ṣ	'S' with full mouth
ت	T	Soft 'T', no 'H' attached	ض	Ḍ	'D' with full mouth, using sides of tongue
ث	TH	'TH' as in 'Thin'	ط	Ṭ	'T' with full mouth
ح	Ḥ	'H' Guttural Sound	ظ	Ẓ	'DH' as in 'Dhuhr' with full mouth
خ	KH	'KH' Very guttural, no usage of tongue	ع	'	Guttural sound - Accompanies vowel
د	D	Soft 'D', no 'H' attached	غ	GH	'GH' Very guttural, no usage of tongue
ذ	DH	'DH' as in 'Adhān'	ق	Q	'K' with back of tongue raised
س	S	'S' only, not 'Z'	و	W	'W' read, not silent
ش	SH	'SH' as in 'Shin'	ى	Y	'Y' only, not 'I'

Note: Double consonants must be pronounced with emphasis on both letters without pause. e.g. Allāhumma should be read al-lāhum-ma.

(سبحانه وتعالى)
Subḥānahū wa ta'ālā
May He be glorified

(صلى الله عليه وسلم)
Ṣallallāhu 'alayhi wasallam
Allāh's peace and mercy be upon him

(عليه السلام)
'Alayhis salām
Peace be upon him

(رضي الله عنه)
Raḍiyallāhu 'anhu
May Allāh be pleased with him

Contents

Syllabus

Coursebook	C 1	C 2	C 3	C 4
Guide Age Range:	6 - 7yrs	7 -8yrs	8 - 9yrs	9 - 10yrs
Fiqh	Basic Introduction to Five Pillars of Islām Shahādah, Ṣalāh, Zakāh, Ṣawm & Ḥajj Introduction to Tahārah Method of Wuḍū'	Methods of Staying Clean: Istinjā', Wuḍū' and Ghusl. Wuḍū' in Detail: Farā'iḍ, Sunan, Mustaḥabbāt, Makrūhāt and Nawāqiḍ. Brief Introduction to Tayammum Method of Ṣalāh for Boys and Girls	Keywords Types of Najāsah Ghusl: Farā'iḍ, Sunan and Method Rak'āt of Ṣalāh Conditions of Ṣalāh Nawāqiḍ of Ṣalāh Method of Ṣalāh Ṣalātul Witr Ṣalātul Musāfir Ṣalātul Mariḍ	Masaḥ 'Alal Khuffayn Masaḥ on Wounds Wajibāt of Ṣalāh Sajdah as-Sahw Ṣawm Tarāwīḥ
Aḥādīth	5 Aḥādīth	5 Aḥādīth	10 Aḥādīth	10 Aḥādīth
	Feeding the Hungry Helping Others Doing Things Slowly Cleanliness Truth	Truth Salām Using the Right Hand Drinking Whilst Sitting Kindness to Neighbours	Ṣalāh, Love for Others, Steadfastness, Life, This World Du'ā', Guests Mercy, Modesty Shukr	Feeding Others, No to Racism, Good Character Thanking Others, Friends, Kindness Trust, Keys to Paradise, Dhikr Du'ā'

CURRENT BOOK

C 5	C 6 Boys	C 6 Girls	C 7	C 8
10 - 11yrs	11 - 12yrs	11 - 12yrs	12 - 13yrs	13 - 14yrs
Miscellaneous Points of Wuḍū', Tayammum in Detail Sunan of Ṣalāh Forbidden and Disliked Times of Ṣalāh Ṣalāh of a Masbūq Qaḍā Ṣalāh 'Īd Ṣalāh Ḥajj and 'Umrah Ziyārah	Types of Water Impurities and Cleaning Methods Maturity in Boys Wājib Acts of Ṣalāh Masā'il of Being an Imām Janā'iz: Method of Ghusl for the Deceased, Shrouding and Burial Jumu'ah Ṣalāh Adhān and Iqāmah	Types of Water Impurities and Cleaning Methods Maturity in Girls Masā'il of Ḥayḍ, Nifās and Istiḥāḍah Wājib Acts of Ṣalāh Janā'iz: Method of Ghusl for the Deceased, Shrouding and Burial	Mustaḥabbāt and Makrūhāt of Ṣalāh Sutrah Sajdah Tilāwah Taḥarrī, Qaṣr Ṣalāh, Ṣalātul Mariḍ and Ma'dhūr, Ṣalātul Kusūf/Khusūf Zakāh, Inheritance I'tikāf, Laylatul Qadr Ḥalāl Foods, Cross Contamination, List of Ḥalāl and Ḥarām Animals, Seafood, Uḍhiyah	Nafl Ṣalāh, Khushū', Ṣalāh with Jamā'ah Nikāh: Choosing a Spouse, Relations Before Marriage List of Maḥārim, Mahr, Walīmah Ṭalāq: Different Types of Ṭalāq, 'Iddah Buyū': Ijārah, Ribā and Gambling Taqlīd: Different Schools of Fiqh, References from Ḥadīth
10 Aḥādīth	15 Aḥādīth	15 Aḥādīth	15 Aḥādīth	15 Aḥādīth
Promises, Tongue Ghībah, Intoxicants Beauty of a Person's Islām, Carrying Tales 99 Names of Allāh سبحانه وتعالى Importance of the Last 3 Sūrah (Mu'awwidhāt) Speaking Good, Good Character	Major Sins, Pride, Good Character, Health and Free Time Truth and Lies, Love for the Messenger صلى الله عليه وسلم Islām is Based upon 5 Pillars, Qur'ān as an Intercessor Ṣalāh at its Correct Time, Kindness to Parents, Gatherings, Good Actions, Ṣadaqah, Ramaḍān, Friendship	Major Sins, Pride, Good Character, Health and Free Time Truth and Lies, Love for the Messenger صلى الله عليه وسلم Islām is Based upon 5 Pillars, Qur'ān as an Intercessor Ṣalāh at its Correct Time, Kindness to Parents, Gatherings, Good Actions, Ṣadaqah, Ramaḍān, Friendship	People of Jannah and Jahannam, Ghībah Siwāk, Not Faulting Food, Modesty, Forgiveness of Sins, Lies Appreciate Blessings, Laylatul Qadr, Durūd, Signs of a Mu'min, Stopping Others from Evil, Ṣalāh with Jamā'ah, Du'ā', Dhikr	Not Having Hatred for Anyone. Spending for the Sake of Allāh سبحانه وتعالى, Disliked Actions, Salām upon Entering Rights of a Muslim, Status of a Mu'min, Reward of Patience, Forgiving Others, True Wealth, Islām is Easy Sweetness of Īmān, Ṣalāh, Closeness to Allāh سبحانه وتعالى, Power of Allāh سبحانه وتعالى, Being Self-sufficient

Syllabus

Coursebook	C 1	C 2	C 3	C 4
Guide Age Range:	6 - 7yrs	7 -8yrs	8 - 9yrs	9 - 10yrs
Sīrah	Childhood of Our Beloved Messenger Muḥammad صلى الله عليه وسلم His صلى الله عليه وسلم Youth. Marriage to Khadījah رضي الله عنها The Children of our Beloved Messenger صلى الله عليه وسلم	In the Cave of Ḥirā The First Revelation The First Believers Open Call to Islām Persecutions Faced by Muslims	Migration to Abyssinia, Two Great Warriors Accept Islām, A Different way, The Boycott The Year of Sadness The Journey to Ṭā'if Inviting the Arab Tribes Al-Isrā' and al-Mi'rāj	The Pledge at 'Aqabah, Hijrah Journey, Arrival in Madīnah Munawwarah Treaties with the Jews, The Hypocrites Battles of Badr, Uḥud & Aḥzāb
Tārīkh	Ādam عليه السلام Nūḥ عليه السلام	Hūd عليه السلام Ṣāliḥ عليه السلام	Ibrāhīm عليه السلام Ismā'īl عليه السلام Isḥāq عليه السلام	Ya'qūb عليه السلام Yūsuf عليه السلام
'Aqā'id	Articles of Faith Qualities of Allāh سبحانه وتعالى Allāh سبحانه وتعالى the Provider, Allāh سبحانه وتعالى The Merciful	Allāh سبحانه وتعالى the Protector, The All Hearing, The All Seeing, The One Angels Revealed Books The Qur'ān	Messengers Qiyāmah Minor Signs List of the Major Signs	Major signs in Detail: Mahdi, Dajjāl, 'Īsā عليه السلام Ya'jūj Ma'jūj, The Beast The Sun Rising from the West, The Smoke, Landslides Blowing of the Trumpet, The Day of Qiyāmah, Mīzān and The Bridge

CURRENT BOOK

C 5	C 6 Boys	C 6 Girls	C 7	C 8
10 - 11yrs	11 - 12yrs	11 - 12yrs	12 - 13yrs	13 - 14yrs
Treaty of Ḥudaybiyyah, Bay'ah ar-Riḍwān, The Message of Islām Spreads, 'Umratul Qaḍā Conquest of Makkah, The Battle of Ḥunain, The March to Tabūk The Farewell Pilgrimage, The Messenger (صلى الله عليه وسلم) Leaves the World	Shamā'il Abū Bakr (رضي الله عنه) His Life and Work The Mothers of the Believers	Shamā'il Abū Bakr (رضي الله عنه) His Life and Work The Mothers of the Believers	Shamā'il 'Umar (رضي الله عنه) His Life and Work	Shamā'il 'Uthmān (رضي الله عنه) 'Ali (رضي الله عنه) Their Life and Work
Mūsā (عليه السلام) 'Īsā (عليه السلام)	Dāwūd (عليه السلام) Sulaymān (عليه السلام) Yūnus (عليه السلام) Introduction to Islamic History The Umayyads	Dāwūd (عليه السلام) Sulaymān (عليه السلام) Yūnus (عليه السلام) Introduction to Islamic History The Umayyads	Zakariyyā (عليه السلام) Yaḥyā (عليه السلام) The Abbāsids	Ayyūb (عليه السلام) Andalusia (Muslim Spain) The Crusades The Ottomans
Death, Journey after death, Jannah, Description, Seeing Allāh (سبحانه وتعالى), Actions that Lead to Jannah Jahannam: Description, Actions that Lead to Jahannam A'rāf, introduction to Taqdīr, our Beliefs with Regard to Allāh (سبحانه وتعالى) Our Beliefs with Regard to the Prophets and the Ṣaḥābah	Ahlus Sunnah wal Jamā'ah, Beliefs with Regard to Prophethood The Ṣaḥābah & their Rankings, Four Khulafā Asharā Mubasharah. The Awliyā', Mu'jizāt and Karāmāt Isrā' and Mi'rāj	Ahlus Sunnah wal Jamā'ah, Beliefs with Regard to Prophethood The Ṣaḥābah & their Rankings, Four Khulafā Asharah Mubasharah. The Awliyā', Mu'jizāt and Karāmāt Isrā' and Mi'rāj	Qaḍā' and Qadr Evil Eye The World as a Place of Means Life after Death Barzakh Resurrection	Attributes (Ṣifāt) of Allāh (سبحانه وتعالى) Istiwā' Īmān Consulting the 'Ulamā'

Syllabus

Coursebook	C 1	C 2	C 3	C 4
Guide Age Range:	6 - 7yrs	7 -8yrs	8 - 9yrs	9 - 10yrs
Akhlāq	Respect Cleanliness Politeness in Speech Smiling Starting from the Right Hand Side	Keeping Promises Being Thankful Spreading Salām Helping in Good Things Kindness to Animals	Thinking Good of Others Sharing Kindness to Parents Speaking the Truth Saying a Good Word	Trust Seeking Permission Before Entering Removing Harm from the Road Being a Good Neighbour
Ādāb	Ādāb of: Eating Drinking Sleeping, Waking up Using the Washroom	Ādāb of: Greeting Entering a House Speaking Sneezing Yawning	Ādāb of: Travelling Studying Qur'ān Walking Masjid	Ādāb of: Du'ā' Dressing Guests & Hosts Sitting in a Gathering Istinjā

CURRENT BOOK

C 5	C 6 Boys	C 6 Girls	C 7	C 8
10 - 11yrs	11 - 12yrs	11 - 12yrs	12 - 13yrs	13 - 14yrs
Asking Advice (Mashwarah) Patience Ties of Kinship Exchanging Gifts and Honouring the Guest Virtues of Dhikr	Oppression and Bullying Envy Ghībah Pride Following the Sunnah	Oppression and Bullying Envy Ghībah Pride Following the Sunnah	Spreading Rumours Value of Time Virtues of Knowledge Benefits of Durūd and Ṣalawāt	Shortness of this Life Taqwā Tawakkul Tawbah Modesty in Gaze
Ādāb of: Ghusl Social Interaction Writing Siwāk Visiting the Sick	Ādāb of: Moderation in Expenditure Importance of a Woman in Society Adhān 'Īdayn Jumu'ah Personal Hygiene	Ādāb of: Adhān Modesty in Dress Moderation in Expenditure Importance of a Woman in Society Personal Hygiene	5 Branches of Faith: Mu'āsharat; Social Manners Taking Oaths, Answering Questions, Using a Mobile Phone and the Internet. Walking with Elders Beginning from the Right when Serving Informing Dependants of one's Whereabouts Interaction with non-Muslims, Condolences	Mu'amalāt: Debate and Discussions Nikāh, Transactions Ādāb for the Seller Ādāb for the Buyer General Ādāb of Shopping

اَلْحَمْدُ لِلّٰهِ رَبِّ الْعَالَمِينَ
وَالصَّلَاةُ وَالسَّلَامُ عَلٰى نَبِيِّنَا مُحَمَّدٍ
وَعَلٰى اٰلِهِ وَصَحْبِهِ أَجْمَعِينَ

بِسْمِ اللّٰهِ الرَّحْمٰنِ الرَّحِيمِ

Fiqh

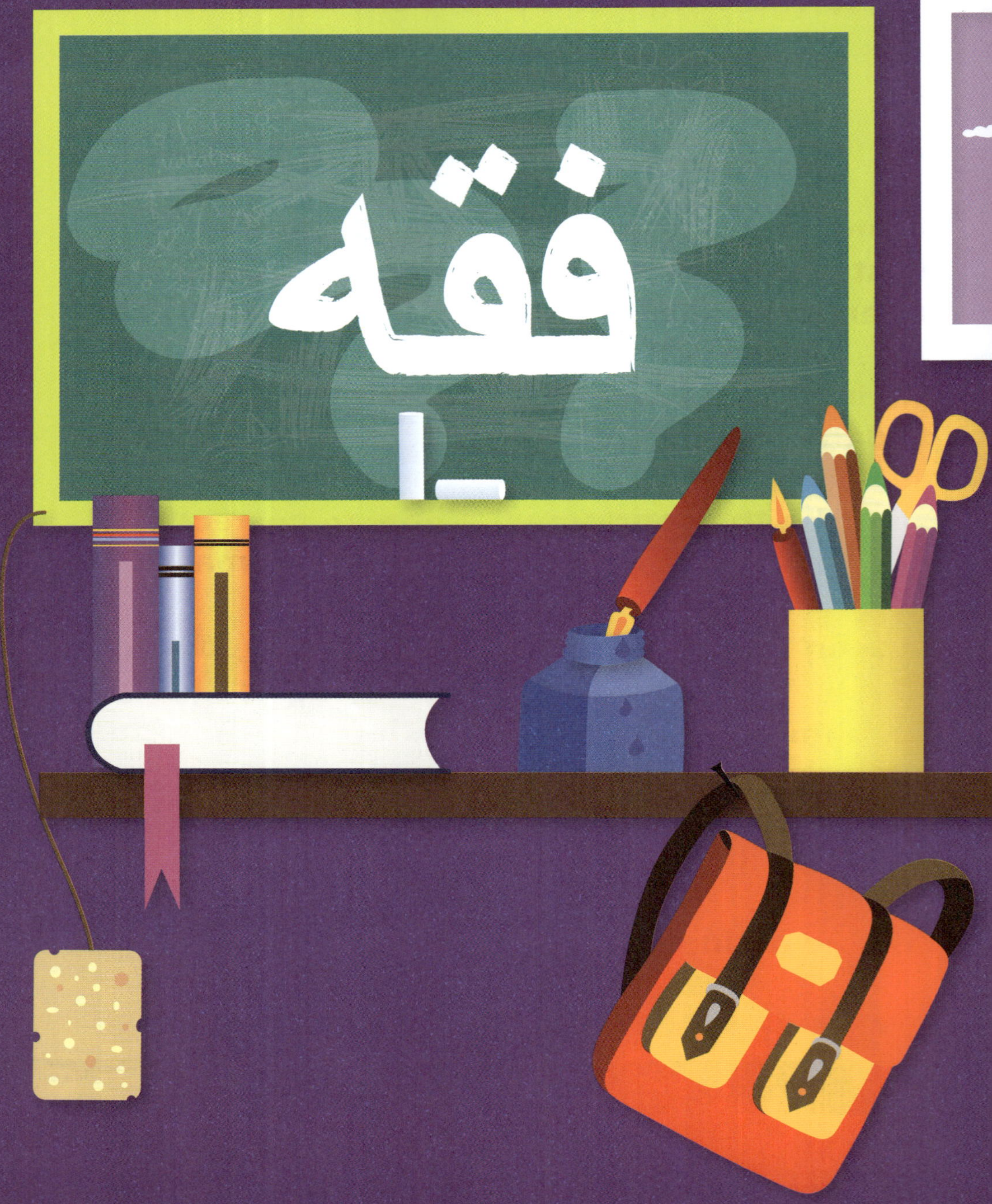

Learning Objectives

Fiqh

At the end of this unit pupils should be able to:

Highlight the miscellaneous points of wuḍū'.

Demonstrate how to perform tayammum, illustrating which parts are farḍ and when tayammum will be nullified.

Distinguish between the sunan of qiyām, rukū', sajdah and qa'dah in ṣalāh.

Describe the conditions of how to correctly integrate into ṣalāh behind an imām (masbūq).

Explain how to compensate for a missed ṣalāh.

Recognise how 'īd ṣalāh is different from other ṣalāh.

Memorise the requirements for 'umrah.

List the actions in each of the five days of ḥajj.

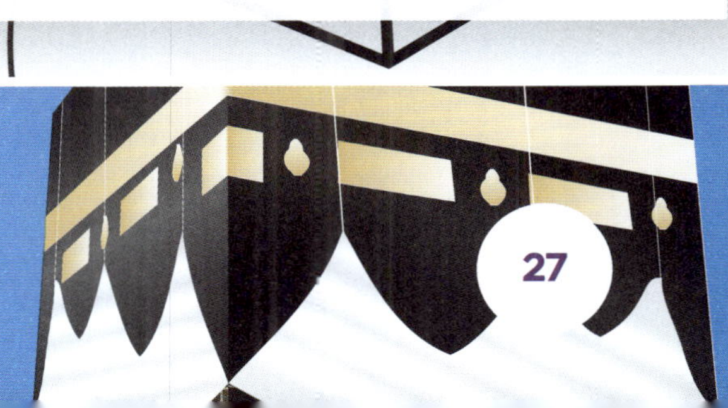

Fiqh

Wuḍū'

Miscellaneous points of wuḍū'

1

A person's wuḍū' will only break if the blood actually flows from its place. If the blood doesn't flow but remains in its place, the wuḍū' will not be broken.

For example, when a person gets scratched and sees some blood on his skin which does not move, with such blood, the wuḍū' will not be broken as it did not flow.

If one bleeds from the teeth or somewhere in the mouth, one's wuḍū' will be broken when the blood is more or the same amount compared to one's saliva. This can be understood if the saliva is yellowish red.

Clotted blood which comes out from the nose will not break wuḍū'.

2

If a person is wearing a tight ring, he must ensure water reaches the skin beneath the ring. This is a wājib requirement.

Wuḍū'

3

If anything sticks onto the skin which stops water from reaching the skin below, it is compulsory to remove that substance. Wuḍū' will not be valid until the substance is removed and water touches the skin. For example, if a person has paint which coats the skin over his fingers, he must first remove the paint stains before doing wuḍū'.

4

If a person laughs in ṣalāh to the extent that another person may be able to hear it, the ṣalāh and wuḍū' are both broken.

If he laughs to the extent that only he himself hears it, only the ṣalāh will be broken.

If a person smiles in ṣalāh, their ṣalāh will not be broken nor will the wuḍū' be broken.

5

If a person falls asleep whilst sitting on the ground cross legged, his wuḍū' will not break. Similarly, if a person leans on something whilst his bottom is firmly on the ground, his wuḍū' will not break.

If a person falls asleep whilst performing sajdah according to the sunnah manner, his wuḍū' will not break.

Wuḍū'

6

If a person has a doubt whether they have wuḍū' or not, they should look to certainty with regard to wuḍū'. If they are sure of performing it earlier and are only unsure about the breaking of wuḍū', then they should consider the wuḍū' unbroken.

7

If a person forgets to wash a limb in wuḍū' and remembers afterwards, it is not necessary to repeat the entire wuḍū'. Washing that limb alone will be sufficient.

8

It is not permissible to touch the Qur'ān except with wuḍū'. Likewise, if a Qur'ān āyah is written somewhere, one cannot touch that part of the paper where the Qur'ān is written except with wuḍū'.

It is not permissible to touch a screen which has the Qur'ān displayed on it without wuḍū'.

9

Wuḍū' is not broken by cutting one's hair or nails.

Wuḍū'

10

If a person has a light beard such that the skin under the beard remains visible, then it is necessary that the water used during wuḍū' reaches his facial skin.

If somebody has a dense beard, he will only wash the hair on the face. He will not have to wash the skin below the beard.

11

If, from the eye or ear, liquid leaks, then one must see whether or not it is from a wound. If the water is from a wound within the eye or ear, one's wuḍū' will break.

12

It is desirable and good to perform fresh wuḍū' for every ṣalāh even if one has wuḍū' already.

13

If one has long nails, it is essential that water reaches under them.

Tayammum

Tayammum means to use soil as a means of attaining purity in the absence of water or being unable to use it due to illness.

Did you know that no other ummah before us had the blessing and advantage of doing tayammum? Allāh سبحانه وتعالى reserved the option of tayammum for us as a way of making it easier to worship Him.

When is tayammum permissible?

If there is no water for an approximate one mile radius.

If one has an illness which will intensify by using water.

If extreme cold weather prevents one from having ghusl with cold water.

If water is nearby but one cannot reach it due to fear.

If water is available but is only enough for drinking.

Tayammum

Three farā'iḍ in tayammum:

Intention before doing tayammum. → Strike both hands and then do masaḥ of the face. → Strike both hands and then do masaḥ of the arms including elbows.

Method of performing tayammum

After making your intention of wanting to become pure, strike both hands on clean soil once.

Pass your hands over your face making sure the hands have covered the area between the forehead and the chin and the area between the two earlobes.

Then strike your hands on clean soil again. Make masaḥ of the arms starting from the fingertips taking it up to and including the elbows by using the left hand for the right arm and the right hand for the left arm.

Tayammum

Items on which tayammum IS permitted:

- Clean soil
- Walls of mud, stone, or brick
- All items coated with a thick layer of dust.
- Sand
- Stone
- Limestone

Tayammum

Items on which tayammum IS NOT permitted:

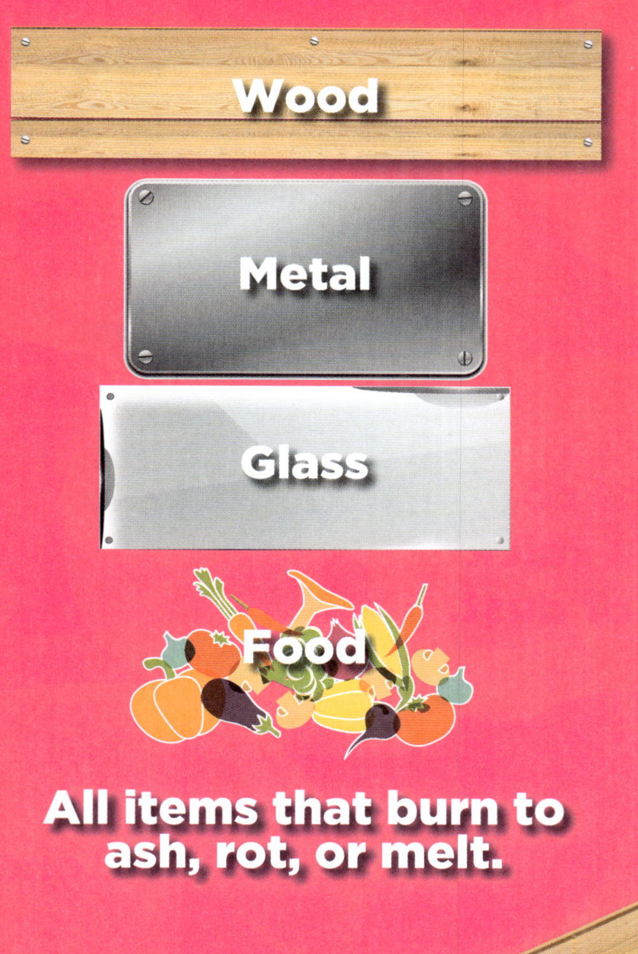

All items that burn to ash, rot, or melt.

Tayammum

Nawāqiḍ of Tayammum

The following actions will break your tayammum.

1. All acts that break wuḍū' break tayammum.

2. Tayammum that is done due to the absence of water shall break if there is access to water.

3. Tayammum that is done due to an illness shall break upon being cured and having the ability to use water.

In point one tayammum can be done again, however, in point two and three, tayammum will no longer be permitted.

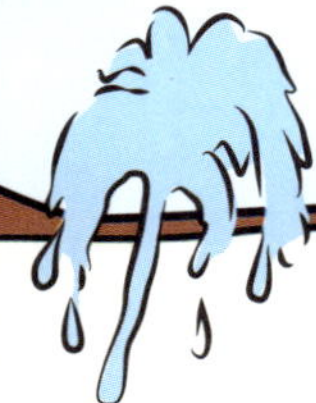

Ṣalāh

Sunan of Qiyām

1. Stand upright facing the qiblah. The head should not be bent. The eyesight should be focused on the place of sajdah.

2. The toes should be pointing towards the qiblah, and one should stand in the normal standing position.

3. When the imām says the Takbīr Taḥrīmah (first takbīr) the 'muqtadī' (one following the imām) should also quietly but audibly say it immediately after the imām.

4. While saying the first takbīr, a male should raise both his hands with the thumbs in line with his earlobes.
   A female should raise her hands in line with her shoulders.

5. The palms of the hands should face the qiblah while saying the Takbīr Taḥrīmah. The hands will be raised for the first takbīr only.

Ṣalāh

6. While raising the hands during the first takbīr the fingers should be kept naturally relaxed (neither completely open nor tightly together).

7. Then, when folding the hands, the palm of the right hand should be placed on the back of the left hand.

8. The males should form a ring around the wrist of the left hand by gripping it with the thumb and the little finger of the right hand. The middle three fingers of the right hand should be close together over the left forearm resting below the navel.

9. The females should place the right hand on top of the left on the chest with both palms facing towards the chest and the fingers kept close together.

10. Then one should recite du'ā' al-istiftāḥ (thanā').

Ṣalāh

Sunan of Qirā'ah

1. After the du'ā' al-istiftāḥ, Ta'awwudh should be recited quietly in the first rak'ah only.
2. After Ta'awwudh, Tasmiyah should be recited quietly and thereafter recited in every rak'ah.
3. After Sūrah al-Fātiḥah, say "Āmīn" softly.
4. To recite from Sūrah al-Ḥujurāt (49) to Sūrah al-Inshiqāq (84) in Fajr and Ẓuhr, and from Sūrah al-Burūj (85) to Sūrah al-Bayyinah (98) in 'Aṣr and 'Ishā', and from Sūrah az-Zalzalah (99) to Sūrah an-Nās (114) in Maghrib Ṣalāh.
5. To lengthen the first rak'ah of the Fajr Ṣalāh.
6. The Qur'ān should not be recited too fast nor too slowly but at a medium pace.
7. Only Sūrah al-Fātiḥah should be recited in the third and fourth rak'āt of each farḍ ṣalāh. In any ṣalāh with jamā'ah, only the imām is to recite the Qur'ān. The followers will be silent.

Ṣalāh

Sunan of Rukū'

1. Takbīr should be said whilst going into rukū'.
2. Males should grasp their knees with their fingers spread in rukū'.
3. Females will touch the knees with the fingers being kept close together.
4. In rukū', the legs should be kept straight.
5. The head and the lower back of the males should be in a straight line. Females will keep the back slightly bent.
6. سُبْحَانَ رَبِّيَ الْعَظِيْمِ (Perfect is my Lord, the Great) should be recited at least three times in rukū'.
7. While getting up from rukū', the imām should say سَمِعَ اللّٰهُ لِمَنْ حَمِدَهٗ (Allāh hears one who praises Him). The muqtadī should then say رَبَّنَا وَلَكَ الْحَمْدُ(Our Lord! All praise be to You). The person praying ṣalāh alone should say both.

Ṣalāh

Sunan of Sajdah

1. Say the takbīr while proceeding for sajdah, placing the knees on the ground first, then the hands followed by the nose, and then the forehead. The fingers should be close together.
2. Place the head between the two hands.
3. In sajdah, males should keep their stomachs separate from their thighs with the toes of both feet pointing towards the qiblah.
4. Males should keep their arms separate from their sides with their elbows raised from the ground.
5. Females should keep the body compact with the arms placed on the ground and with the thighs and stomach touching. Both the feet should face the right.
6. سُبْحَانَ رَبِّيَ الْأَعْلٰى (Perfect is my Lord, the Most High) should be read at least three times.
7. Reciting the takbīr, rise from sajdah by lifting the forehead first, followed by the nose, then the hands and knees. Sit with ease between the two sajdahs.

Sunan of Qa'dah

1. In qa'dah, males should keep their right foot up whilst the toes should face the qiblah and let the left foot lie flat whilst sitting on it. Females should sit on the floor with both feet facing towards the right, with the right thigh on the left thigh.
2. Both hands should be placed upon the thighs.
3. In tashahhud, the forefinger should be raised while reciting أَشْهَدُ أَنْ لَّا إِلٰهَ and should be lowered while reciting إِلَّا اللهُ.
4. Recite Durūd Ibrāhīm in the last qa'dah.
5. After Durūd Ibrāhīm, a du'ā' from the Qur'an or ḥadīth should be read.
6. Make salām on both sides to the extent that the cheeks can be seen by the person behind saying اَلسَّلَامُ عَلَيْكُمْ وَرَحْمَةُ اللهِ with the right side first.
7. The imām should make the intention of salām to the congregation, angels and pious jinns.

Ṣalāh

8. The congregation should make their intention of salām for the imām, angels and pious jinns and they should also make the intention for the rest of the people on their right and left respectively.

9. The person praying alone should only make the intention of salām for the angels.

10. The congregation should make their salām at the same time as that of the imām.

11. The imām should not stretch salām, and should say the second salām in a softer tone than the first salām.

12. The person who has joined jamā'ah late should wait for the imām to say his second salām before getting up to perform the missed rak'āt.

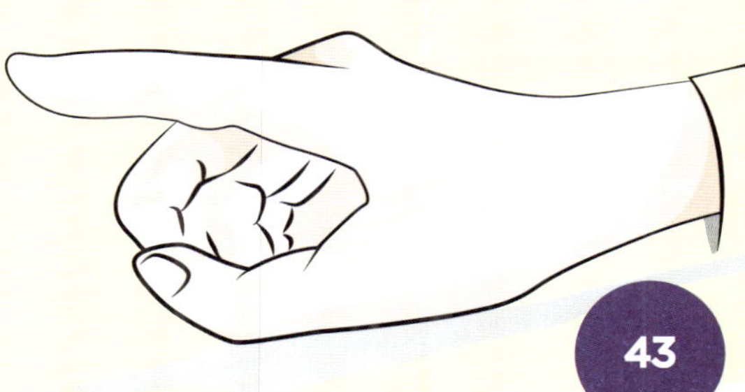

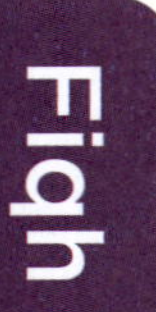

Ṣalāh

Times when ṣalāh is not permitted

There are three times at which it is not permissible to perform any ṣalāh at all:

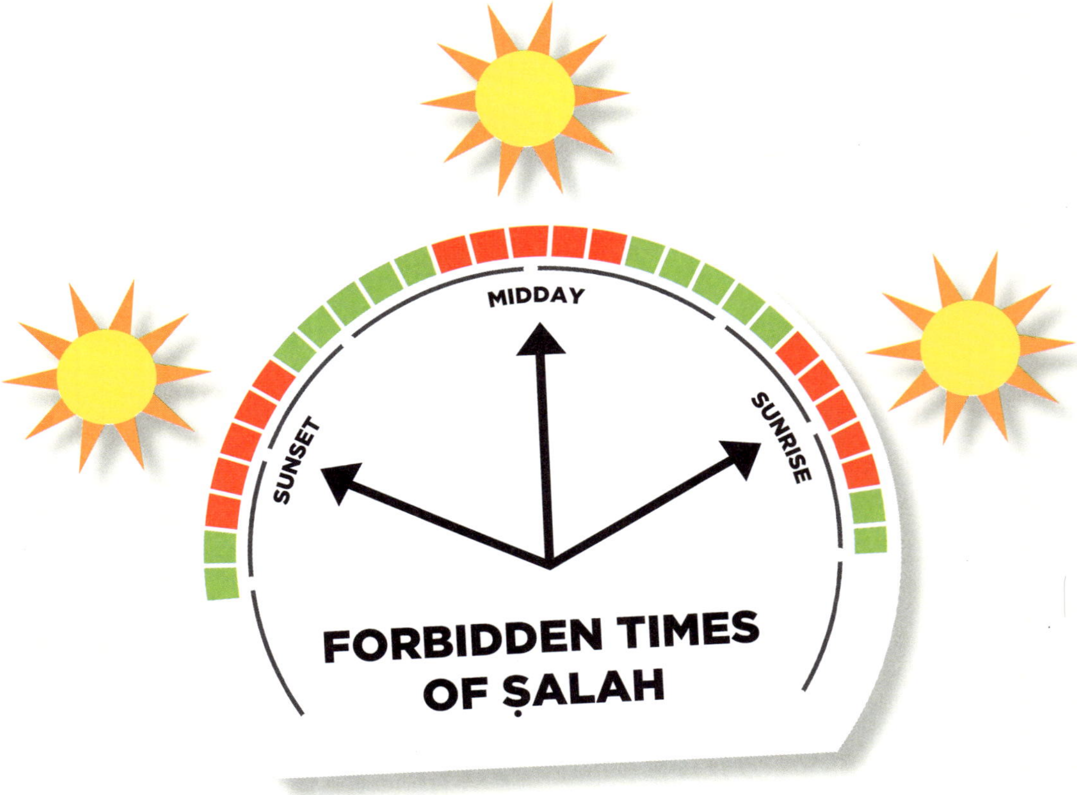

MIDDAY
SUNSET
SUNRISE

FORBIDDEN TIMES OF ṢALAH

Ṣalāh

1) Whilst the sun is rising.

2) Whilst the sun is at its peak. This is usually a few minutes before zawāl time.

3) Whilst the sun is setting. One may only perform 'Aṣr prayer of that day if they have not yet done so.

Ṣalāh

Time when nafl ṣalāh is disliked

It is makrūh to perform nafl (voluntary) prayers at the following times:

Once Fajr time starts one should not perform any nafl. Only the Sunnah of Fajr should be performed.

After the Farḍ of Fajr, one should not perform any nafl prayer until the sun has fully risen.

After the 'Aṣr prayer, no nafl should be performed.

Ṣalāh

Ṣalāh of a Masbūq

Our Beloved Messenger صلى الله عليه وسلم said: "Whoever performs ṣalāh for Allāh سبحانه وتعالى for forty days in congregation, catching the first takbīr, two protections are written for him: protection from the Fire, and protection from hypocrisy." (Tirmidhī)

1

Masbūq is a person who has missed one or more rak'āt behind the imām.

2

If you join the jamā'ah whilst the imām is in qiyām, you should join in by saying the takbīr and stand quietly.

3

If the imām is in rukū', say the takbīr and stand for a moment in qiyām before going into rukū'.

4

If you join the ṣalāh after the imām has stood up from rukū', then that rak'ah has been missed.

5

Always follow the imām's actions as soon as you stand in the ṣaff (row). Do not stand and wait for the imām to stand up from sajdah.

6

If the imām is sitting in the 2nd or 4th rak'ah, you should say the takbīr and join in straight away.

7

Once the imām performs both salāms, stand up to make up the rak'āt you have missed.

Ṣalāh

What do you do if you have missed a rak'ah or a few rak'āt?

Rak'ah with imām	Rak'ah missed	How
3	1	Stand up after the imām has made salām. **Recite:** • Du'ā' al-Istiftāḥ, Ta'awwudh & Tasmiyah • Sūrah al-Fātiḥah and a sūrah Complete the rest of the rak'ah. After the sajdah, sit & recite tashahhud, durūd & du'ā'.
2	2	Stand up after the imām has made salām. **Recite:** • Du'ā' al-Istiftāḥ, Ta'awwudh & Tasmiyah • Sūrah al-Fātiḥah and a sūrah Stand up for the last rak'ah after sajdah. **Recite:** • Tasmiyah, Sūrah al-Fātiḥah and a sūrah Sit after sajdah & complete ṣalāh as normal.
1	3	Stand up after the imām has made salām. **Recite:** • Du'ā' al-Istiftāḥ, Ta'awwudh & Tasmiyah • Sūrah al-Fātiḥah and a sūrah Sit down after sajdah & recite tashahhud only, then stand up for the next rak'ah **Recite:** • Tasmiyah, Sūrah al-Fātiḥah and a sūrah Do not sit down after the sajdah but stand straight up for the last rak'ah **Recite:** • Tasmiyah and Sūrah al-Fātiḥah After the sajdah sit and complete ṣalāh as normal.
0	4	Stand up after the imām has made salām and pray as you are praying a normal four rak'ah ṣalāh.

Ṣalāh

What to do if you have missed a rak'ah or a few rak'āt in Maghrib Ṣalāh?

Rak'ah with Imām	Rak'ah missed	How
2	1	Stand up after the imām has made salām. Recite: • Du'ā' al-Istiftāḥ, Ta'awwudh & Tasmiyah • Sūrah al-Fātiḥah and a sūrah Complete the rest of the rak'ah. After the sajdah, sit & recite tashahhud, durūd & du'ā'.
1	2	Stand up after the imām has made salām. Recite: • Du'ā' al-Istiftāḥ, Ta'awwudh & Tasmiyah • Sūrah al-Fātiḥah and a sūrah Sit down after sajdah & recite tashahhud only, then stand up for the next rak'ah Recite: • Tasmiyah, Sūrah al-Fātiḥah and a sūrah After the sajdah sit and complete ṣalāh as normal.
0	3	Stand up after the imām has made salām and pray as you are praying a normal three rak'ah ṣalāh.

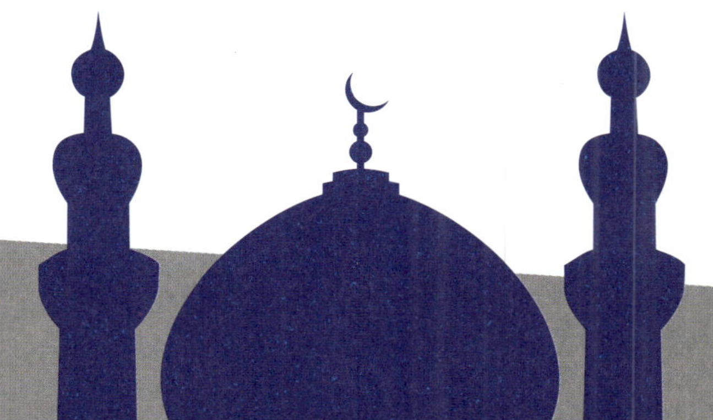

Ṣalāh

Qaḍā' ṣalāh

Qaḍā' means to make up the ṣalāh which has been missed. Qaḍā' is only for the farḍ and witr ṣalāh.

There is no fixed time for qaḍā' ṣalāh. One should perform it as soon as possible, however the three forbidden times must be avoided.

"The first thing a person will be questioned about on the Day of Judgement will be ṣalāh" (Sunan Nasa'ī)

We should never ever miss ṣalāh. If a person mistakenly oversleeps or fails to perform ṣalāh in its correct time, they will have to perform qaḍā'.

Our Beloved Messenger Muḥammad صلى الله عليه وسلم said: "He who forgets the prayer, or he slept (and it was missed), its repayment is that he should perform it when he remembers it." (Ṣaḥīḥ Muslim)

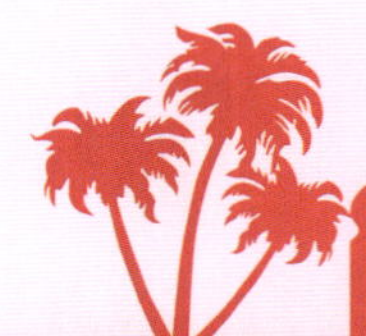

Ṣalāh

Is there qaḍā' for sunnah ṣalāh?

The performance of all sunnah ṣalāh is highly emphasised especially the two sunnah of Fajr. The Prophet صلى الله عليه وسلم said: "The two rak'ah before the dawn (Fajr) prayer are better than this world and all it contains." (Ṣaḥīḥ Muslim)

The sunnah ṣalāh cannot be made up if they were missed, however if a person misses Fajr Ṣalāh and makes qaḍā' of it before midday, they should also make qaḍā' of the sunnah of Fajr. If qaḍā' is made after midday, only the farḍ ṣalāh should be performed.

If there was not enough time left for Fajr Ṣalāh and they therefore only read the farḍ, it is preferable to offer the sunnah after the sun has risen fully but before midday.

The other sunnah ṣalāh which can be performed after it's time is the four rak'ah sunnah of Ẓuhr. If somebody missed the four rak'ah sunnah of Ẓuhr before the farḍ, they may perform it after the two rak'ah sunnah of Ẓuhr but within the time of Ẓuhr.

Besides the Fajr and Ẓuhr sunan, none of the other sunan or nawāfil can be performed after the expiry of their designated time.

Fiqh

Ṣalāh

Qaḍā' ṣalāh

If a person has missed fewer than six ṣalāh, they must perform them first in order before performing any other ṣalāh.

For example, if a person missed **Ẓuhr**, **'Aṣr** and **Maghrib**, then before performing his **'Ishā'**, they must perform **Ẓuhr**, **'Aṣr** and **Maghrib**.

If a person has missed six or more farḍ ṣalāh, it is not necessary to perform them in order and it is not necessary to perform them first before performing other farḍ ṣalāh.

If many ṣalāh are missed, one should try their best to work out the exact number. If they cannot work out the exact number, a proper estimation should be made.

Thereafter, one should try their best to complete all their qaḍā' ṣalāh.

If a ṣalāh was missed intentionally, along with doing qaḍā', one should beg Allāh سبحانه وتعالى for forgiveness.

Ṣalāh

'Īd Ṣalāh

The Muslims have two major days of celebration. These are called 'Īd al-Fiṭr and 'Īd al-Aḍḥā. Muslims have been given a special ṣalāh on these days to express their happiness and gratitude to Allāh سبحانه وتعالى for giving them a day of celebration.

The two 'Īd Ṣalāh are performed in a special way. There are six extra takbīrs in 'Īd Ṣalāh. The six extra takbīrs are wājib.

Before going for 'Īd Ṣalāh, it is mustaḥabb to do the following:

- Do ghusl.
- Use miswāk.
- Apply fragrance.
- Wear one's best clothes.
- Give Ṣadaqah al-Fiṭr before 'Īd al-Fiṭr.
- Express happiness.

It is sunnah to eat something sweet before 'Īd al-Fiṭr Ṣalāh.

It is sunnah to eat qurbāni meat after 'Īd al-Aḍḥā Ṣalāh

The giving of Ṣadaqah al-Fiṭr becomes compulsory upon an individual who has the sufficient amount of wealth with the break of dawn on the day of 'īd al-Fiṭr. The goal of Ṣadaqah al-Fiṭr is to enrich the poor and suffice their need. The amount of Ṣadaqah al-Fiṭr is the value of 1.662kg of wheat.

Ṣalāh

This is how you pray 'Īd Ṣalāh:

First Rak'ah

Say Takbīr Tahrīmah then fold your hands

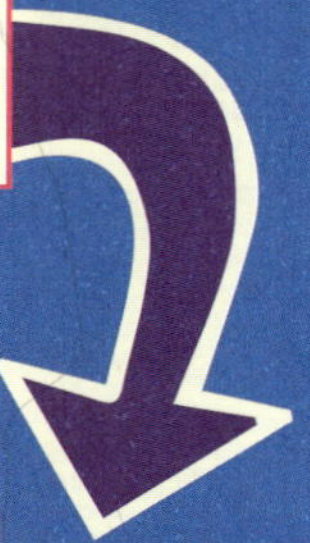

Recite Du'ā' al-Istiftāḥ

Raise your hands saying the takbīr then drop them

Raise your hands saying the takbīr then drop them

Raise your hands saying the takbīr then fold them and listen to the qirā'ah

Remember: FOLD, DROP, DROP, FOLD!

Remember to say the Takbīr each time you raise your hands

Start Second Rak'ah

Second Rak'ah

Listen to the qirā'ah (Sūrah al-Fātihah and a sūrah)

Raise your hands saying the takbīr then drop them

Raise your hands saying the takbīr then drop them

Raise your hands saying the takbīr then drop them

Down into rukū'

Remember: DROP, DROP, DROP, DOWN!

'Īd Ṣalāh for both 'Īds is the same. In 'Īd, the ṣalāh takes place first, then the khuṭbah. In Jumu'ah Ṣalāh, the khuṭbah takes place first, then the ṣalāh.

'Umrah and Ḥajj

The Prophet صلى الله عليه وسلم said: "The performance of 'umrah erases the sins committed between it and the previous one. And the reward for ḥajj mabrūr (pilgrimage accepted by Allāh) is nothing but Paradise." (Ṣaḥīḥ al-Bukhārī)

Iḥrām

People generally refer to the white clothing as iḥrām. However, iḥrām in reality is a state wherein certain ḥalāl things become ḥarām for a temporary period. The white clothing is a sign that a person is in this state.

Before entering into iḥrām, one should:

- Take a bath
- Clip nails
- Apply fragrance
- Perform 2 rak'ah ṣalāh.

'Umrah and Ḥajj

How do you enter this 'state'?

Niyyah (intention) + Talbiyah = State of Iḥrām

One must have the intention to enter into this sacred state of iḥrām before entering the mīqāt.

Mīqāt is the boundary at which iḥrām becomes compulsory for those intending to perform ḥajj or 'umrah.

At the time of making intention, one should recite:

Talbiyah:

لَبَّيْكَ اللّٰهُمَّ لَبَّيْكَ، لَبَّيْكَ لَا شَرِيْكَ لَكَ لَبَّيْكَ،

إِنَّ الْحَمْدَ وَالنِّعْمَةَ لَكَ وَالْمُلْكَ، لَا شَرِيْكَ لَكَ

"Here I am at Your service, O Allāh, here I am. Here I am, you have no partner, here I am. Truly, all praise, favours and sovereignty are Yours. You have no partner."

'Umrah and Ḥajj

Clothing of Iḥrām:

Men will wear two sheets of cloth which should preferably be white. No other garments should be worn during iḥrām.

Men should wear slippers which do not cover the **instep of the foot**.

Women will wear an 'abāyah and scarf. They should just make sure that nothing touches the face physically. They should cover their faces with special caps fitted with veils. Women may wear normal shoes.

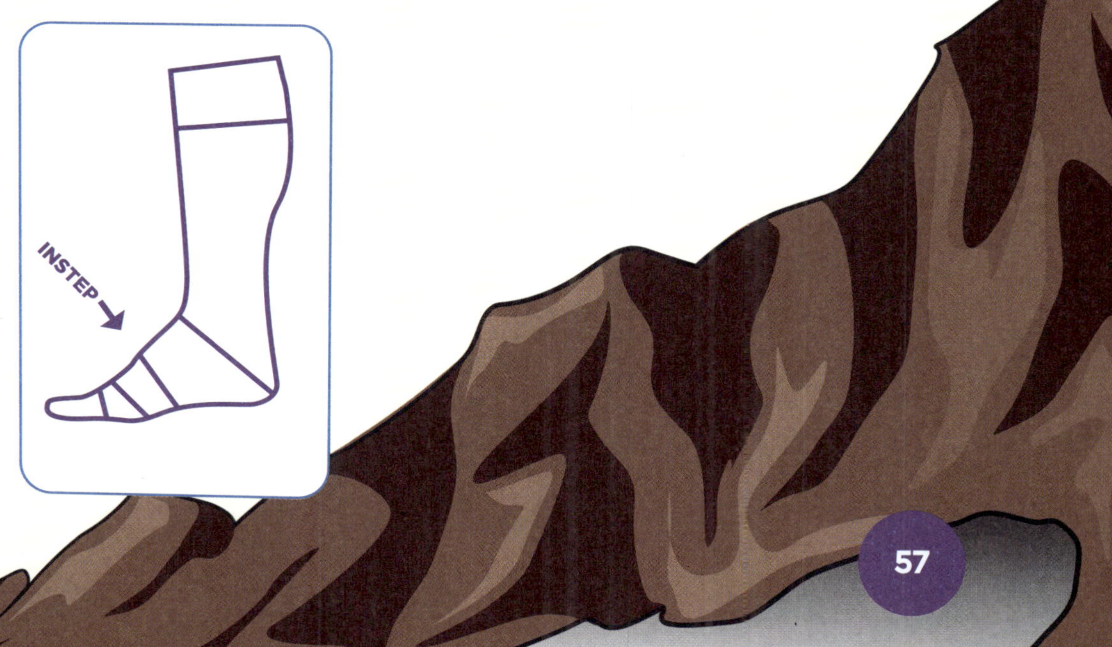

'Umrah and Ḥajj

Forbidden acts in iḥrām:

- Using fragrance
- Cutting/shaving hair
- Cutting nails
- For a male to wear normal clothes
- For a male to cover his face or head with something touching it
- For a female to let a cloth cover her face in a manner that it is touching her face.

Permissible acts in Iḥrām:

- Having a shower for purification or for coolness
- Using unscented soap. However, it is preferable not to do so
- Injections
- Wearing bandages
- Wearing glasses or sunglasses
- Wearing a wristwatch
- The whole body can be covered in a blanket, except the face for females and the head and face for males.
- Wearing a belt/pouch
- To kill scorpions, snakes, mosquitoes and wasps.

'Umrah

'Umrah is a sunnah of our Beloved Messenger Muḥammad صلى الله عليه وسلم. The method of 'umrah is:

Sunnah	Make ghusl for iḥrām Pray two rak'āt before iḥrām
Farḍ	Enter the state of iḥrām with intention and talbiyah Perform ṭawāf
Wājib	Perform sa'y Ḥalaq (shaving)/qaṣr (trimming) of the hair on the head.

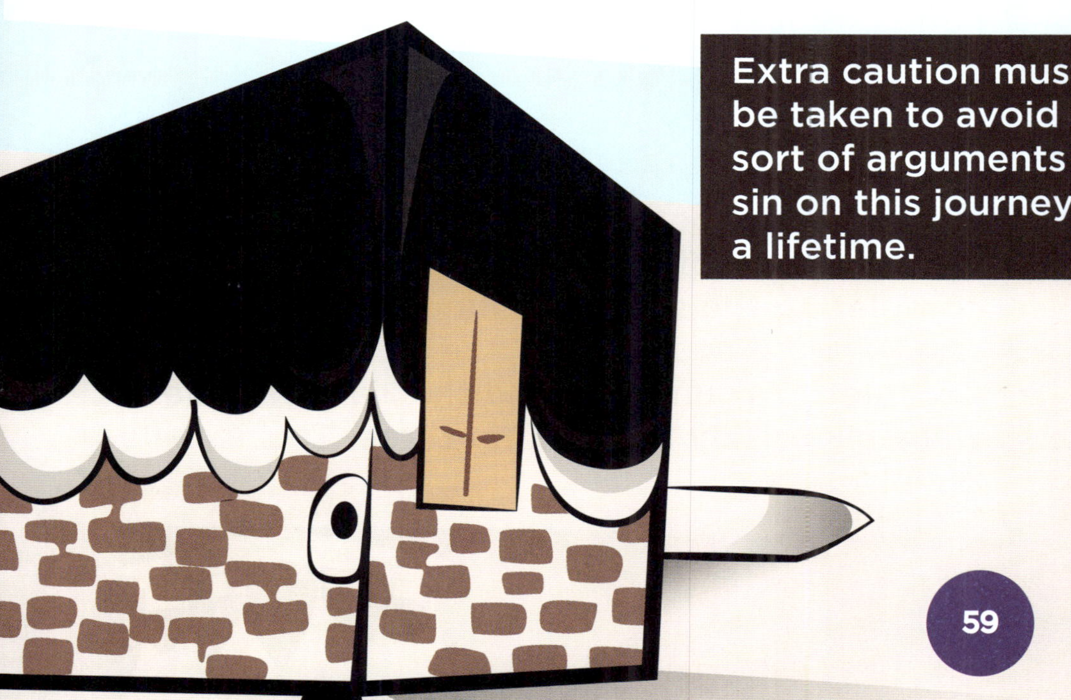

Extra caution must be taken to avoid any sort of arguments or sin on this journey of a lifetime.

'Umrah

How to perform Ṭawāf:

- To begin ṭawāf, stand in front of the Ka'bah facing al-Ḥajar al-Aswad (the Black Stone).
- Men should do iḍṭibā': uncovering of the right shoulder just before ṭawāf.
- Step in line with the Black Stone with the body facing it, and whilst raising the hands to the earlobes, say:

اَللهُ أَكْبَرُ لَا إِلٰهَ إِلَّا اللهُ

- Thereafter, do istilām by touching and kissing the Black Stone. If this is not possible then one may raise the hands towards it and kiss the hands. Whilst doing istilām say:

بِسْمِ اللهِ اَللهُ أَكْبَر

- Istilām will be performed a total of 8 times: at the beginning of every round in ṭawāf and after completing the seventh round.

- Complete 7 rounds around the Ka'bah. Males will walk briskly for the first three. This is called 'Raml.'

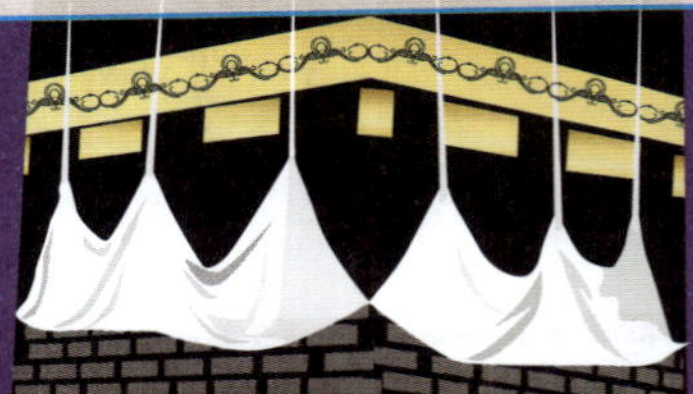

'Umrah

Rukn
Yamānī
al-Ḥajar
al-Aswad
Maqām Ibrāhīm
Start
&
End Point
Ṣafā and Marwah

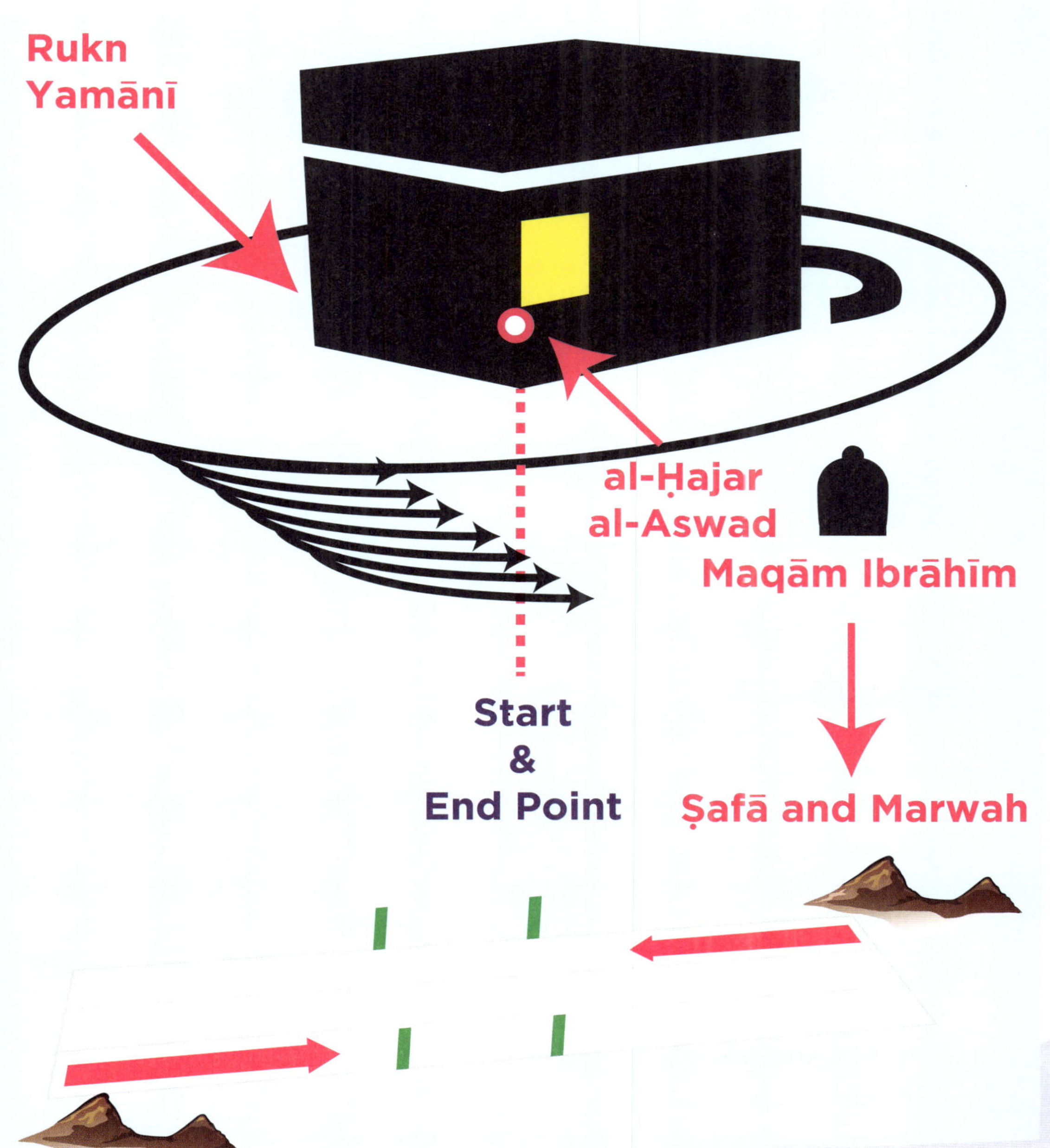

'Umrah

It is wājib to perform two rak'āt after ṭawāf. Before going for sa'y, perform istilām again. Thereafter begin sa'y. Sa'y is performed by walking between these two hillocks seven times, starting at Ṣafā and ending at Marwah.

It is a sunnah for men to run between the area marked with green lights.

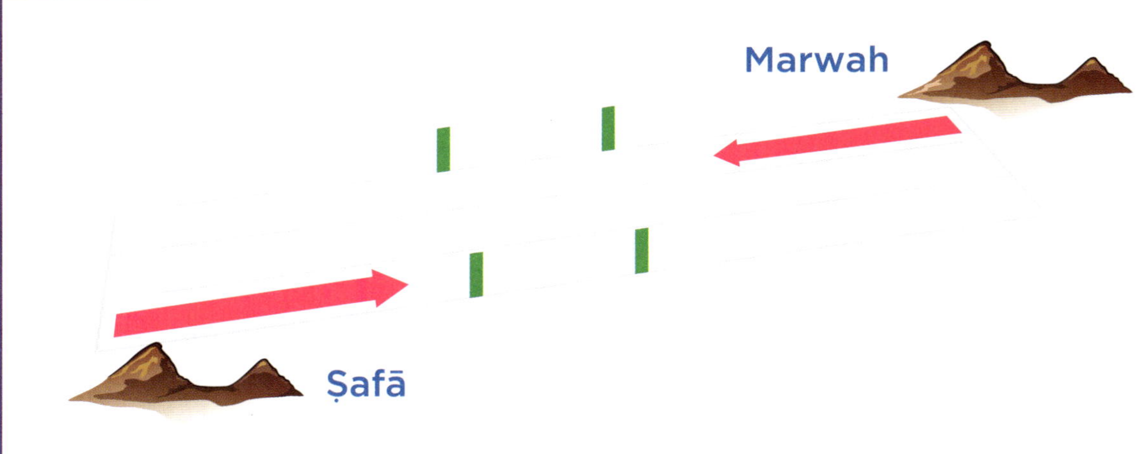

Shaving or trimming the hair is wājib for men to be able to come out of the state of iḥrām.

A woman must only cut an inch of her hair and no more. She can cut it herself.

Once a person cuts their hair, they are free from the laws of iḥrām and the 'umrah is complete!

Ḥajj

Ḥajj is the fifth pillar of Islām

The Prophet صلى الله عليه وسلم said, "Whoever performs ḥajj to this house – Ka'bah – and does not commit any wrongdoing, they will return as the day they were born – pure from sins." (Ṣaḥīḥ al-Bukhārī)

Ḥajj is farḍ once in a lifetime. It only becomes farḍ if one has the money needed to perform ḥajj and is able to travel to Makkah. For a woman, she must have her husband or a close male family member (maḥram) to accompany her on ḥajj.

Types of Ḥajj

Ḥajj can be performed in different ways.
There are three types of ḥajj:

- Ḥajj Qirān = Ḥajj + 'Umrah in one iḥrām.
- Ḥajj Tamattu' = Ḥajj + 'Umrah in two iḥrāms.
- Ḥajj Ifrād = Only ḥajj.

Farā'iḍ of Ḥajj

- Iḥrām for Ḥajj
- Wuqūf at 'Arafah
- Ṭawāf az-Ziyārah

Wājibāt of Ḥajj

- Wuqūf at Muzdalifah
- Pelting the Jamarāt
- Animal sacrifice
- Ḥalaq or Qaṣr
- Sa'ī
- Ṭawāf al-Wadā'

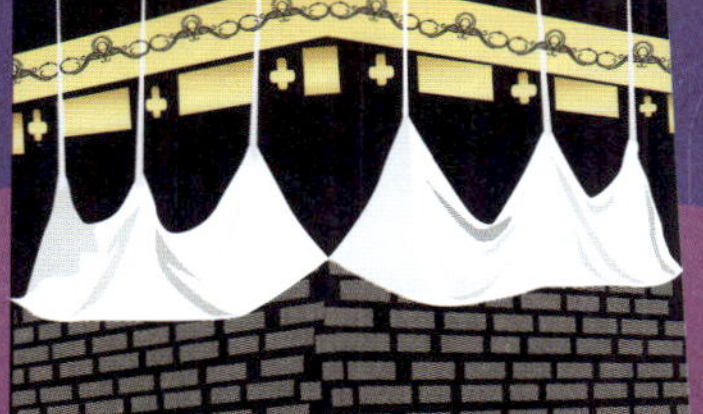

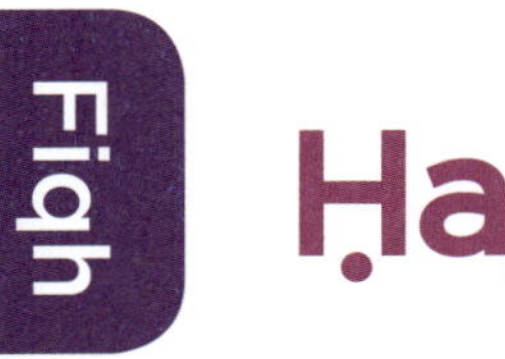

Ḥajj

How to perform ḥajj:

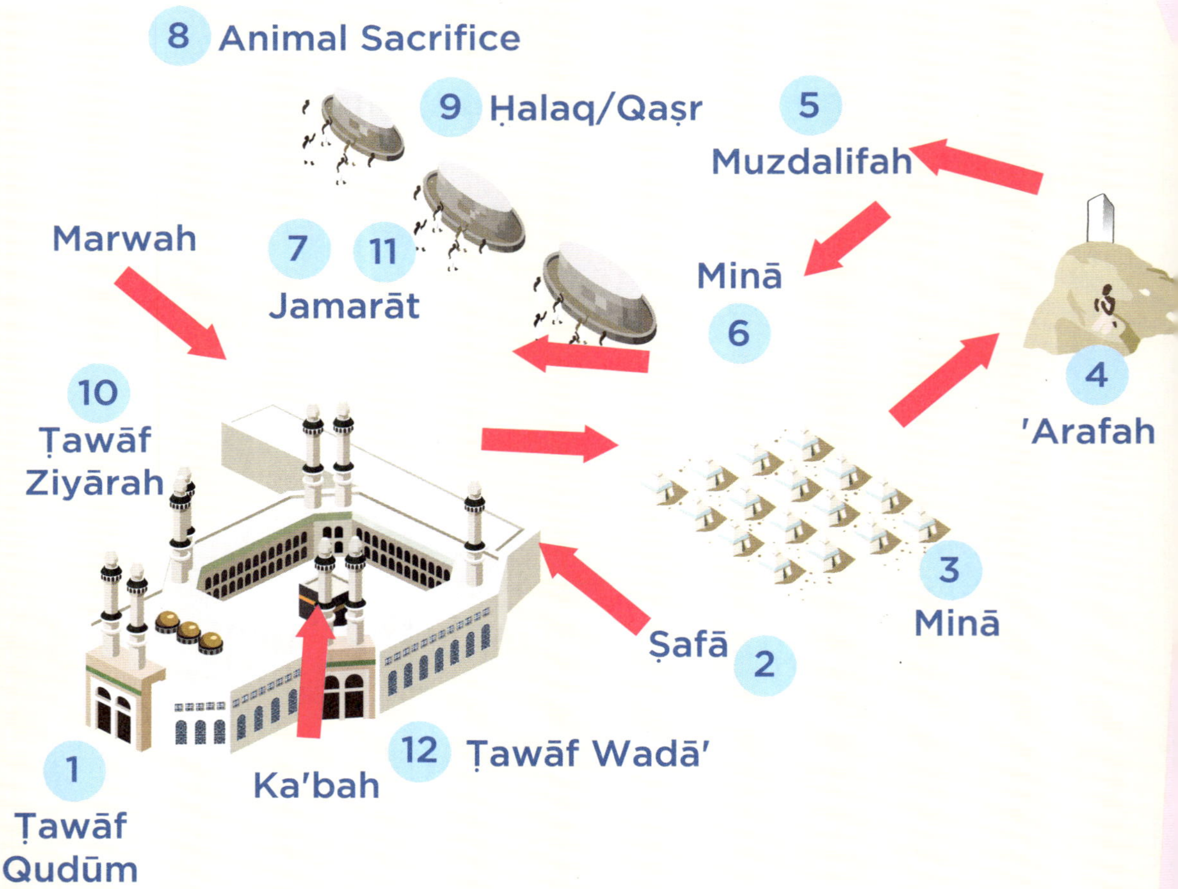

1 Ṭawāf Qudūm
Ka'bah
2 Ṣafā
Marwah
3 Minā
4 'Arafah
5 Muzdalifah
6 Minā
7 Jamarāt
8 Animal Sacrifice
9 Ḥalaq/Qaṣr
10 Ṭawāf Ziyārah
11 Jamarāt
12 Ṭawāf Wadā'

Ḥajj

Ḥajj: day by day

If you are planning to perform Ḥajj Tamattu', complete your 'umrah before the 8th of Dhul Ḥijjah. On the 8th of Dhul Ḥijjah, come in to the state of Iḥrām for ḥajj.

Day 1: 8th Dhul Ḥijjah – Minā (Yawm at-Tarwiyah)

- Leave for Minā from Makkah after sunrise.
- Perform five ṣalāh in Mina (Ẓuhr, 'Aṣr, Maghrib, 'Ishā' and Fajr of the 9th).
- Stay in Minā overnight.

Day 2: 9th Dhul Ḥijjah – 'Arafah & Muzdalifah

- Leave Minā after sunrise.
- Wuqūf (staying and stopping over) at 'Arafah lasts from zawāl until sunset.
- Engage in du'ā' and 'ibādah.
- Perform Ẓuhr and 'Aṣr.
- Leave after sunset without performing Maghrib.
- Go to Muzdalifah.
- Perform Maghrib and 'Ishā' together.
- Collect 70 pebbles.
- Spend the night in Muzdalifah.
- It is wājib to be in wuqūf (remain) at Muzdalifah for a period between Fajr and sunrise.

Ḥajj

Ḥajj: day by day

Day 3: 10th Dhul Ḥijjah – Minā

- Leave Muzdalifah before sunrise and proceed to Minā.
- The following must be done in order: (Remember the key word 'PAS')
  - Pelting (Jamarah al-'Aqabah: seven pebbles)
  - Animal sacrifice
  - Shaving or trimming of hair
- You are now free from iḥrām and its restrictions.
- Perform Ṭawāf Ziyārah and the wājib sa'y of ḥajj.
- Spend the night at Minā.

Day 4: 11th Dhul Ḥijjah – Minā

- Pelt all three jamarāt (7 pebbles each).
- The timing for ramy (pelting) is between zawāl and sunset.
- If you have not done the animal sacrifice, ḥalaq/qaṣr or Ṭawāf Ziyārah you may do it today.
- You cannot free yourself from iḥrām until ḥalaq/qaṣr has been done.
- Stay in Minā.

Ḥajj

Day 5: 12th Dhul Ḥijjah – Minā

- Pelt all three jamarāt (7 pebbles each).
- If you have not done the animal sacrifice, ḥalaq/qaṣr or Ṭawāf Ziyārah you may do it today.
- Leave Minā before sunset to Makkah.

Day 6: 13th Dhul Ḥijjah – Minā

- It is optional, however virtuous to stay in Minā and pelt the three jamarāt on this day also.

After returning to Makkah, perform Ṭawāf Wadā' before you leave for Madīnah or to come back home.

That's your ḥajj done!

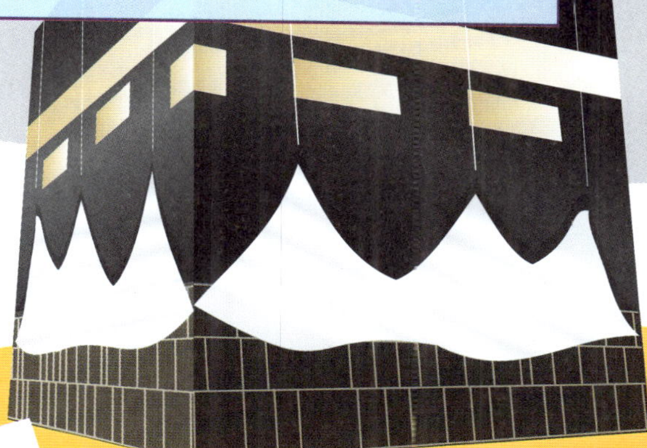

It is advisable to visit a ḥajj workshop or consult a scholar before going for ḥajj.

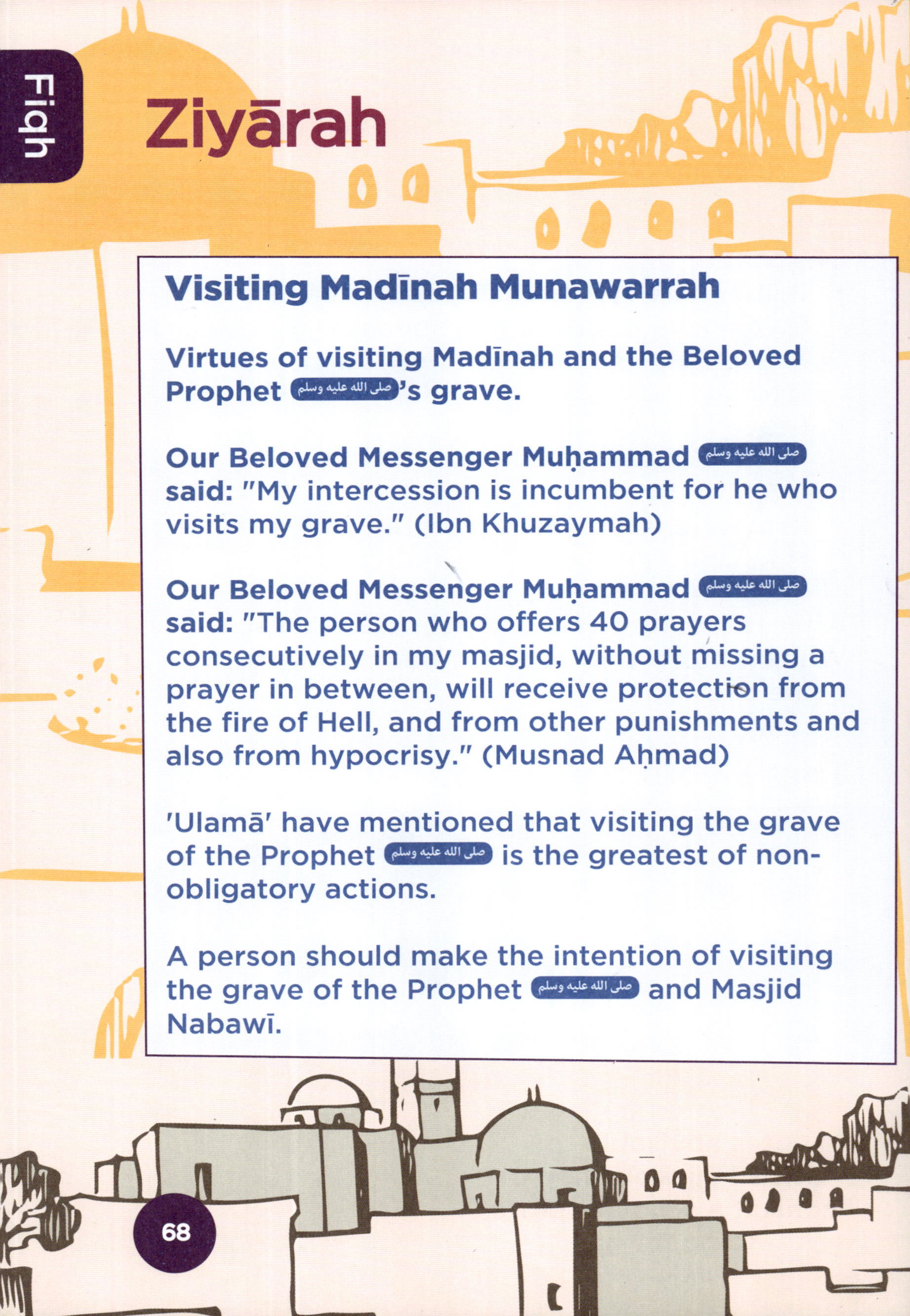

Ziyārah

Visiting Madīnah Munawarrah

Virtues of visiting Madīnah and the Beloved Prophet صلى الله عليه وسلم's grave.

Our Beloved Messenger Muḥammad صلى الله عليه وسلم **said:** "My intercession is incumbent for he who visits my grave." (Ibn Khuzaymah)

Our Beloved Messenger Muḥammad صلى الله عليه وسلم **said:** "The person who offers 40 prayers consecutively in my masjid, without missing a prayer in between, will receive protection from the fire of Hell, and from other punishments and also from hypocrisy." (Musnad Aḥmad)

'Ulamā' have mentioned that visiting the grave of the Prophet صلى الله عليه وسلم is the greatest of non-obligatory actions.

A person should make the intention of visiting the grave of the Prophet صلى الله عليه وسلم and Masjid Nabawī.

Ziyārah

Method of entering Madīnah and the Masjid

- Recite as much ṣalawāt (durūd) as possible.
- Take care of necessary arrangements upon reaching the blessed city such as accommodation.
- Perform mustaḥabb ghusl and wear one's best clothing.
- Men should apply fragrant perfume.
- Try to give some money in ṣadaqah.
- Try to enter from Bāb al-Jibra'īl whilst reciting:

بِسْمِ اللهِ، وَعَلٰى مِلَّةِ رَسُوْلِ اللهِ، رَبِّ أَدْخِلْنِيْ مُدْخَلَ صِدْقٍ، اَللّٰهُمَّ صَلِّ عَلٰى مُحَمَّدٍ، وَعَلٰى اٰلِ مُحَمَّدٍ، وَاغْفِرْ لِيْ ذُنُوْبِيْ، وَافْتَحْ لِيْ أَبْوَابَ رَحْمَتِكَ وَفَضْلِكَ

- Perform two rak'āt Taḥiyyatul Masjid in the Rawḍah al-Jannah if possible or anywhere convenient if it is not makrūh time for ṣalāh.

Ziyārah

Greeting the Prophet صلى الله عليه وسلم, Abū Bakr رضي الله عنه and 'Umar رضي الله عنه

Upon reaching the blessed room where the Prophet صلى الله عليه وسلم, Abū Bakr رضي الله عنه and 'Umar رضي الله عنه are buried, one should stand will full respect.

Standing in line with the Prophet صلى الله عليه وسلم's grave, one should say:

اَلصَّلٰوةُ وَالسَّلَامُ عَلَيْكَ يَا رَسُوْلَ اللهِ

"Mercy and Peace be upon you, O Messenger of Allāh."

Take one step to the right, in line with the blessed grave of Abū Bakr رضي الله عنه and say:

اَلسَّلَامُ عَلَيْكَ يَا خَلِيْفَةَ رَسُوْلِ اللهِ

"Peace be upon you, O khalīfah of the Messenger of Allāh."

Take another step to the right, in line with the blessed grave of 'Umar رضي الله عنه and say:

اَلسَّلَامُ عَلَيْكَ يَا أَمِيْرَ الْمُؤْمِنِيْنَ

"Peace be upon you, O leader of the Believers."

Thereafter make du'ā' to Allāh سبحانه وتعالى facing the qiblah.

Ziyārah

Places to visit in Madīnah

The Rawḍah al-Jannah (The Garden)

The masjid of the Prophet صلى الله عليه وسلم has many beautiful and sacred areas. From among them is the Rawḍah.
The Prophet صلى الله عليه وسلم said: "The area between my house and my mimbar is a garden from the gardens of Paradise." (Ṣaḥīḥ al-Bukhārī)

Jannatul Baqī'

Jannatul Baqī' is the famous graveyard of Madīnah. There are hundreds of Ṣaḥābah and pious people buried in this graveyard. One should visit this graveyard as often as possible.

Masjid al-Qubā'

The first masjid that was built by the Prophet صلى الله عليه وسلم in Madīnah was Masjid al-Qubā'.
The Prophet صلى الله عليه وسلم said: "Whoever goes to this masjid and prays there, will have a reward like that of an 'umrah." (Nasa'ī)
The Prophet صلى الله عليه وسلم would go every Saturday to Masjid al-Qubā'. (Ṣaḥīḥ al-Bukhārī)

Actions to perform whilst in Madīnah

- Spend as much time as possible in the masjid with the intention of nafl i'tikāf.
- Try to perform ṣalāh in the Rawḍah area of the masjid.
- Recite ṣalawāt (durūd) upon the Prophet صلى الله عليه وسلم as much as possible.
- Have the utmost respect for everything in Madīnah.
- Give ṣadaqah to the people of Madīnah.

Aḥādīth

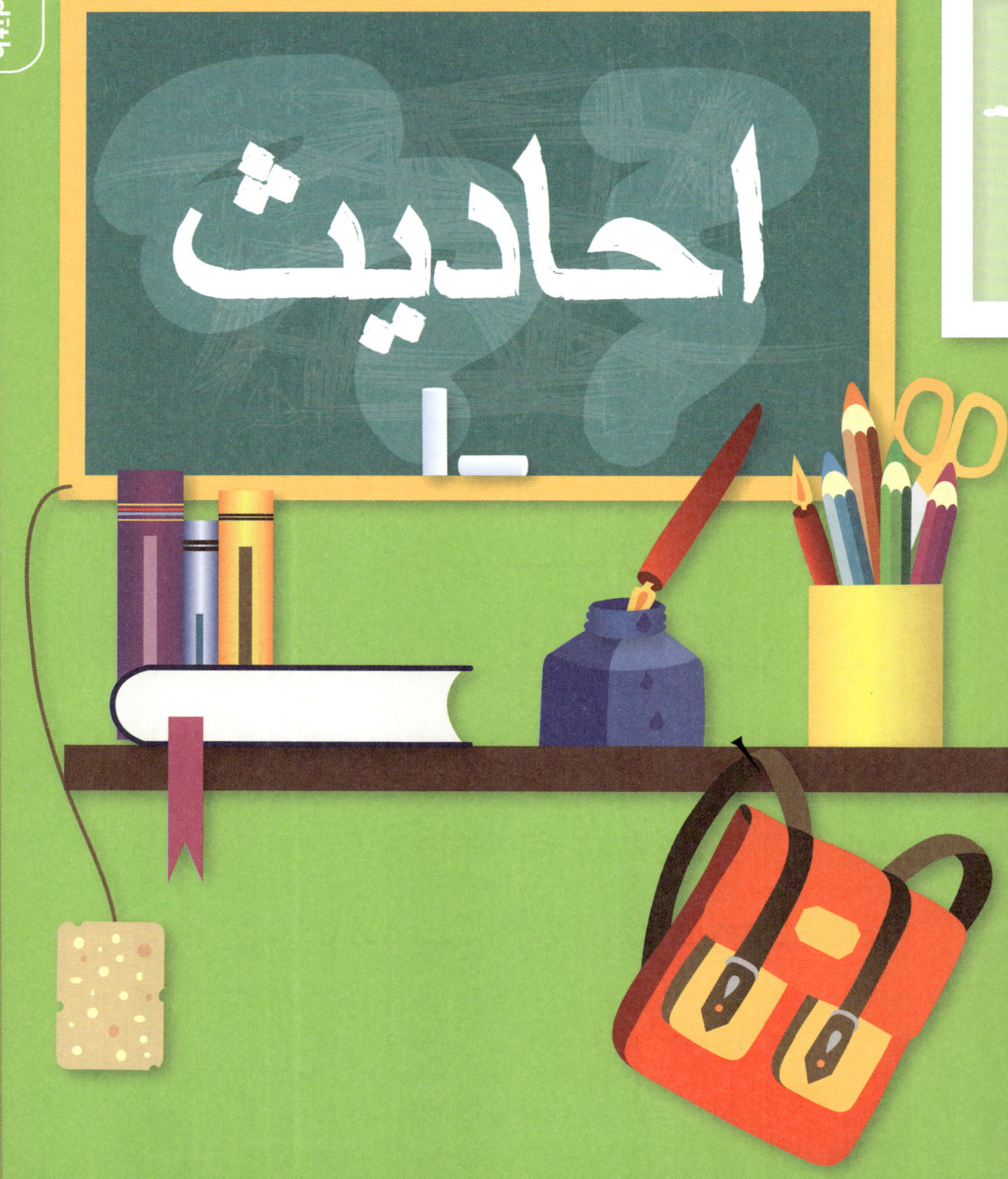

Aḥādīth

لَا دِيْنَ لِمَنْ لَّا عَهْدَ لَهُ

اِحْفَظْ لِسَانَكَ

اِيَّاكُمْ وَالْغِيْبَةَ

كُلُّ مُسْكِرٍ حَرَامٌ

مِنْ حُسْنِ اِسْلَامِ الْمَرْءِ تَرْكُهُ مَا لَا يَعْنِيْهِ

لَا يَدْخُلُ الْجَنَّةَ نَمَّامٌ

اِنَّ لِلّٰهِ تَعَالٰى تِسْعَةً وَّتِسْعِيْنَ اِسْمًا مَنْ اَحْصَاهَا دَخَلَ الْجَنَّةَ

اِقْرَأْ قُلْ هُوَ اللّٰهُ اَحَدٌ وَالْمُعَوِّذَتَيْنِ حِيْنَ تُمْسِيْ وَحِيْنَ تُصْبِحُ ثَلَاثَ مَرَّاتٍ تَكْفِيْكَ مِنْ كُلِّ شَيْءٍ

مَنْ كَانَ يُؤْمِنُ بِاللّٰهِ وَالْيَوْمِ الْاٰخِرِ فَلْيَقُلْ خَيْرًا اَوْ لِيَصْمُتْ

اِنَّ مِنْ اَحَبِّكُمْ اِلَيَّ اَحْسَنُكُمْ اَخْلَاقًا

Promises

Aḥadīth

قَالَ رَسُوْلُ اللهِ صَلَّى اللهُ عَلَيْهِ وَسَلَّمَ

Rasūlullāh صلى الله عليه وسلم said:

لَا دِيْنَ لِمَنْ لَّا عَهْدَ لَهُ

"A person who does not keep his promise does not have (complete) religion (dīn)." (Aḥmad)

A promise is made to show that you will definitely carry out an action. Once you make a promise, you have made a verbal contract which you must fulfil. A person who breaks his promise is a liar, for he said something which he was not going to do.

"O you who believe! Why do you say that which you do not do? Most hateful it is with Allāh that you say that which you do not do." (Qur'ān 61:2-3)

Before we make a promise we must think: "Can I really carry this action out?" If the answer is "yes" then we should make the promise and try our utmost best to carry it out and if the answer is "no", then we should kindly excuse ourselves from making the promise.

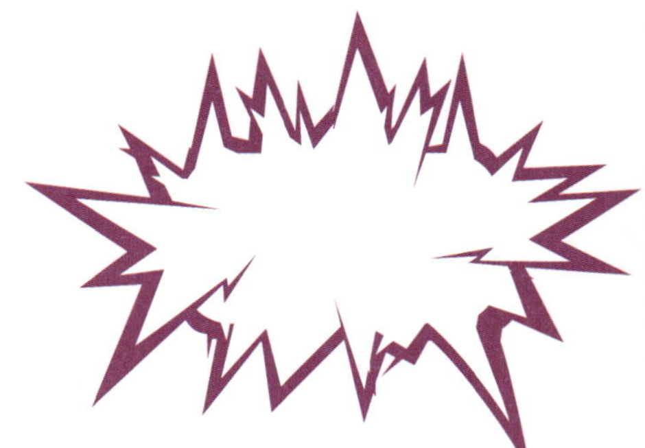

Tongue

قَالَ رَسُوْلُ اللهِ صَلَّى اللهُ عَلَيْهِ وَسَلَّمَ

Rasūlullāh صلى الله عليه وسلم said:

اِحْفَظْ لِسَانَكَ

"Safeguard your tongue." (Ṭabarānī)

The tongue is a boneless piece of flesh, yet it is very powerful. The tongue can join nations and it can even break hearts.

A wise person always thinks then speaks, whilst a foolish person speaks then thinks. Words are like arrows: once released they cannot be stopped. But as long as they remain unspoken, they are under our control. So we must always think before we speak.

In another ḥadīth, Rasūlullāh صلى الله عليه وسلم said: "A person utters a word pleasing to Allāh without thinking much of it for which Allāh raises his ranks (in Jannah); another one speaks a word displeasing to Allāh without thinking much of it, and for this reason he will sink down into Jahannam." (Ṣaḥīḥ al-Bukhārī)

Ghībah

Aḥadīth

قَالَ رَسُوْلُ اللهِ صَلَّى اللهُ عَلَيْهِ وَسَلَّمَ

Rasūlullāh صلى الله عليه وسلم said:

إِيَّاكُمْ وَالْغِيْبَةَ

"Save yourself from ghībah." (Ṭabarānī)

Ghībah is to say something bad about your brother or sister in their absence. When we take part in ghībah, our good actions are taken from us and given to the person whom we spoke about. Ghībah will not be forgiven until the person forgives us. If we have made ghībah about someone, we must ask for their forgiveness. If they have passed away or we cannot find them, then we must continue to make du'ā' for them until we feel we have paid them back.

Our Beloved Messenger Muḥammad صلى الله عليه وسلم said: "A muflis (bankrupt) is one who comes on the Day of Judgement with prayers, fasting, and zakāt, but finds himself bankrupt on that day as he has finished his funds of virtues by abusing others, making false statements, unlawfully consuming wealth, shedding blood and beating others; his virtues will be credited to the account of those who suffered at his hand. And if his good deeds fall short of balancing the account, then the other person's sins will be entered into the muflis's account, and he will be thrown into the Fire." (Ṣaḥīḥ al-Bukhārī)

Intoxicants

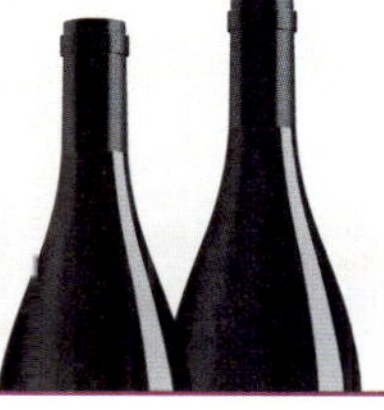

قَالَ رَسُوْلُ اللهِ صَلَّى اللهُ عَلَيْهِ وَسَلَّمَ

Rasūlullāh صلى الله عليه وسلم said:

كُلُّ مُسْكِرٍ حَرَامٌ

"Every intoxicant is forbidden." (Ṣaḥīḥ Muslim)

Intoxicants are ḥarām whichever form they may be in. This includes drugs, alcohol, or any substance that clouds our senses.

The Prophet صلى الله عليه وسلم said, "Every intoxicant is unlawful. Allāh has taken a promise upon himself for the one who takes intoxicating drinks, that he will make him drink from 'Ṭīnatul Khabāl.' They asked, "O Messenger of Allāh صلى الله عليه وسلم, what is Ṭīnatul Khabāl?" He said, "The sweat of the inmates of Hell or the pus (impurities) of the inmates of Hell." (Ṣaḥīḥ Muslim)

This is just one of the many punishments a person will face in the Ākhirah. In this world he will suffer, as the effects of drugs and intoxicants affect a person mentally too. We should say "No" to drugs and alcohol. May Allāh سبحانه وتعالى protect us all. (Āmīn)

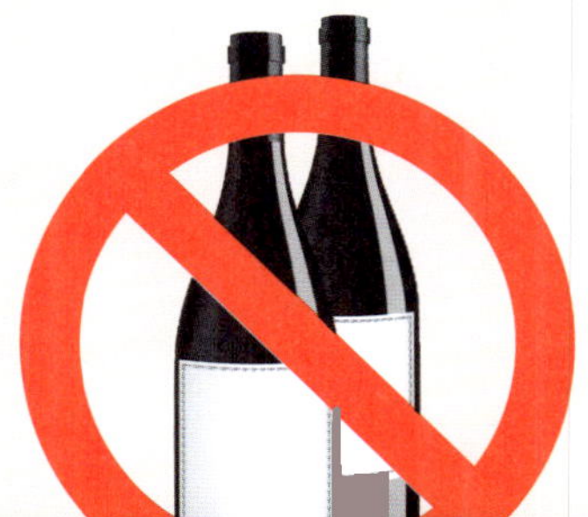

Beauty of a Person's Islām

Aḥadīth

قَالَ رَسُوْلُ اللهِ صَلَّى اللهُ عَلَيْهِ وَسَلَّمَ

Rasūlullāh صلى الله عليه وسلم said:

مِنْ حُسْنِ إِسْلَامِ الْمَرْءِ تَرْكُهُ مَا لَا يَعْنِيْهِ

"It is part of the beauty of a person's Islām to leave that which does not concern him." (Tirmidhī)

In this ḥadīth our Beloved Messenger صلى الله عليه وسلم is informing us how to beautify our dīn by leaving those things which do not benefit us in this world or the Ākhirah.

We should rather spend our time in doing and saying those things that will be of benefit to us or others. He صلى الله عليه وسلم said: "The best person is he who benefits others." (Ṭabarānī) Indeed our time in this world is short. Imām Shāfi'ī رحمه الله said: "Life is a moment so make it a moment of obedience."

If something is not to do with us, we should not be nosey and try to find out what is happening as this is of no benefit to us.

However, if we see someone doing something wrong then we should remember that it is our duty to encourage others to do good and stop them from doing wrong.

Carrying Tales

Aḥadīth

قَالَ رَسُوْلُ اللهِ صَلَّى اللهُ عَلَيْهِ وَسَلَّمَ

Rasūlullāh صلى الله عليه وسلم said:

لَا يَدْخُلُ الْجَنَّةَ نَمَّامٌ

"He who carries tales shall not enter Jannah."
(Ṣaḥīḥ Muslim)

Tale-bearers are liars. They tell lies to different people and through these lies they spread fitnah (corruption) and divide the Ummah. Such people are the cause of much corruption.

That is why we are reminded if someone comes to us with some news, we must always verify it as we don't know whether or not they are speaking the truth. This includes messages that we may receive regarding a particular person or incident.

Imagine the severe consequences of acting on some news which was not true!

We must always remember that a person who spreads false rumours will be deprived from entering the everlasting, beautiful gardens of Paradise.

Names of Allāh

Aḥadīth

قَالَ رَسُوْلُ اللهِ صَلَّى اللهُ عَلَيْهِ وَسَلَّمَ

Rasūlullāh صلى الله عليه وسلم said:

اِنَّ لِلّٰهِ تَعَالٰى تِسْعَةً وَّتِسْعِيْنَ اِسْمًا مَنْ اَحْصَاهَا دَخَلَ الْجَنَّةَ

"Allāh سبحانه وتعالى has such 99 names, whoever does 'iḥṣā' (comprehends) of them shall enter Jannah." (Tirmidhī)

"For Allāh there are the most beautiful names. So, call Him by them" (Qur'ān 7:180)

We should try to use the names of Allāh when we supplicate to him.

Allāh سبحانه وتعالى has many names of which there are 99 such names that whoever does 'iḥṣā' (fully comprehends) of them shall enter Jannah.

The word 'iḥṣā' includes the following:
1) To understand and know the names
2) To make du'ā' to Allāh سبحانه وتعالى using the names
3) To act according to the names; for example we know Allāh سبحانه وتعالى is the All Hearing so we should think of this when we speak that Allāh سبحانه وتعالى can hear us and we know Allah is the All Seeing, we should think of this when we do something that the All Seeing is watching me.

Names of Allāh

هُوَ اللّٰهُ الَّذِي لَآ اِلٰهَ اِلَّا هُوَ

الرَّحْمٰنُ الرَّحِيمُ الْمَلِكُ الْقُدُّوسُ السَّلَامُ الْمُؤْمِنُ الْمُهَيْمِنُ

الْعَزِيزُ الْجَبَّارُ الْمُتَكَبِّرُ الْخَالِقُ الْبَارِئُ الْمُصَوِّرُ الْغَفَّارُ

الْقَهَّارُ الْوَهَّابُ الرَّزَّاقُ الْفَتَّاحُ اَلْعَلِيمُ الْقَابِضُ الْبَاسِطُ

الْخَافِضُ الرَّافِعُ الْمُعِزُّ الْمُذِلُّ السَّمِيعُ الْبَصِيرُ الْحَكَمُ

الْعَدْلُ اللَّطِيفُ الْخَبِيرُ الْحَلِيمُ الْعَظِيمُ الْغَفُورُ الشَّكُورُ

الْعَلِيُّ الْكَبِيرُ الْحَفِيظُ الْمُقِيتُ الْحَسِيبُ الْجَلِيلُ الْكَرِيمُ

الرَّقِيبُ الْمُجِيبُ الْوَاسِعُ الْحَكِيمُ الْوَدُودُ الْمَجِيدُ الْبَاعِثُ

الشَّهِيدُ الْحَقُّ الْوَكِيلُ الْقَوِيُّ الْمَتِينُ الْوَلِيُّ الْحَمِيدُ

الْمُحْصِي الْمُبْدِئُ الْمُعِيدُ الْمُحْيِي اَلْمُمِيتُ الْحَيُّ الْقَيُّومُ

الْوَاجِدُ الْمَاجِدُ الْواحِدُ الاَحَدُ الصَّمَدُ الْقَادِرُ الْمُقْتَدِرُ

الْمُقَدِّمُ الْمُؤَخِّرُ الأَوَّلُ الآخِرُ الظَّاهِرُ الْبَاطِنُ الْوَالِي

الْمُتَعَالِي الْبَرُّ التَّوَابُ الْمُنْتَقِمُ العَفُوُّ الرَّؤُوفُ مَالِكُ الْمُلْكِ

ذُوالْجَلَالِ وَالإِكْرَامِ الْمُقْسِطُ الْجَامِعُ الْغَنِيُّ الْمُغْنِي اَلْمَانِعُ

الضَّارَّ النَّافِعُ النُّورُ الْهَادِي الْبَدِيعُ اَلْبَاقِي الْوَارِثُ

الرَّشِيدُ الصَّبُورُ

Mu'awwidhāt

قَالَ رَسُوْلُ اللهِ صَلَّى اللهُ عَلَيْهِ وَسَلَّمَ

Our Beloved Messenger Muḥammad صلى الله عليه وسلم said:

اِقْرَأْ قُلْ هُوَ اللهُ اَحَدٌ وَ الْمُعَوِّذَتَيْنِ حِيْنَ تُمْسِيْ وَحِيْنَ تُصْبِحُ ثَلَاثَ مَرَّاتٍ تَكْفِيْكَ مِنْ كُلِّ شَيْءٍ

"Read Sūrah al-Ikhlās, Sūrah al-Falaq and Sūrah an-Nās three times in the evening and in the morning. These shall suffice you from everything." (Abū Dāwūd)

Our Beloved Messenger صلى الله عليه وسلم is informing us of a way of protecting ourselves from all things that may harm us. These sūrahs should be recited ten times altogether each day;

- Once after the farḍ ṣalāh of Ẓuhr, 'Aṣr and 'Ishā' (3)
- Three times after Fajr and after Maghrib (6)
- Once before sleeping (1)

We need to hold on to this advice and make it a practice to recite these daily.

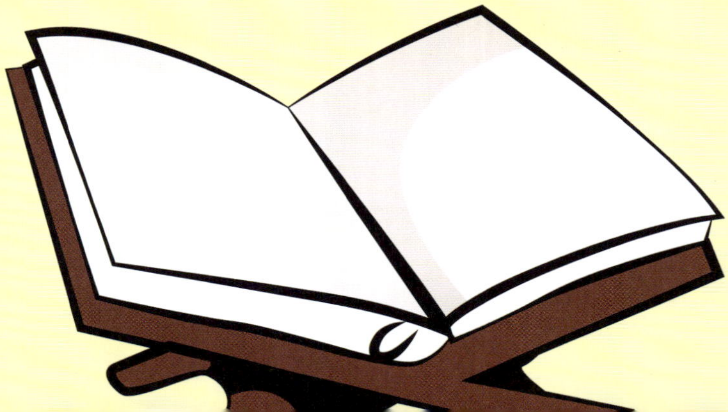

Speaking Good

قَالَ رَسُوْلُ اللهِ صَلَّى اللهُ عَلَيْهِ وَسَلَّمَ

Our Beloved Messenger Muḥammad صلى الله عليه وسلم said:

مَنْ كَانَ يُؤْمِنُ بِاللهِ وَالْيَوْمِ الْاٰخِرِ فَلْيَقُلْ خَيْرًا اَوْ لِيَصْمُتْ

"He who truly believes in Allāh and the Last Day should speak good or keep silent." (Ṣaḥīḥ al-Bukhārī)

Sometimes we say things which we regret. A true believer should always think before they speak. If it is worthwhile, then speak, otherwise it is better to stay silent. In another ḥadīth our Beloved Messenger صلى الله عليه وسلم said that "He is saved who remained silent" (Tirmidhī), which means a person can be saved from many evils of this world and the Ākhirah if he just stays quiet. Today people communicate a great deal, especially through mobile phones and texts; we must think before we type or say something over the phone.

The mention of the Last Day is a reminder to us that every action and word will have to be accounted for on the Day of Judgement. Therefore we need to recall that we should speak only good, for any wrong things we utter may be held against us on the Day of Reckoning.

Good Character

Aḥadīth

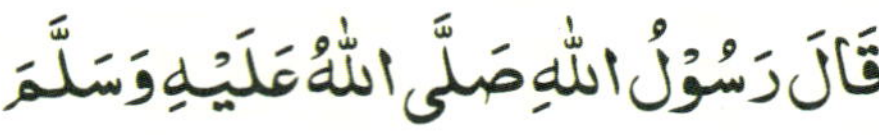

قَالَ رَسُوْلُ اللهِ صَلَّى اللهُ عَلَيْهِ وَسَلَّمَ

Our Beloved Messenger Muḥammad صلى الله عليه وسلم said:

إِنَّ مِنْ أَحَبِّكُمْ إِلَيَّ أَحْسَنُكُمْ أَخْلَاقًا

"Verily the dearest to me from amongst you are those who have the best character." (Ṣaḥīḥ al-Bukhārī)

A person who is dear to the Beloved Messenger Muḥammad صلى الله عليه وسلم is indeed dear to Allāh سبحانه وتعالى; a person who is dear to Allāh سبحانه وتعالى will surely enter Jannah.

Subḥānallāh, Allāh سبحانه وتعالى has made it so easy for us to enter Jannah; all we need to do is have good character, and the way to achieve that is to follow the Sunnah of our Beloved Messenger Muḥammad صلى الله عليه وسلم.

Muḥammad صلى الله عليه وسلم had the best manners. Anas رضي الله عنه says: "I served him for ten years, and he never said 'Uff' (an expression of dislike) to me. He never said 'why did you do that?' for something I had done, nor did he ever say 'why did you not do such-and-such' for something I had not done. (Ṣaḥīḥ al-Bukhārī)

Our Beloved Messenger صلى الله عليه وسلم never became angry for any personal reason. He left a beautiful example for us. It is through the good character of his Ṣaḥābah that Islām spread across the world. We must make an intention today, after learning this ḥadīth, that we will always follow the sunnah and show the best of character.

Sīrah

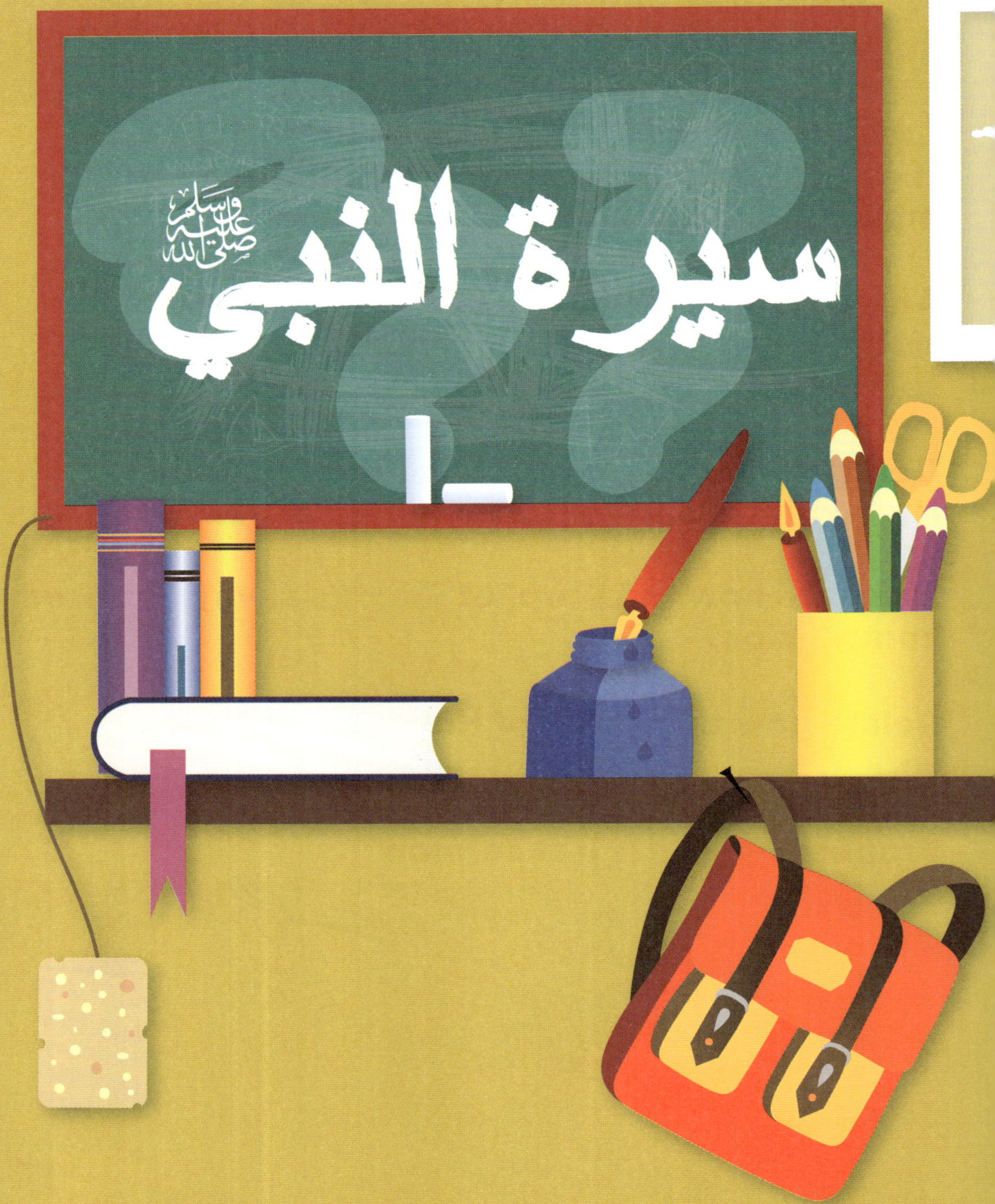

Learning Objectives

Sīrah

At the end of this unit pupils should be able to:

Create the link of the Treaty of Hudaybiyah to the ambassadors of Islām spreading the message across the Arabian Peninsula.

Analyse the finer points of the Treaty of Hudaybiyah where Islām gained and where a sacrifice was made.

Describe how the breaking of the Treaty of Hudaybiyah lead to the conquest of Makkah.

Illustrate how the Prophet صلى الله عليه وسلم always showed compassion.

Relate how the Battle of Ḥunayn occurred.

Recall the points brought forward in the Beloved Prophet صلى الله عليه وسلم 's last sermon.

Sīrah so far...

In the year following Isrā' and Mi'rāj, the twelfth year of Prophethood, a group of twelve people came from Yathrib (Madīnah). They pledged to believe in one Allāh and to attest that Muḥammad صلى الله عليه وسلم is His Messenger. They promised not to steal, kill, or to commit any other acts of evil. This pledge is known as the Pledge of 'Aqabah.

The Messenger صلى الله عليه وسلم sent Muṣ'ab ibn 'Umayr رضي الله عنه to Madīnah Munawwarah as the first Muslim teacher. The next year, during the pilgrimage season, Muṣ'ab ibn 'Umayr رضي الله عنه returned to Makkah along with seventy new Muslims.

After the second pledge of 'Aqabah, the Messenger صلى الله عليه وسلم announced that the Muslims of Makkah Mukarramah were to migrate (move) to Madīnah Munawwarah. This was called the 'Hijrah.' The Muslims left everything in Makkah and slowly, one at a time, or in small groups, began to migrate to Madīnah. The Quraysh saw it as their last chance to plot to kill our Beloved Messenger Muḥammad صلى الله عليه وسلم.

Sīrah

Allāh سبحانه وتعالى protected him and he صلى الله عليه وسلم arrived in Madīnah Munawwarah safely. There in Madīnah, our Beloved Messenger صلى الله عليه وسلم created mu'ākhāt (Islamic brotherhood) between the Anṣār and Muhājirūn.

The Battle of Badr took place in the second year of Hijrah in which many leaders of Quraysh, such as Abū Jahl, were killed. The following year, the Battle of Uḥud took place which was followed by the Battle of Aḥzāb in the fifth year after hijrah.

In Madīnah, there were some people who declared their Islām openly, but in their hearts they did not believe. These people were known as the 'Munāfiqūn.'

Our Beloved Messenger صلى الله عليه وسلم made treaties with the Jewish tribes that lived in Madīnah. They, however, broke these treaties and sided with the Quraysh to hurt our Beloved Messenger صلى الله عليه وسلم.

The Treaty of Ḥudaybiyah

Dhul-Qa'dah 6 AH

Sīrah

In the sixth year of Hijrah, the Messenger صلى الله عليه وسلم saw a dream in which he had entered the Ḥaram at Makkah with the Ṣaḥābah, and performed 'umrah. The Messenger صلى الله عليه وسلم informed the Ṣaḥābah of this dream and they were overtaken with joy. A prophet's dream is part of divine inspiration.

The Messenger صلى الله عليه وسلم set out for Makkah in the month of Dhul Qa'dah, with fourteen or fifteen hundred Muslims, with the intention of performing 'umrah. At a place called Dhul Ḥulayfah, he ordered that all the people enter the state of iḥrām: this made them safe from any attack.

The Messenger صلى الله عليه وسلم then moved on towards Makkah, but he was soon informed that the people of the city had blocked the way. Taking this new information into account, the Messenger صلى الله عليه وسلم changed his route and eventually camped at Ḥudaybiyah.

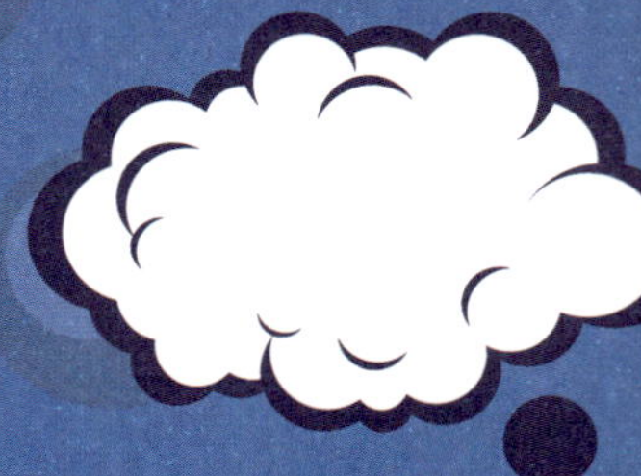

The Treaty of Ḥudaybiyah

The Quraysh sent a tribal chief by the name of Budayl to find out about the Prophet صلى الله عليه وسلم's intentions. The Messenger صلى الله عليه وسلم told him that they were there to perform 'umrah and not to fight. He returned to the Quraysh who were unwilling to let the Messenger صلى الله عليه وسلم enter Makkah.

Discussions between the Messenger صلى الله عليه وسلم and the Quraysh went on, but without success. The Messenger صلى الله عليه وسلم eventually decided to send 'Uthmān ibn 'Affān رضي الله عنه to Makkah on his behalf to talk to the nobles of Quraysh. 'Uthmān رضي الله عنه was chosen because he belonged to the most powerful family in Makkah and none would dare harm him.

'Uthmān رضي الله عنه arrived in Makkah and visited the nobles, informing them of the Prophet صلى الله عليه وسلم's intentions: he was there to perform 'umrah and worship in the sacred Ḥaram and had no intention of fighting. The Quraysh would not back down in refusing the Muslims permission to enter Makkah. They, however, granted 'Uthmān رضي الله عنه permission to perform 'umrah but he declined saying: "How is it I perform 'umrah whilst the Messenger صلى الله عليه وسلم is denied it?"

The Treaty of Ḥudaybiyah

Bay'ah ar-Riḍwān

'Uthmān رضي الله عنه's arrival back at the Muslim camp was delayed and a rumour spread that he had been murdered by the Quraysh. The Muslims were now worried for the safety of 'Uthmān رضي الله عنه. They took a promise at the hand of the Messenger صلى الله عليه وسلم that they would not turn back but fight till their death to avenge the murder of 'Uthmān رضي الله عنه.

This promise is known as Bay'ah ar-Riḍwān.

"Allāh was pleased with the believers when they were pledging allegiance with you (by placing their hands in your hands) under the tree, and He knew what was in their hearts, so He sent down tranquility upon them, and rewarded them with a victory, near at hand." (Qur'ān 48:18)

'Uthmān رضي الله عنه later returned safely. The Quraysh finally came to their senses and decided to come to an agreement with the Messenger صلى الله عليه وسلم. They sent Suhayl ibn 'Amr to make the agreement. It went as follows:

1. The Muslims would return to Madīnah without performing 'umrah. They would return next year to do 'umrah, but would only stay in Makkah for three days.

2. All war would be stopped between the two parties for ten years.

3. The Arab tribes were free to enter into friendship with whichever party they liked.

4. If any Muslim of Makkah was to go to Madīnah without the permission of his guardian, he must be sent back to Makkah, but should any Muslims return to the Quraysh, he would not be returned.

Miswar رضي الله عنه narrated the account of the treaty of Ḥudaybiyah in which 'Urwah came to the Prophet صلى الله عليه وسلم to negotiate its terms and when he returned to his people he said, "O people! By Allāh, I have been to the kings and to Qayṣar, Kisrā and Najāshī, yet I have never seen any of them respected by their people as much as Muḥammad is respected by his companions." (Ṣaḥīḥ al-Bukhārī)

The Message of Islām Spreads

Although this agreement seemed to be against the Muslims, Allāh سبحانه وتعالى brought much goodness out of the treaty. The Messenger صلى الله عليه وسلم was able to spread the Message of Islām not only in the Arabian Peninsula, but also in the courts of the kings. Messengers were chosen and despatched in all directions.

'Abdullāh ibn Ḥudhayfah رضي الله عنه took a letter of invitation to the court of the Persian king, the Khusrau. He became angered with the letter and tore it into pieces. When the Messenger صلى الله عليه وسلم heard what he had done, he said, "May Allāh tear his kingdom to pieces also." Soon after, his son murdered him and his kingdom was destroyed. Diḥyah ibn al-Kalbī رضي الله عنه was instructed to hand the letter of the Prophet صلى الله عليه وسلم to the Governor of Baṣrah who in turn would send it to Caesar, the Roman emperor.

Ḥaṭib ibn Abī Balta'ah رضي الله عنه was chosen to take the letter to the King of Egypt called Muqawqis. Other letters were sent out to the various rulers of Bahrain, Yamāmah, Damascus and Oman.

"It could be that you dislike something, when it is good for you; and it could be that you like something when it is bad for you. Allah knows, and you do not know." (Qur'ān 2:216)

'Umrah al-Qaḍā'

At the end of the seventh year of Hijrah, the Messenger صلى الله عليه وسلم set out for 'umrah along with the Ṣaḥābah as was agreed in the Treaty of Ḥudaybiyah the year before. The Messenger صلى الله عليه وسلم stayed in Makkah for three days then returned to Madīnah.

The Conquest of Makkah

According to the agreement made at Ḥudaybiyah, all Arab tribes were free to join into friendship with either the Muslims or the Quraysh. The tribe of Banū Bakr joined themselves with the Quraysh and the tribe of Khuzā'ah joined the Muslims. They lived in peace for a few years but soon the old hatred came up again. Banū Bakr attacked Khuzā'ah with the help of the Quraysh. The Khuzā'ah went into the Ḥaram for safety but the Ḥaram was not respected and many from the tribe of Khuzā'ah were killed.

The Quraysh were the first to break the agreement. Realising what they had done, they immediately sent Abū Sufyān to Madīnah to try and revive the treaty, but this did not work.

The Messenger صلى الله عليه وسلم immediately prepared to leave for Makkah. Every precaution was taken to keep the Quraysh unaware of the arrival of the Muslim army. On the 10th of Ramaḍān 8 AH, the Messenger صلى الله عليه وسلم left Madīnah with ten thousand soldiers. The Muslims camped at a place called Marruẓ Ẓahrān. Abū Sufyān came to investigate there in the evening, and met the Prophet صلى الله عليه وسلم's uncle 'Abbās رضي الله عنه before reaching the Messenger صلى الله عليه وسلم. He encouraged Abū Sufyān to accept Islām and persuade the Quraysh to surrender. Abū Sufyān then went to meet the Prophet صلى الله عليه وسلم along with 'Abbās رضي الله عنه. There, in the presence of the Messenger صلى الله عليه وسلم, Abū Sufyān accepted the faith he had rejected for so long.

The Conquest of Makkah

The Muslim army victoriously entered Makkah on the morning of Tuesday, 17th Ramaḍān 8 AH. The Quraysh all surrendered without any resistance.

They then gathered in the Ḥaram awaiting the arrival of the Messenger صلى الله عليه وسلم. He entered not like a triumphant, victorious conqueror, but as a humble servant with his head lowered. He knew full well that only Allāh سبحانه وتعالى had granted him victory in the holy city that had previously driven him out.

He now asked the Quraysh, "What do you expect at my hands?" They replied, "Kindness and piety, O gracious brother, gracious nephew."

The Messenger صلى الله عليه وسلم replied, "So be it. There shall be no revenge. May Allāh سبحانه وتعالى forgive you, and he is the most Merciful of those who show mercy."

The Messenger صلى الله عليه وسلم purified the Ka'bah of the 360 idols that lay within it by making sure that they were all destroyed.

Read this chapter carefully and think! Look at how much the Messenger صلى الله عليه وسلم went through from the beginning till this day. Today, he has all the power over the people who hurt him, and drove him and his Ṣaḥābah out of the city, and what did he do? Did he take revenge? No! He forgave them. Subḥānallāh. We must also learn to forgive other people and not to keep hatred in our hearts.

The Battle of Ḥunayn

After the Quraysh had all accepted Islām, the nearby tribes of Hawāzin and Thaqīf rejected. They thought of themselves as being higher. The chief of the Hawāzin, Mālik ibn 'Awf invited the neighbouring tribes and raised a huge army to harm Islām. When the Messenger صلى الله عليه وسلم received the news of this threat, he prepared an army of 12,000 men, which included 2,000 Quraysh, and they marched towards the valley of Ḥunayn.

Some people in the Muslim army felt proud thinking that they could never be beaten because they had such a large army. Allāh سبحانه وتعالى did not like this and wanted to show them that it is Allāh سبحانه وتعالى alone who grants victory regardless of appearance and numbers.

At dawn, the Muslim army advanced in to the valley: awaiting them there was the army of Hawāzin.

The Battle of Ḥunayn

They were renowned for their skill in archery and they showered arrow after arrow upon the Muslim army. This caused great confusion and disorder amongst the Muslim ranks. The Muslims retreated.

As for the Messenger صلى الله عليه وسلم, he stood firm and called out, "I am the Messenger undoubtedly; I am the (grand) son of 'Abdul Muṭṭalib." Those who stood firm beside him were a few kinsmen and emigrants.

The Prophet صلى الله عليه وسلم ordered his uncle, 'Abbās رضي الله عنه, to call out to the Believers to return to the battlefield. The test from Allāh سبحانه وتعالى was over and the enemy was then quickly defeated.

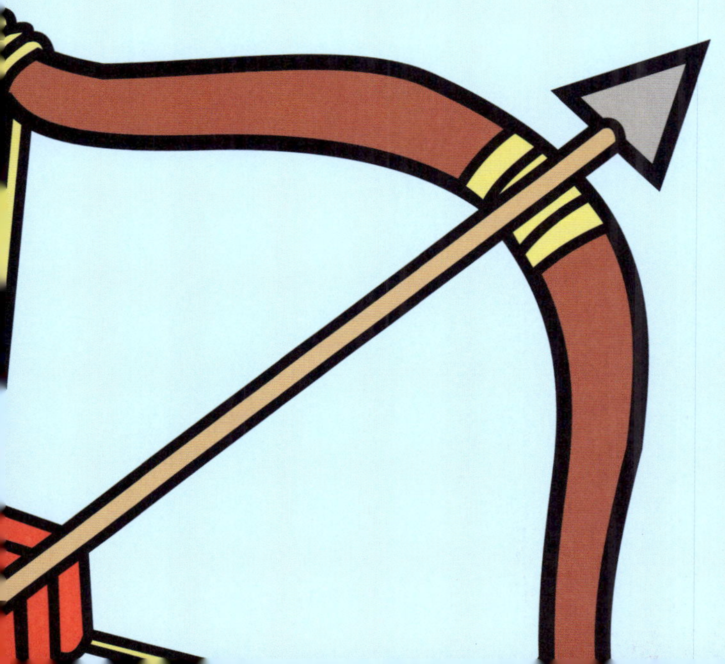

The March to Tabūk

The growing power of Islām was a discomfort for the Roman ruler of Syria. He decided to crush this growing power in the Arabian Peninsula. To do this he gathered a huge army.

Sirah

The news of this great army gathering on the border reached Madīnah, by way of merchants who arrived from Syria. This had an adverse effect on its residents. Muslims were now in constant fear of the arrival of this enormous army.

The Messenger صلى الله عليه وسلم saw the enormity of the situation, and ordered the Muslims to prepare for battle. He sent for the Quraysh and other Arab tribes asking for assistance.

The Messenger صلى الله عليه وسلم told the people of their intended destination before their departure, which was contrary to his habit, so that they may fully prepare for the long hard journey which was before them in the heat of the summer.

The March to Tabūk

30,000 men were ready to go and defend their faith. The Messenger صلى الله عليه وسلم encouraged the Companions to give generously in the way of Allāh سبحانه وتعالى. 'Uthman رضي الله عنه gave 10,000 dinars (gold coins) and 3,000 camels. 'Umar رضي الله عنه gave half of his entire wealth to the cause. Abū Bakr رضي الله عنه came before the Prophet صلى الله عليه وسلم and gave everything he owned, and when the Prophet صلى الله عليه وسلم asked him what he had left for his family, he replied, "Allāh and his Messenger صلى الله عليه وسلم."

The Muslim army left Madīnah and marched towards Tabūk. Upon learning of the Muslim army advancing, the Romans and their allies turned back and fled into their own territory. The Prophet صلى الله عليه وسلم stayed in Tabūk for twenty days where he made treaties with local tribes. He then returned to Madīnah: this was to be the Prophet صلى الله عليه وسلم's last expedition.

The Farewell Pilgrimage

In the tenth year of Hijrah, the Messenger صلى الله عليه وسلم announced his intention to perform ḥajj. People from all over Arabia gathered to perform the ḥajj with the Prophet of Allāh صلى الله عليه وسلم. On a Saturday of the last four days of Dhul Qa'dah, the Messenger صلى الله عليه وسلم departed from Madīnah. He arrived in Makkah on the morning of Sunday, the fourth of Dhul Ḥijjah. During the ḥajj, at 'Arafah he addressed 124,000 companions.

Read this page carefully as this is part of the Last Sermon which was one of the last advices of the Messenger صلى الله عليه وسلم given to us, his ummah.

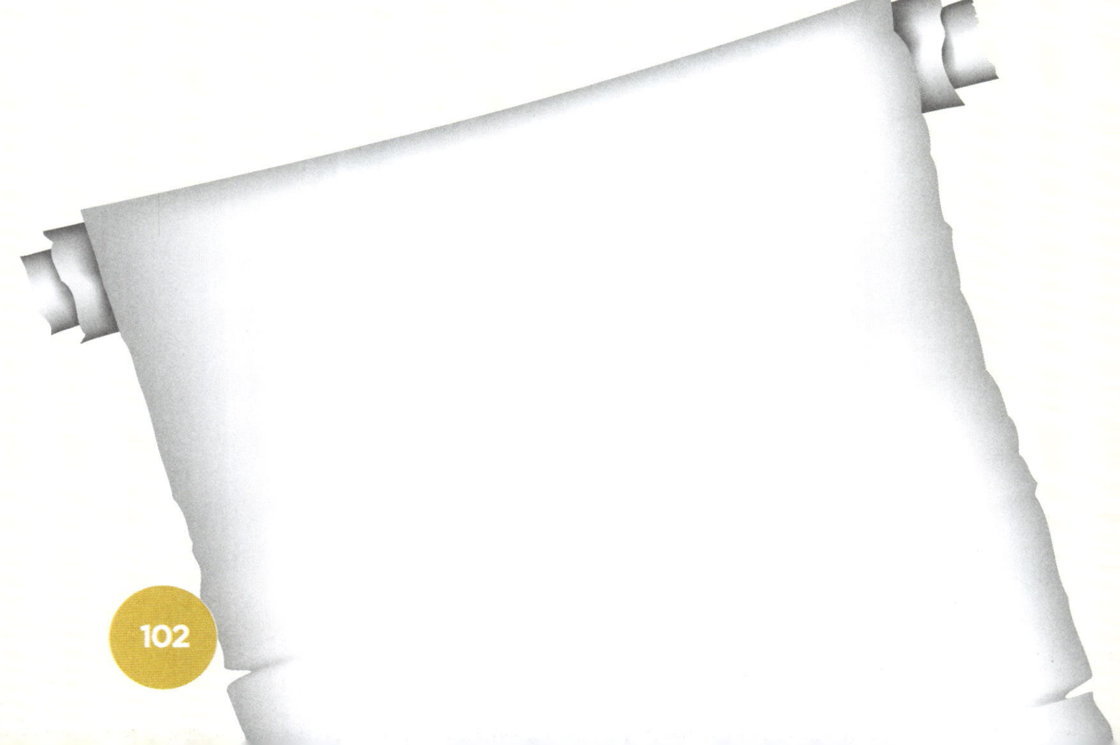

The Farewell Pilgrimage

"O people, listen carefully for I know not whether I shall be with you after this year. Therefore, pass the words on to those who are not here today. O people, just as you respect this day, this month, and this city, similarly respect the life and property of every Muslim. Return the things entrusted to you. Hurt no one so no one may hurt you. Remember that you will indeed meet your Lord and He will ask you about what you did. Beware of Shayṭān for the safety of your religion.

O people, it is true that you have certain rights over your women but they also have rights over you. Remember that you have taken them as your wives only under Allāh's trust and with His permission. If they abide by your right then to them belongs the right to be fed and clothed in kindness. Do treat your women well and be kind to them, for they are your committed helpers. And it is your right that they do not make friends with anyone of whom you do not approve, as well as never to be unchaste. O people, listen to me carefully: worship Allāh, perform your daily prayers, fast during the month of Ramaḍān, and give your wealth in zakāh. Perform ḥajj if you can afford to.

All mankind is from Ādam and Ḥawwā'. No Arab has any superiority over a black or a black over any white, except through piety and good action. Learn that every Muslim is a brother to every Muslim and that the Muslims make one brotherhood. O people, no prophet or messenger will come after me and no new faith will be born. I leave behind me two things: the Qur'ān and my Sunnah, and if you follow these you will never go astray."

The Farewell Pilgrimage

Sīrah

At the end he asked them, "All of you will be asked about me. What will you say?" They replied, "We bear witness that you have conveyed the message and fulfilled your mission." The Messenger صلى الله عليه وسلم raised his forefinger skywards and then moved it down towards the people saying, "O Allāh! Bear witness."

After sunset, the Prophet صلى الله عليه وسلم arrived in Muzdalifah where he spent the night. In the morning he set out for Minā where he completed the ḥajj. He stayed in Minā for the 11th, 12th and 13th of Dhul Ḥijjah. Upon completing the rituals of ḥajj, the Messenger صلى الله عليه وسلم headed for Madīnah.

The Messenger of Allāh صلى الله عليه وسلم Leaves the World

The Messenger صلى الله عليه وسلم returned from Makkah. He saw his mission successful. From the trials and torture of Makkah, from being driven out of his home city, to this happy victorious day, the Beloved Messenger صلى الله عليه وسلم had been through much and now it was time to meet his Lord, Allāh سبحانه وتعالى.

Being a human, it was time for him to leave this world, and the Messenger صلى الله عليه وسلم sadly fell severely ill at the end of Ṣafar in the eleventh year of hijrah.

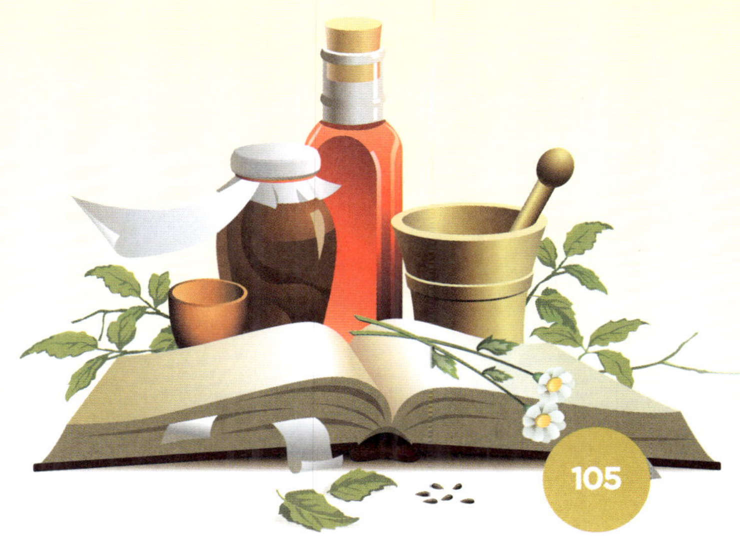

The Messenger of Allāh صلى الله عليه وسلم Leaves the World

The Ṣaḥābah were greatly worried and could not bear to think of what might happen to their Beloved Messenger صلى الله عليه وسلم who had been more compassionate and kind than a father to them. He had taken the whole of humanity as his own; the thought of separation was unbearable.

The illness increased and the hearts of those around him began to cry. It was on a Monday, the 12th of Rabi' al-Awwal, 11 years after the migration to Madīnah from Makkah, that the kindest man on earth left this world. It was the saddest day. The Ṣaḥābah were in extreme shock and they did not know how to take the news to their hearts.

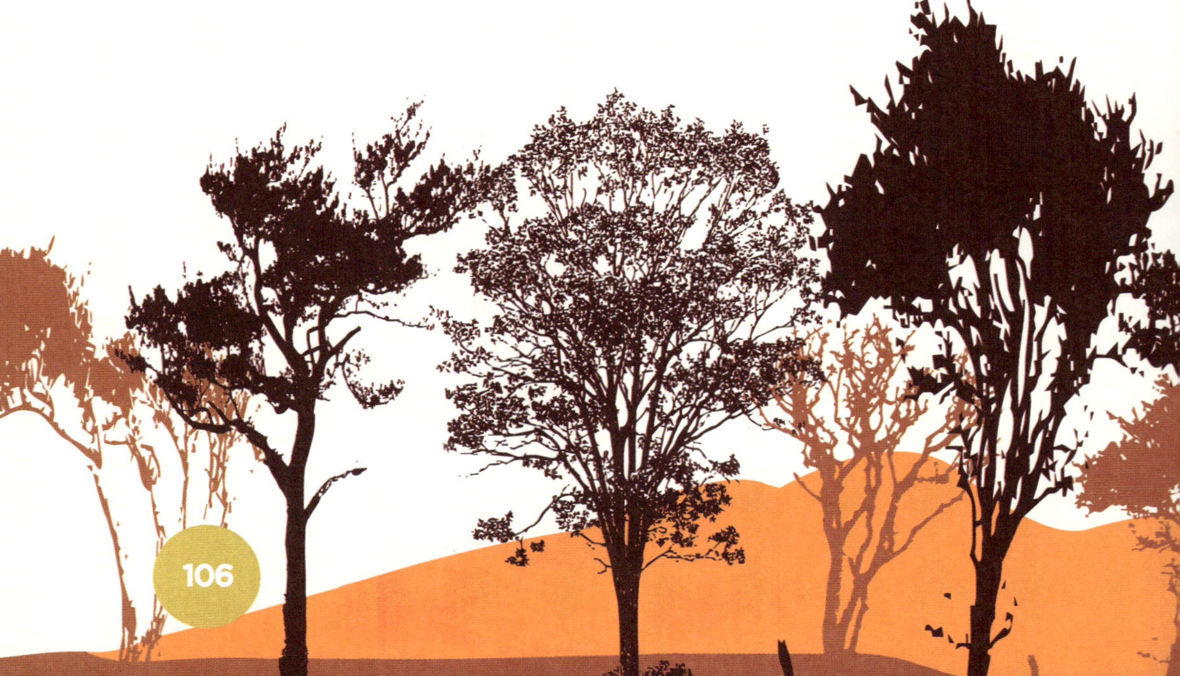

The Messenger of Allāh صلى الله عليه وسلم Leaves the World

Finally Abū Bakr رضي الله عنه gained strength and took hold of the situation by addressing all the Ṣaḥābah. He explained that Muḥammad صلى الله عليه وسلم was a human and that the messengers that came before him had also passed away.

"Muhammad is but a messenger, there have been messengers before him. So, if he dies or is killed, would you turn back on your heels? Whoever turns back on his heels can never harm Allāh in the least. Allāh shall soon reward the grateful." (Qur'ān 3:144)

إِنَّا لِلّٰهِ وَإِنَّا إِلَيْهِ رَاجِعُوْنَ

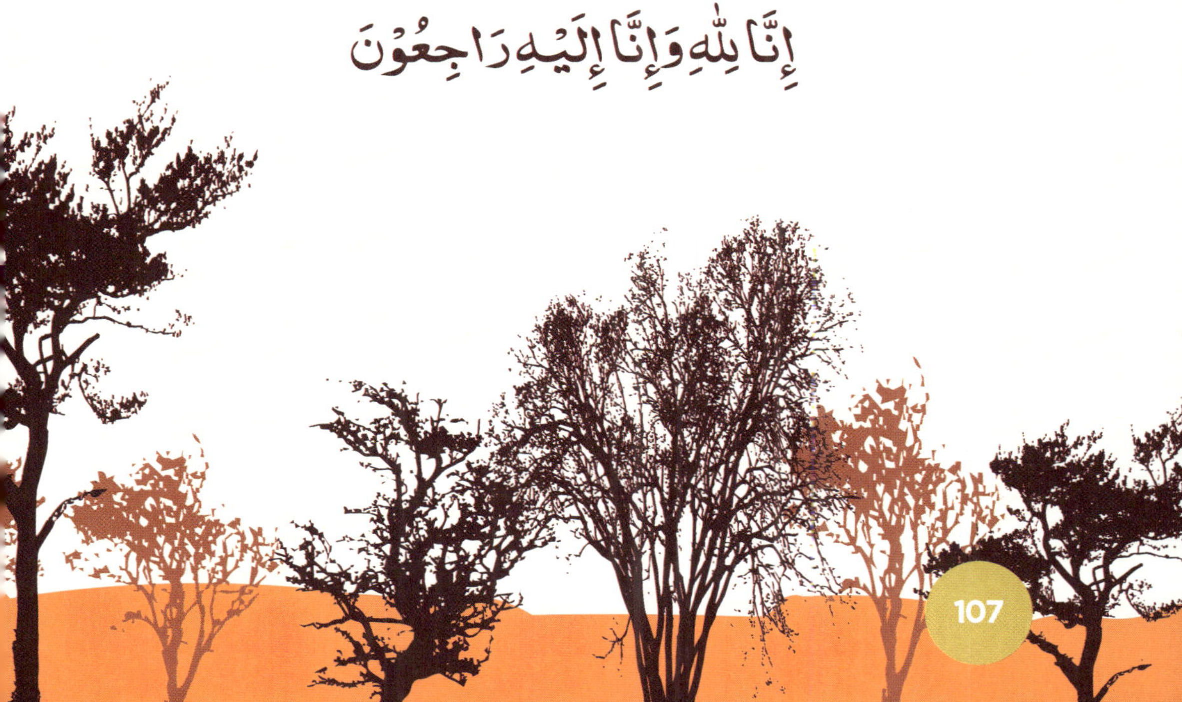

Tārīkh

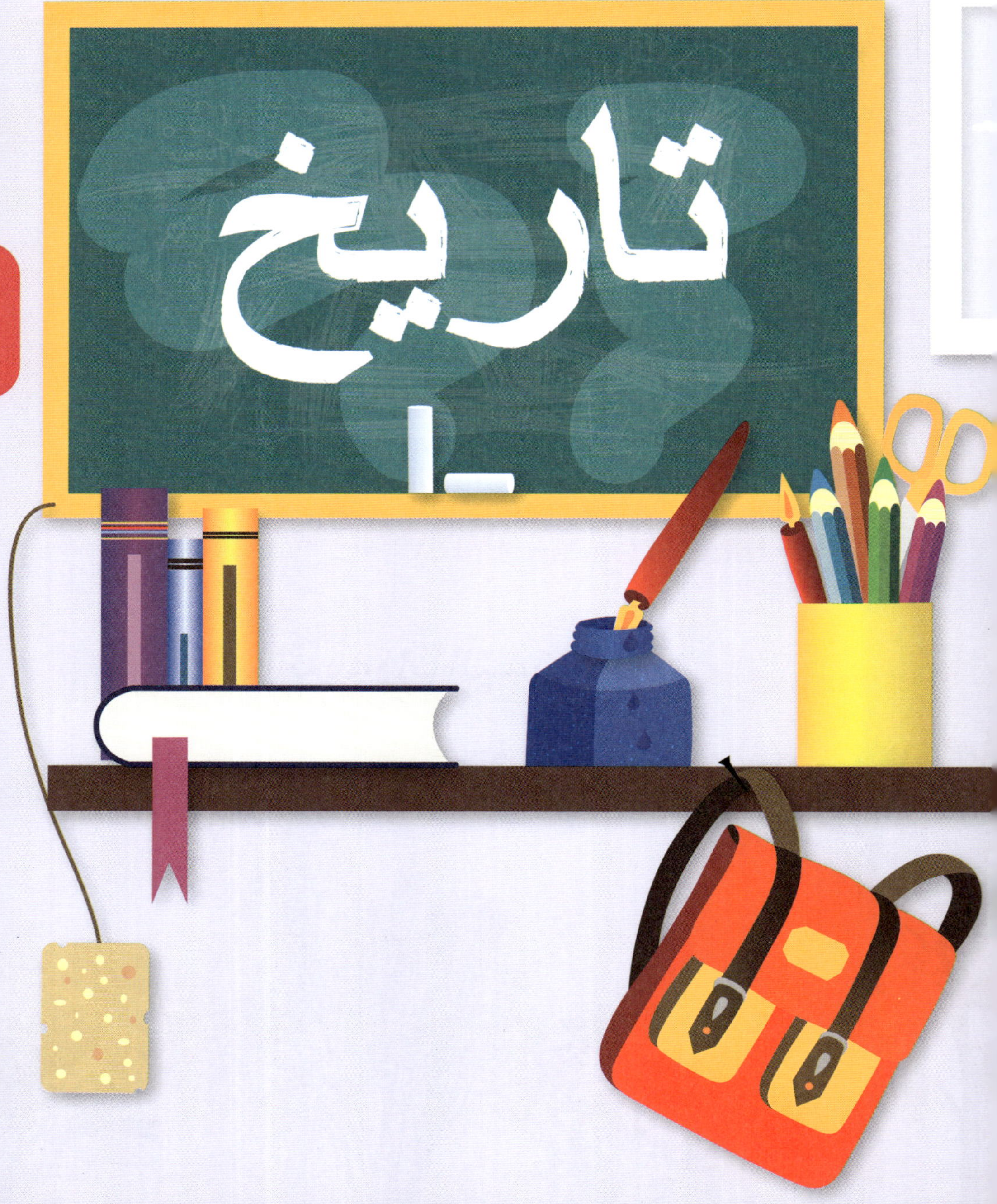

Learning Objectives

Tārīkh

At the end of this unit pupils should be able to:

Explain how Allāh سبحانه وتعالى returned Mūsā عليه السلام to his mother.

Describe how Mūsā عليه السلام had to take shelter outside Egypt.

Describe the miracles bestowed upon Mūsā عليه السلام from Allāh سبحانه وتعالى.

Illustrate how Fir'awn's arrogance lead to his destruction.

Summarise the events that led to the miraculous birth of 'Īsā عليه السلام.

List the miracles given to 'Īsā عليه السلام.

State our beliefs in regards to 'Īsā عليه السلام.

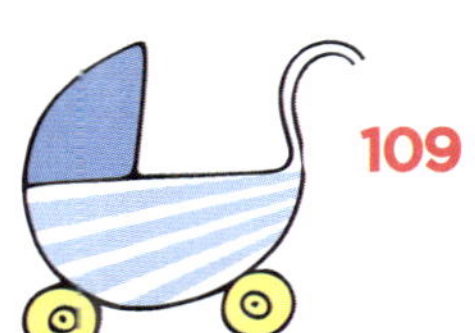

Mūsā عليه السلام

The brothers of Yūsuf عليه السلام stayed in Egypt and since their father Ya'qūb عليه السلام was known as Isrā'īl, they and their progeny came to be known as the Banū Isrā'īl (the children of Isrā'īl). The other people who lived in Egypt became known as the Qibṭī (Coptics). The Qibṭīs used to look down on the Banū Isrā'īl.

The Qibṭīs were the rulers of Egypt. Their leader was called Fir'awn, and he was a very evil king who claimed to be the Lord and commanded people to worship him. One day, some people told him that a child would be born among the Banū Isrā'īl who would destroy his kingdom. When Fir'awn heard of this he became furious and began killing all the male children that were born to the Banū Isrā'īl.

When the mother of Mūsā عليه السلام gave birth to him, she was very worried about his life. Allāh سبحانه وتعالى inspired her to place baby Mūsā عليه السلام in a basket and put him in the river. Allāh سبحانه وتعالى strengthened her heart for this.

Mūsā عليه السلام

Fir'awn and his wife, Āsiyah, were walking on the bank of the river when they spotted a basket floating towards them. They opened it and were shocked to see a young boy inside. Fir'awn immediately ordered that the boy be killed in case he was the boy the people had warned him about.

Āsiyah pleaded with Fir'awn saying:
"He will be a coolness of the eyes for me and for you. Don't kill him. He may be of benefit to us, or we may adopt him as our son." (Qur'ān 28:9)

Mūsā عليه السلام's sister was following the box and she saw that it had been picked up by Fir'awn. The baby became hungry. It would not take milk from any lady. Mūsā عليه السلام's sister stepped forward and said, "I know of a very good lady who will be able to give this child milk."

Mūsā عليه السلام's mother was called and immediately Mūsā عليه السلام began drinking milk from her. Fir'awn asked her to take him and return him after a couple of years when he was able to eat food.

Look how Allāh سبحانه وتعالى returned Mūsā عليه السلام to his mother.

Mūsā عليه السلام

After a few years Mūsā عليه السلام was returned to the palace of Fir'awn where he grew up and saw how his people were mistreated. They would have to do all the work for the Qibṭīs. Mūsā عليه السلام was very strong.

One day Mūsā عليه السلام was walking in the market and saw a fight between a Qibṭī and a man from his people, the Banū Isrā'īl. The Isrā'īlī asked Mūsā عليه السلام for help. Mūsā عليه السلام struck the Qibṭī. The strength of Mūsā عليه السلام was so intense that the Qibṭī died immediately.

Mūsā عليه السلام was very upset as he did not intend to kill the Qibṭī at all. News spread that a man from the people of Fir'awn had been killed by a man from the Banū Isrā'īl.

The next day Mūsā عليه السلام saw the same person from his tribe fighting and knew that this person was the one who was starting the fights. When Mūsā عليه السلام tried to stop the Qibṭī, the man from Banū Isrā'īl became worried that Mūsā عليه السلام will reprimand him for his actions so he said loudly, "O Mūsā! Will you kill me as you killed a person yesterday?" (Qur'ān 28:19) The people heard this and the news got to Fir'awn's palace that it was Mūsā عليه السلام who had killed the Qibṭī.

Mūsā عليه السلام

Mūsā عليه السلام left Egypt in fear, looking over his shoulder, as word had reached him that Fir'awn was looking to kill him. He arrived in the city of Madyan, and saw upon entering the city that some people were giving water to their animals. The Qur'ān mentions this and what happened later in great detail:

'And when he arrived at the water of Madyan he found there a group of men watering (their flocks), and besides them he found two women who were keeping back (their flocks). He said: "What is the matter with you?" They said: "We cannot water (our flocks) until the shepherds take (their flocks). And our father is a very old man." So he watered (their flocks) for them, then he turned back to a shade, and said: "My Lord! truly, I am in need of whatever good that You bestow on me!"

Then there came to him one of the two women, walking shyly. She said: "Verily, my father calls you that he may reward you for having watered (our flocks) for us."

The father who was Shu'ayb عليه السلام talked to Mūsā عليه السلام and reassured him by telling him not to fear as he had escaped from the wrong-doers.

Mūsā عليه السلام

One of the daughters suggested to her father to hire Mūsā عليه السلام so he could help the family as he was strong and trustworthy. Shu'ayb عليه السلام saw Mūsā عليه السلام had great qualities and decided to ask Mūsā عليه السلام to marry one of his daughters. He said: "I intend to wed one of these two daughters of mine to you, on condition that you serve me for eight years, but if you complete ten years, it will be (a favour) from you. But I intend not to place you under a difficulty. If Allāh سبحانه وتعالى wills, you will find me one of the righteous." (Qur'ān 28:27) Mūsā عليه السلام agreed to this and fulfilled the term.

Sometime after, he was travelling with his family back to Egypt. They left on a cold dark night but got lost on the way. Mūsā عليه السلام saw a fire which was, in actual fact, nūr (Divine Light) in the direction of Mount Ṭūr. He stopped his family and notified them that he had seen a fire and perhaps he may bring news or something to warm them. Mūsā عليه السلام went close to the direction of the fire and was called from the right side of the valley, in the blessed place from the tree: "O Mūsā! Verily I am Allāh the Lord of the 'Ālamīn (mankind, jinn and all that exists)." (Qur'ān 28:30)

Allāh سبحانه وتعالى spoke to Mūsā عليه السلام and selected him to be a messenger to the people of Fir'awn. Mūsā عليه السلام was ordered to throw his stick which turned into a snake. Mūsā عليه السلام became afraid but was reassured by Allāh سبحانه وتعالى.

Mūsā عليه السلام

Then Mūsā عليه السلام was told to put his hand under his arm: when he did it came out shining.

These were the two main signs Allāh سبحانه وتعالى granted Mūsā عليه السلام. Miracles were always given to the prophets according to the time. At that time magic was very common. Allāh سبحانه وتعالى gave Mūsā عليه السلام such a miracle that the magicians could not match.

Allāh سبحانه وتعالى commanded Mūsā عليه السلام to invite Fir'awn and his people to Allāh سبحانه وتعالى as they had become very rebellious; they were not accepting the truth and continued hurting people.

Mūsā عليه السلام had become fearful that the Coptics would come and kill him as he had accidentally killed one of their people.

He spoke to Allāh سبحانه وتعالى about his fears and then said "My brother Hārūn, he is more eloquent in speech than me, so send him with me as a helper to confirm me. I fear that they will not listen to me." (Qur'ān 28:34)

Allāh سبحانه وتعالى accepted this request and Mūsā عليه السلام along with his brother Hārūn were sent to Fir'awn.

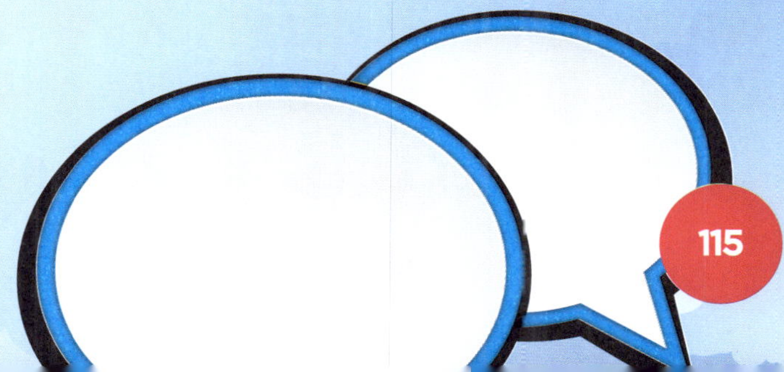

Mūsā عليه السلام

When he arrived back at Fir'awn's palace, now as a messenger, Fir'awn said, "What is this? This is nothing but magic!" (Qur'ān 28:36) Fir'awn was very arrogant and said to Hāmān, his chief advisor, "Build for me a block of towers so I can peek to the Lord of Mūsā عليه السلام for I think he is lying." (Qur'ān 28:38) Fir'awn placed a challenge before Mūsā عليه السلام: to compete with all his magicians to see who would win!

The day was set and everyone gathered to see what would happen. Many magicians arrived for the challenge. They asked Fir'awn "Will we get a reward if we win?" (Qur'ān 26:41) Fir'awn said, "Yes! Indeed and you will also become amongst my close ones." (Qur'ān 26:42)

The magicians asked Mūsā عليه السلام, "Will you go first or shall we?" (Qur'ān 20:65) Mūsā عليه السلام told them to go first. They placed their ropes and said, "With the honour of Fir'awn, we shall be victorious." (Qur'ān 26:44) Mūsā عليه السلام felt a little fear in his heart. Allāh سبحانه وتعالى told him not to worry as His help was with him.

When Allāh سبحانه وتعالى sends a messenger, he grants them miracles that challenge the people of the time and what is common amongst them. For the people of Egypt, this was magic. Allāh سبحانه وتعالى gave Mūsā عليه السلام such a miracle which overpowered all their illusions and magic.

Mūsā عليه السلام

Mūsā عليه السلام threw his stick and it turned into a huge python which ate all the small snakes up. These small snakes were the results of illusions the other magicians had put before the people. When the magicians saw Mūsā عليهما السلام working with Allāh سبحانه وتعالى's help, they knew this was not magic. This was something far more powerful than any kind of magic. They all at once fell into prostration to Allāh سبحانه وتعالى and said altogether, "We have believed in the Lord of Hārūn and Mūsā عليهما السلام." (Qur'ān 20:70)

Fir'awn was furious. He stood up and sat down, then stood up again and sat down. He said, "Have you believed before I gave you permission? I will surely cut off your hands and legs in opposite directions!"

The magicians had seen something which had made them understand that this life is so short, and the life to come in the Ākhirah is the real life. They said to Fir'awn, "Do as you please for we have turned to Allāh سبحانه وتعالى in repentance to him for all the evil you forced us to do. You can only hurt us in this world. The Ākhirah is everlasting." Allāh سبحانه وتعالى had protected Mūsā عليه السلام and shown the people the power of Allāh سبحانه وتعالى. Fir'awn was very angry after this defeat and so increased the torture of the Banū Isrā'īl.

Mūsā عليه السلام

Allāh سبحانه وتعالى commanded Mūsā عليه السلام to speak kindly to Fir'awn, even though he was so evil. But when he did not take heed and continued to rebel along with the Qibṭīs oppressing the Banū Isrā'īl, Allāh سبحانه وتعالى sent a series of signs and punishments. The Qur'ān tells us of these:

Allāh سبحانه وتعالى sent down a flood, locusts, lice, frogs, and blood coming one after the other. Regardless of these punishments Fir'awn and his people remained arrogant and continued sinning.

When the punishments occurred they would tell Mūsā عليه السلام to pray to Allāh سبحانه وتعالى so he would remove the punishment from them and after this the people said they would believe in Allāh سبحانه وتعالى and they would stop tormenting the Banū Isrā'īl.

However, they lied. When Allāh سبحانه وتعالى removed the punishment they broke their word. Allāh سبحانه وتعالى then commanded Mūsā عليه السلام to take the Banū Isrā'īl to the Blessed Land and away from the oppression of Fir'awn. Allāh سبحانه وتعالى wanted the Banū Isrā'īl to be free from the oppression of Fir'awn and his people. Mūsā عليه السلام took them all with him.

Mūsā عليه السلام

When Fir'awn found out that they had all gone, he prepared his army and set out to chase them. The Banū Isrā'īl reached a dead end! In front of them they saw the sea and behind them they could hear the hooves of the approaching horses coming to attack. They said, "We have been caught." Mūsā عليه السلام reassured them by saying, "Never! My Lord is with me, he shall guide me." With the command of Allāh سبحانه وتعالى Mūsā عليه السلام hit the water with his stick and suddenly twelve pathways opened up, one for each tribe of the Banū Isrā'īl.

When Fir'awn arrived he said, "Look how the water has opened for me." He went into the pathways with his whole army thinking he was going to reach the Banū Isrā'īl. When they got to the middle, Allāh سبحانه وتعالى commanded the waters to come crashing down on them: he and his army were drowned. Such was the end of the king who called himself God.

Allāh سبحانه وتعالى had saved the Banū Isrā'īl from the evil of Fir'awn. The water threw the body out of the sea and Allāh سبحانه وتعالى said: "So this day We shall save your (dead) body that you may be a sign to those who come after you! And verily, many among mankind are heedless of Our signs." (Qur'ān 10:92)

The Banū Isrā'īl were saved from the plots of Fir'awn. Allāh سبحانه وتعالى then revealed the Tawrāh to Mūsā عليه السلام.

'Īsā عليه السلام

There lived among the Banū Isrā'īl, a man named 'Imrān. 'Imrān and his wife Hannah longed for a child of their own. They vowed to dedicate this child for the service of Masjid al Aqṣā. Allāh سبحانه وتعالى answered their prayers and blessed them with a daughter whom they named Maryam. Maryam was placed under the care of her uncle, Zakariyyā عليه السلام, who was a prophet.

One day, when he visited Maryam رضي الله عنها in her chamber inside Masjid Al Aqṣā, he saw fruits that were not available at that time. He asked her in amazement, "O Maryam how did you get these?" She replied, "They are from my Lord."

Upon seeing this, Zakariyyā عليه السلام asked Allāh سبحانه وتعالى to bless him with a child of his own too. For he saw that Maryam was receiving fruits which were not in season, so Allāh سبحانه وتعالى could definitely bless him with a child in his old age.

Allāh سبحانه وتعالى answered his prayers and blessed him with a son called Yaḥyā. Yaḥyā was a very pious boy who was blessed with prophethood too. May Allāh سبحانه وتعالى send mercy on Zakariyyā and Yaḥyā عليهما السلام, and may Allāh سبحانه وتعالى send mercy on all the messengers.

'Īsā عليه السلام

Maryam رضي الله عنها grew up to be a very pious and chaste lady. She was dedicated to the worship of her Creator. One day, an angel approached her and said, "Allāh سبحانه وتعالى is going to bless you with a child without you ever marrying." This was to be a miracle of Allāh سبحانه وتعالى on the Earth. For Allāh سبحانه وتعالى, nothing is impossible. He created Ādam عليه السلام without a mother and father so why can't he create a child without a father?

Maryam رضي الله عنها was worried about what the people would say. She felt the time approach for the baby to come, so she took rest under a date tree.

Allāh سبحانه وتعالى said to her: "Do not grieve; your Lord has placed a stream beneath you. Shake the trunk of the palm-tree towards yourself, and it will drop upon you ripe fresh dates." (Qur'ān 19:24-25)

Maryam رضي الله عنها was also told that if she met anyone she should say to them "I have promised to keep a fast for Allāh سبحانه وتعالى so I will not talk with any human being."

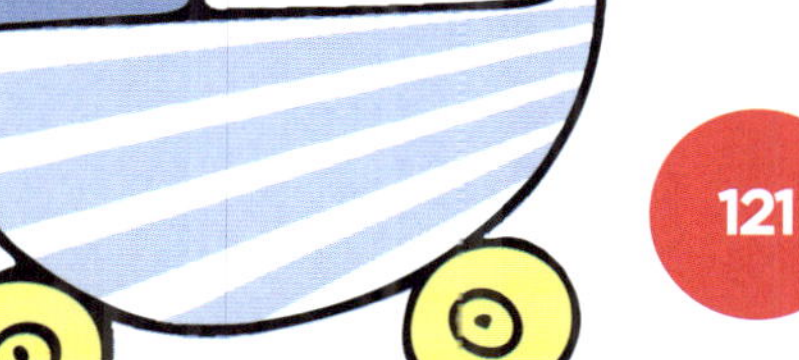

'Īsā عليه السلام

The people were shocked, for they knew Maryam رضي الله عنها was not married - so how could she have had a child? The Angel Jibra'īl عليه السلام had told her to point at the child if people questioned her. Maryam pointed at the baby and Allāh سبحانه وتعالى willed for 'Īsā عليه السلام to talk whilst he was still in the cradle.

He said: "Verily I am the servant of Allāh. He has given me the Book, and made me a Prophet, And He has made me a blessed one wherever I be, and has enjoined ṣalāh and zakāh upon me as long as I am alive, and (He has made me) good to my mother, and he did not make me oppressive (or) ill-fated. And peace is upon me the day I was born, the day I shall die, and the day I shall be raised alive again."

The people were even more shocked when they heard this, a baby speaking! This was clearly a miracle of 'Īsā عليه السلام.

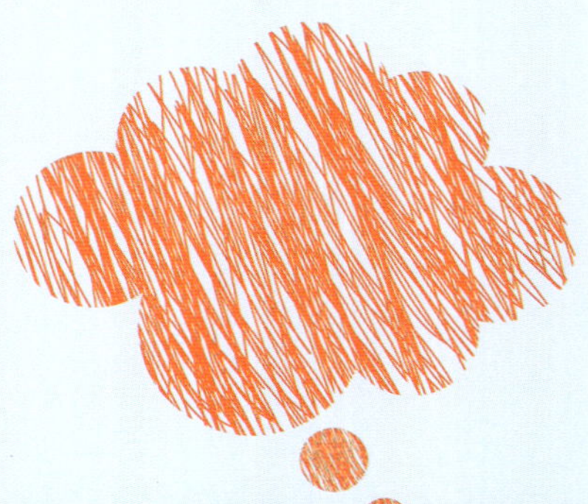

'Īsā عليه السلام

As 'Īsā عليه السلام grew up, evil had spread all around him, and the people had forgotten the message brought to them by Mūsā عليه السلام and other prophets; they had become corrupt. 'Īsā عليه السلام invited them to the worship of Allāh سبحانه وتعالى; he explained to them the message of Allāh سبحانه وتعالى. But they did not like what he said. Allāh سبحانه وتعالى blessed 'Īsā عليه السلام with many miracles. Allāh سبحانه وتعالى mentions the story of 'Īsā عليه السلام, along with the miracles He gave 'Īsā عليه السلام, in the Qur'ān:

"I have come to you with a sign from your Lord, that is, I create for you from clay something in the shape of a bird, then I blow in it, and it becomes a living bird by the will of Allāh سبحانه وتعالى; and I cure the born-blind and the leper, and I cause the dead to become alive by the will of Allāh سبحانه وتعالى; and I inform you of what you eat and what you store in your homes. In this there is surely a sign for you if you are believers." (Qur'ān 3:49)

Through the permission of Allāh سبحانه وتعالى 'Īsā عليه السلام could do all these things. 'Īsā عليه السلام came and told the people to worship the one Allāh and not associate partners with him. When he sensed they were not listening, he asked "Who are my helpers for the sake of Allāh سبحانه وتعالى?"

A group of people who were known as Ḥawāriyyūn (the disciples) listened to him said "We are the helpers of (the dīn of) Allāh سبحانه وتعالى. We believe in Allāh سبحانه وتعالى; so be our witness that we are Muslims. Our Lord, we have believed in what You have revealed, and we have followed the Messenger. So, record us with those who bear witness (to the Truth)". (Qur'ān 3:52-53)

'Īsā عليه السلام

When the leaders saw that some people were following 'Īsā عليه السلام, they felt threatened. They worried that their grip over weaker and poorer people would weaken. So they went to the Roman leaders and warned them, saying that if they did not stop 'Īsā عليه السلام, he would soon take over their kingdom. They gathered and surrounded the house of 'Īsā عليه السلام so that they could send a guard to arrest him.

Tārīkh

"They (the opponents of 'Īsā عليه السلام) devised a plan, and Allāh devised a plan. And Allāh is the best of all planners." (Qur'ān 3:54)

Allāh raised 'Īsā عليه السلام up to the heavens and changed the face of the guard so that he looked like 'Īsā عليه السلام. When a group of soldiers who had been waiting outside, to make 'Īsā عليه السلام's arrest complete, grew impatient they chose to barge into the house. Thinking this guard was 'Īsā عليه السلام, they seized and crucified him. He screamed that he was not 'Īsā عليه السلام, but they took this as normal practice: an arrested person usually chants his innocence.

We are told in the Qur'ān that 'Īsā عليه السلام was not killed nor crucified. The people were deluded by resemblance. The people who argued about this matter were unsure themselves. They had no knowledge of it. It has been made very clear to us that 'Īsā عليه السلام was not killed. Instead Allāh سبحانه وتعالى lifted him towards Himself. Allāh سبحانه وتعالى is All-Mighty, All-Wise.

'Īsā عليه السلام

'Īsā عليه السلام will one day come back to Earth near the time of the Day of Judgement. He will come back as a follower of our Beloved Messenger Muḥammad صلى الله عليه وسلم. He will kill the Dajjāl and live in the world for a period of time after which he shall die a physical death and be buried next to our Beloved Messenger Muḥammad صلى الله عليه وسلم, in Madīnah Munawwarah.

Here are some important points to remember in regards to our belief of 'Īsā عليه السلام:

- 'Īsā عليه السلام is one of the great messengers of Allāh سبحانه وتعالى. He was a human just like all the prophets.
- 'Īsā عليه السلام was born miraculously without a father. His mother Maryam رضي الله عنها was a virgin and never married.
- Like all messengers, 'Īsā عليه السلام performed many miracles through the help of Allāh سبحانه وتعالى.
- 'Īsā عليه السلام has not died a physical death nor was he killed or crucified. Almighty Allāh سبحانه وتعالى raised him whilst he was alive into the heavens where he is to this day.

‘Aqā’id

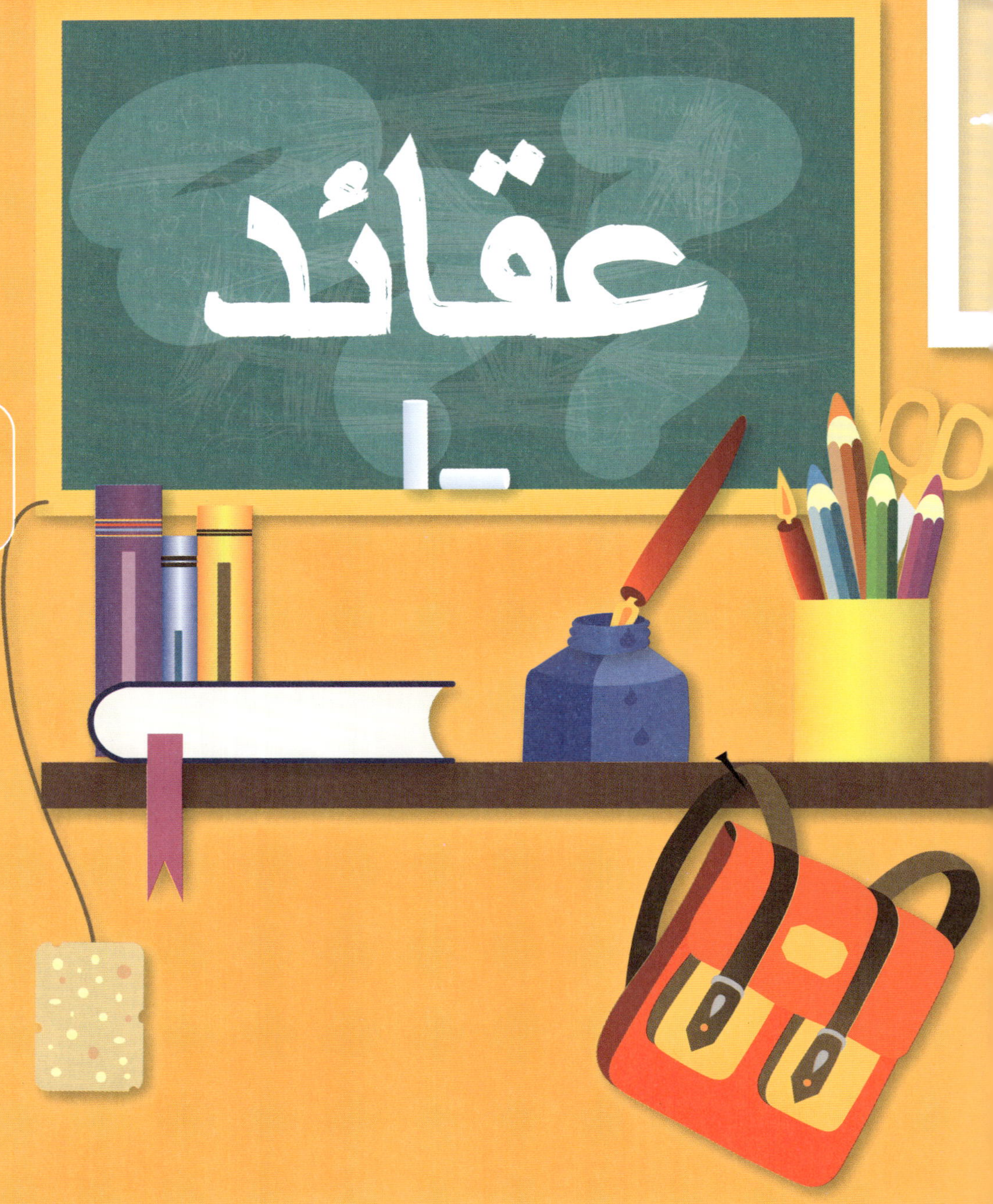

Learning Objectives

'Aqā'id

At the end of this unit pupils should be able to:

Describe how one's deeds have a direct effect on the type of death.

Specify which questions will be asked in the grave and how ones's answers will affect one's final destination.

Portray some of the description of Jannah and Jahannam described by the Qur'ān and aḥādīth.

Differentiate the actions that will lead towards Jannah and Jahannam.

Explain using the Qur'ān and ḥadīth how fate is ordained by Allāh سبحانه وتعالى.

State what A'rāf is.

Explain what taqdīr (fate) is through the words of our Beloved Prophet Muḥammad صلى الله عليه وسلم.

State our beliefs with regard to Allāh سبحانه وتعالى.

Outline our beliefs with regard to the prophets and ṣaḥābah.

Death

Everyone has to leave this world. We are, in reality, just travellers. Both the fittest person who goes to the gym for three hours a day and the laziest person who sleeps so many hours a day will die. Both the doctor and the patient will die.

Allāh سبحانه وتعالى states:
"Every soul has to taste death. It is on the Day of Judgement that you shall be paid your rewards in full. So, whoever has been kept away from the Fire and admitted to Paradise has really succeeded. " (Qur'ān 3:185)

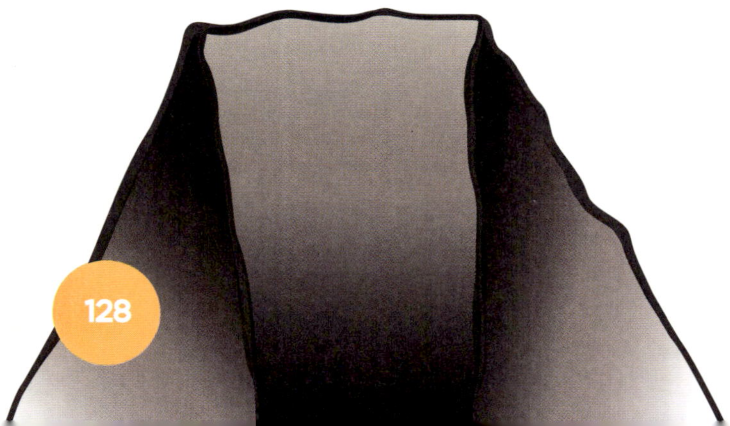

Death

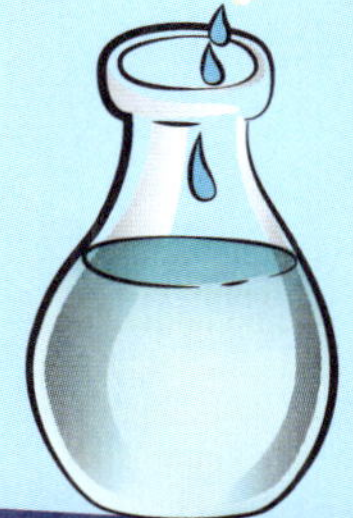

The Prophet صلى الله عليه وسلم explained to us what happens at the time of death clearly.

For a good person who believed in Allāh سبحانه وتعالى and obeyed His commands, death will come in the following manner:

"Verily when the believing slave (of Allāh) is at the point of departure from the worldly life, and is about to enter the next life, angels descend from Heaven. Their faces are white (and bright) like the sun. They carry with them a shroud from the clothes of Paradise, and perfume from the fragrance of Paradise. They sit away from him at the limit of his eyesight. The Angel of Death then arrives, sits by his head and says, "O good and peaceful soul, depart to Allāh's forgiveness and pleasure!" On hearing this, the soul leaves the body (as easily) as water pours out from the spout of a water-skin container, and he (the Angel of Death) takes it... the sweetest smell of musk ever to exist on the surface of the Earth emanates from the soul." (Aḥmad)

Death

A person who did not believe in the truth from Allāh سبحانه وتعالى will have the following death:

"And verily, when a disbelieving slave (of Allāh) is at the point of departure from the worldly life, and is about to enter the Hereafter, strong hulking angels with dark faces descend to him from the Heavens. They bring with them coarse fabric from the Fire. They sit away from him at the limit of his eyesight.

The Angel of Death arrives, sits by his head and says, "O malicious soul, depart to the wrath and anger of Allāh!" On hearing this, it becomes terrified, and clings to the body, but he extracts it by force, like a thorny skewer is pulled from wet wool. The soul releases the most repugnant odour of a decaying corpse that ever existed on the surface of the Earth." (Aḥmad)

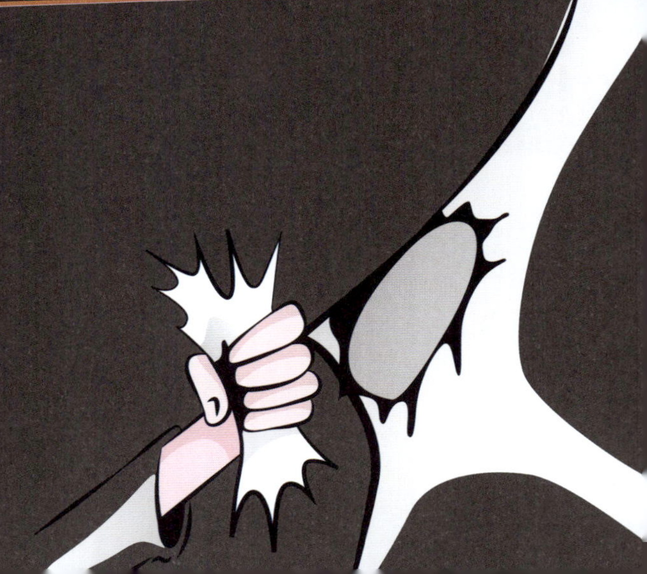

The Journey after Death

After the soul comes out of the body, it travels towards the Heavens. The Prophet صلى الله عليه وسلم described the journey of the two types of souls in the following manner:

"The angels then ascend with it (the believer's soul). As they pass by gatherings of angels, they are asked, "What is this good soul? They (the angels holding it) reply, "This is so and so, the son (or daughter) of so and so," using the best names with which he had been addressed in the worldly life. When they reach the Lowest Heaven, they ask for permission to enter, and the gates open for them.

The most elite (angels) of each heaven escort him to the next one, until the soul reaches the Seventh Heaven. Allāh then says, "Write My servant's records in 'Illiyyūn. And what will make you know what 'Illiyyūn is? A register inscribed. To which bear witness those who are nearest (to Allāh, i.e. the angels)" (Qur'ān 83:19-21).

Thus, the soul's records are inscribed in 'Illiyyūn, and the angels are told, "Take him back to the Earth, because I promised them that: 'from it (earth) I created them, into it I shall return them, and from it I shall resurrect them once again.'" (Qur'ān 20:55) He is returned to Earth, and his soul is returned to his body, so that he hears the thumping of his companions' shoes as they walk away from his grave..."

The Journey after Death

"The angels then ascend with it (the disbeliever's soul). As they pass by gatherings of angels, they are asked, "What is this malicious soul? They (the angels holding it) reply, "This is so and so, the son (or daughter) of so and so," using the worst names with which he had been addressed in the first life.

When they reach the Lowest Heaven, they ask for permission to enter, and the gates are not opened for him. "For them (the disbelievers), the gates of Heaven will not be opened, and they will not enter Paradise until the camel goes through the eye of a needle!" (Qur'ān 7:40)

Allāh سبحانه وتعالى then says, "Write his records in Sijjīn in the Lowest Earth." And the angels are told, "Take him back to the Earth, because I promised them that; 'from it (Earth) I created them, into it I shall return them, and from it I shall resurrect them once again.' (Qur'ān 20:55)" His soul is cast down to Earth without regard, and his soul falls into his body. "As for the one who joins partners with Allāh, it is as if he plunges down from the skies, whereupon birds snatch him off, or the wind casts him away to a remote place (away from Allāh سبحانه وتعالى's Mercy)." (Qur'ān 22:31)

His soul is restored to his body, so that he hears the thumping of his companions' shoes as they walk away from his grave..." (Aḥmad)

The Questioning in the Grave

After a person's burial is complete and the people leave his graveside, two angels descend to the person in the grave. The names of these angels are Munkar and Nakīr.

A person's soul is returned to his body. He is thereafter asked the following questions:

'Who is your Lord? What is your religion? Who is the man who was sent to you?'

A believer will reply,
"My Lord is Allāh. My religion is Islām. That is the Messenger of Allāh."

A disbeliever will reply,
"Alas, I don't know. Alas, I don't know. Alas, I don't know."

No matter if a person is buried in a grave or drowns in the sea, they will still be questioned by these angels.

The Life of the Grave (Barzakh)

Death is not the end of a person: it is just the beginning. For Muslims, the real life is the life after death. That life is forever.

As part of our Īmān, we believe that a good person is blessed in the grave with various bounties and an evil person is punished in a manner which Allāh سبحانه وتعالى wills.

The Prophet صلى الله عليه وسلم said:
"The grave is a garden from the gardens of Paradise or a pit from the pits of Hell." (Tirmidhī)

A believer who passed the test of Munkar and Nakīr will be given a bedding from Jannah, he will be clothed with the clothing of Jannah and a gateway to Jannah will be unveiled. He will be soothed and cooled with the fragrant scent of Jannah in his grave.

A person who failed the test of Munkar and Nakīr will be given a bedding of fire, clothing of fire and a gateway to the Hellfire will be unveiled. The scorching heat and blistering hot winds will be let loose upon him from this gateway.

The Life of the Grave (Barzakh)

After the first time the Trumpet is blown, no one will remain except Allāh سبحانه وتعالى. Allāh سبحانه وتعالى will then command Isrāfīl عليه السلام to rise and blow the Trumpet a second time, through which the whole world will be recreated by the command of Allāh سبحانه وتعالى. But this time it will be different from before.

Afterwards Allāh سبحانه وتعالى will command everyone to rise and all the bodies will come back to life to stand before the Lord of the Universe, and answer for their actions.

"And they shall be presented lined-up before your Lord. (It will be said to them,) 'You have certainly come to Us just as We had created you for the first time, while you claimed that We would not make any appointed time for you.'" (Qur'ān 18:48)

"Then, as for him whose scales (of good deeds) are heavy, he will be in a happy life (Jannah)." (Qur'ān 101:6-7)

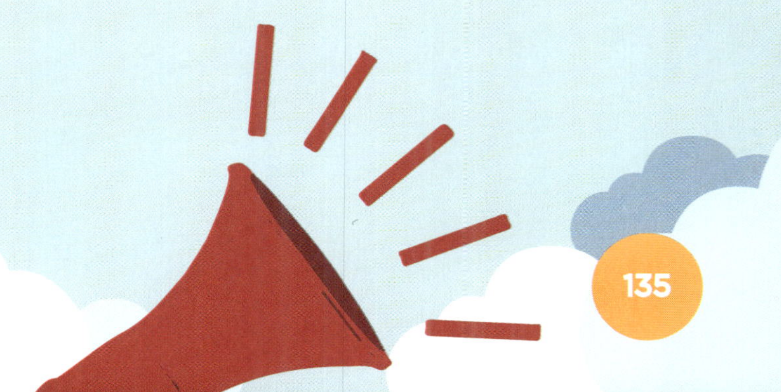

Jannah

Jannah is a beautiful and peaceful place which Allāh سبحانه وتعالى has prepared for the Believers. It is such a beautiful place that no eye has ever seen, no ear has ever heard of, and no mind has ever imagined.

Just before the Believers enter Jannah, they will come by a fountain in which each and every one of them will make ghusl (bath), by which their faces will shine and look very radiant. The men will become extremely handsome and the women will become so beautiful that even the ḥūrs (women of Jannah) will envy them.

Angels will welcome the Believers into Jannah. The people entering Jannah will wear crowns. The ummah of our Beloved Prophet Muḥammad صلى الله عليه وسلم will enter Jannah first, after which everyone else will follow. The atmosphere will be joyous, peaceful and ecstatic.

The highest of the degrees of Paradise is al-Firdaws. It was narrated that Abū Hurayrah رضي الله عنه said that the Messenger of Allāh صلى الله عليه وسلم said, "When you ask of Allāh, ask Him for al-Firdaws, for it is in the best part of Paradise and is the highest part of Paradise, and above it is the Throne of the Most Merciful, and from it spring forth the rivers of Paradise." (Ṣaḥīḥ al-Bukhārī)

Jannah

There are four rivers in Jannah:

1. Water
2. Milk
3. Wine
4. Honey

These rivers will not be like those of this world. The water and milk will not taste like that of this world. The honey will be pure. The wine will not intoxicate nor will it cause any harm to our bodies; it will be pure.

There will be a market in Jannah known as Sūq al-Jannah. Anas ibn Mālik رضي الله عنه narrated that the Prophet صلى الله عليه وسلم said:

"Verily in Paradise there is a market which the people of Paradise will come to every Friday. The north wind will blow and scatter fragrances on their faces and clothes. This will add to their beauty and attractiveness. They will then go back to their families after having an added lustre to their beauty and attractiveness. Their families will say to them, "By Allāh, you have been increased in beauty and loveliness after leaving us," and they will say, "By Allāh you too have increased in beauty and attractiveness after us." (Ṣaḥīḥ Muslim)

Seeing Allāh

"Many faces, that day, will be glowing, looking towards their Lord." (Qur'ān 75:22-23)

The greatest blessing of Jannah will be seeing Allāh سبحانه وتعالى. Our Beloved Messenger Muḥammad صلى الله عليه وسلم said, "When the people of Jannah shall enter Jannah, and the people of Jahannam shall enter Jahannam, a caller shall call: "O people of Jannah, Allāh سبحانه وتعالى is inviting you to a gathering in which He wishes to reward you."

The people of Jannah shall say, "Has He not illuminated our faces? Has He not saved us from the Fire? Did He not make our scales heavy?" (Implying that He has given them so much, so what more could there be?)

Then the veils will be lifted and they shall look at the countenance of Allāh سبحانه وتعالى. The people of Jannah will not be given any reward greater than viewing the countenance of Allāh سبحانه وتعالى.

Jannah

The description of Jannah through the Qur'ān and aḥādīth:

"And Allāh سبحانه وتعالى will reward them with Paradise, and silken garments, because they were patient. Reclining on raised thrones, they will not see therein neither excessive sunlight nor extreme bitter cold, (the climate shall be just right).

The shade will be close upon them, and bunches of fruit will hang low within their reach. Vessels of silver and cups of crystal will be passed around amongst them, crystal-clear, made of silver, measured by those (who filled them) with due measure. They will be given a cup (of wine) mixed with Zanjabīl, a fountain called Salsabīl.

And circling around them will be serving boys, blessed with eternal youth. If you see them, you would think they are scattered pearls. When you look there (in Paradise) you will see a delight (that cannot be imagined), and a Great Kingdom. Their garments will be of green sundus (a kind of fine silk), and of istabraq (a kind of thick silk), They will be adorned with bracelets of silver, and their Lord will give them a pure drink." (Qur'ān 76:12-21)

Jannah

"Verily, the dwellers of Paradise that Day will be busy in joyful things. They and their wives will be in pleasant shade, reclining on thrones. They will have therein fruits (of all kinds), and all that they will ask for. (It will be said to them): "Salām" (Peace be on you), a word from the Lord, Most Merciful."
(Qur'ān 36:55-58)

Abū Mūsā al-Ash'arī رضي الله عنه narrated that the Prophet صلى الله عليه وسلم said, "Verily, for the Believers in Paradise, are tents made of a single hollow pearl, the length of which will be sixty miles."
(Ṣaḥīḥ Muslim)

Abū Hurayrah رضي الله عنه said that the Messenger of Allāh صلى الله عليه وسلم said,"There is not a tree in Paradise, except that its trunk is made of gold." (Tirmidhī)

'Aqā'id

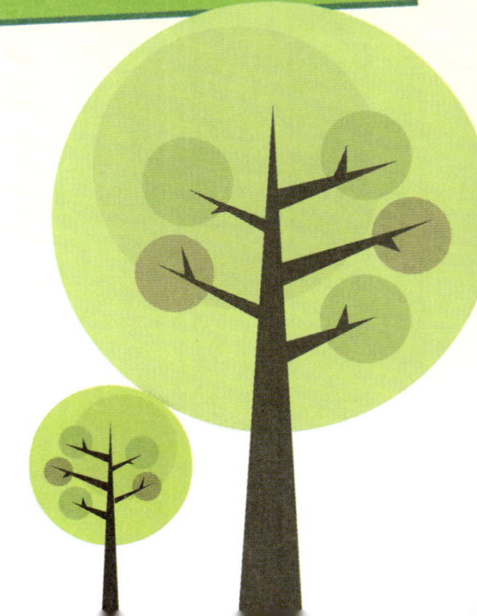

Actions that will Lead us to Jannah

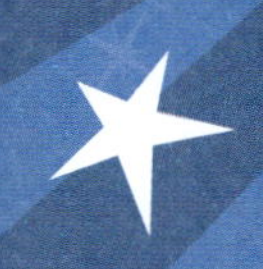

Belief in Allāh and doing good actions

"Whoever believes in Allāh, and does so righteously, He will write off his evil deeds, and will admit him to gardens beneath which rivers flow, where they will live forever. That is the great achievement." (Qur'ān 64:9)

Visiting the sick

The Messenger صلى الله عليه وسلم said, "Whoever visits a sick person or visits a brother in Islām, a caller cries out to him, "May you be happy, may your walking be blessed, and may you occupy a dignified position in Paradise!" (Tirmidhī)

Spreading Salām.
Feeding people
Praying ṣalāh at night (tahajjud)

Abdullah ibn Salām رضي الله عنه said the first words from the Messenger صلى الله عليه وسلم when he arrived in Madīnah were, "O people! Spread peace... share food... pray during the night while people sleep... and you will enter Paradise in peace." (Tirmidhī)

Actions that will Lead us to Jannah

- In Sūrah al-Mu'minūn Allāh سبحانه وتعالى informs us that the people who come to stay in Jannah al-Firdaws will be those that:

  - Concentrate in their humility when offering ṣalāh
  - Keep away from vain things
  - Give zakāh
  - Protect their chastity and modesty
  - Look after their trusts
  - Look after their promises
  - Are consistent in ṣalāh

Those are the inheritors of al-Firdaws (the Paradise).

Whoever offers 12 rak'āt in the day and night, Allāh سبحانه وتعالى will build for him a house in Jannah.

- 2 Rak'āt before Fajr
- 4 Rak'āt before Ẓuhr
- 2 Rak'āt after Ẓuhr
- 2 Rak'āt after Maghrib
- 2 Rak'āt after 'Ishā'

(Ṣaḥīḥ Muslim)

'Asharah Mubasharah

There are ten Ṣaḥābah who were given the glad tidings of Paradise in this world in one gathering by our Beloved Messenger صلى الله عليه وسلم. He صلى الله عليه وسلم said, "Abū Bakr will be in Paradise, 'Umar will be in Paradise, 'Uthmān will be in Paradise, 'Alī will be in Paradise, Ṭalḥah will be in Paradise, az-Zubayr will be in Paradise, 'Abdur Raḥmān ibn 'Awf will be in Paradise, Sa'd (ibn Abi Waqqāṣ) will be in Paradise, Sa'īd (ibn Zayd) will be in Paradise, and Abū 'Ubaydah ibn al-Jarrāḥ will be in Paradise." (Tirmidhī)

These ten Ṣaḥābah were known as the 'Ashrah Mubasharah (the ten people who were given the glad tidings of Jannah).

May Allāh سبحانه وتعالى be pleased with them and grant us all Jannah al-Firdaws.

Jahannam

"Surely Jahannam (the Hell) lurks in ambush. It is an abode for the rebellious people who will be abiding in it for ages. They will taste nothing cool in it, nor a drink, except boiling water and pus: this being a punishment fully commensurate (with their deeds). They did not expect (to face) accounting (of their deeds), and they rejected Our signs totally. And everything (from their deeds) is thoroughly recorded by Us in writing. So now taste! We will add nothing to you but torment." (Qur'ān 78:21-30)

Jahannam is a place of misery, pain, and grief, a place which has been prepared for the non-believers and the people whose sins outweighed their good deeds.

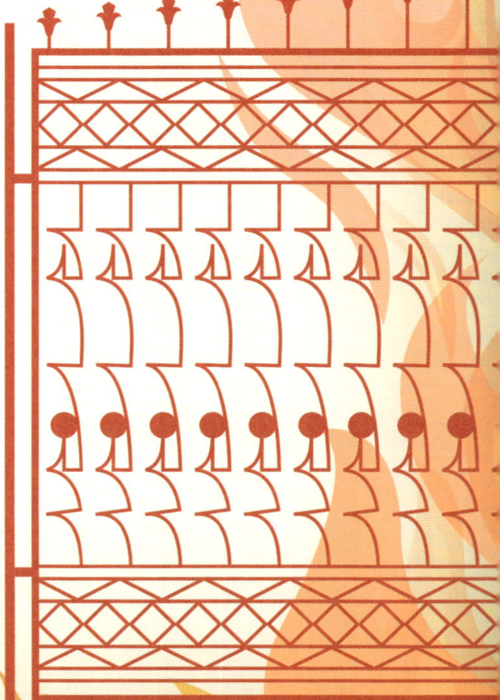

Jahannam

"Jahannam was heated for a thousand years and its fire turned red. It was then heated for another thousand years and it became white. It was again heated for another thousand years and it turned black. At present, Jahannam is pitch black and dark." (Tirmidhī)

"Your fire (the fire of this world) is one part from seventy parts of the fire of jahannam, each part of it is like the heat of this world." (Tirmidhī)

"For each gate there is a group apportioned from them." (Qur'ān 15:44)

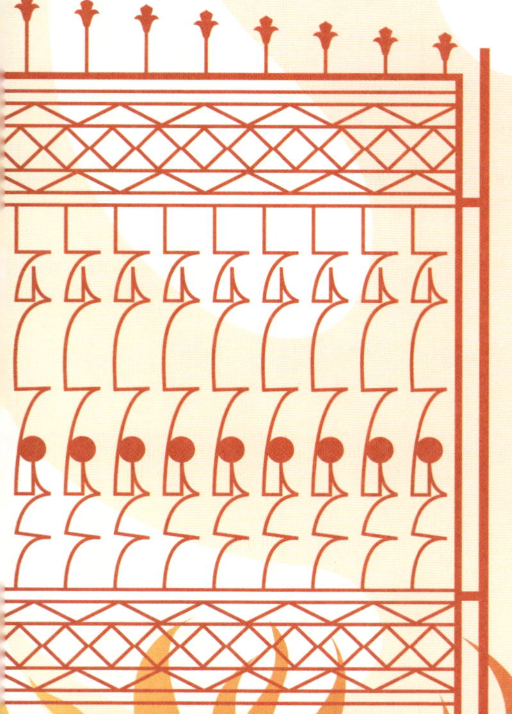

Jahannam

There are seven gates of Jahannam. The types of punishments in Jahannam mentioned in the Qur'ān and Ḥadīth are as follows:

Creatures: "Verily, there are long-necked camel-like snakes in Jahannam. If anyone of these bites a person of Jahannam, he will feel the pain for 40 years.... Verily, there are donkey-size scorpions in Jahannam. If anyone of these stings a person of Jahannam, he will feel pain for 40 years." (Aḥmad)

"On the Day of Resurrection, a neck will come out from Jahannam, having two eyes, two ears and one tongue to see, hear and speak. It will say that it has been designated for three types of people:

a. every rebellious and stubborn one.
b. everyone who made an associate with Allāh سبحانه وتعالى.
c. the one who draws pictures (of living beings)." (Tirmidhī)

Jahannam

Food: "Boiling water will be poured on their heads and it will pierce their skulls until it reaches their stomachs; this will make their guts melt and go down to their feet, then everything will be returned to its original condition again." (Aḥmad)

"Indeed the tree of Zaqqūm, is the food for the sinful. Like murky oil, it boils within bellies, like the boiling of scalding water." (Qur'ān 44:43-46)

"The dwellers of Jahannam will experience such intense hunger that this alone will be equal to the terrible torment which will be rendered. Then they will seek for food and they will be given food that will stick to the throat (i.e. it will neither go in nor come out)." (Tirmidhī)

Jahannam

Iron and Chains: "And there will be rods of iron (to punish) them. Every time they wish to get away therefrom, due to anguish, they will be forced back, and (it will be said): "Taste you the chastisement of burning!" (22:21-22)

"If the rod of iron is placed on the ground, all men and jinn put together will not lift it." (Aḥmad)

"But soon shall they know, when the shackles (shall be) round their necks, and the chains; they shall be dragged along, in the boiling stinging fluid, then in the Fire shall they be burned." (Qur'ān 40:70-72)

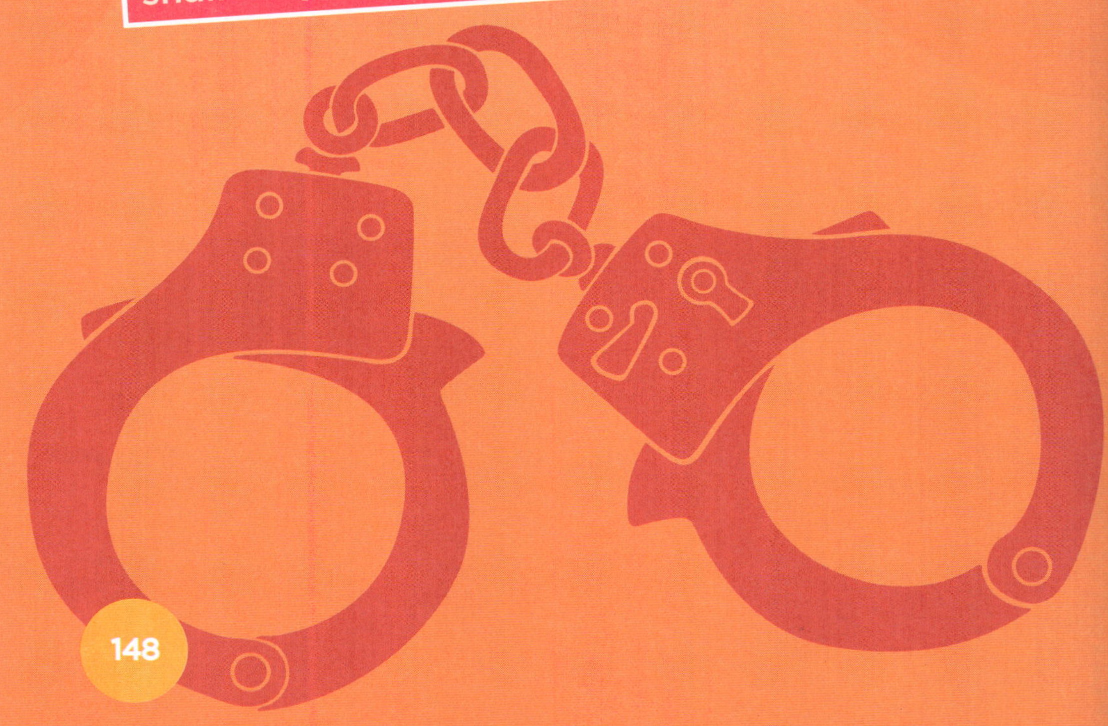

Garments: "Their garments of qaṭirān (pitch), and their faces covered with fire." (Qur'ān 14:50)

According to Ibn 'Abbās رضي الله عنه, qaṭirān means melted brass. The people of Jahannam will be made to wear this clothing which is extremely hot. (Ibn Kathīr)

"The dwellers of Jahannam will cry so much that ships would be able to sail in their tears, and their tears will be of blood" (Ḥākim).

"Verily the tongue of the unbeliever will be pulled out up to one or two 'farsakh' (three miles) and the people will walk over it. The distance between two shoulders of an unbeliever will be so wide that it will take three days if a horse covers it rapidly: his jaw-tooth will be equal to mount Uḥud, and the thickness of his skin will be equal to the passage of three days." (Ṣaḥīḥ Muslim)

"Those who reject Our Signs, We shall soon hurl them into the Fire: as often as their skins are roasted through, We shall replace these for fresh skins, that they may taste the chastisement: for Allāh is Exalted in Power, Wise." (Qur'ān 4:56).

"The least among the people of Hell in punishment is one whose sandals and laces are of fire from which his brain boils as a pot of water would boil (when set on fire): he will not think that there is anyone being punished more than him, but in reality, he is the least in punishment." (Ṣaḥīḥ al-Bukhārī)

Actions that Lead to Jahannam

Hypocrisy – acting as a Muslim outwardly but having disbelief inwardly

"Indeed Allāh will gather the hypocrites and disbelievers in Hell all together." (Qur'ān 4:140)

'Abdullāh ibn 'Amr رضي الله عنه reports that the Beloved Messenger Muḥammad صلى الله عليه وسلم said, "If anyone has four characteristics, he is a pure hypocrite, and if anyone has one of them, he has an aspect of hypocrisy until he gives up: when he is trusted, he betrays his trust; whenever he speaks, he lies; when he makes an agreement, he breaks it; and when he quarrels, he behaves in an insulting manner." (Ṣaḥīḥ al-Bukhārī)

Actions that Lead to Jahannam

Lying
Our Beloved Messenger Muḥammad صلى الله عليه وسلم has said: "Lying leads to deviance and deviance leads to the Fire." (Ṣaḥīḥ al-Bukhārī)

Spreading tales
Our Beloved Messenger Muḥammad صلى الله عليه وسلم said, "A talebearer shall not enter Jannah." (Ṣaḥīḥ Muslim)

Being two faced.
Our Beloved Messenger Muḥammad صلى الله عليه وسلم said, "You will find the worst person on the day of Judgement to be the two-faced person." (Ṣaḥīḥ al-Bukhārī)

A two-faced person is like a hypocrite: in front of some people he says something and he then goes to other people and says the total opposite.

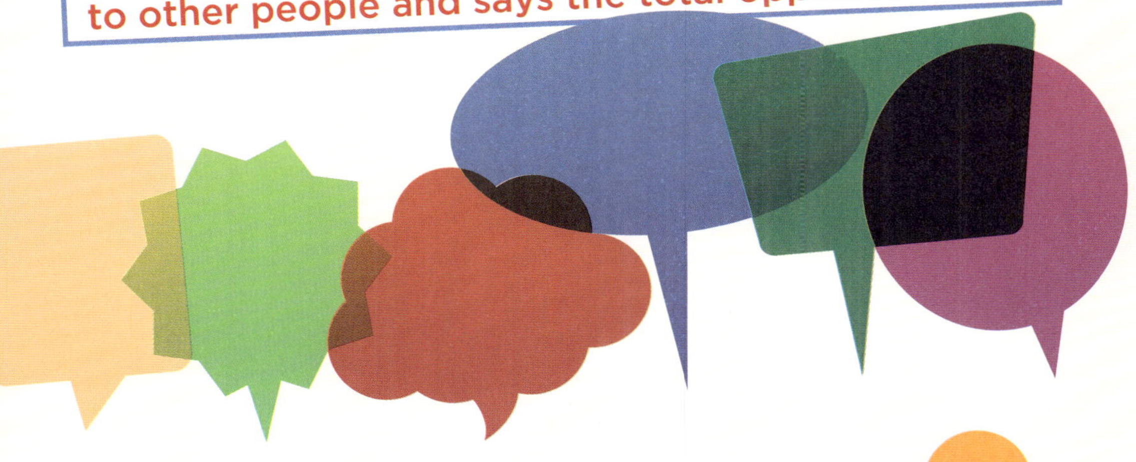

Actions that Lead to Jahannam

Being arrogant and proud
Our Beloved Messenger Muḥammad صلى الله عليه وسلم said, "He shall not enter Jannah in whose heart there is an atom's weight of pride." (Ṣaḥīḥ Muslim)

Picture makers who draw pictures of animate and living beings.
Our Beloved Messenger Muḥammad صلى الله عليه وسلم said, "The picture makers will be given the severest punishment." (Ṣaḥīḥ al-Bukhārī)

One who breaks family ties
Our Beloved Messenger Muḥammad صلى الله عليه وسلم said "The person who breaks family ties will not enter Jannah." (Ṣaḥīḥ al-Bukhārī)

May Allāh سبحانه وتعالى protect us all from Jahannam.

Āmīn.

'Aqā'id

A'rāf

A'rāf is a place between Jannah and Jahannam. Those people who have the same amount of good and bad deeds will be sent here. Eventually they will enter Jannah. The Qur'ān informs us of the people of A'rāf in the following verse:

"Between the two groups there will be a barrier. And on A'rāf (the Heights) there shall be people who will recognize each group through their signs, and they will call out to the people of Paradise, "Peace on you." They will not have entered it, yet they will hope to.

When their eyes will be turned to the people of the Fire, they will say, "Our Lord, do not join us with the unjust people."

The people of A'rāf will call out to the people (of the Fire) whom they will recognise through their signs: "Your masses were not of any help to you, nor was the arrogance you used to show. Is it these (people of Paradise) about whom you swore that Allāh would not allow His mercy to reach them?"

(It will be said to such people): "Enter Paradise - there will be no fear for you, nor shall you grieve." (Qur'ān 7:46-49)

Al-Qadr (Fate)

'Abdullāh ibn 'Abbās رضي الله عنه reported that "One day I was behind the Prophet صلى الله عليه وسلم and he said to me:

"O young man, I shall teach you some words of advice: Be mindful of Allāh, and Allāh will protect you. Be mindful of Allāh, and you will find Him in front of you. If you (have need to) ask, ask of Allāh; and if you seek help, seek help from Allāh. Know that even if a nation (or the whole community) were to gather together to benefit you with something, they would not benefit you with anything except that which Allāh has already recorded for you, and that if they gathered together to harm you with something, they would not be able to harm you with anything except that which Allāh has already recorded against you. The pens have been lifted and the pages have dried." (Tirmidhī)

"It could be that you dislike something, when it is good for you, and it could be that you like something when it is bad for you. Allāh knows, and you do not know." (Qur'ān 2:216)

Al-Qadr (Fate)

"Surely, it is Allāh with whom rests the knowledge of the Hour, and He sends down the rain, and He knows what is in the wombs. No one knows what he will earn tomorrow, and no one knows in which land he will die. Surely, Allāh is All Knowing, All Aware." (Qur'ān 31:34)

"With Him are the keys of the unseen. No one knows them but He. He knows what is in the land and the sea. No leaf ever falls but that He knows about it, and there is no grain in the dark layers of the earth, or anything fresh or dry that is not recorded in a manifest book." (Qur'ān 6:59)

From this we should learn and understand that all power and might is with Allāh سبحانه وتعالى. Allāh سبحانه وتعالى knows everything. Allāh سبحانه وتعالى loves us, and although sometimes something may happen to us which we may not like, when we look back we see that it was truly good for us. This is part of our faith, that we must believe that everything is from Allāh سبحانه وتعالى.

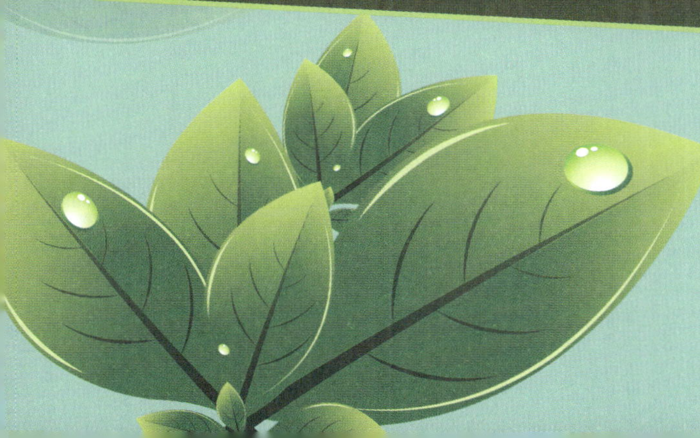

Our Beliefs with Regard to Allāh سبحانه وتعالى

- We declare Allāh سبحانه وتعالى's oneness believing, without doubt, that Allāh سبحانه وتعالى is One, without any partners.
- There is nothing like Him (neither in quality, nor in reality).
- There is no God other than Him.
- He is the Eternal without a beginning and the Enduring without end (He is free from the restrictions of time).
- He will never perish.
- Nothing happens except by His will.
- He is living and never dies.
- He neither slumbers nor sleeps.

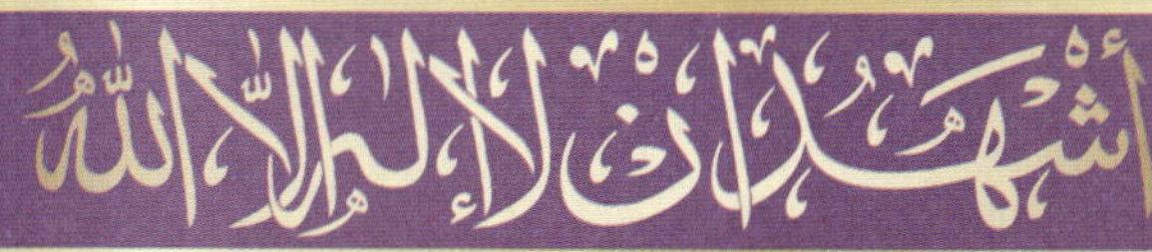

Our Beliefs with Regard to Allāh سبحانه وتعالى

- He has the power to do everything.
- Everything is dependent on Him, everything is easy for Him, and He is in need of nothing.
- He created creation with His knowledge.
- He ordered them to obey Him and forbade them from disobeying Him.
- He has absolute knowledge of everything.
- No one can change His decree, put back His command, or overpower His affairs.
- We believe in all of this and are certain that everything comes from Him (be it good or bad).

Our Beliefs with Regard to the Messenger Muḥammad صلى الله عليه وسلم

- We believe that Muḥammad صلى الله عليه وسلم is Allāh سبحانه وتعالى's chosen servant, selected Prophet, and His Messenger with whom Allāh سبحانه وتعالى is well-pleased.

- He is the seal of the prophets, the leader of the God-fearing, the most honoured of all the Messengers, and the Beloved of the Lord of all the Worlds.

- Every claim to prophethood after him is false and deceitful.

- He is the one who has been sent to all the Jinn and all mankind with truth and guidance.

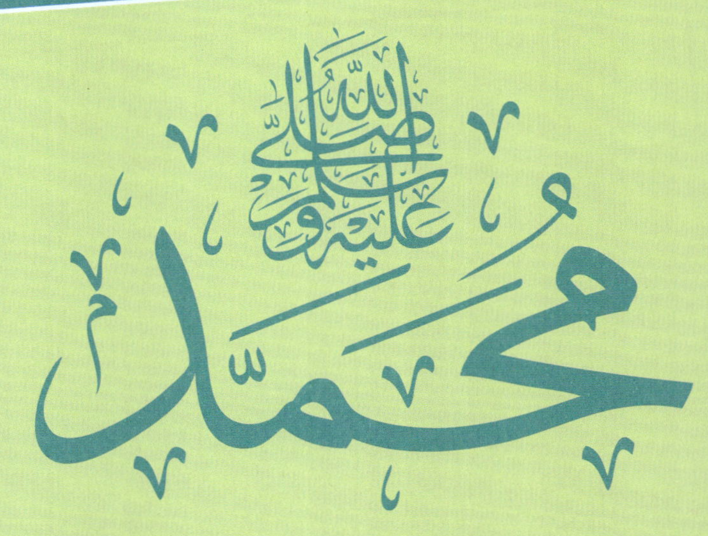

Our Beliefs with Regard to the Prophets

- Our belief in the prophets and messengers is firm. We accept that all of them are free from sins.
- We believe Allāh سبحانه وتعالى is pleased with all of them.
- The mistakes they have made have been forgiven by Allāh سبحانه وتعالى. Mistakes are not the same as sins.
- We do not worship any of them.
- Nor do we say that they share any of the divine qualities of Allāh سبحانه وتعالى.
- We do not give any one of them a higher status than another except as revealed by Allāh سبحانه وتعالى.

Our Beliefs with Regard to the Ṣaḥābah

- The Ṣaḥābah were the beloved Companions of the Messenger Muḥammad صلى الله عليه وسلم.

A Ṣaḥābī is someone, who in the state of īmān, met the Beloved Messenger Muḥammad صلى الله عليه وسلم in the Messenger صلى الله عليه وسلم's lifetime and thereafter died with īmān. 'Ṣaḥābah' is plural for 'Ṣaḥābī.'

- We love the Ṣaḥābah but we do not take our love for any one individual among them to excess nor do we disown any of them.

- We only speak well of them.

- Love for all of them is part of Islām.

- Hatred for them is hypocrisy and rebelliousness.

Our Beliefs with Regard to the Ṣaḥābah

- We confirm that, after the death of the Messenger Muḥammad صلى الله عليه وسلم, the khilāfah (successorship) went first to Abū Bakr رضي الله عنه, thus proving his excellence and superiority over the rest of the Muslims, then to 'Umar ibn Al-Khaṭṭāb رضي الله عنه, then to 'Uthmān ibn 'Affān رضي الله عنه, and then to 'Alī ibn Abī Ṭālib رضي الله عنه. These are the Rightly-Guided Khulafā'.

- We believe all the wives of our Beloved Messenger Muḥammad صلى الله عليه وسلم were righteous and pious. They are the Mothers of the Believers (Ummahātul Mu'minīn).

We ask Allāh سبحانه وتعالى to guide us all on the right path, and save us from falling prey to ignorance and the deceit of Shayṭān and that of our own selves, Āmīn.

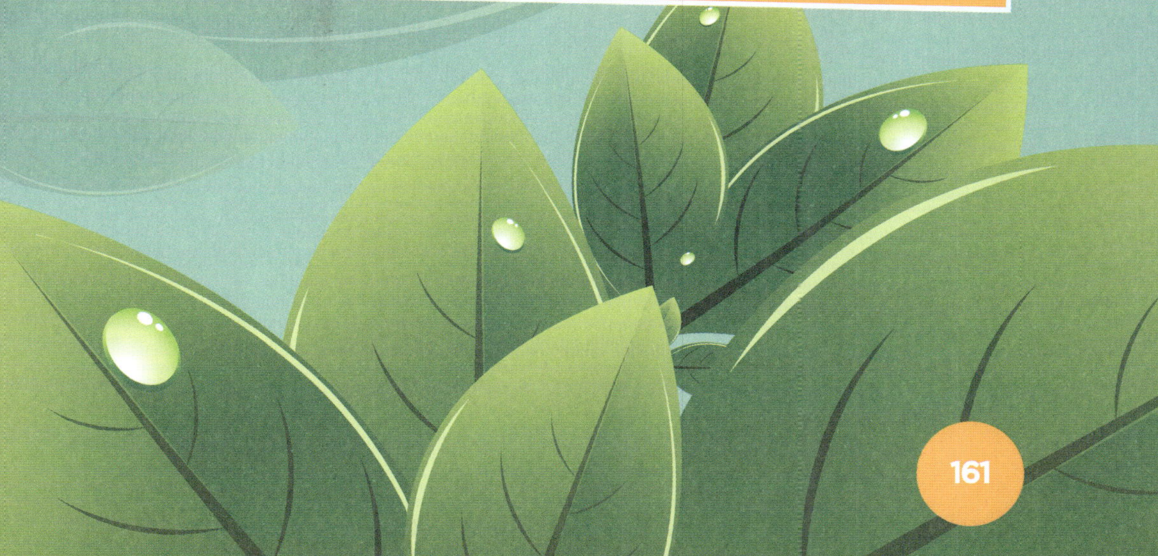

Akhlāq

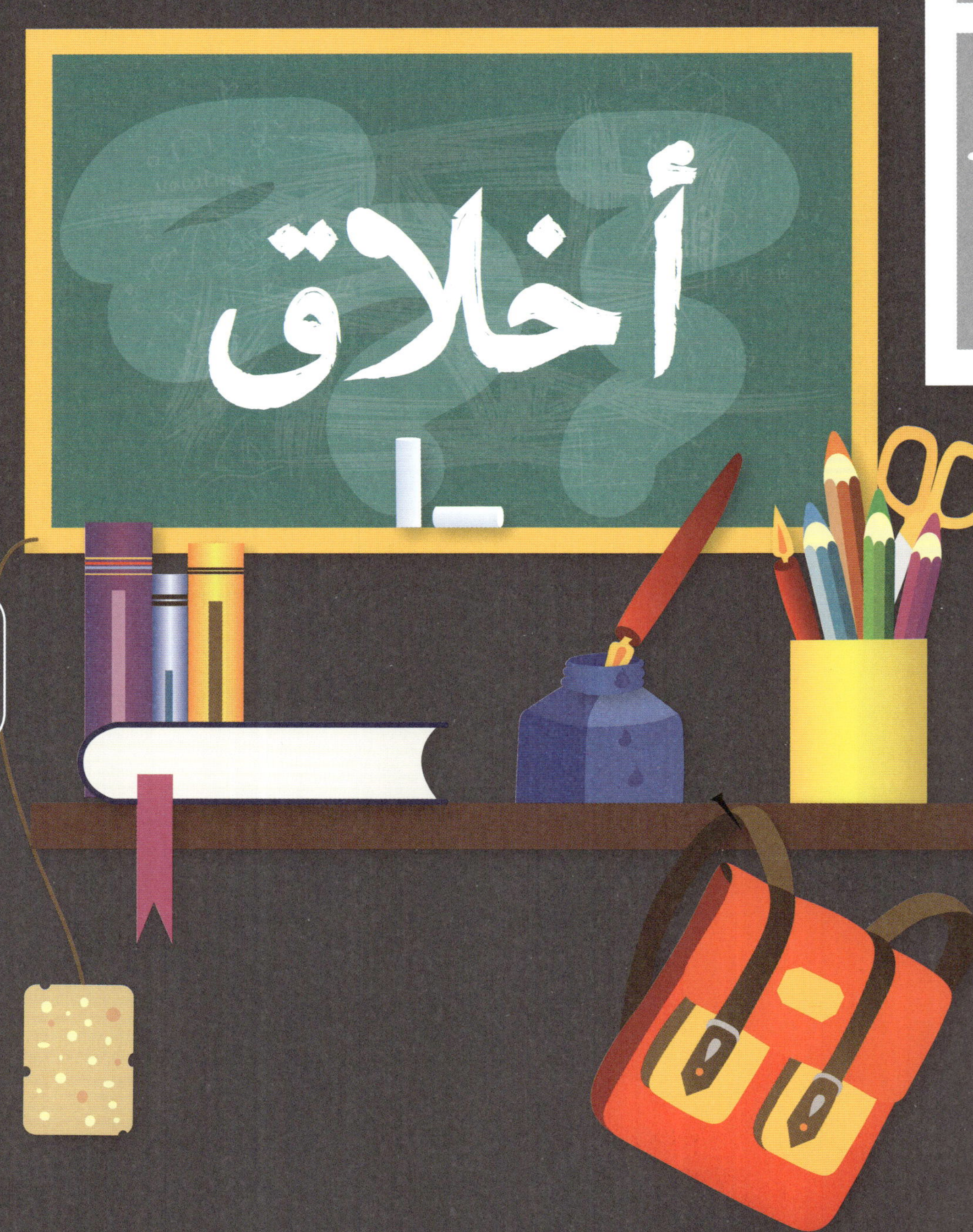

Akhlāq

Learning Objectives

Akhlāq

At the end of this unit pupils should be able to:

Describe the occasions of mashwarah and the people with whom it should be done.

Expand on 'someone who is consulted is in a position of trust' in relation to the responsibilities of giving mashwarah.

With examples, describe the three types of ṣabr.

Propose situations on how to keep and bring families together and the reward associated with keeping ties.

Describe the importance of exchanging gifts and honouring the guest.

List the virtues of dhikr.

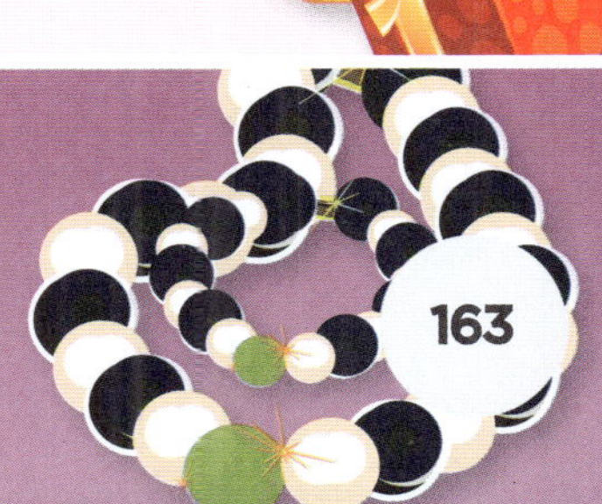

Mashwarah

"Consult them in the matter and, once you have taken a decision, place your trust in Allāh. Surely, Allāh loves those who place their trust in Him." (Qur'ān 3:159)

"And those who have responded to their Lord (in submission to Him), and have established ṣalāh, and whose affairs are (settled) with mutual consultation between them, and who spend out of what We have given to them." (Qur'ān 42:38)

Abū Hurayrah رضي الله عنه reports that the Messenger of Allāh صلى الله عليه وسلم said, "Anyone who gives his Muslim brother misguided advice when he consults has betrayed him." (Adab al-Mufrad lil-Bukhārī)

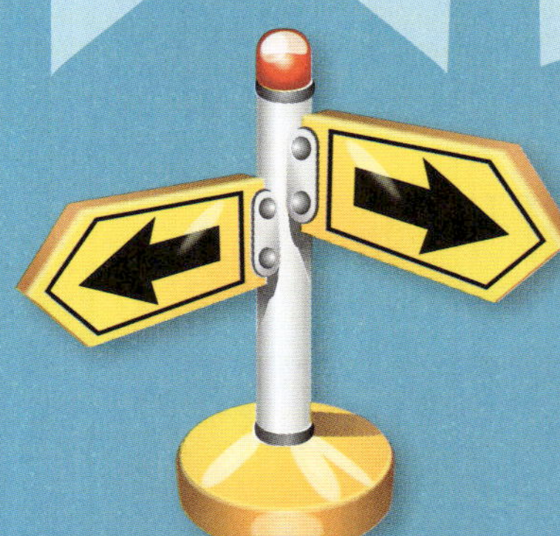

Mashwarah

'Mashwarah' means to consult other people. Asking others is, and should be, an essential part of our daily life. It was the practice of our Beloved Messenger صلى الله عليه وسلم, the Ṣaḥābah, and those that followed them. Through asking other people's opinion, we gain a better understanding of the task that is to be undertaken. It makes us humble because we realise that we are not always right in everything, and it creates love and unity between the Muslims, as they feel part of the journey and not left out.

Mashwarah should be done with those who may be younger than us too: again this will create love and affection as well as train them on the importance of asking other people's advice before they carry out something.

Allāh سبحانه وتعالى places more blessings in a decision or action when we make mashwarah, as hearts become united and togetherness is created. Our Beloved Messenger صلى الله عليه وسلم has said that Allāh سبحانه وتعالى's assistance is with the group. (Ṣaḥīḥ al-Bukhārī)

Mashwarah

Many a time we feel that the course of action we are undertaking is the correct one and there can be no other way, but when we ask the advice of others we see that there is a better way to do something. We should make mashwarah with those people who have experience. We tend to ask our friends a lot but forget to ask our elders or our parents. Remember: our parents have seen much more of life than we have and their advice and guidance can be priceless. Let us take advantage of the elder generation amongst us and ask their advice on the important matters in our lives.

When making collective mashwarah in a group, an amīr should be appointed. The amīr will then ask advice from some people.

If someone comes to ask us for advice we must remember the guidelines of our Beloved Messenger Muḥammad صلى الله عليه وسلم who said, "Someone who is consulted is in a position of trust." (Tirmidhī)

Mashwarah

We should ensure that we give the best possible advice we are aware of and on no account should we give any incorrect information or advice. If someone accepts our mashwarah we should not be boastful and think big of ourselves but, on the other hand, if our mashwarah is not taken we should not become upset. Remember: giving mashwarah is giving advice and an opinion - it is not an order or command.

Allāh سبحانه وتعالى gives us a beautiful example of the benefits of mashwarah in the story of Yūsuf عليه السلام, when the king of Egypt saw a dream. The people beside him said it was merely a nightmare but when he asked the advice of one who had experience and knowledge (Yūsuf عليه السلام), he was told totally different. By making mashwarah and taking the advice, the king, along with his people and many others living around, was saved from the effects of severe droughts and famine. If he had decided to act on his own, the story would have been very different.

Ṣabr

"Do not lose heart and do not grieve, and you are the upper-most if you are believers." (Qur'ān 3:139)

"O you who believe, be patient, compete with each other in patience, and guard your frontiers, and fear Allāh so that you may be successful." (Qur'ān 3:200)

"Certainly those who observe patience will be given their reward in full, without measure." (Qur'ān 39:10)

"...and be patient. Surely, Allāh is with the patient." (Qur'ān 8:46)

"And give glad tidings to those who patiently persevere – who say, when afflicted with calamity: 'To Allāh we belong, and to Him is our return' – they are those on whom descends blessings from their Lord and mercy, and they are the ones that receive guidance." (Qur'ān 2:155-7)

"And seek assistance through patience and prayer." (Qur'ān 2:45)

"Undoubtedly, along with the hardship there is ease." (Qur'ān 94:6)

Ṣabr

'Patience' in Arabic is called 'ṣabr.' There are three types of ṣabr:

1. Obedience
2. Abstinence
3. Endurance

Let us look at each one individually. Ṣabr in the form of obedience means being patient in obeying our Creator. Here is an example: It is ṣalāh time and we don't feel like waking up from our bed. But in rising and praying, we were patient! Another example is that it is time to pay zakāh. We don't feel like giving but we go ahead and give in charity. We have made ṣabr in the form of obedience!

Ṣabr with abstinence means being patient in staying away from sins. Our desires invite us to look at something we are not supposed to, however we control ourselves: therefore we have made ṣabr. Another example would be: people around us are engaged in doing ghībah. They ask us to join the discussion, and we feel like gossiping too. But we control our tongues and walk away or tell them to stop: we have made ṣabr!

Ṣabr

Ṣabr by means of endurance through difficulties means being patient when hardships may come our way. Sometimes we laugh, sometimes we cry - they say times have changed, but it's people who change. One minute someone is your best friend. You know no one better than him. The next minute he is your worst enemy. Every single limb in your body wants to hurt him. Why? What happened? Something he did or said changed everything (and here we have a friendship problem).

Another example is: everything was going really well at school: you're the star pupil, top of the class in all the subjects, adored by every teacher, then one day you happen to be in the wrong place at the wrong time. You get blamed for something you never dreamt of doing, and everything has gone. Whoever you pass by begins to whisper and they point fingers at you. Blamed, accused, you and your reputation go down the drain.

A third example is that you love going home from school to see and meet your mum and dad: you love them very dearly but you feel so hurt when they begin to quarrel and it is left unresolved: each one is trying to shout the other down or it's a one-way shout. You just sit in your room hoping they would understand each other, wishing they knew how you felt, praying you could do something to help.

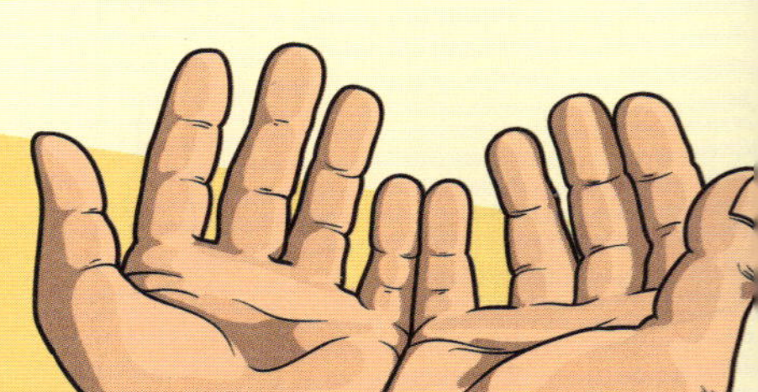

Ṣabr

Everyone everywhere has problems. If life was always as happy as we wished it to be, then this would no doubt be Jannah. It can't be Paradise! This is the world where things are different.

One thing we should never forget is that whatever the problem, however severe it gets, we are never alone and never will be, because Allāh سبحانه وتعالى knows everything.

"Not a leaf falls except that He knows. There is not a grain in the darkness (or depths) of the earth, nor anything fresh or dry (green or withered), but it is inscribed in a clear book." (Qur'ān 6:59)

Once a lady was doing ṭawāf of the Ka'bah, singing some couplets, "O Allāh سبحانه وتعالى, had You not given me the strength to bear all the difficulties that came crumbling onto me like a mountain, I would have been no more. O Allāh, I thank You for helping me throughout these hard times." Someone hearing her voice asked, "What were those difficulties that you sing of?" She said, "O be gone! I have never told anyone of my problems." The questioner persisted and the lady felt forced to narrate the following incident.

"It was in the days of 'Īd al-Aḍḥā. My husband, having slaughtered a lamb for us had come inside to dine. One of my sons said to the other, 'Come let me show you how father cut the lamb.' In doing so he accidentally killed his brother. Seeing what he had done, he ran off into the mountains. My husband went in search for him while I looked in shock at my dead son.

Ṣabr

I waited for a long time but my husband did not return. I came out of the house to enquire and saw a man running down from the mountain. When he came close, he told me that my son was killed by a wolf and my husband, trying to save him, had fallen from the cliff. I was so startled to hear this news that I forgot I had left my six-month-old child in the house. Entering the home I saw he had crawled into the water pot and scalded his whole body. He also died instantaneously. My sister, hearing the news, came and, when she saw my state, screamed and died in shock. I was left alone with no one except my Allāh سبحانه وتعالى." (Rawḍatur Rayyāḥīn)

When we're drowning in our problems, remember there's someone out there in a worse situation than us. Be patient: 'Verily, with every difficulty there is relief.' (Qur'ān 94:6)

At the end of the dark tunnel, light awaits us.

Anas ibn Malik رضي الله عنه narrated that the Beloved Messenger صلى الله عليه وسلم said: "The greatest reward comes with the greatest trial. When Allāh loves people He tests them. Whoever accepts that wins His pleasure but whoever is discontent with that earns His wrath." (Ibn Mājah)

Ṣabr

Look at the story of Yūsuf عليه السلام. A messenger of Allāh سبحانه وتعالى, yet look how he was tested. In his early teens he was taken away from his father by his own flesh and blood, thrown into a well, sold as a slave, accused of something he never did, and placed in jail for fourteen years. Then light came, and he was made the King of Egypt. Subḥānallāh, he was then reunited with his father after forty long years. At the end of the story Yūsuf عليه السلام says:

"Verily my Lord understands best the mysteries of all that He plans to do. For verily, He is full of knowledge and wisdom." (Qur'ān 12:100)

It may be that Allāh سبحانه وتعالى is planning something better for us.

"It is possible that you dislike a thing whereas it is good for you, and that you love a thing whereas it is bad for you. But Allāh knows and you do not know." (Qur'ān 2:216)

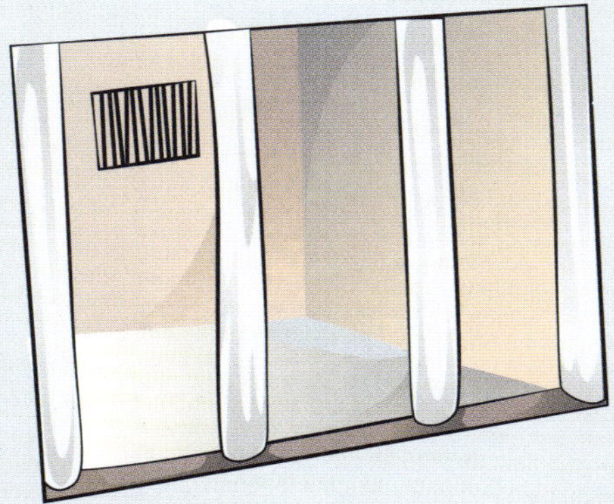

Ṣabr

There was once a minister who was in the habit of always saying, "Whatever has happened is good." One day he went on a hunting trip with the king. Upon arriving at the destination, the king pulled out his bow and arrow pricking himself in the process, which caused him to bleed. The minister immediately said "Whatever has happened is good." The king became furious, saying, "I am in pain and you say it's good! I am arresting you right now. You will be thrown into prison until I return!"

As he was being taken away he uttered the same sentence, "Whatever has happened is good." The king continued his hunt alone and soon he was deep into the jungle where he was cornered by cannibals. They carried him and took him to their master, where a ceremony was taking place and these cannibals had long been in search of a human to sacrifice. They placed the king on the slab ready for sacrifice and as he lay there trembling from head to toe the chief called out, "Check the body, it must be free from any type of cuts and bruises!" When they inspected the king's body they saw that his finger was cut and so let him go.

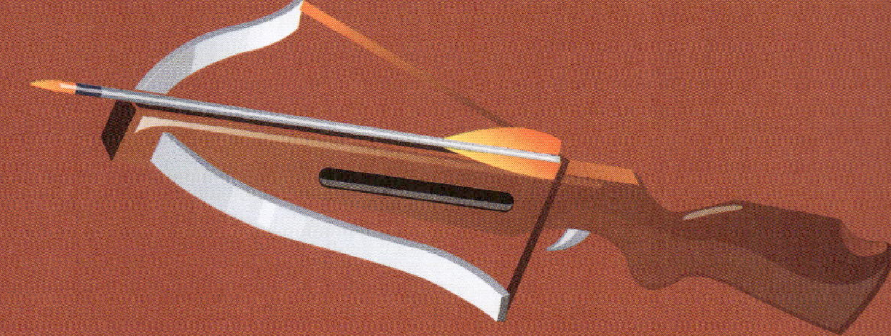

Ṣabr

The king ran for his life, and upon arriving at the palace called for the minister immediately. "I now understand the reality of your statement regarding me, but when I sent you away you said the same. What good was in that?" The minister explained, "Well it's obvious sir, I hadn't received a cut so, if I had stayed with you, I would have become their meal."

Let us be strong and look on the bright side, whatever the problem may be. Emotional changes happen to everyone.

Ṣabr

Look at the weather: sometimes it rains and rains like it is never going to stop, and sometimes it is so hot that the sun's rays feel doubled in strength. You've just got to keep going and bear everything that comes your way. Be firm on your feet just as a rock stands amidst the ever-rising waves of the ocean. This alternation of the day and night, happiness and sadness is a lesson for us all. The one who is drowning in the river of misery should know that the break of dawn is near. And the one who thinks he has got it all and is oppressing and troubling the creation of Allāh سبحانه وتعالى, beware the night will soon be upon us.

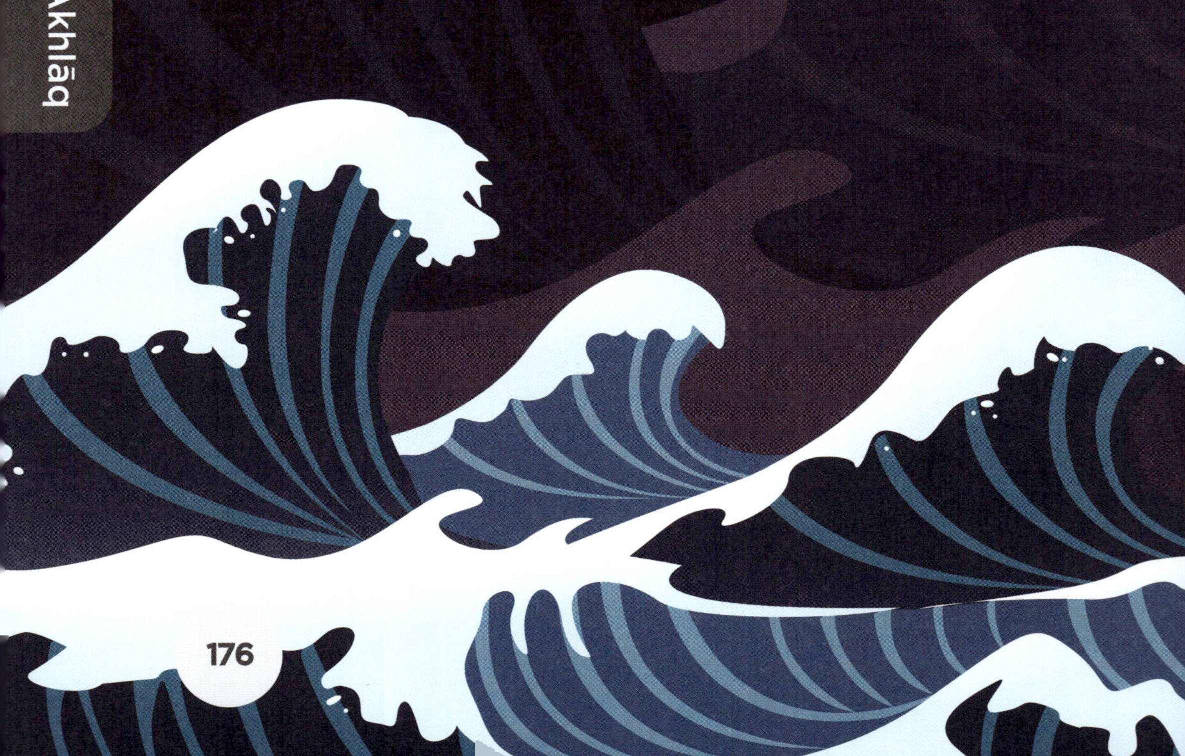

Keeping Ties of Kinship

"Fear (the violation of the rights of) the womb-relations. Surely, Allāh is watchful over you." **(Qur'ān 4:1)**

"As for those who break their pledge with Allāh after it has been made binding, and cut off the relationships Allāh has commanded to be joined, and make mischief in the land, those are the ones for whom there is the curse, and for them there is the evil abode." **(Qur'ān 13:25)**

The Messenger of Allāh صلى الله عليه وسلم **said,** "Whoever would like his rizq (provision) to be increased and his life to be extended, he should uphold the ties of kinship." **(Ṣaḥīḥ al-Bukhārī)**

A Bedouin asked the Prophet صلى الله عليه وسلم, "O Messenger of Allāh صلى الله عليه وسلم, tell me something that brings me closer to Paradise and takes me further away from the Hell Fire." The Prophet صلى الله عليه وسلم said, "Submit to Allāh سبحانه وتعالى only and do not take partners with Him, establish prayers, pay zakāt and establish good relations with your relatives." When the bedouin left, the Prophet صلى الله عليه وسلم said, "If he holds onto what I have told him, he will enter Paradise." (Ṣaḥīḥ al-Bukhārī)

Keeping Ties of Kinship

The Prophet صلى الله عليه وسلم said, "Al-Rahim (Kinship) is hung to the throne of Allāh سبحانه وتعالى (al-'Arsh) saying, "Whoever connects me, Allāh سبحانه وتعالى will connect him, and whoever cuts me off, Allāh سبحانه وتعالى will cut him off." (Ṣaḥīḥ al-Bukhārī)

We can understand the importance of maintaining ties with our relatives. We must make a point of visiting them regularly and sitting with them. Keeping ties with our relatives brings many benefits to us and to the people around us.

- It brings the pleasure of Allāh سبحانه وتعالى.
- It is a means of pleasing another Muslim, which itself is a great action.
- It creates love and unity amongst the people.
- It brings blessings to our life and sustenance.

How unfortunate it is that we see many people that don't talk to their own family members because of something that might have occurred many years ago. Remember our Beloved Messenger صلى الله عليه وسلم said to "join with one who cuts from you". (Aḥmad)

We need to be forgiving like the great examples we have seen.

Exchanging Gifts and Honouring the Guest

"Give each other gifts and you will love each other." (Ṣaḥīḥ al-Bukhārī)

"Whoever believes in Allāh and the Last Day let him honour his guest." (Ṣaḥīḥ Muslim)

Islām is a complete way of life. It also teaches a person how to live a peaceful and harmonious life in this world by abiding to the commands of Allāh سبحانه وتعالى.

When a person is at peace with people, when he is not fighting with his brothers and sisters, when there are no squabbles going on, he is at peace and can worship Allāh سبحانه وتعالى with ease and comfort. However, when there is fighting and hatred amongst the people, then a person cannot focus on his worship totally but rather he is always preoccupied with other people's worries - how will they react? What will they say next? etc.

Exchanging Gifts and Honouring the Guest

Through the two ḥadīth at the beginning of this chapter, our Beloved Messenger صلى الله عليه وسلم is showing us two great ways of creating this love amongst ourselves. The first aspect is giving gifts to each other. A gift is a thing given willingly to someone without payment. It can be something very small. The price or size does not matter. Many a time we create this image that a gift has to be wrapped up and it has to be expensive. No, a gift is from the heart. It is truly the thought that counts. We should give a gift for the sake of Allāh سبحانه وتعالى and not for name or fame. A little gift with the right intention can mean so much.

When someone receives a gift, immediately they are softened and touched by the giver of the gift as it is something they have received without expecting it or without asking for it.

Akhlāq

When we give a gift we must not expect a gift in return nor should we ask or wait for appreciation. Allāh سبحانه وتعالى speaks about when the people of Paradise had given others gifts in the world they would say: "We feed you only for the sake of Allāh; we have no intention of (receiving) either a return from you or thanks." (Qur'ān 76:9)

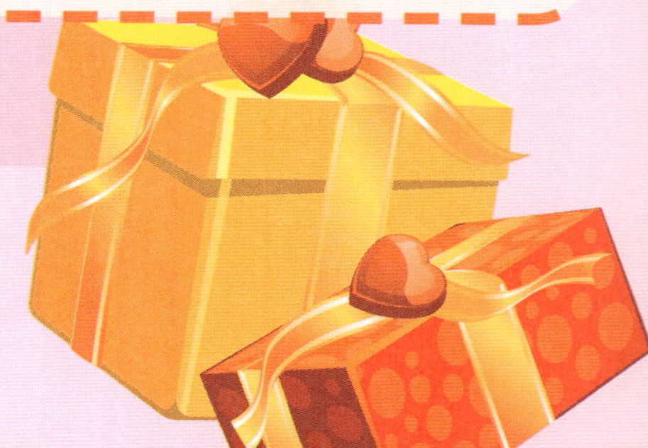

Exchanging Gifts and Honouring the Guest

There are a few etiquettes of giving gifts such as ensuring you don't broadcast that you gave such and such a gift. Once a gift is given, one should not ask for it back as it defeats the purpose of gifts. Also, bear in mind not to give such gifts that a person will find difficulty in accepting.

The second aspect mentioned is honouring the guest. Again, when someone comes to our house and we honour them, we prepare the best food available for them. If we sit and talk with them, how will such a guest feel? Very privileged of course! This in turn will create love for the host. This guest may visit again, and if he/she is a close relative, then the ties of kinship shall be strengthened.

On the other hand, if a host mistreats the guest by ignoring their needs and does not entertain them, most definitely hatred and ill feeling will be created.

Subḥānallāh, in following the simple guidelines of Islām, so much can be gained. We have distanced ourselves from these beautiful teachings and thus have fallen. We see other cultures have begun to adopt the beautiful way of Islām and benefit from it.

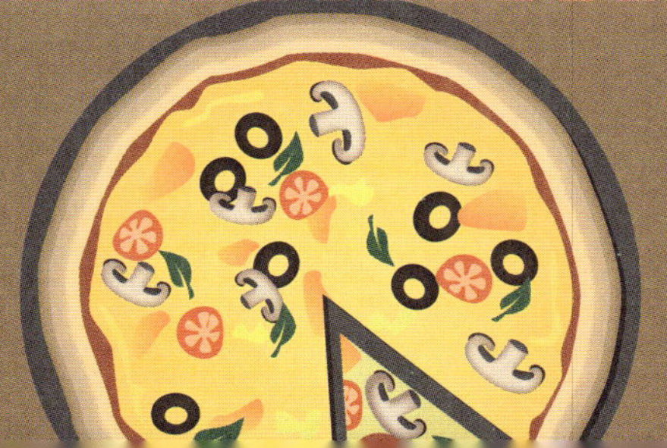

Dhikr

"O you who believe, remember Allah abundantly, And proclaim His purity morning and evening." (Qur'ān 33:41-42)

"Listen! By the remembrance of Allāh the hearts will find peace." (Qur'ān 13:28)

"...Those men and women who engage much in Allāh's praise, for them Allāh has prepared forgiveness and a Great Reward." (Qur'ān 33:35)

"When any group of people remember Allāh, angels surround them and mercy covers them, tranquillity descends upon them, and Allāh mentions them to those who are with Him." (Ṣaḥīḥ Muslim)

The likeness of the one who remembers his Lord and the one who does not remember Him is like that between the living and the dead." (Ṣaḥīḥ al-Bukhārī)

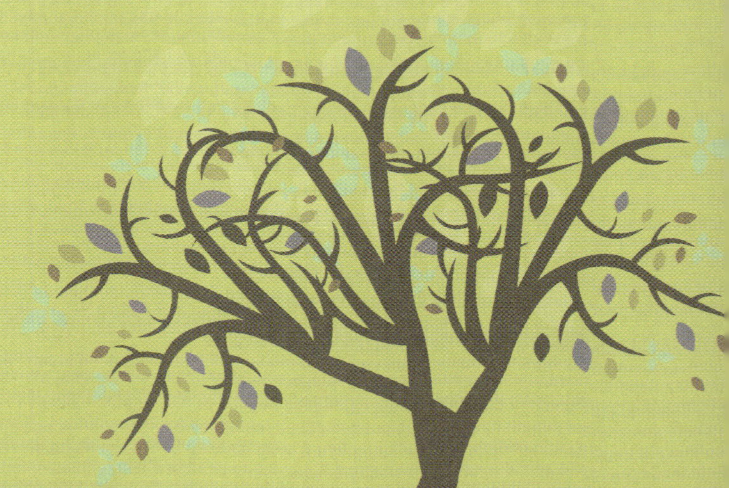

Dhikr

Ḥāfiẓ Ibn al-Qayyim رحمه الله, a well-known muḥaddith (a scholar of ḥadīth) has listed many benefits of dhikr.

1) Dhikr keeps away the Shayṭān and weakens his strength.

2) It is the cause of Almighty Allāh سبحانه وتعالى's pleasure.

3) It relieves the mind from anxieties and worries.

4) It produces joy and happiness in the heart.

5) It strengthens the body and mind.

6) It brightens the face and heart.

7) It attracts one's sustenance.

8) It is the key to the nearness of Almighty Allāh سبحانه وتعالى. The more abundant the dhikr, the closer one will get to Allāh سبحانه وتعالى.

9) Dhikr of Allāh سبحانه وتعالى causes one's mention in the court of Allāh سبحانه وتعالى, as is mentioned in the Qur'ān:

فَاذْكُرُونِىٓ أَذْكُرْكُمْ

"Remember me, and I will remember you." (2:152)

10) It is food for the heart and soul: to deprive them of dhikr is like depriving these vital organs of their food.

11) It cleanses the heart of its rust. It has been mentioned in the ḥadīth that everything rusts according to its nature. In the same way, the heart rusts with worldly desires: to purify it dhikr is necessary.

Ādāb

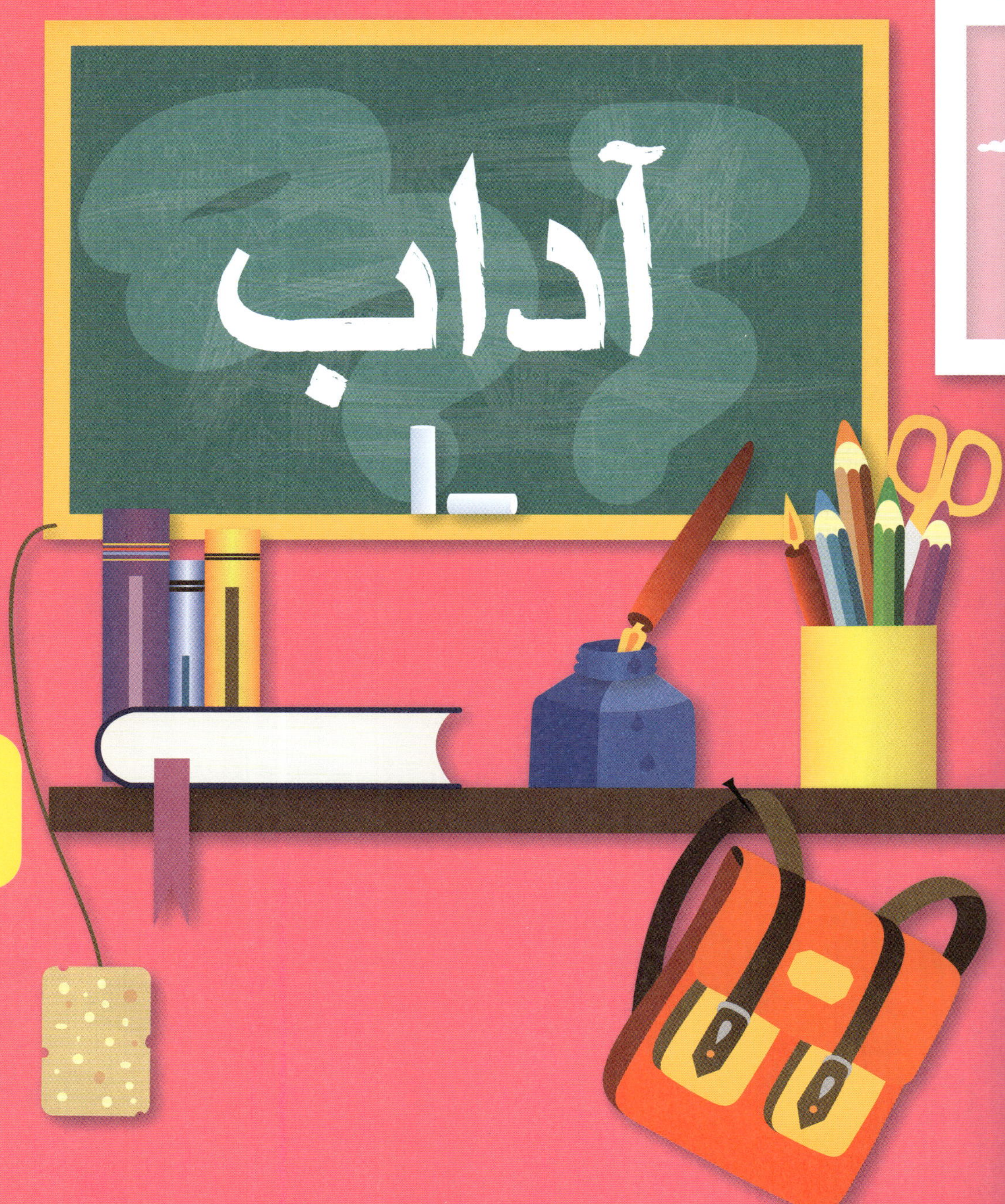

Ādāb

Learning Objectives

Ādāb

At the end of this unit pupils should be able to:

- List the ādāb of ghusl.
- Carry out appropriate interactions with people.
- Apply the ādāb when writing.
- State the benefits of using a miswāk.
- Explain the virtues and manners of visiting the sick.

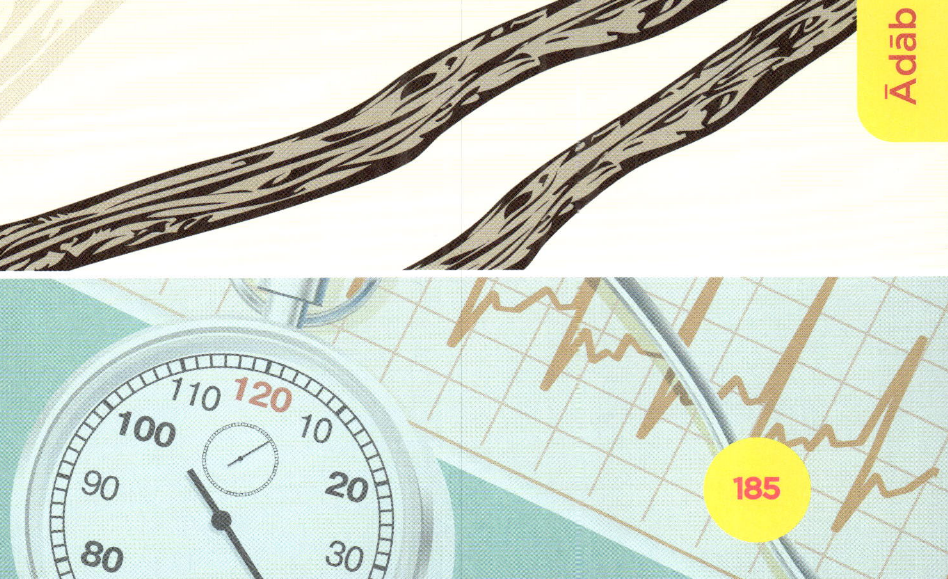

Ādāb of Ghusl

"And (He) sent down upon you water from the heavens, so that He may purify you with it." (Qur'ān 8:11)

"We have sent down purifying water from the heavens." (Qur'ān 25:48)

Water is a gift from Allāh: it is a way of purifying ourselves. The Prophet صلى الله عليه وسلم said, "It is Allāh's right on every Muslim that he should take a bath (at least) once in seven days." (Ṣaḥīḥ al-Bukhārī)

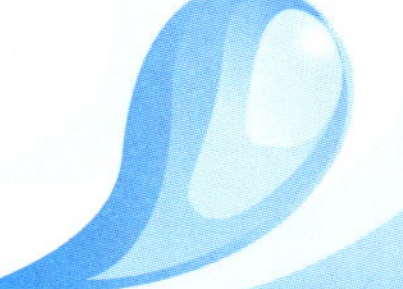

Ādāb of Ghusl

Ādāb of Ghusl:

- Wash both hands including the wrists.
- Remove any impurities from the body.
- Wash the private parts.
- Perform wuḍū'.
- Wash the head.
- Pour water over the right shoulder followed by the left side three times.
- Ensure water reaches every part of the body.
- Do not forget the main parts of ghusl and the obligatory acts: rinsing the mouth and nose.
- Rotate or remove any rings or earrings to ensure water reaches all portions of the body.
- Do not waste water.
- Hasten to cover yourself.
- Do not talk whilst doing ghusl.
- Ensure privacy is maintained.

Ādāb of Social Interaction

"Surely, Allāh does not like those who are arrogant, proud." (Qur'ān 4:36)

"Let whosoever believes in Allāh and in the Last Day either speak good or be silent." (Ṣaḥīḥ al-Bukhārī)

The way we interact with other people is very important. Keep in mind the following points:

- Speak only the truth.
- Speak politely, in a moderate voice.
- Talk humbly and not arrogantly.
- Talk at the level of the person. For example, if you are talking to an elder, speak with words that suit an elder.
- Do not prolong your speech: keep to the point.
- Think before you speak.
- Do not boast and brag about yourself.
- Do not use inappropriate language.
- Never interrupt a conversation.

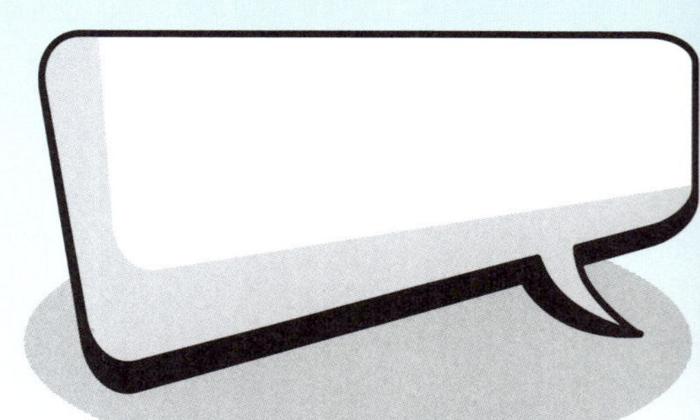

Ādāb of Social Interaction

- Do not isolate a person in a gathering.
- Do not engage in idle talk.
- Talk about those things which will benefit you and others.
- Remember to mention the name of Allāh سبحانه وتعالى.
- Do not backbite.
- Remember to listen to the other person.
- Give your full attention to people when interacting with them.
- Do not make fun of each other: remember that excessive joking leads to enmity.
- Do not laugh too much.
- Do not quarrel or argue even if you feel you are right.

Practising such things will create love and unity amongst the ummah.

Ādāb

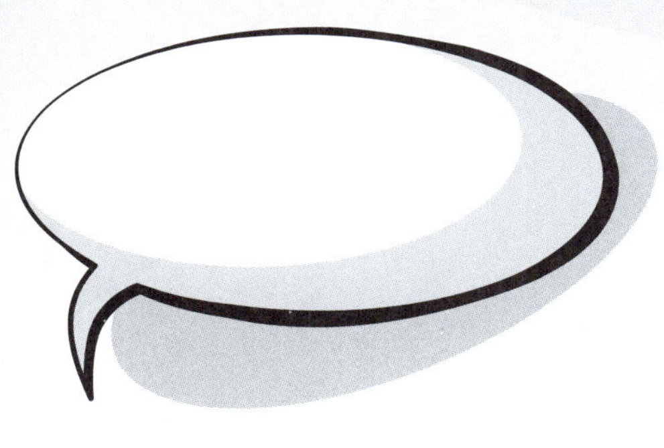

Ādāb of Writing

When writing to someone for the first time, clearly state the purpose.

Always have your name and address clearly visible.

If you have requested a reply, it is a good gesture to provide a stamped envelope with your address written on it.

Do not prolong the message unnecessarily.

Begin and end with pleasantries such as: "I pray you are well and please remember me in your prayers."

When writing to an elder, remember to use the most respectful words possible.

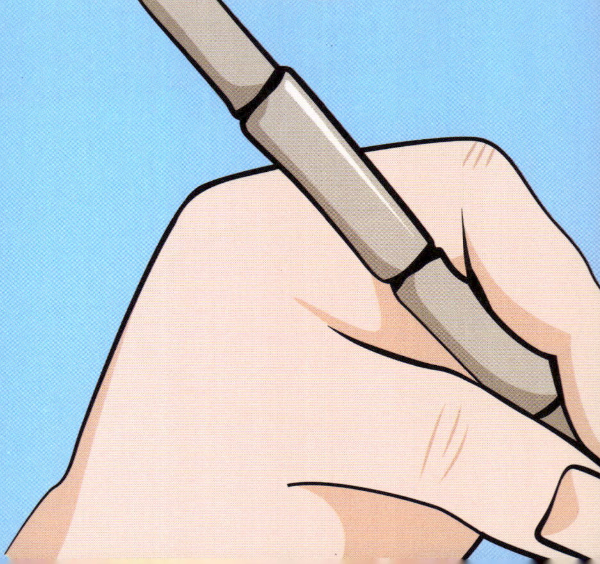

Ādāb of Writing

Do not be blunt in asking them to do something - rather write it as a request.

Make sure you write a date on it.

When writing to someone you know, make sure you read the letter before sending it.

When writing to a friend or relative, inform them of your health and state, as that is what they would most likely want to hear about.

Try not to write any bad news in a letter, as you don't know when the letter will be opened and it may be taken as a shock.

Do not fill it with too many questions.

Begin with salām.

End with a du'ā' and salām.

Ādāb of Miswāk

"Say (O Prophet), 'If you really love Allāh سبحانه وتعالى, then follow me, and Allāh سبحانه وتعالى shall love you and forgive you your sins. Allāh is Most-Forgiving, Very Merciful.'" (Qur'ān 3:31)

'Ā'ishah رضي الله عنها narrates that the Beloved Messenger صلى الله عليه وسلم said, "The miswāk is a means of purifying the mouth and pleasing the Rabb." (Nasa'ī)

'Ā'ishah رضي الله عنها narrates that whenever the Beloved Messenger صلى الله عليه وسلم slept in the night or day, as he awoke, he would brush his teeth with miswāk before performing wuḍū'. (Abū Dāwūd)

The many benefits of using miswāk are as follows:

- Strengthens the gums and prevents tooth decay.
- Assists in eliminating toothaches and prevents further increase of decay which has already set in.
- Creates a fragrance in the mouth.
- A cure for illness.
- Eliminates bad odours and improves the sense of taste.
- Sharpens the memory.
- A cure for headaches.

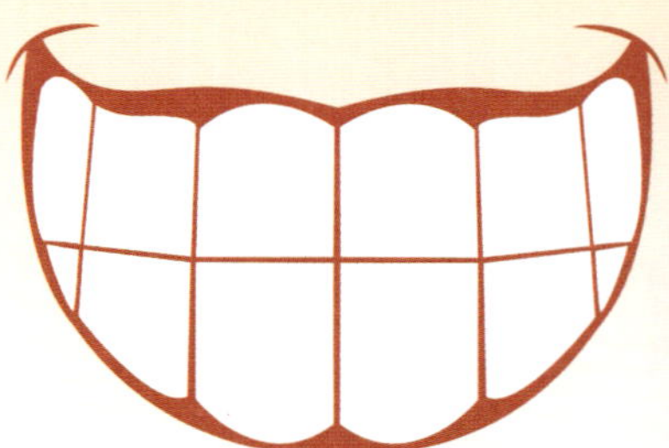

Ādāb of Miswāk

- Creates lustre (nūr) on the face of the one who continually uses it.
- Causes the teeth to glow.
- Strengthens the eyesight.
- Assists in digestion.
- Clears the voice.
- It is a means of dying with īmān.
- The greatest benefit of using miswāk is gaining the pleasure of Allāh سبحانه وتعالى.

The miswāk should be used regularly and especially on the following occasions:

- Recitation of the Qur'ān.
- At the time of wuḍū'.
- Before going for ṣalāh.
- Before sleeping.
- Upon awakening.
- After entering one's home.
- When the signs of death are apparent on a person.

Abū Hurayrah رضي الله عنه said, "I have used the miswāk before sleeping, after rising, before eating and after eating, ever since I heard the Beloved Messenger صلى الله عليه وسلم advising so." (Aḥmad)

The miswāk should be held with the small finger and thumb below and the remaining fingers on top.

Ādāb of Visiting the Sick

In a Ḥadīth Qudsi, our Beloved Messenger Muḥammad صلى الله عليه وسلم said that Allāh سبحانه وتعالى will say on the Day of Judgement:

'"O son of Ādam I was sick and you did not visit Me." He will say: "O Lord how can I visit You? You are the Lord of the worlds." He will say: "Did you not know that My servant so-and-so was sick yet you did not visit him? Did you not know that if you had visited him you would have found Me with him?"' (Ṣaḥīḥ Muslim)

"There is not a Muslim that visits another in the morning except that 70,000 angels ask forgiveness for him until the night, and if he visits him at night then 70,000 angels ask forgiveness for him until the morning, and he will have earned a garden in Paradise." (Tirmidhī)

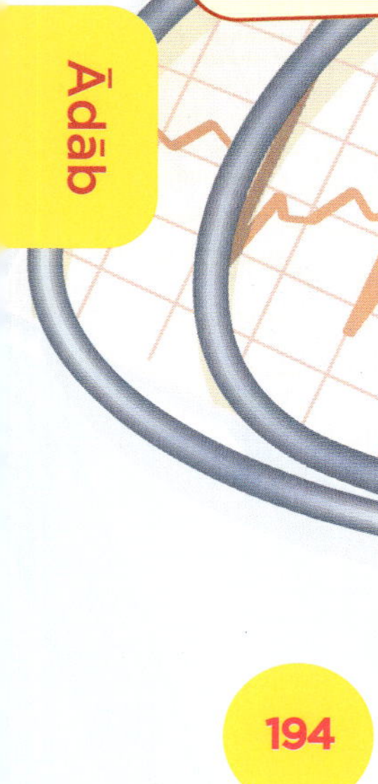

Ādāb of Visiting the Sick

When visiting an ill person, remember to encourage them and be careful not to scare them.

Our Beloved Messenger Muḥammad صلى الله عليه وسلم would recite the following du'ā' when visiting the sick:

لَا بَأْسَ طَهُورٌ إِنْ شَاءَ اللهُ

'Do not be afraid, if Allāh wills, this will be a way of cleansing' (Tirmidhī)

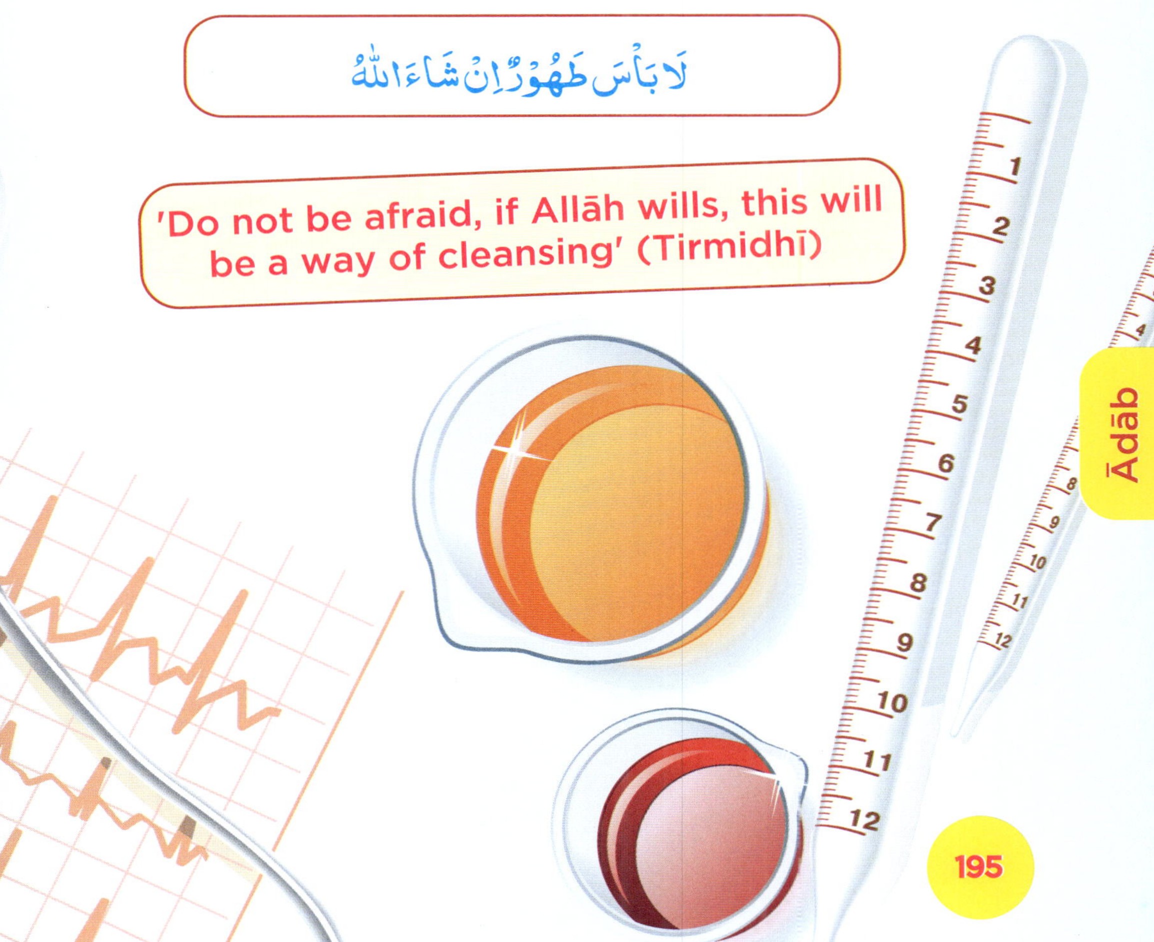

Ādāb of Visiting the Sick

Make a du'ā' for the sick person.

Our intention should be to gain the pleasure of Allāh سبحانه وتعالى.

Do not force the sick person to eat or drink.

Request them to make du'ā' for you, as an ill person's du'ā' is like the du'ā' of the angels. (Ibn Mājah)

Do not stay for too long whilst on your visit, as this may burden the patient. Convey your salām, ask the sick how they are feeling, pray for their recovery, and then leave.

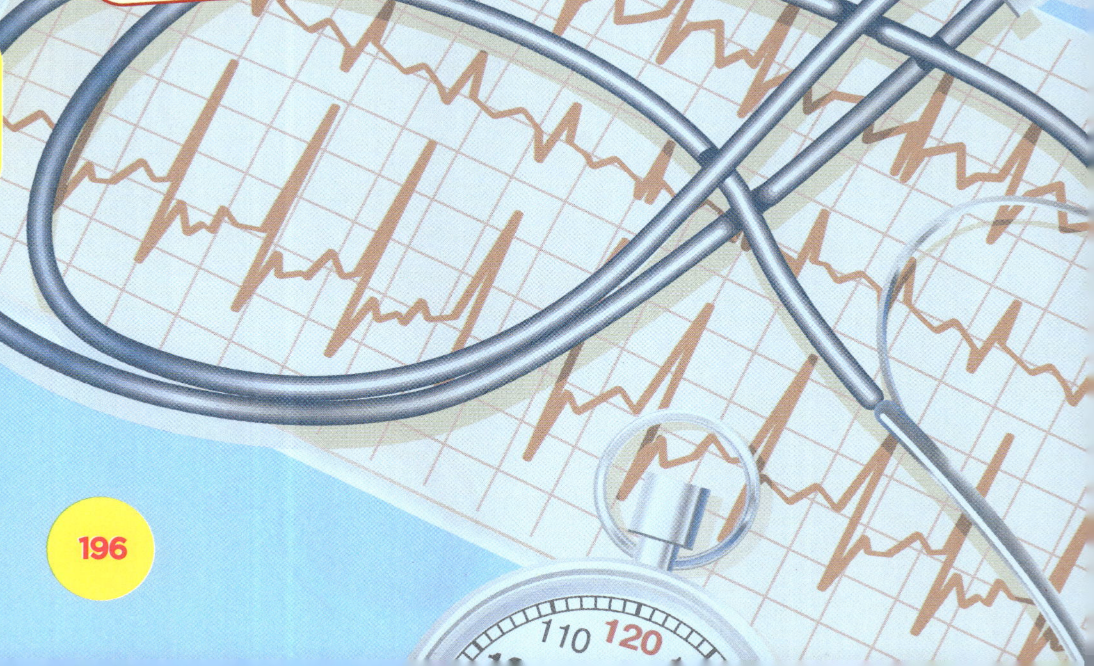

Ādāb of Visiting the Sick

Do not ask too many questions.

Speak of good things and not of other things which may upset the sick patient.

أَسْأَلُ اللهَ الْعَظِيمَ رَبَّ الْعَرْشِ الْعَظِيمِ أَنْ يَشْفِيَكَ

The Prophet صلى الله عليه وسلم said, "He who visits a sick person who is not on the point of death and supplicates seven times with the above du'ā' (I beseech Allāh the Great, the Rabb of the Great Throne, to heal you), Allāh will certainly heal him from that sickness." (Tirmidhī)

Abū Hurayrah رضي الله عنه reported that the Messenger صلى الله عليه وسلم said that "Whoever visits a sick person, a caller calls from the skies and says, 'You have done well and your walk was good also, and you have earned a place in Paradise.'" (Tirmidhī)

Bibliography

Fiqh Section

'al-Sughdi (d.461AH), **"al-Nutaf fi 'al-Fatāwā'**, Dar 'al-Furqān, 1984

'al-Samarqandi(d.540AH), **'Tuḥfat 'al-Fuqahā''**, Dār 'al-Kutub 'al-'ilmiyyah, 1994

'al-Kāsānī (d.587AH), **'Badā'i' 'al-ṣanā'i' fī al-Tartīb al-Sharā'ī'**', Dār 'al-Kutub 'al-ilmiyyah, 1986

'al-Marghinānī (d.593AH), **"al-Hidāyah fī sharh bidāyah 'al-mubtadī'**, Maktabah 'al-Bushra, 2007

'al-Bukhāri, Burhān 'al-Dīn (d.616AH), **"al-Muḥīṭ 'al-Burhānī fi 'al-Fiqh 'al-Nu'mānī'**, Idārah 'al-Qur'ān, 2004

'al-Mawṣilī (d.683AH), **"al-ikhtiyār li ta'līl 'al-Mukhtār'**, 'al-Halabī, 1937

Khusrū (d.885AH), **'Durar 'al-Ḥukkām Sharh Gurar 'al-Aḥkām'**, Dar 'ihyā' 'al-Kutub

Ibn Nujaym (970AH), **"al-Baḥr 'al-Rā'iq Sharh Kanz 'al-Daqā'iq'**, Dār 'al-Kitāb 'al-Islāmī

A-Qudūrī (d.428 AH), **'Mukhtasar 'al-Qudūrī'**, Dār Qubā', 2003

'al-Ṭaḥṭāwī (d.1321 AH), **'Ḥāshiyah 'al-Ṭaḥṭāwī 'alā Marāqī 'al-Falāḥ'**, Dār 'al-Kutub 'al-'ilmiyyah, 1997

Ibn 'Ābidīn (d.1252 AH), **'Radd 'al-Muḥtār'**, H.M.Saeed

Ḥaydar, Alī (d.1353 AH), **'Durar 'al-Ḥukkām Fī Sharh Majallah 'al-Aḥkām'**, Dār 'al-Jiyal, 1991

Niẓām 'al-Dīn et al, **"al-Fatāwā 'al-Hindiyyah'**, Maktabah 'al-Rashīdiyyah

Ludhyānwi, Mufti Rashīd Ahmed (d.2002 CE), **'Aḥsan 'al-Fatāwā'**, H.M Saeed, 1979

Gangohi, Mufti Maḥmūd 'al-Ḥasan (d.1996 CE), **'Fatāwā 'al-Mahmudiyyah'**, Idārah 'al-Farūq, 2008

Mufti Radhā' 'al-Haq et al, **'Fatāwā Dār 'al-Ulūm 'al-Zakariyyā'**, Zamzam Publishers, 2007

'al-Tatwī, Muhammad Hāshim (d.1174 AH), **'Fākihat 'al-Bustān'**, Dār 'al-Kutub 'al-'ilmiyyah, 2012

Bibliography

Aqīdah Section

'al-Taftāzānī, Sa'd 'al-Dīn (791 AH), '**Sharh 'al-Aqā'id 'al-Nasafiyyah'**, Dār 'al-Bayrūtī, 2007

'al-Ghaznawī (d.773 AH), **'Sharh 'al-Aqīdah 'al-Ṭaḥāwiyyah'**, Dār 'al-Kuraz, 2009

'al-Māturīdī (d.333 AH), **'Kitāb 'al-Tawhīd'**, Dār ṣādir,

'al-Maydānī (d.1298 AH), **'Sharh 'al-Aqīdah 'al-Ṭaḥāwiyyah'**, Dār 'al-Fikr, 1995

'al-Bayjūrī (d.1276 AH) , **'Tuḥfat 'al-Murīd 'alā Jawharah 'al-Tawhīd'**, Dār 'al-Salām, 2002

'al-Qārī, Mulla 'Alī (d.1014 AH), **'Minaḥ 'al-Rawdh 'al-Azhar Fī Sharh 'al-Fiqh 'al-Akbar'**, Dār a;-Bashā'ir 'al-islāmiyyah, 1998

'al-Qārī, Mulla 'Alī (d.1014 AH**), 'Dhaw' 'al-Ma'ālī 'alā Manẓūmah Bad'a 'al-amālī'**, Dār 'al-Bayrūtī, 2006

'al-Bayhaqī (d.458 AH), **'Kitāb 'al-Asmā' wa 'al-ṣifāt'**, 'al-Maktabah 'al-Azhariyyah li 'al-Turāth

'al-Shahrastānī (d.548 AH), **"al-Milal wa 'al-Niḥal'**, Dār 'al-Kutub 'al-'ilmi-yyah, 1992

'al-'Āṣrī, Saif ibn 'Alī, **"al-Qawl 'al-Tamām bi Ithbāt 'al-Tafwīdh Madhaban li 'al-Salaf 'al-Kirām'**, Dār 'al-Fath, 2010

Kan'ān, Muḥammad Aḥmad, **'Jāmi' 'al-La'ālī Sharh Bad'a 'al-'Amāli'**, Dār al-Bashā'ir al-Islāmiyyah', 2010

'Al-Nawawī (d.676 AH), **' 'al-Mināj Sharh Ṣaḥīḥ Muslim ibn al-Ḥajjāj'**, Dār 'Ihyā' al-Turāth

Hadīth Section

'al-Bukhārī, Muḥammad ibn Ismā'īl (d.256AH), **'Ṣaḥīḥ al-Bukhārī'**, Dar Ṭūq al-Najāh, 2001

Muslim, Muslim ibn al-Ḥajjāj (d.261AH), **'Ṣaḥīḥ Muslim'**, Dār 'iḥyā al-Turāth al-'Arabī,

Nasa'ī, Aḥmad ibn Shu'ayb (d.303AH), **'Sunan al-Nasa'ī'**, al-Risālah, 2001

Abū Dāwūd, Sulaymān ibn al-'Ash'ath (d.275AH), **'Sunan Abī Dāwūd**, Dār al-Risālah al-'ālamiyyah, 2009

Bibliography

'al-Tirmidhī, Muḥammad ibn 'Īsā (d.279AH), **'Sunan al-Tirmidhī'**, Dār al-Gharb al-'islāmī, 1996

'Ibn Mājah, Muḥammad ibn Yazīd (d.273AH), **'Sunan Ibn Mājah'**, Dār al-Risālah al-'ālamiyyah, 2009

Ibn Ḥanbal, Aḥmad (d.241AH), **'Musnad Aḥmad**, Mu'assah al-Risālah, 2001

Al-Ṭabarānī, Sulaymān ibn Aḥmad (360AH), **'al-Mu'jam al-Kabīr'**, Maktabah ibn Taymiyyah,

Al-Ṭabarānī, Sulaymān ibn Aḥmad (360AH), **'al-Mu'jam al-Awṣaṭ'**, Dār al-Ḥaramayn

'al-Bazzār, Aḥmad ibn 'Amr (d.292 AH), **Musnad al-Bazzār'**, Maktabah al-'Ulūm wa al-Ḥikam, 2009

Ibn Ḥibbān, Muḥammad ibn Ḥibbān (d.354 AH), **'Ṣaḥīḥ Ibn Ḥibbān'**, Mu'assah al-Risālah, 1988

Al-Ḥākim, Muḥammad ibn Abdullah (d.405 AH), **'al-Mustadrak alā al-Ṣaḥīḥayn'**, Dār al-Kutub al-'ilmiyyah, 1990

Al-Bayhaqī, Aḥmad ibn al-Ḥusain (d.458 AH), **'al-Sunan al-Kubrā'**, Dār al-Kutub al-'ilmiyyah, 2003

Tārīkh Section

Ibn Kathīr (d.774 AH), ' **'al-Bidāyah wa al-Nihāyah'**, Dār 'Ihyā al-Turath', 1988

Al-Dhahabī (d.748 AH), **'Siyar al-'A'lām al-Nubalā''**, Mu'assah al-Risālah, 1985

'al-Sarjānī et al, **'al-Mawsū'ah al-Muyassarah fī al-Tārīkh al-'islāmī'**, Mu'assasah Iqra', 2014

Alkhateeb, Firas, **'Lost Islamic History'**, Hurst Publishers, 2014

'Al-Hassani, Salim et al, **'1001 inventions: Muslim Heritage in Our World'**, Foundation for Science Technology and Civilisation, 2006

Bibliography

Credits

Mawlānā Muḥammad Yaḥyā ibn Fārūq
Director

Mawlānā Muḥammad Qāsim Manjra
Project Manager

Mawlānā Harūn Makda, Mawlānā Isḥāq Boodi and Mawlānā Ẓahīr Sidat
Consultation Panel

'Irfān Chhatbar
Design & Artwork

Shakīl Zikr
Illustration

'Ābid Russell, Rachel Larson & Khadījah Vania
Editing

Bakh Sumira Sulṭān
Workbooks & Extension Activities

Media Jamshidi
Vectorisation

Rest of the team at An Nasihah Publications

May Allāh سبحانه وتعالى reward them all abundantly in this world with blessings and grant them all Jannat al-Firdaws with His everlasting pleasure in the next.

Āmīn.

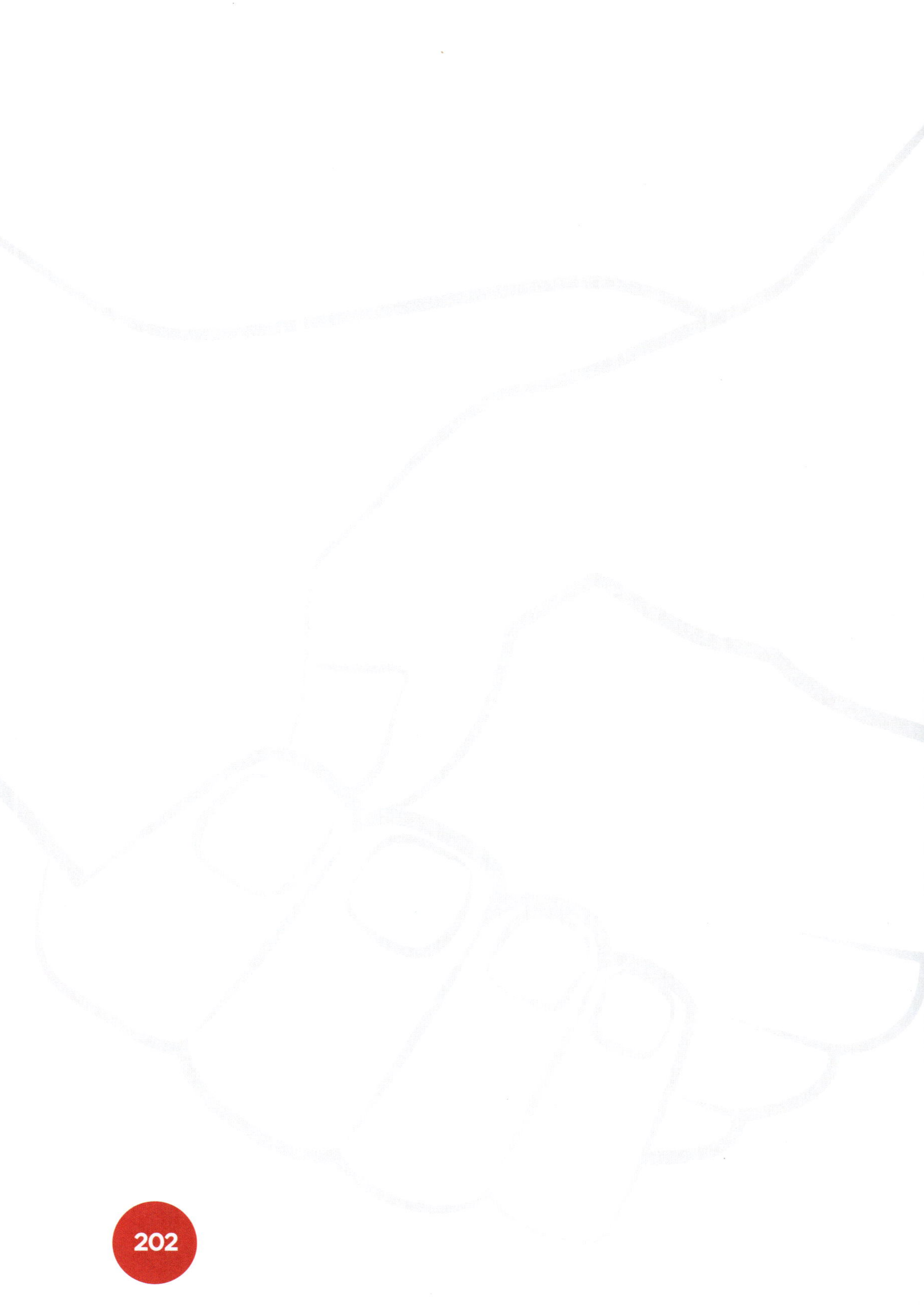